Dictionary
of
Newfoundland and Labrador

A unique collection of language and lore

By Ron Young

Editors
Janice Stuckless and Lila Mercer Young

Illustrator
Mel D'Souza

Cover Design
Vince Marsh

Copyright ©2006 by Downhome Publishing Inc.
43 James Lane
St. John's, NL, Canada, A1E 3H3
Tel: 1-888-588-6353
Fax: 1-709-726-2135
Web site: www.downhomelife.com
E-mail: mail@downhomelife.com

Printed in Canada

ISBN: 1-895109-22-1

Thank You

to the following for reading the manuscript for this book and editing it in their areas of expertise: Stanley Baldwin, Anne Brown, Tim Brown, David Clarke (Phd, marine history), Austin Davis, Meta Dawe, Frank Galgay, Alma Hardy, Phillip Hiscock (Phd, Professor of Folklore, Memorial University), Eric Keats, Dwayne LaFitte, Melanie Martin, Dee Murphy, George Pike, Bev Pope, Clar Pope, Captain Joe Prim, Ed Smith, Jack Troake and Ivan Young.

Thank you to the following who made multiple contributions to this book by mail, fax, e-mail, or phone: Jennifer Anthony, Peggy Antle, Deana Armstrong, Janet Badcock, Walter Badcock, Maude (Whiffen) Barnes, Danny Bath, Mike Breen, Joan Brown, Bob Canning, Darrel Carew, Bruce Chafe, Madonna Cole, Dave Connolly, Hilda (White) Cooper, Aiden Crewe, Meta Dawe, Thomas Dillon, Wil Dooling, Douglas Dove, Walt Forsey, Ross Fowler, Ron Fowlow, Jennifer Fudge, Trent Fudge, Cathy Gale, Evelyn Gullage, Tammy Hammond, Marie Dunphy Harding, Henry Hart, Terry Hart, Frances B. Healey, Edith and Sam Hill, Jennifer Hill, Hubert Hillier, Wilson Hiscock, Debbie Hynes, Fred Hynes, Mel Hynes, Stella Hynes, Teresa Ivy, Jack Jenkins, Josephine Jenkins, Eric Keats, Frank Keefe, Karen Kennedy, Barbara Laing, Amanda Lake, Marilyn Lannon, Jackie Locke, Darren Long, Mario MacDonald, Leona (Fitzpatrick) Machan, Karen Manning, Winnie (Abbott) Martin, Emily Marshall, Stanley Martin, Jack McBeth, Elaine McGrath, Glen Moore, Bob Morgan, Glen Morry, Derek Moulton, Kevin Murray, Cyril Nash Jr., Beverly Newhook, Stan Noftall, Lawrence Normore, Joan Oxford, Tony Oxford, Dave Peckford, Bill Penney, Douglas Penney, Howard E. Penney, Nichole Phillips, Harold G. Piercy, Barbara E. Pilgrim, Raymond Pilgrim, Norm Pinhorn, Bev Pope, Clar Pope, Joe Prim, Archie Rideout, Alex Rowe, John Rowe, Sybil Rowe, Jamie Senior, Marion Shea, Rita Smart, Laura Spurrell, Rosalind Stoyles, Garry Tizzard, Edith Toope, Eugene Toope, Aleen Torraville, Garry Troake, Bonnie (Stuckless) Vardy, Nadine Avery Vey, Petley Vey, Angela Warford, Clara Watkins, Don Weatherbee, Gerald Wells, Dorothy Wheeler and Effie J. White.

Thank you to all those who made single contributions to this book, sometimes via Downhome magazine, sometimes verbally and sometimes inadvertantly.

And thank you to Wayne Curnew, for his advice on rabbit snaring and logging; to Mickey Michael and Barbara Laing, for their information on piddely; to Gerry Prim, for her information on the Southern Shore; and to Douglas Roberts, for his information on cod traps.

Also, thank you to Pat Hayward for inspiring me to finish this project.

And a special thank you to the many wonderful people I've met in Newfoundland and Labrador over the years who didn't know how closely I was listening to what they said to me.

And, of course, a big thank you to Mel D'Souza, whose great illustrations bring these pages to life.

D^{EDICATION}

This book is dedicated to my son, Grant Young,
who shares my interest in informing and
entertaining with the written word.

Index

Introduction

The Canadian province of Newfoundland and Labrador is a land of colourful scenery, colourful people and a colourful language. Photographs that have appeared in *Downhome* magazine over the years attest to the spectacular scenery of the province. The rugged beauty of its coastline against backdrops of imposing mountain ranges would easily earn it a top rating as one of the most scenic places in the world.

Complementing the scenery are the people of Newfoundland and Labrador. They are delightfully unsophisticated, self-confident, outgoing and famously hospitable. Their heritage is a potpourri of Irish, English, Scottish, French, other European, and Native ancestry, with a dash of Americana introduced by the U.S. Armed Forces during and after WWII.

Likewise, the language is comprised of a concoction – and contortion – of the English vocabulary garnished with insightful and humorous sayings, many of which are made up on the spur of the moment with a facility that is intrinsic to Newfoundlanders and Labradorians. This flair for creating their own descriptive words and colourful sayings has given a new dimension to the English language, and one that is in a constant state of growth.

Newfoundland and Labrador's English colloquialisms have been a source of interest to linguists and great amusement to visitors to the province (including the descendants of Newfoundlanders seeking a connection with their roots). Newfoundlanders speak with a flourish and their speech is not always readily understood. In fact, it's not uncommon to see strangers turn to another Newfoundlander to ask for an interpretation of what was said, and then show their appreciation with a chuckle or even hearty laughter.

This book began about 10 years ago when I asked readers of *Downhome* magazine to send in the words and expressions they remembered from their part of the province for publication in this book. Submissions that arrived by mail, fax, phone and, in more recent years, e-mail have all been included in this book. Many words used in this publication are part of my own vocabulary, words I learned in the geographical areas in which I grew up. I also spent many hours researching books and other material to make the collection complete. Because our readers are from different parts of the province, the words and meanings are varied. In cases where one word has more than one meaning, I have included all the meanings of which I am aware.

I have long had a fascination with the spoken and written word, particularly with those words used in Newfoundland and Labrador, the language I grew up with. I was first intrigued when I discovered that people in different places said things differently. People from Twillingate did not speak like people from Grand Falls and Windsor. I had gone "mummering" in Twillingate before I left there in 1950, but when I did it in Windsor, it was called "janneying." Many other words were also unique to Central Newfoundland. And when we moved to Stephenville in 1958, I heard Newfoundland English spoken with a French accent for the first time. "Me, I come from the Crossing on a dog team, me. God damn, no snow!" is an expression I remember hearing there. The community of Sheave's Cove on the Port au Port Peninsula was pronounced "*SHE - vis - cove.*"

In 1962 Labrador City was growing when I moved there along with workers from other parts of Canada. The different words I learned in Labrador West probably prepared me somewhat for Toronto when I moved there in 1963.

In Toronto I had difficulty understanding the many non-Newfoundlanders I met, but I had more trouble being understood by them – sometimes to the point of embarrassment. In Toronto you can't call a kettle a slut, even if you've called it that all your life. You don't say a picture is squish, because they may think you're squatting a bug; and you don't say "squatting a bug" because they think "squat" means to coopie down. (They don't know what "coopie down" means either). You never say your "arse is gone dunch" or that the bread is "fousty" in Toronto. You never ask for "turps" at a hardware store if you're looking for something to clean your paint brush with. And if your daughter is teething, at the drug store you ask for a "soother," not a "dumb tit."

From the many Newfoundlanders I met over my 34 years in Toronto, I learned many words and expressions from this province I had never heard before. From a fellow from Conception Bay, I learned that what we call a "grump" in Notre Dame Bay, they call a "gump," which is a hitching post on a wharf. Collecting these colloquialisms has become a hobby of mine. I've studied their origins, their varied areas of use and meanings. Inspired by the Newfoundland language, I also studied certain aspects of other languages.

All languages currently in use in the world are known as "living languages" that change over time. To explain further, let me tell you about a dead language.

Latin was the language of the ancient Romans and is now as dead as the Roman Empire itself. That means it is no longer used anywhere in everyday conversation. Because it isn't in use, the language never grows and the words never take on added meanings. Because the meanings of the words always stay the same in Latin, it is still used in several areas including law, medicine and science. In the legal field this prevents loopholes in the interpretation of the letter of the law. The Latin term *mens rea* means "guilty mind." In every criminal trial in the democratic world no one can be convicted without *mens rea* being proven in court. Although new interpretations may be added to the English meaning of "guilty mind," or the meaning may change altogether, in Latin *mens rea* will always mean that the person knew he was committing a wrong.

In medicine, Latin is used to specifically identify each drug, as many drugs are commonly known by different names, and sometimes different drugs are commonly known by the same name. Using Latin prevents errors in the exacting science of that profession.

Latin is also used in science in recording the various species of flora and fauna. Each species is known by many names in different parts of the world, which causes confusion, so the Latin name is applied to specifically identify each species. For that reason I have used them when referring to flora and fauna in this book

The living language spoken by residents of Newfoundland and Labrador is one that evolved from other languages. Our language came mostly from English (with Irish, Scottish, Welsh and West Country English accents), some French and, to a lesser degree, native, as well as a number of others to a much lesser degree.

Like other living languages, ours evolved and changed over the years. Because there was very little communication between residents of Newfoundland and Labrador and the outside world for many years, our language took a different direction than did languages in other areas of the English-speaking world.

In the case of some words, however, our language didn't evolve at all. One example is the past tense of *dig*. In this province this is sometimes *digged*, and not the dictionary definition, *dug*. *Digged* was proper English in 1603 when King James VI of Scotland became King James 1 of England and had the Bible translated into the language of the day. The word *digged* is used 38 times throughout the Old and New Testaments, and the word *dug* is not used once. One example of this is found in Luke 6:48. It reads, "He is like a man which built an house, and *digged* deep, and laid the foundation on a rock." There are many examples of older English words in past and current use in this province dating back to that English era which can be found in the Scriptures.

To some residents, especially those of English descent, the *h* at the beginning of certain words is silent. This was also the case at the time of England's first King James, when the literate of England also left the pronunciation of the *h* off many words. The phrase *an house* is used 79 times in the Bible, while *a house* is used only eight times. In certain parts of this province a *hat* becomes an *at*. Sometimes the opposite occurs: "I'm going to give the *orse* some *hoats*." This is a form of over-correction or over-compensation, which is familiar to university professors on the subject.

Though some words remained the same, possibly from a biblical influence, many evolved into other words. Since the language of this province was seldom written down, it is not hard to understand how it evolved into what it is in such a relatively short number of years. The words used were passed on orally and sometimes the word was not pronounced properly or was not comprehended properly. I can understand that. For years I interpreted the song lyrics "mares eat oats and does eat oats and little lambs eat ivy" as "mairzy dotes and dozy doats and little lamsey divy." At Christmas I would sing at the top of my lungs," a far tree, juniper tree," when the words actually were "a partridge in a pear tree." Without seeing the words written down it is easy to mispronounce them, as our ancestors often did. *Barricade* can become *battycatter*, or *blackguard* can become *blaygert* in a generation or two.

As in other cultures, sometimes when words that end in *ing* are used the *g* is left off. *Bringing* becomes *bringin*, *laughing* becomes *laughin* etc.

Quite often the *th* sound is pronounced as a *t* and sometimes as a *d*. The main reason for this is that in the Gaelic language of Ireland, which had a large influence on the development of speech patterns in Newfoundand and Labrador, there is no *th* sound. Another factor was the reality that here, as in other cultures where life was hard and taking the proper care of one's teeth was not a priority, many people lost their teeth at an early age. This makes it almost impossible to pronounce the *th* sound. Without top teeth to press one's tongue against, the *th* comes out sounding like a *d*, a *t* or an *f*. (You can put your dentures back in now.)

Even when people kept teeth longer, the language they used was the one they learned from birth, from older generations who sometimes had no teeth, so the pronunciation was upheld. This was true to a certain extent in Newfoundland and Labrador. *This* becomes *dis*, *three* becomes *tree*, *bath* becomes *bat*, and *teeth* becomes *teef*. The word *teef* also means *thief* in this province, as it does in the English-speaking countries of the Caribbean, where the residents have a similar background.

In Newfoundland and Labrador the letter *i* is sometimes pronounced *ee*, for instance, the word *skiff*, is pronounced *skeef*.

Sometimes when *o* appears before *r* it becomes *a*: *forty* becomes *farty*; *corn*, *carn*; *morning*, *marning* etc.

Often people, particularly those whose roots are in West Country England, will use an *f* instead of a *v*, and vice versa. Sometimes people say *vin* when they mean *fin*, and *fan* when they mean *van*.

The *s* sound is often replaced with a *z* sound – the word *send* becomes *zend*.

The *d* sound at the end of a word is often left off the pronunciation, turning the word *round* into *roun* and *hold* into *hole*.

The letter *s* is sometimes added to verbs, and sometimes left off nouns. "I *gets* as good a time now as I used to get 24 *year* ago."

The *oi* sound often becomes an *i* sound, *point* is reduced to *pint* and *boil* to *bile*. "Every time you *pints* your finger at me, me blood fair *biles*."

Sometimes the past tense of a verb that differs from universal and conventional English is used. For instance, the word *cotched* is used as the past tense of *catch*. "He was ahead of me, but I cotched up to him."

Since life in Newfoundland and Labrador revolves around the ocean, I have included a number of nautical words and terms that are, or were, in common or casual use in this province.

Where necessary, I have used sentences to put the words in their proper context. To do this I have sometimes used colloquialisms to put the terms in perspective. Other times I have not because colloquialisms would not better explain the meaning of the word or phrase.

I have also given explanations of the word where necessary and its origins or possible origins when known. Where necessary I have also included pronunciation instructions in an effort to preserve the sound of the language. Instead of the standard dictionary form of phonetics to sound out the words (which not everyone may understand), I have used single-syllable, common words to represent the sound of each syllable of the Newfoundland words. I have also used rhyming words to sound out single-syllable and multiple-syllable words.

To aid researchers using this book, words that have the exact same meaning are cross referenced. As in all dictionaries, socially unacceptable words are also included. In cases where I wasn't sure of the meaning of a phrase, or where the meaning is obvious, I have left the meanings out.

This book reflects the language used by peoples of Newfoundland and Labrador from the time of settlement to the present day. It also reflects the influences of living in isolation in coves, on the sides of cliffs and on islands in remote locations. In many of those outports the only people a person saw, apart from the residents of that community, were those close enough to visit by rowboat. In these places the evolution of the language was rather insular, so much so that many words varied greatly from outport to outport. This can be seen in this book by the many different words and terms that mean the same thing.

This is by no means a complete dictionary of the words and expressions ever used in this province, but it is very extensively researched and gives the broadest overview of the language and culture of Newfoundland and Labrador of any book to date. I am hoping that this collection will inspire even more useful information for a second, more complete edition.

To fully understand the language and lifestyle, I felt readers should know something about the people who used and use the language, and lived and live the lifestyle, so the first chapter is a brief history of the province called "How We All Got Here."

Read and enjoy.

Ron Young

Mail submissions for the Second Edition to:
Dictionary of Newfoundland and Labrador
43 James Lane
St. John's, NL, A1E 3H3
or E-mail: ron@downhomelife.com

How We All Got Here

O f all the people who ever lived in this land now known as Newfoundland
and Labrador, every one of them came from somewhere else. Beginning
with the first people who migrated from western North America when the world
was still in the caveman era, to the last refugee who jumped ship or plane here
and decided to take up residence, we, or our forebears, came from somewhere
else. Among the different peoples who came here to live over the centuries
were the Maritime Archaic people, the Dorset Eskimo and, in more recent centuries, the Beothuk. The Vikings came and stayed for a few years around the
turn of the last millennium. But they left. There is evidence that between that
time and the time of Columbus and Cabot, fishermen from European nations
came here to fish. Many of these fishermen didn't consider they had found a
new continent, but simply a place where fish were plentiful, even though it took
many days to reach it. In those days, longitude was unheard of, but navigators
knew about latitude and could always tell how far north they were by the stars.
These sailors always tried to stay on the same latitude while travelling east and
west, so getting back to a place after you found it was just a matter of staying
on the same latitude for as long as it took. None of these earlier visitors stayed,
they just filled their boats with fish and sailed home.

When Cabot returned to England after his first voyage, he brought news of
fish so plentiful that one could catch them merely by "lowering a basket into the
water." Shortly after that, more people started coming. Some of them stayed.
Collectively, over the years, the ones who stayed became who we are today.

Our forebears came from a number of lands in the eastern Atlantic to settle
in Terra Nova – or as the early English called it, the New Founde Lande.
Although this wild new land, far across the sea, would hand these earliest settlers hardships of the worst kind, these brave pioneers sought one of the most
important needs of mankind — freedom. This commodity, so foreign yet so valued by them, was enough for them to put everything, even their lives, on the
roulette wheel of life for it.

Life for the poor in England was wretched and things were no better in the
neighbouring countries. The people of Ireland, Scotland and Wales toiled the
land every day so their landlords could live a life of ease. Serfdom, the way of
life which made the masses virtual slaves to the land owners, lasted in the
British Isles until the 1600s and in France until 1789. The "Feudal System,"
which gradually replaced Serfdom, gave a certain amount of freedom to the
peasants. But they were still peasants and, for the most part, still slaves to
poverty, as well as to the land owner.

The new found land where fish was plentiful and there was free access to
land was a big attraction to these impoverished people, and a number of them
found their way here. They were few in number at first, but they kept coming.
They came from the counties of West Country England, southwestern Ireland,
northwestern France; and from the Channel Islands, Scotland, Wales, Spain,
Portugal and other places.

Apart from the people living where Royal Licence was in place, such as

Cupids, Ferryland and Placentia, many of these earlier settlers were here illegally in the eyes of one or more countries. Some came with a mercantile company and stayed on in Newfoundland after their indentured time was up, while some were ship jumpers. These included naval deserters and indentured servants who ran away from masters. Some were escaped prisoners. Some were just lucky enough to secure a passage here by whatever means to escape the way of life they had previously been forced to live.

There were many deserters from the Royal Navy in Newfoundland's early years. Many sailors on those ships were not volunteers but had been captured by the "press gangs," who were often little more than thugs used to enforce laws which had existed in England since Anglo-Saxon times. The Impress Service sent out gangs of eight to 12 men, with an officer, to locate anyone between 18 and 55 with sea experience, and try to convince them to join the navy. Very few could be persuaded, so they were forced into navy service. Knocked unconscious, threatened with sword, pistol and musket, and plied with alcohol: just some of the different techniques used to secure crews for the King's ships.

In *England Under Queen Anne, vol. 1*, G. M. Trevelyan writes: "The navy, as the more essential service of the two, also enjoyed the right, denied to the army, of forcibly seizing any of the subjects of the land to man the Royal ships in time of war. The sight of honest citizens waylaid, knocked down and marched off manacled to serve the Queen at sea, was strangely out of keeping with the free and lawful spirit of the English polity. The interruption of trade was even more loudly complained of, for merchant fleets ready to leave port often lost so many of their crews to the press-gang that they could not sail."

Used extensively under Elizabeth I, Charles I and Oliver Cromwell, press gangs forcibly seized and carried individuals into service; frequently subjects of foreign countries were taken. Impressment was not used exclusively to obtain crews for naval ships, but for merchant ships as well, for many years. This happened often in spite of the fact that the practice, as well as the action of taking foreigners – even for the Navy – was illegal.

In 1800 the Royal Navy consisted of 130,000 men, only half of which were English. A large number of Irish, Scots and blacks from the West Indies and the Americas served in the navy. The Royal Navy didn't care whether you were a free man or a slave, or what your native language or your skin colour was. As long as you were able-bodied and would follow orders you were eligible.

Able men in Newfoundland were also subject to be pressed. The *New York* and *Boston* were two well-known Royal Navy impressment ships at one time. In their era the impressment laws had relaxed to the point that certain men were "protected." These included apprentices already indentured to a master, seamen with less than two years experience at sea, fishermen, and others associated with maritime trade and industry such as riggers, shipwrights and sailmakers. These men were essential to the economic well-being of the empire and were not to be conscripted by press gangs. However, simply identifying oneself as a member of a protected segment of British society was not enough to guarantee one's freedom. Each "protected man" was required to carry with him a document called a "protection" that identified him and his trade. If he could not produce his protection on demand by the press gang, he could be pressed without further question.

In his book *Pathways Through Yesteryear*, Michael P. Murphy writes about the *Boston* in St. John's: "On the afternoon of October 24th, the ship being due to sail the next day, Captain Morris ordered two lieutenants and a boat's crew of seamen to go ashore as a press gang. The First Lieutenant of the *Boston*, Mr. Lawry, a slim, dark young man with a good record in the Navy, was in charge of the party, No trouble was encountered on shore and a large number of fishermen and others were seized and taken aboard the *Boston*.

"In the morning of the following day, October 25th, the impressed men were examined by the ship's doctor and a number of them, apprentices and such, were released when their employers on shore came to claim them. Eight men, however, were taken into service and as they were not employed at the time they expressed themselves as willing to join the Navy and to take the bounty (of cash, known as the King's Shilling) then being offered."

The vast amount of shipping inspired by the Newfoundland fishery brought another hardship for the earlier settlers. Pirates of many nationalities, far from the reach of any law, often plundered ships and sometimes settlements. Some of these pirate ships started out as privateers, captained by men who had been given licence to plunder ships of an enemy nation in times of war. Among the bounty taken from captured ships was a supply of fresh crew members to take the place of pirates lost in battle. Many an honest sailor were forced into piracy by the blood-thirsty pirate captains and forced to commit crimes out of fear for their own lives. If they were lucky enough to escape, going back to their own country to live was often not an option. Some of these found refuge in isolated places around the new colony.

But whether they were deserters or they were fleeing from the press gangs in England, which many did, or they came for some other reason, these settlers were few in numbers in the early years. By 1650, there were only about 2,000 settlers who lived year-round in the colony. The rest came here during the summer months to make themselves enough to live the rest of the year back in their native country on the eastern side of the Atlantic.

There are a number of reasons for the earlier slow population growth. For one thing, the merchants of West Country England saw settlement in Newfoundland as a possible loss to their lucrative fishing businesses. They believed that settlement in Newfoundland would shift the focus of trade from their port cities, such as Bristol and Poole, to somewhere in Newfoundland. The large revenues generated by the Newfoundland fish trade were very important to the counties of Dorset, Devon, Hampshire, Cornwall and Somerset. By 1630, as many as 300 ships were leaving West Country to spend four months or more in the fish-catching and curing business on the other side of the Atlantic. Sail, net and rope-making factories flourished, as did ship-building and manufacturing of all items necessary for the fishing businesses, including lamps, lanterns, dishes, etc. Farmers and other food producers also felt the positive affect of the trade. Newfoundland was more important to England's economy than the New England colonies, and even more than Canada after 1763, when that vast land was added to the British Empire. British and other European merchants, fishermen and statesmen continually talked of the value of the Newfoundland fishery and made often extravagant claims for it.

In 1713, for example, French merchants said it was "absolutely necessary for the support of the Kingdom in general and more particularly for the Maritime Provinces of Western France where thousands of families would be reduced to beggary in case that fishery be taken from them." In 1784 an English politician proclaimed that the fishery "was a more inexhaustible and infinitely more valuable source of wealth than all the mines in the world." Of course he didn't know about modern technology, and the effect it would have in devastating the fish stocks, when he made that statement.

Because of the value of the new-world fishery, the pressure the West Country English counties were able to use to lobby Parliament and the Crown brought about such laws as William III's Anti-Chimney Act, which forbade the building of houses within six miles of the shoreline. The following poem from that era, written by Hugh Scott, demonstrates, not only one of the results of this law, but also the very reason why freedom was so important to these wretched souls in the first place.

Whipping Post

Born in a tenement home,
Our guts were racked with hunger;
My parents tried their Christian best,
To keep us all alive.
But poverty does as poverty will,
My father stole a red hen
To make a soup for supper time,
But guards came to the door.
They cried ..

"Tie him to the whipping post,
Crack the cat and flay;
Tie him to the whipping post,
By God, we'll make him pay."

On the birthday of my thirteenth year,
I joined the Royal navy;
Small, frail and tired of death,
I set off to see the world;

My Captain ruled with an iron fist,
His justice made me shudder;
Though small and frail I did protest,
The advances of that old bugger.
And he yelled...

"Tie him to the whipping post,
Crack the cat and flay;
Tie him to the whipping post,
By God, we'll make him pay."

And when I was just twenty-one,
I sailed out for the new world;
With good intent to settle down,
I made for Newfoundland.
Foundation built a home of wood,
A chimney for the fire;
The Fishing Admiral came around,
Said, boy you broke the law.

"Tie him to the whipping post,
Crack the cat and flay;
Tie him to the whipping post,
By God, we'll make him pay."

They burnt the whole house to the ground,
They tore down my fine chimney;
They dragged me to the Admiral's ship,
And tied me to the mast.
The Admiral read the charges out,
"No squatters and no chimneys!"
A pound of flesh tore from my back,
As warning to them all!
They heard...

"Tie him to the whipping post,
Crack the cat and flay;
Tie him to the whipping post,
By God, we'll make him pay."

The second reason why settlement was slow starting in Newfoundland was
that France and England were at war, on and off, for many years and ownership
of Newfoundland was very much in dispute. The French, Spanish and
Portuguese had been sending ships to Newfoundland, possibly even before

Cabot's 1497 voyage, to prosecute the fishery here. France in particular continued to send more ships and men than England did for several centuries after that.

In his *History of Newfoundland and Labrador*, the late Dr. Fred Rowe writes: "According to Innis, of the 128 vessels listed as sailing to Newfoundland from western Europe prior to 1550, 93 were French and only 11 were English. In the next century France annually sent out hundreds of ships with thousands of fishermen."

For all the larger numbers of French who came to these shores, now for the most part only the names remain. Notre Dame Bay, Port aux Choix and Fleur de Lys are but a few. Yet in spite of their French names, these places are populated by English-speaking people today.

Being on the losing end of wars with England, France gave up all claim to Newfoundland in the Treaty of Utrecht in 1713, but she still retained fishing rights to what was known as the French Shore. By far larger than the English Shore, no one was allowed to settle on the French Shore, but the Treaty allowed the French to erect "stages made of boards, and huts necessary and usual for drying of fish."

Clause 13 of the Treaty went on to say, "... it shall be allowed to the subjects of France to catch fish, and to dry them on land, in that part only, and to no other besides that, of the said island of Newfoundland, which stretches from the place called Cape Bonavista to the northern point of the said island, and from thence, running down the western side to Point Riche."

In spite of the Treaty, some English fishermen, and some French as well, settled in restricted areas. This sometimes lead to disputes in some areas.

By 1750, Newfoundland's population had only reached about 8,000. Except for a few French ship-jumpers in the Cape St. George area and a few other pockets of French settlers, most of the residents were English-speaking. This is somewhat surprising when you consider that the French were coming here longer and much more often than the English. Dr. Rowe believed that the price and availability of salt was one of the biggest factors in this development.

"There was one fundamental and crucial difference between the English fishery in Newfoundland and the fisheries of the French, Spanish and Portuguese," he writes. "The Europeans had available to them plentiful supplies of relatively cheap salt, something that England lacked. The southern nations operated a 'green' or 'wet' fishery, one where the fish was heavy-salted and stored in the vessel's hold and taken back to Europe, where it could be further processed or disposed of as desired."

The unavailability of salt made it imperative that the fish caught by English fishermen be light-salted and cured in Newfoundland. That meant the English had to build fish flakes for drying their catch and "ship's rooms" for storing and further processing and packaging the fish. Some of these earlier fishing businessmen would pay employees to winter-over to look after the premises while the owner was away in England. This gave, first the English, and later the Irish fishermen a stronger attachment to the new land than it did their mainland European counterparts.

But salt was not the only factor. As years went on, the French also began curing fish in Newfoundland and taking it back ready for market. This may have been because dried cod is less heavy and less bulky than "wet fish" and would have allowed them to transport a much more valuable cargo on the long trip home. In any event they were forbidden by treaty to settle and only stayed for the duration of the fishing season.

Although the French were only seasonal settlers, they did play a role in settlement by English-speaking fishermen and their families. To insure against looting, vandalism, or damage by natural causes, many French fishermen, hired English-speaking fishermen as "guardiens" or care-takers over the winter. Some of the people they hired were already living year round on the French Shore, even though it was as forbidden to them as it was to the French.

Some of the French fishermen also broke the law and became full-time residents. There may have been many more of them who eventually stayed, in spite of the law, but in 1756 the Seven Years' War broke out between England and France, and the French stopped coming to Newfoundland to fish. In their absence the encroachment by English and Irish settlers on the forbidden shore escalated. This was particularly true in Bonavista Bay and into Notre Dame Bay as far as Cape John, including such island settlements as Exploits, Fogo and Twillingate. After the war the French fishermen resumed the Newfoundland fishery, but the number of ships that made the venture were fewer than before the war.

At the end of the 1700s and the early decades of the 1800s, during and immediately after the Napoleonic Wars, there was a period that saw a large influx of settlers from southwestern England and southwestern Ireland

By the early 1800s, the earlier fears of the West Country merchants were realized by the growing number of fish merchants who had set up businesses in Newfoundland. Although by that time there weren't as many new settlers arriving, the population of the colony grew substantially as more and more children were being born in the new colony. As these children became adults they would spread out to find new areas to fish and found new settlements until there were more than 1,400 settlements in remote parts of the Island as well as on the Labrador coast. Although many of the earliest settlers came from West Country England, there was also such a large influx of people from certain Irish counties that, for a while, the Irish settlers outnumbered all others.

Before the year 1900 the population of Newfoundland and Labrador had reached 220,000. Most of these earlier settlements consisted of only a few families. Long-distance transportation was mostly unavailable or unaffordable so many of these families led rather insular lives, in regular contact with only the closer communities. They had traded their life of deprivation in the old country for one of isolation in the new one. Yet they marked out their spots as close as possible to their source of sustenance, the ocean, and they stayed. Fishing was what it was all about, and even when the 1870s rolled around it still accounted for more than 95 per cent of the colony's exports.

In spite of the fact that they had new freedom, the way of life was hard in outport Newfoundland. A. C. Laut, a journalist who visited Newfoundland in the late 1800s, writes, "Almost hidden behind the perpendicular cleavages are the lagoons where the fishing hamlets cluster. More isolated, lonely places could not be imagined. The cabins huddle close to the water's margin, or stick like toys on a peg to a bare steep cliff. The rocks, rising on every side, forbid access to the unknown and unexplored interior. Except for the stunted growth of moss and trees, whose roots grip the very fissures of rock, not a vestige of green appears against the granite wall....There is no provender for stock, and generations of the people have never seen cattle...When winter closed, there were families with less than a barrel of flour and only a few fagots of cod for six months' supplies. Men, women and children have scarcely enough clothing to hide their nakedness. Coarse duck coats are worn till they literally fall away in tatters. Blankets, bedding, overcoats and flannels are unknown and undreamed-of luxuries....Little dilapidated cottages, barely high enough for a man to stand upright, cling to the steep hillside or perch on some lofty ridge directly above the watery tumult..."

Mr. Laut's observations were made in the late 1800s, as coastal boats were just starting to provide some sort of regular service. By that time there were areas in Newfoundland where people were much better off, and some who were somewhat affluent. Yet for most of the hundreds of small outports around this vast shoreline, the bleak picture Laut paints is probably close to the truth.

Although descendants of Irish and English make up the largest portion of today's population, they are not the only groups who were here for some time. These include several groups of French, Basques, Spanish, Portuguese and Mi'kmaq, as well as others. Most experts believe that also mixed in our bloodline is that of the Beothuk, who are no longer with us as an identifiable race. Like the Beothuk, Dorset and Maritime Archiac people before them, each group of newcomers had it as hard as the other in finding their way here and making a life for themselves when they got here. Their struggles are part of what makes the sons and daughters of this place what they are today.

Words and Meanings

Not all the words that appear here are exclusive to Newfoundland and Labrador, but most are, and all have been in general usage in this province at one time or another. The words found in this section are a collection of words sent in by readers of *Downhome* magazine; from the author's personal knowledge; and a large number of publications, particularly the Dictionary of Newfoundland English, by G. M. Story, W. J. Kirwin and J. D. A. Widdowson.

a ~ of. "Give me a slice a that bread."

aaron's rod ~ a plant of the rosewood or roseroot family *[Sedum rosea]*.

aback ~ behind. "The cellar is aback of the house."

abaft ~ a nautical term meaning behind the beam line of a vessel.

abeam ~ the beam is an imaginary line drawn across the width of a vessel at its widest point. Anything this line crosses by extending it to starboard or port is said to be abeam of the vessel.

abroad ~ apart. "Don't pick that mat abroad."

according to ~ in equal measure. "I'll give you some logs according to the number you saw into lumber for me."

adikey also **dickey** ~ a hooded garment.

adikey

admiral's room ~ the choice land given to the skipper of the first English fishing vessel to arrive in a Newfoundland harbour in the 1600s and 1700s.

adze ~ a cutting tool used in ship-building. Similar to an axe with the blade at right angles like a hoe.

adze

afeard ~ afraid.

afore ~ forward of, before.

aft ~ 1. the back portion of a vessel. 2. toward the rear. "Jargie Bath went back aft, he tripped on the paddle and broke off the gaff."

after ~ 1. to have completed. "I know all about the Grand Banks because I was after being there." 2. to the rear. "I was standing on the after deck."

after-room ~ a fish-holding compartment located in the stern of a boat.

aftmost ~ closest to the stern of a vessel.

ag-rode {pronounced: *AG - rod*} ~ See **hag-rode**.

airsome ~ cold, fresh and bracing.

alder ~ a small deciduous tree or sapling.

alder bird ~ the common redpoll *[Acanthis flammea flammea]*.

alee ~ towards, or on, that side of a ship that is fartherest from the direction of the wind. "Black Island is alee of us."

alexander ~ 1. the Scotch lovage, *[Ligusticum scotchicum]*, a medicinal herb. 2. a dumpling seasoned with the herb.

alley-coosh ~ to go to bed. From the French "aller coucher" meaning the same.

alleys also **glass alleys, glassells** ~ marbles, especially the clear marbles which often encased a design that resembled the flight on a dart. See also **Alleys** on page 203.

all in ~ fatigued. "I've been digging potatoes for ten hours straight and I'm all in."

altered ~ of an animal, castrated.

American man ~ See **naked man**.

American Shore ~ the stretch of coast from Ramea Islands on the south coast, westward around Cape Ray and up the west coast to Quirpon Island on the tip of the Northern Peninsula. The Treaty of Paris, in 1783, gave American fishermen the right to take bait and other fish on this coast.

ampery ~ sore and infected. "I cut my finger and now it's right ampery."

anchorage ~ a body of water protected by land which affords shelter for vessels.

andramartins ~ silly pranks and tricks.

aneist ~ See **anigh**.

angashore also **hangashore** ~ 1. a weak, miserable, antisocial or sickly person. 2. a lazy, shiftless person. From those who are too lazy to go to sea and would rather stay on the land or "hang ashore."

angashore

angish ~ very poor.

angle-dog ~ a worm used for bait when trouting.

anigh also **anighs, anighst, aneist,**

aninst ~ 1. next. "Your turn is anigh." 2. near, beside.

anighs ~ See **anigh**.

anighst ~ See **anigh**.

aninst ~ See **anigh**.

anse ~ a cove. Probably from the French word "anse," meaning "cove."

apast ~ past. "April Fools is gone apast and you're the biggest fool at last."

aport ~ towards the port or left side of a vessel. "Captain Guy swung the *Polina* hard aport."

apple ~ a type of potato of high quality.

apse ~ 1. a festering boil on the arm or leg. 2. the aspen tree.

apsy ~ an area thick with aspen trees.

ar also **either** ~ any. "I left the house without ar breakfast this mornin'."

Arctic Current also **Labrador Current** ~ the ocean current flowing from Davis Strait, along the coast of Labrador and Newfoundland.

arctic hare ~ See **mountain hare**.

arctic steak ~ whale meat.

arg ~ to argue. "Don't arg with me. I know what I'm talking about."

arm ~ a deep and comparatively narrow inlet from the sea.

arn ~ ever a one, any. "When you went out in the bight shooting turrs, did you get arn?"

arse ~ rear. "The arse is gone right out of her."

arse end ~ the back end of something. "I fell over the arse end of the rodney."

arse foremost ~ backwards. "You've got your sweater on arse foremost."

arse over kettle ~ to fall down, to go head over heels.

arse up ~ 1. backwards. 2. upside down.

article ~ a naughty person. "He's quite the article."

ar udder ~ another. "I don't suppose we'll have ar udder man in Newfoundland like Joey Smallwood." Probably derived from "any other."

ash cat also **ashy cat** ~ a person who fears the cold.

ashy cat ~ See **ash cat**.

a-starboard ~ toward the starboard or right side. "Swing the wheel hard a-starboard."

athwart also **atirt** ~ across.

atirt ~ See **athwart**

aunt ~ the title given any mature woman in Newfoundland and Labrador, whether blood-related or not. "I was talking to my mother's friend, Aunt Sophie."

awash ~ having water washing over. "The decks are awash."

awful ~ 1. very. "That blueberry pie was awful good." 2. exceptional. "He was an awful feller for telling jokes."

awl ~ a tool used with tacker in making or repairing footwear, or other leather or canvas items.

awl

aye b'y ~ I agree.

babbage also **babbish** ~ a narrow strip of dried seal, moose or caribou skin used as filling for snowshoes. "The dogs only went and chewed the babbage out of my rackets."

babbish ~ See **babbage**.

bacallao ~ 1. the Spanish name for Newfoundland and its adjacent islands.

baccalieu skiff ~ a skiff or small schooner used in the fishery off Baccalieu Island.

baccy ~ tobacco.

bachelor buttons ~ the name given to a number of wild flowers including the wild daisy.

backanswer ~ 1. an unfavourable reply from a child who is being scolded. "Don't you backanswer me you young maneen." 2. to reply disrespectfully to anyone.

back-burn ~ a back load, especially a back load of firewood.

back house also **back kitchen, back pantry** ~ a room, usually off the kitchen, used for storage, especially of food items such as sacks of flour, bottled preserves and food in pickle barrels. On really cold nights sometimes hens were kept in the back kitchen overnight, or longer if necessary.

back kitchen ~ See **back house**.

back-load ~ the amount of firewood or other items that may be carried on the shoulder at one time.

back-on ~ turned with one's back to someone or something.

back-paddle ~ See **sheave**.

back pantry ~ See **back house**.

back shore ~ the innermost part of a harbour.

back tilt ~ a temporary shelter in the woods with an open front facing away from the wind where a fire was lit.

backwash also **wake** ~ the churning water left behind a moving vessel.

backwater ~ See **sheave**.

bad like ~ resembling. "He's not bad like his brother."

badness ~ mischievous behavior intended in fun. "My youngest boy was right full of his badness this morning."

baffed out ~ 1. exhausted. 2. getting old.

baint ~ am not or are not. "I baint going to go to school tomorrow." Originated in West Country England, from the compounding of the words "be not."

baiser ~ a large trout.

bait box ~ a container to hold a fisherman's bait.

bait depot ~ a cooled shed where bait is stored.

bait fish ~ small fish used as bait for larger fish.

bait-fishing ~ catching fish on a hand-line or trawl, which used bait.

bait hauler ~ a fisherman engaged in catching bait.

bait jack ~ See **bait tub**.

bait skiff ~ a skiff used for catching capelin and other bait fish.

bait tub also
bait jack ~ a
wooden tub
used to hold
bait.

bait tub

bakeapple ~
the cloudberry, dwarf mulberry,
salmonberry, or creeping raspberry
[Rubus chamaemorus], a yellow-
orange clusterberry, similar in appearance to
the raspberry and
found in bogs
and marshes.
Containing
from 50 to
over 150 mg
of ascorbic acid
per 100 g of
fruit, this berry has a very tart taste.
It has been used in the prevention
of scurvy by Norwegian sailors and
North American Inuit.

bakeapple

bake pot ~ a cast iron pot used for
baking and cooking.

baker's fog ~ See **fog**.

bald ~ refers to a cutting tool with
the edge worn down or nicked.

bald coot ~ the surf scoter
[Melanitta perspicillata].
Measuring 36 cm (14 in) in length
and having an 84 cm (33 in)
wingspan, a diving duck found in
mixed flocks with other scoters off
the coast, and sometimes inland.

ballast ~ rocks, sand, pig iron or
any heavy objects used to stabilize
a ship.

ballast bed ~ a
part of a wharf. A
square wooden
crib filled with
rocks and some-
times other heavy materi-

ballast bed

al to hold the crib to the ocean bottom. A number of ballast beds were
laid on the bottom in a row, some
distance apart, each farther from
shore than the previous. The deck
of the wharf was then built to cover
and connect the ballast beds.

ball gun ~ a muzzle-loading gun
loaded with a ball instead of shot.

ballicatter {pronounced: *BAL - ee
CAT - ter*} also **battycatter, barricader** ~ a band of ice formed along
the beach from the spray of the
ocean. Probably derived from the
word barricade, which became barricader and so on.

ballirag {pronounced: *BAL - ee -
RAG*} ~ to abuse or scold.

ball mold ~ a device into which hot
lead is poured to make a gun ball or
bullet.

ballroom ~ a humorous name for a
crew's quarters on a sealing vessel.

ball tag ~ a game in which a
sponge or rubber ball is thrown by
one member of a group to tag other
members.

bander ~ a copper coin, a half-
penny.

bangbelly ~ a pancake made with flour and fatback pork, often served with molasses.

banger ~ an overcoat.

bank also **fishing bank** ~ an undersea elevation of land where fish feed and may be caught.

bank cod also **bank fish** ~ the codfish caught offshore on a fishing bank.

banker also **banking schooner** ~ 1. a schooner once used to fish the offshore banks using dories which were stacked on deck, as opposed to schooners which fished the Labrador coast and seldom used dories. 2. a man who fishes the offshore banks from dories.

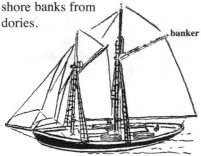
banker

bank fish ~ See **bank cod**.

bank fisherman ~ a man who fishes the offshore banks.

bank-fishing also **banking** ~ catching fish on a fishing bank.

bank herring ~ herring caught on the offshore banks.

banking ~ See **bank-fishing**.

banking anchor also **fisherman's anchor** ~ an anchor with a wooden stock used in bank fishing.

banking dory ~ a stackable dory used in bank fishing.

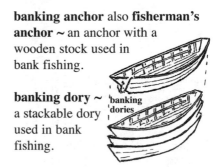
banking dories

banking fleet ~ a number of vessels engaged in bank fishing.

banking schooner ~ See **banker**.

bank weather ~ damp, foggy weather.

banniken ~ 1. a small drinking cup. 2. a tin cup.

banniken

bannock ~ a small round cake of bread.

banshee wind ~ a death omen. See also **Bad Luck** on page 280.

bar ~ 1. to set a net across a river to catch fish. 2. to enclose a school of fish inside a net. 3. the crossmember on a snowshoe. 4. a chocolate bar.

barachois also **barrasway, barrachois, barrisois, barasway, barrisway** ~ 1. a delta or sand bar at the mouth of a river. 2. the sheltered harbour formed by same.

barasway ~ See **barachois**.

barbel {pronounced: *BARB - ull*} also **barvel** ~ a fisherman's apron which covers the breast to the knees, usually made of canvas, sheepskin or other animal skins.

barbel

barber ~ 1. the mist rising from the water on a frosty day. 2. a cold, cutting wind.

bare buff ~ 1. naked from the waist up. 2. completely naked.

bare-legged cup of tea ~ a cup of tea served without food offered.

bare poles ~ a ship's masts when no sails are set.

barge ~ a large vessel used to collect fish from Labrador fishing schooners and process them.

bark ~ 1. tree rind. 2. a liquid made from boiling bark and tree buds in water. 3. to boil fish nets, sails or leather in a mixture of water and tree bark to preserve them from rotting. 4. a simile for bad-tasting tea. "That tea is just like the bark."

bark pot ~ a large cast iron cauldron used to preserve fish nets and sails.

barley over ~ See **bar rover**.

barmp ~ honk the car horn.

barnicle ~ 1. a funny-looking rock sticking out of the ocean. 2. a vicious person or animal.

barnystickle ~ See **thornback**.

barrachois ~ See **barachois**.

barrack ~ a structure for storing hay.

barrasway ~ See **barachois**.

barrel ~ 1. a measurement of uncured fish. 2. the look-out post on the masthead of a ship, the crow's nest.

barrel chair ~ a chair made from a barrel.

barrel chair

barrel-heater ~ a stove used by coopers to temper the wood in the construction of barrels.

barrel-man ~ 1. the sailor designated to man the ship's look-out barrel. 2. a radio show hosted by Joseph Roberts Smallwood.

barrels ~ plenty, lots. "Don't give the youngsters any more peppermint knobs, they've had barrels of 'em."

barrel over ~ See **bar rover**.

barrens ~ a plateau with low vegetation where berries often grow.

barricader ~ See **ballicatter**.

barrisois ~ See **barachois**.

barrisway ~ See **barachois**.

bar rover also **barley over, barrel over** ~ a children's game of hide-and-seek.

barter shop ~ a small shop that trades product for fish.

bar tight ~ being taut, without any slack whatsoever and under great strain. "The wind was so strong that the anchor chain went bar tight." From the English term "bar taut," meaning the same.

barvel ~ See **barbel**.

bas also **baz** ~ 1. to throw with force. 2. to throw pitch or toss marbles so that they hit other marbles. Often used in association with games in which stones, marbles, etc., are tossed. "The young one had to bas a stone to get my attention."

basin ~ an artificially enclosed space of water in which ships are placed for loading, unloading or being repaired.

bastard ~ 1. a codfish too small to have real resale value.

bat ~ a club with an iron hook and spike used to kill and take seals.

batant ~ the piece of wood that runs along the edge of a door or window or the hatch of a ship.

bath ~ to cook lobster or salmon in water at a cannery.

batsman ~ a sealer who uses a club.

battant also **batten** ~ 1. a metal strip with a hole in either end, used to secure the hatch cover on a ship. 2. a piece of wooden weather-stripping around a door or window.

batten ~ See **battant**.

batten down ~ to securely cover a hatch with tarpaulins.

batter ~ the action of a bird flapping its wings along the water to take light. "I was just bring up me gun when the turrs battered away."

battery ~ 1. a fortified area where larger guns are mounted to repel an attack. 2. a caribou blind.

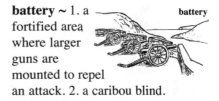
battery

batticatter ~ See **ballycatter**.

batty ~ a boatload of codfish. Probably from the French "bateau," meaning boat.

bauk ~ See **bawk**.

baulk ~ See **bawk**.

bautom ~ a ball of yarn.

bavins ~ 1. slivers of wood cut from a dry stick and used to start a fire. 2. pieces of dry brushwood.

bawk also **bauk, baulk, hagdown** ~ the greater shearwater *[Puffinus gravis]*, or the sooty shearwater *[Puffinus griseus]*, often seen in the company of the Alantic Fulmar.

These are very much ocean birds who mostly come ashore in foggy weather. Bawks can stay aloft by gliding for a long period of time.

bawk

bawn ~ 1. a natural flake of turf or stones on which salt fish are spread to dry. 2. a grassy meadow in a settlement.

bay boy ~ a lad from an outport.

bayman ~ a male who lives somewhere outside St. John's.

bay noddy ~ a derogatory term for an outport dweller.

bay price ~ the price the local outport merchant paid for fish.

bay salmon ~ a variety of salmon with a limited migration range.

bay seal also **harbour seal, jar** ~ the common seal *[Phoca Vitulina]*, a non-migrating seal found in coastal waters. These vary in colour from black, brown, grey or tan, with darker patches. The pattern is unique to the individual. They have a relatively large head with a short body and flippers. Males measure 1.4-1.9 m (4.6-6.2 ft) in length, and weigh 55-170 kg (121-375 lb), while females are 1.2-1.7 m (3.9-5.6 lb) long and weigh 45-105 kg (100-230 lb).

bay seal

bay tilt ~ a winter cabin built at the bottom of a bay.

bay wop ~ a derogatory term for an outport dweller. The word "wop" is an acronym for "Without Papers," referring to an illegal foreigner.

baz ~ See **bas**.

bazzom ~ a blueish-purple-coloured bruise.

beach bird ~ a variety of plover found along beaches.

beach bird

beach rock ~ a rock or stone rounded and made smooth by the action of the waves.

beach room ~ a beach large enough for processing fish.

beal ~ 1. the beak or bill of a bird. 2. the bib of a cap or hat.

beal

beam ~ 1. a supporting cross-member of a ship, especially the one at her widest point. 2. the width of a ship.

beam ends ~ the port and starboard sides of a ship at deck level. "In the storm the schooner hove out nearly on her beam ends and we thought she was going to capsize."

bear ~ safely frozen, capable of supporting a certain weight. "Is the ice on the pond bear yet?"

bear dog ~ the old name for the Newfoundland dog.

beat ~ to drive a sailing vessel against wayward winds and currents.

beater ~ 1. a young harp seal just out of the whitecoat stage. 2. a wayward woman.

beatle board ~ a board or paddle used to beat mats or clothes.

beatle board

beat out ~ to be tired and out of breath. "I've been running for hours and I'm beat out."

Beaver ~ 1. a once-popular brand of chewing and pipe tobacco in Newfoundland and Labrador. 2. a drink of rum at 11:00 a.m.

beaver hat ~ See **gun cap**.

bed ~ wooden rollers used to launch and haul up a boat.

bed

beddamer ~ See **bedlamer**.

bedding ~ 1. the planks to which a boat engine is secured. 2. the floor of a stage or store.

bedlamer also **bellamer, beddamer, bedlemer, bedlimer** ~ 1. a two-year-old harp seal. 2. a teenage

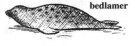

bedlamer

boy. Possibly from the old English word, "bedlamer," meaning, "one who creates bedlam, havoc or chaos." Also, possibly, from the French, "bête de la mer," which means, "beast of the sea."

bedlemer ~ See **bedlamer**.

bedlimer ~ See **bedlamer**.

bed rock ~ a stone heated and covered in cloth to be used as a bedwarmer.

bees ~ 1. go. "I bees berrypickin' sometimes." 2. am. "I bees in Change Islands sometimes."

belay ~ 1. to scull or steer a small boat with a sculling oar. 2. to make fast with a rope.

belk ~ to burp or belch. Probably derived from the word "belch."

belks ~ plenty, lots. "We won't run out of gas, we have belks of it to drive the whole distance."

belly-flop ~ to make an improper dive into the water and land on one's chest and stomach.

belly keg ~ the stomach.

belong to ~ come from, to be a native of. "Where do you belong to?"

bend ~ See **bend on**.

bender ~ the branch or sapling bent over to make the spring of a rabbit snare. See also **Rabbit Catching** on page 256.

bending horse ~ the structure used by coopers to bend barrel hoops into shape.

bend on also **bend** ~ to attach a sail to a spar, mast or boom.

Beothick ~ See **Beothuk**.

Beothuck ~ See **Beothuk**.

Beothuk also **Beothick, Beothuck** ~ a member of the now-extinct indian tribe that inhabited Newfoundland when the first Europeans arrived.

Beothuk

berry bank ~ a hill or incline bearing wild berries.

berry box ~ a wooden box used to transport berries from the berry hills.

berry hills ~ the hills where berries grow in abundance.

berry note ~ a receipt given to a berry picker for berries received.

berry ocky ~ 1. a home-made drink of wild berries, especially partridge-berries. 2. a drink of water mixed with jam.

berth ~ 1. a space on a sealing vessel as a sealer to share in profits of voyage. 2. a particular codfishing

spot for trap fishing. "We drew lots and I got the Spillers Rock berth this year." 3. food and lodging given in exchange for cutting timber. 4. a docking area where a vessel may tie up.

berth free ~ a berth allowed a sealer without a fee.

berth money ~ the fee charged a sealer for a berth on a sealing ship.

berth ticket ~ the ticket showing authorization of a berth aboard a sealing vessel.

best kind ~ in great condition, healthwise and otherwise.

bib ~ 1. the peak of a cap. 2. the spout of a teapot or kettle.

bibber also **bivver** ~ to shiver, tremble or shake, especially with the cold, and especially the lips.

bibby also **quickie. quicknie, hot ass, piper, pompey, slut, smut** ~ a locally-made tin or copper camp ket-tle which is small at the top and big at the base.

bibby

bide ~ to stay. "You bide here and I'll check to see if the ferry is coming in." Originated in British Isles.

bide-in feast ~ a big meal celebrating a newborn child.

big ice ~ a large field of tightly-packed ice.

bilk ~ a pile of wood (roughly about a pick-up truck load).

bill ~ 1. a promissory note showing the earnings of a member of a sealing crew or fishing crew at the end of a voyage after deductions. "I'm going to the ice to make a bill, and all the crew will join me." 2. the narrow tip of a headland.

billet ~ a junk of wood cut to fit a stove. "I just bought a load of birch billets."

billy gale ~ a term used by eastern mainlanders to refer to a Newfoundlander.

billy knocker ~ a policeman's nightstick or baton.

billy tub ~ a tub made by cutting a barrel in two.

billy tub

bim-bye also **bin-bye, bum-bye, bun-bye** ~ after a while. "I'll be there bim by." Derived from the expression, "by and by."

bin-bye ~ See **bim-bye**.

binder {rhymes with *finder*} ~ a rope used to fasten wood to a sled.

binicky ~ moody and cross.

binnacle ~ the wooden or brass box which contains the compass.

birch bark also **birch rind, birch rine** ~ the bark of a birch tree used as insulation, as a covering and to light fires.

birch broom ~ a broom home-made by shaving down a birch stick, or by tying birch twigs to a stick.

birch brooms in the making

birch rind ~ See **birch bark**.

birch rine ~ See **birch bark**.

birch tree ~ refers to either the paper birch, or American white birch *[Betula papyrifera]* or yellow birch *[Betula lutea]* tree.

birch wood ~ the firewood obtained from a birch tree.

bird ~ the penis.

birding ~ hunting sea birds.

bis ~ are, or is. See also **bissen**.

biscuit box house ~ a two-storey wooden house that was bigger than a salt-box house and had a saddle roof that sloped gently and was almost flat. See also **Houses and Other Buildings** on page 231.

bissen ~ are not, or is not. "You bissen in bed already bis you?" Originated in West Country England, probably derived from "bees not."

bitch ~ a female seal.

bitting stick ~ a stick twisted around a binding rope to tighten it.

bivver ~ See **bibber**.

black ~ a Roman Catholic term for a Protestant, whose soul, being non-Roman Catholic, was considered to be black.

black art book ~ a book, owned by witches and wizards, believed to enable these sorcerers to perform their supernatural enchantments.

blackberry also **moss berry** ~ the crowberry *[Empertrum nigrum]*. The blackberry is almost completely devoid of natural acid and its sweet flavour generally peaks after frost. These berries are a staple of the Inuit, who call them, "Fruit of the North."

blackberry heath ~ the leaves and twigs of the blackberry used for home remedies. Also used to insulate cellars.

blackenin' ~ 1. shoe polish. "Oh, the moon shines bright on Charlie Chaplin, hees shoes are crackenin', for the want of blackenin'." 2. stove polish.

blackfish ~ See **pothead**.

blackjack molasses also **blackstrap molasses** ~ a type of West Indian molasses.

black man ~ a name given to the devil and often used to threaten misbehaving children.

black psalm ~ 1. a curse. 2. a text thought to have magical and sinister powers.

black pudding ~ See **blood pudding**.

blackstrap molasses ~ See **blackjack molasses**.

bladder ~ a blister on the flesh, often caused by a burn or chafing.

blanker ~ See **flanker**.

blare ~ yell loudly. "Don't blare at me, I can hear you."

blast ~ a wound received by supernatural means. "He was taken by fairies and came back with a blast on his back."

blasty bough ~ a dead evergreen bough after the needles have turned red.

blather ~ nonsensical talk.

blaygard also **blaygert** ~ foul language. "He's always using blaygard so I hates to see him come to the door." From the word blackguard, meaning a scoundrel. A scoundrel would likely be the type of person to use foul language.

blaygert ~ See **blaygard**.

bleacher ~ a young unmarried woman.

blear ~ an ignorant person.

blessed virgin's leaf ~ the lady's thumb plant *[Polygonum persi-caria]*, having clusters of very small pinkish flowers and growing to a height of one metre (3 ft).

blind buck and davy also **bonna winkie** ~ a game of blind man's bluff. See also **Blind Buck and Davy** on page 205.

blind mush ~ a soup made of cabbage and other vegetables but no meat.

blocked solid ~ so full that nothing can move. "The ice was blocked solid in the harbour." "After the accident the highway was blocked solid."

blood pudding also **black pudding** ~ a large black sausage made from parts of an animal carcass including blood.

blossom ~ a large snow flake.

blow ~ a rest. "I'm tired of sawing wood so I'm going to take a blow."

blowey ~ windy.

blow hole also **seal hole** ~ a breathing hole in the ice made by seals.

blown cod ~ a split cod, half dried by exposure to the wind.

blubber ~ 1. the fat of seals or whales. 2. decomposing cod livers used to make cod liver oil.

blue note ~ a receipt from a merchant for fish received.

blue peter ~ a seaman's coat.

Blue Puttee ~ a member of the first contingent of Newfoundland volunteers for WWI. See also **War Heroes** on page 269.

blue puttee

bluff ~ abruptly rising land, especially a headland.

bluff

boat a net ~ to bring in a fish net and reset it.

boat fisherman ~ an inshore fisherman.

boat hook ~ a long-handled gaff.

bobber ~ a float used in trouting.

bobby rooter ~ See **rusty tom rooter**.

bob sled ~ a sled, similar to a catamaran but having only one seat or cross-member and only two horns. When hauling wood, the back end of the logs bob along on the ground behind.

bob sleds ~ two bob sleds connected in tandem by a rope or chain so that the distance between them can be adjusted to accommodate long and short loads, without the load dragging. See also **double sled**.

bob sleds

bog ~ peat, especially removed from marsh-land and used to improve soils.

bogan {rhymes with *stow - gan*} ~ the backwater from a river or stream.

bogey

bogey {rhymes with *stogie*} ~ a small cooking stove used in the galley of a boat.

bogey-warped ~ cramped from sitting in one position. Possibly from sitting beside a bogey, the stove in a vessel's galley, which was often cramped for space.

boggan {rhymes with *noggin*} ~ the crossbar behind a horse to which the traces are tied,

boiler ~ a large pot for heating or boiling water.

boil proof ~ embroidery thread.

boil-up ~ a meal in the woods.

boil up

bond store ~ a liquor store.

boneen also **bonnif** ~ a piglet.

bonfire ~ any large open fire.

bonfire night ~ November 5, a celebration that saw a number of bonfires attended by different groups in every Newfoundland and Labrador community. See also **Bonfire Night** on page 199.

bonna winkie ~ See **blind buck and davy**.

bonnet ~ the hood of a motor vehicle. Originated in the British Isles.

bonnif ~ See **boneen**.

boo ~ a head louse.

boo-bagger ~ 1. a head louse. 2. dried nasal mucus. 3. the devil. 4. an imaginary figure used to threaten children who were misbehaving.

boogeyman ~ the devil.

book ~ 1. the grade or reading level a child has aspired to. "Are you in book three this year?" 2. to misdeal playing cards so some are facing each other.

booked ~ while shuffling playing

cards, having one or more cards face the wrong way.

booshy ~ See **cooty**.

boot-legger ~ a large timber fly.

born days ~ a lifetime up to now. "I never saw the like in all my born days."

borned ~ gave birth to. "The old sheep borned three lambs."

Boston states ~ the United States.

bostoon ~ 1. to complain loudly. 2. an ignorant person.

bots ~ a grub-like parasite that causes chronic indigestion in horses.

bottom ~ 1. the innermost part of a bay, harbour or inlet. 2. a low-lying area, usually swampy.

bottomer ~ a thin cake.

bough bed ~ a bed that used boughs as a mattress. "We always slept on bough beds when we worked in the lumber woods, and when they got too hard we cut fresh boughs."

bough fence ~ a fence made of spruce or fir boughs interwoven with saplings.

bough whiffen also **whiffen** ~ a lean-to or shelter made with poles from fir or spruce trees and boughs from the same trees. The poles

would be placed at an angle and the back and sides filled in. The front was left open to accommodate a campfire. These were temporary shelters built by people spending time in the woods.

boulder ~ a large marble.

bow {rhymes with *cow*} ~ the fore end of a vessel.

bow {rhymes with *go*} ~ the curved part of a snowshoe.

bow drill ~ a drill that rotated by the up and down movement of a "bow"
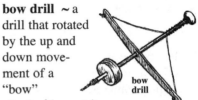
attached by a string. This drill cut in both clockwise and counter-clockwise rotation. It was helpful in drilling holes because a man could put his whole body into the effort, not one arm against the other as when using a brace and bit.

box cart ~ a two-wheeled vehicle fitted with a box for holding product, especially coal.

boxey ~ the tough and gnarled part of a tree which is hard to chop into firewood.

boy ~ 1. an inexperienced man on his first fishing voyage to Newfoundland from England or Ireland. 2. the frequent term of address for a male of any age.

brace ~ two, especially two rabbits.

brace and bit ~ a hand tool for boring holes, consisting of a cranking handle and interchangeable drilling bits.

brace and bit

brack ~ a crack in a dish, furniture or other item.

brackety ~ spotted or speckled, especially in the colouring of domestic animals.

brackish water ~ See **breachy water**.

brail ~ 1. lines tied to the edges of sails or nets to truss them up. 2. a device for coiling twine on a ship. 3. a rough, amateurish sewing job. 4. to truss up sails or nets using brail. 5. to sew or stitch carelessly.

branch ~ a tributary of a river or main stream.

brandies ~ 1. an iron tripod for holding a pan in place over a fire. 2. a shoal of rocks that are above water at low tide.

brazen ~ impudent, saucy. "She's a brazen little brat."

breach ~ 1. the action of a fish jumping out of the water. 2. a school of fish or sea mammals on the water's surface.

breach of mackeral ~ a school of mackerel swimming with their "snouts" partly out of water, mak-ing their presence known only on a calm sea. "I haven't seen either breach of mackerel around yet this year."

breachy water {pronounced: *BREE - chee - WA - ter*} also **brackish water** ~ fresh water with a salty taste.

bread and cheese ~ a name applied to a rocky, barren hill.

bread and cheese nuts ~ the May Blossom, May Day Flower or White Thorn *[Crataegus oxyacantha]*, the red berries of the hawthorn tree. Primary chemical constituents of this herb include Vitamin C, flavonoids (quercetin, quercetrin), glycosides, proanthocyanidins, anthocynaidins, saponins, tannins and cratetegin (most prevalent in the flowers, then leaves, then berries). The berries have been used to lower high blood pressure and high cholesterol, as well as increase low blood pressure.

bread box ~ See **grub box**.

bread poultice ~ a medication incorporating bread and hot water, applied externally. See also **Home Remedies and Cures** on page 228.

breaker ~ a large ocean wave that breaks into foam.

breaking water ~ water that is churning and causing whitecaps.

bream ~ to melt the existing tar on a vessel's bottom with a torch, then add new tar to the old to seal the seams.

breastner ~ See **breastney**.

breastney also **bresna, breastner, bresney, brishney** ~ 1. an armful or bundle of firewood. 2. dry twigs gathered to start the fire.

breeches ~ See **britches**.

breeze ~ press down hard. "Breeze down on the end of that plank while I saw off a piece!"

bresna ~ See **breastney**.

bresney ~ See **breastney**.

brewis {pronounced: *BREWS*} ~ hard tack, also known as ships biscuits, soaked in water to soften. Probably from the English words "brewis" and "brevis," meaning "bread soaked in broth or gravy."

brewis bag ~ a bag used to soak hard bread.

bride knot ~ the floral arrangement worn by the bride.

bridge also **flatform**, **platform** ~ a patio, or wooden (and sometimes concrete) structure outside the entrance to a house. "Be sure to sweep the snow of your boots on the bridge before you comes in the house."

bridge

bridle ~ a piece of string attached to the top and bottom of a kite, to which the flying line was attached. See also **Flying Kites** on page 216.

briggs ~ heavy trousers that puff out from the sides at the thighs. From the Scottish, breeks.

briggs

brin bag ~ a burlap sack. "We used to carry our potatoes in brin bags."

bring ~ carry. "Bring your soft drink bottle back to the store so you can get your deposit back."

bring up ~ 1. a sudden stop. "Don't run down the garden after it gets dark because you might bring up in the clothesline." 2. ideal thing. "My shed is the real bring up."

bring up standing ~ to come to an abrupt stop while remaining erect.

brishney ~ See **breastney**.

britches also **breeches, fish breeches** ~ cod roe still in its sack.

broach ~ to open a container. "Why don't you broach that barrel of herring?"

broad day ~ a fine day.

brochet ~ a male caribou in its second year.

brooker also **grouse, browser partridge** ~ the Allen's willow ptarmigan *[Lagopus lagopus alleni]*, a bird of the ptarmigan family, which prefers ore moist and better vegetated country than its cousin, the rock ptarmigan. The male grows to a length of 43 cm (17 in) and a weight of 560 g (20 oz), while the smaller female grows to a length of 40 cm (16 in) and weighs up to 450 g (15 oz). It feeds primarily on mosses and lichens, and berries when available.

brooming ~ the act of raising a broom on a ship's masthead to show that the vessel is for sale.

brough {rhymes with *stuff*} ~ easily breakable.

browal ~ a swelling on the head, often the forehead or brow.

brown sally ~ a muzzle-loading gun.

browse {rhymes with *house*} ~ the tips of tree branches on which wild and domestic animals sometimes feed.

browser partridge ~ See **brooker**.

browsy {rhymes with *mousey*} ~ a particularly wild taste in rabbits that feed on browse.

brush ~ a sudden gust of wind.

bubble walker ~ a log driver

bubble walker

skilled at walking on the moving logs in a river.

bud of the lug ~ the chin.

buddy ~ See **buddywhatisname**.

buddywhatisname also **buddy** ~ referring to a person whose name is unknown or can't readily be recalled. "I was talking to buddywhatsisname – you know him – the feller who used to shoe the horses."

buck saw ~ a saw with a wooden or metal handle and replaceable blade, used to cut logs.

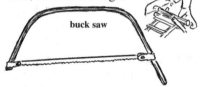

buck saw

bulkhead ~ a vertical partition or wall in a ship to divide it into compartments.

bullamarue ~ 1. an outspoken, noisy person who insists on having his own way. 2. a show-off.

bull bird also **john bull**, **nunchie**, **pigeon diver**, **gilly** ~ the common dovekie *[Platus alle]*. Measuring 20-25 cm (8-10 in), and having a wingspan of 30-33 cm (12-13 in), these birds were too small to make a meal by themselves

bull bird

and were often hunted and used to make soup. Nesting in Greenland, millions of these birds over-winter on the coasts of Newfoundland and Labrador. The community of Bay Bulls got its name from this bird.

bull cook ~ a lumberwoods cook's helper.

bullnozer ~ a bulldozer. "What, a bullnozer here in Herring Neck? That's only something else to get in the garden and eat the cabbage!"

bulls eyes ~ hard candy made in Newfoundland.

bully bagger ~ an imaginary figure used to threaten children who were misbehaving.

bully boat ~ a large sailing boat with gaff topsails.

bultow ~ fishing trawl.

bulwarks ~ that part of a ship's hull which rises above the main deck and forms a wall around the deck.

bum boat ~ a boat which meets a ship coming into a harbour to purchase or barter for some of her cargo to sell or trade.

bum-bye ~ See **bim-bye**.

bumper load ~ a full load. "We had a bumper load of fish last voyage."

bumps ~ having your friends hold you and bounce your bottom off the floor for every year of your age on your birthday, and then once more for good luck.

bun ~ 1. one of the three sections of a loaf of homemade bread. 2. a tea biscuit.

bun-bye ~ See **bim-bye**.

bunch ~ a lump or raised area on the body caused by a blow or something else. "I got a big bunch on my head when I fell on the ice."

bunk ~ 1. the cross-member or seat on a bobsled or catamaran sled. 2. a bed aboard ship or in a logging or other bunkhouse. See also **crossbar**.

bunk chain ~ the chain used to fasten a load on a bobsled or catamaran.

bunker also **locker, slab** ~ the kitchen counter top.

bunkhouse ~ a sometimes roughly constructed building in the woods in which loggers slept. See also **The Lumberwoods** on page 263.

bunkum ~ nonsense. "Don't tell me the Liberals are any good in government, that's bunkum."

buoy {pronounced: *BOY*, as well as *BOO - ee*} ~ a float used to mark the position of nets, traps, trawls, moorings, shipping channels, etc.

buoy pole ~ a stick extending up from a buoy to enable it to be seen from a distance above the curvature of the ocean.

buoy pole

burgoo ~ oatmeal porridge.

burned ~ frostbitten.

burning weather ~ being cold enough to cause frostbite. "It's some burning weather out tonight."

burny ~ in a marble game, two marbles that are touching after they are tossed.

burry ~ berry.

burryin' ~ picking berries. "I was burryin' in on the White Hills and got two gallons of partridgeberries."

bush born ~ the name given by English and Irish settlers to persons born in Newfoundland.

busk ~ to beg food and clothing.

butter bitch ~ the man in charge of a ship's stores.

butter churn ~ a wooden device used to churn cream into butter.

butter churn

butter pot ~ a prominent rounded hill.

butter teeth ~ the two top, front teeth.

button, button ~ a children's game. See also **Button, Button** on page 205.

buttow {pronounced: *BUT - toe*} ~ a trawl or long line of fish hooks.

b'y {pronounced: *BY*} ~ 1. a young male person, a boy. 2. any male person, regardless of age. "Have another piece of cake, my dear, the b'ys are working."

by and by ~ later. "We'll come visit you by and by."

by boats ~ the fishing boats of various sizes left in Newfoundland when the owners returned to West Country England for the winter.

by rights ~ strictly speaking. "By rights I should have been here sooner."

cadder ~ a quilt or eiderdown.

cadgy ~ See **catchy**.

cairn ~ See **naked man**.

cal ~ money, cash.

callabogus ~ a drink containing rum mixed with other ingredients, including spruce beer, molasses etc.

calm {rhymes with *ma'am*, also rhymes with *mom* in some parts of Newfoundland and Labrador} ~ 1. the absence of wind. 2. having no agitation on the water's surface.

Candlemas cake ~ 1. a type of sweetened bread baked for party on February 2 or Candlemas Day. 2. the party itself.

canker ~ 1. a type of potato wart. 2. a sore on the mouth.

cankery ~ 1. tarnished. 2. messy.

cant ~ to lean to one side.

canterbury bells ~ See **pink bells**.

canting ~ gossiping or telling yarns. "There was a lot of canting going on at the Home League meeting last night."

canvas ~ a cheap, thin type of linoleum used as a floor covering.

cape ~ a projecting headland or tip of a peninsula.

cape ann also **linkum** ~ a fisherman's hat similar to a sou'wester, except that it is made of rubber instead of oilcloth or oilskin, and originated in the United States. The word "linkum" is probably derived from "Lincoln" and probably originated in the New England States.

cape ann

capelin also **caplin** {pronounced: *CAPE - lynn*} ~ a slender, translucent olive coloured, small-scaled fish of the *Osmeridae* family of smelts that grow to a maximum length of 25 cm (10 in) *[Mallotus villosus]*. Capelin make excellent

capelin

bait fish and were also once used as fertilizer for the vegetable gardens. They are sometimes cleaned and fried for dinner and often salted (or smoked) whole and dried to be roasted later. Although capelin sometimes spawn offshore, the females often come ashore to leave their eggs, which are fertilized by the males who also come ashore to procreate with the females on the pebbled beaches. The spawning process leaves the capelin quite vulnerable to predators, especially humans. They are seined offshore by long-liners and caught in capelin traps. On the beaches they can be caught by hand, in a dip net, or even a bucket. But the best way to catch them onshore is with a cast net. See also **cast net**.

capelin cart ~ a two-wheeled cart hauled by a horse or donkey and used to carry capelin.

capelin scull ~ the migration of capelin schools from the deep water to spawn on beaches. From "capelin school."

capelin trap ~ a box-like trap of netting used to catch capelin.

capelin weather ~ cold misty weather. This is the kind of weather usually experienced at capelin-spawning time.

caplin ~ See **capelin**.

capstan ~ 1. a vertical spindle turned by a handle that acts as a lever to lighten the load when hauling in ropes, chains or cables aboard ship. 2. a similar device used onshore to haul up smaller boats.

capstan

cap stick ~ a ball game.

captain's ticket ~ a sea-captain's certificate of competency.

car ~ a floating wooden box in which live lobster are stored before being sold.

caravel built ~ See **carvel built**.

carawat ~ 1. idle talk among a group of people. 2. to gossip.

carbuckle ~ See **carbunkle**.

carbunkle also **carbuckle** ~ 1. a sore, similar to a boil, usually on the neck, but sometimes appearing on the armpits. 2. a boil or collection of boils close together.

carcass ~ the living body of a person. "Get up here to thy supper or I'll crack the skin on thy skull and haul thy carcass up through."

card ~ 1. a wooden template that determines the size of mesh in a net or trap. 2. to draw raw wool into long fibers before spinning it into yarn.

cardeen ~ the way the accordion is often jocularly referred to in Newfoundland and Labrador.

cardeen

carey's chicken also **mother carey's chicken** ~ one of two species of small petrels: the storm petrel *[Procellaria pelagica]*, and Leach's storm petrel *[Oceanodroma leucorhoa]*. Petrels measure about 20 cm (8 in) to the tip of their tails with a wingspan of about 47 cm (18.5 in), and weigh 40-50 g (1.5-1.8 oz). The Leach's storm petrel is bigger than the storm petrel, with longer, more pointed and distinctively angled wings and a longer, forked tail. On land, they crouch on bent legs and move with shuffling gait. In the air, the flight is erratic with swoops, bounces, flutters and skimming motions. Most petrels feed on crustaceans, molluscs, small fish etc., while some will follow ships, feeding in the wake for disturbed organisms or scraps.

caribou berry ~ 1. the berry of the white mandarin plant *[Streptopus amplexifolius]*. 2. the berry of the rose mandarin plant *[Streptopus roseus]*.

caribou fly ~ 1. the deer fly *[Chrysops exitans]*.

cark ~ See **cork**.

carpenter ~ 1. a small land crustacean of the *Oniscus* family that is about 14 mm (9/16 in) in length, a woodlouse or sow bug. 2. a similar creature found in the ocean.

carrying-on also **driving-works** ~ misbehaving, acting up, engaged in horseplay or just plain boisterously having fun. "You youngsters better stop that carrying on or someone might get hurt."

carry off ~ to steal. "Someone carried off my new hammer."

cart ~ a sled.

carteel boat ~ See **cartel boat**.

cartel boat also **carteel boat** ~ an auxiliary boat used to transport fish.

carter ~ the driver of a dog team.

carvel built also **caravel built, plank boat, seam boat** ~ a boat with planks that abut, rather than overlap, each other.

carver ~ a person who splits codfish.

case hardened ~ stubborn.

cast ~ 1. to throw, especially to throw a net. 2. to add up figures.

cast net ~ a small, round, handheld net with lead balls around the outside, used for catching capelin in shallow water. The

cast net

net is flung over a school of capelin, trapping them as the lead balls sink to the bottom. A string, attached to a number of other strings that are attached to the circumference of the net is then drawn in, causing the lead balls to come together and create a bag, sometimes holding a hundred or more capelin.

cast net ball ~ a lead ball with a hole through the middle, used as a weight on a cast net.

cat also **cat-o-nine-tails** ~ a vicious whip that, when used to flog the bare backs of law-breakers or disobedient sailors or other workers, it would cut through the flesh and leave scars that sometimes lasted for life. See also **Whipping Post** on page 17.

catamaran {pronounced: *CAT - ah - mar - AN*} also **dog-cat, horn-slide** ~ a sled with two runners, two cross seats and four horns (upright round sticks for holding logs on the sled).

catamaran

cat berry ~ the wild lily-of-the-valley *[Maianthemum canadense]*.

catch ~ the quantity of fish caught. "We had a good catch yesterday."

catchy also **cadgy, kedgy** ~ a person who does odd jobs.

cat house ~ 1. a covering over a wild animal trap, especially a pine marten or lynx trap. 2. a whorehouse.

cat-o-nine-tails ~ See **cat**.

cat trap ~ a trap to capture lynx or pine marten. The lynx is a member of the cat family, while the marten is a member of the weasel family. In Ireland martens are referred to as cats, which is where the Newfoundland term most likely originated.

cattywampus ~ crazy.

caubeen ~ a cap or hat. Origin: Ireland.

caudle ~ to work in a careless manner.

caudler ~ a person who does everything wrong.

caught over ~ beginning to freeze over. "It must have been cold last night because the harbour caught over." NOTE: The future or present tense of this word was never used. ie: One would never say, "The harbour will catch over tonight," or "The harbour is catching over."

cavalance ~ a type of bean.

cellar ~ a structure, apart from a dwelling, built partly underground or into the side of a hill and covered in sods, and used to keep vegetables from freezing in winter and from rotting on warm summer days.

CFA ~ See **come from away**.

chamber pot ~ a ceramic or enamel pot with a handle that was kept under every bed at night for the purpose of urination.

chamber pot

champkin ~ a champion.

change ~ 1. cash. 2. to tender for exchange. "I went to the bank to change my cheque but they said I didn't have enough ID."

changling ~ a child left in exchange by fairies. See also **Fairylore** on page 283.

charm ~ 1. noise. "There's some charm when the youngsters play bar rover." 2. to cure illnesses and remove warts by other than medical means. "I got a toothache so I'm going to see a charmer and have it charmed away."

charmer ~ the seventh son of a seventh son, believed to be able to cure illnesses by other than medical means. In some areas people believed that one was a charmer simply by being the seventh son.

chart ~ a map-like representation of a part of an ocean or sea, showing depths and contours, used for navigation.

chaw and glutch ~ bread and tea.

chebacco boat ~ a sailing vessel with a high, narrow stern once used in the Newfoundland fishery. Named after a small river in Massachusetts.

cheek ~ the fleshy part of a cod's head, considered something of a delicacy.

cheek music also **chin music** and **mouth music** ~ the mouthing of the notes of a tune when a musical instrument is not available.

cheem ~ the V-shaped notch in the ends of barrel staves into which the top and bottom fit.

chesterfield ~ a sofa.

chimbe {pronounced: *CHIME*} ~ the part of the barrel staves that go beyond the head of the barrel.

chimbe hoop ~ the hoop near the ends of a barrel to protect the chimbe.

chimbley ~ See **chimley**.

chimley also **chimbley** ~ a chimney.

chinch also **chink, stog** ~ to stuff. "Make sure you chinch that oakum in the seams tight or the boat will leak."

chin cough ~ the whooping cough.

chink ~ See **chinch**.

chinkers ~ a material used to fill in the gaps between the boards or logs of a house.

chin music ~ See **cheek music**.

chip chip ~ a children's guessing game. See also **Chip, Chip** on page 207.

chips ~ french fries.

chisel ~ a lively variation of the lancers dance.

choby also **chopy, chovy, mop head, shovy** ~ kindling that is shaved so thin that pieces curl out to make them as easy to light as paper or birch bark. A chobie was sometimes used to light one's pipe or cigarette by igniting it from the kitchen stove.

chobies

chocolate root ~ the water avens, indian chocolate, cure all and water flower *[Geum rivale]*. an erect perennial plant having pinnate leaves and few nodding flowers with brown-purple calyx and orange-pink petals. The root of this plant has a powerfully astringent action that is beneficial in passive hemorrhage and diarrhea.

chook ~ 1. a pig. 2. a call to pigs. "Here chook, chook, chook!"

chops ~ the mouth.

chopy ~ See **choby**.

choule ~ the jaw.

chovy ~ See **choby**.

Christian ~ a human being as opposed to an animal.

Christmas ~ the food and drink served over the twelve days of Christmas. "Come on in and have a bit of Christmas."

Christmas box ~ 1. a Christmas gift. 2. a box containing gifts, which might include food or money. 3. a box used to collect money for those in need at Christmas.

Christmas fish ~ the salt cod eaten on Boxing Day.

Christmas time ~ a party, often with dancing and skits and other entertainment, before or after Christmas Day.

chuck ~ to throw or toss.

chuckle ~ 1. to grasp someone by the throat. 2. a gentle blow to the chin.

chuckle-head ~ a fool. From Devon, England.

chuckley-muck ~ a wheel nailed to a stick which children pushed around while making oral noises to emulate an engine. Some models had a shorter

chuckley-muck

stick nailed to the longer stick which served as a gear stick.

chucks ~ the cheeks. From Devon, England.

chummy also **chummywatchacallit** ~ referring to a person (or an item) whose name is unknown or can't readily be recalled. "Have you seen chummy, the feller you went down on the Labrador with, lately?

chummy-jigger also **machine**, **thingamabobber**, **thingamajig**, **whatchamacallit** ~ referring to an item, the name of which is unknown or can't readily be recalled. "Hand me that chummer jigger there on the bench, will you?"

chummywatchacallit ~ See **chummy**.

chute {pronounced: *SHOOT*} ~ an inclined trough down which coal or other substances may slide.

civil ~ referring to the weather on a good day. "There's not a draft of wind. It looks like we're going to have a civil day."

clamper also **clumper** ~ an ice pan.

Clarenville boat ~ a boat built at Clarenville.

clave {rhymes with *save*} also **cleave** {rhymes with *sleeve*} ~ to split by chopping

claving wood

with an axe. "Could you go out and clave some splits to light the fire tomorrow morning?"

clavey {rhymes with *savy*} ~ 1. a mantlepiece or shelf. 2. a storage place in a fireplace chimney.

clear airs ~ the name applied to settlers of Newfoundland from Tipperary, Ireland.

clear thing ~ the ideal thing. "When you're not feeling good that Brick's Tasteless is the clear thing to perk you up."

cleave ~ See **clave**.

clergy ~ a priest or minister of the church.

clever ~ 1. handsome. "That's some clever-looking boyfriend you got there, my maid." 2. robust and healthy. "Sure he's clever enough to load 45 gallon drums of oil aboard the schooner his self."

clever-looking ~ handsome.

clew ~ the corner of a sail.

clew up ~ to settle accounts. "When I went to clew up with the merchant last year I had enough for a plug of baccy and a few candies fer the youngsters."

clew-up time ~ the time in autumn when a fisherman settled his account with the merchant. This was probably the most important

time of year for those involved in the fishery. This was the time when a fisherman found out if he had earned enough money to pay off his debt to the merchant. This was a constant worry for him, but was somewhat alleviated by the fact that most merchants would carry them over the next year and, in many cases, year after year.

cliff rock ~ a sharp rock as opposed to a rounded beach rock.

clink ~ 1. a jail. 2. a blow or slap. 3. to strike someone, especially on the head. "If you say that one more time I'm going to clink you upside the head."

clinkerbell ~ See **ice candle**.

clinker built ~ a method of constructing wooden vessels so that each strake of side planking on the hull overlaps the one below it. This type of hull was usually found on smaller vessels, particularly lifeboats.

clinker together ~ to construct in a very rough and unskillful manner. "After he got home from fishing, Bert clinkered together a few sticks, just enough to keep the sheep out, and his wife quiet."

clint ~ to secure a driven nail by bending the protruding end over with a hammer. Probably from the word "clinch," meaning the same.

clip ~ a bobby pin.

clobber ~ 1. in an untidy state of things. 2. to strike or beat.

clom also **clum, glom** ~ to clutch and hold. "Clom onto that stick of wood while I saw it."

close {rhymes with *dose*} ~ humid and hot. "It's so close today I've had to change me shirt three times."

close to the floor ~ a fast jig. "Give us one close to the floor." See also **Dancing** on page 211.

clot ~ a clump of earth or sod. From "clod."

cloud ~ a lady's shawl, scarf or head covering.

clout ~ to hit, or strike someone hard. "Bring back my bike or I'll clout you so hard you'll think your father was your mother."

club ~ to put an extra sole on a shoe or boot.

club-footed ~ a person with one leg longer than the other.

clum ~ See **clom**.

clumper ~ See **ice pan**.

clutch ~ a brood of chickens.

CN bus ~ officially called the Roadcruiser service when it started in 1968. It was operated by Canadian National and replaced the passenger service that had been previously provided by the train from Port aux Basques to St. John's. This service was later taken over by the present operators, DRL, a private company out of Triton, Newfoundland.

coach box ~ a box for carrying passengers on a komatik. See also **woman's box**.

coady ~ a sauce, particularly one made of molasses, to spread over dough boys or puddings.

coal fees ~ school fees. One of the major expenses in child education at one time was having to pay for coal to keep the pot-bellied stove in the classroom heated to the point where students were warm enough to be able to study and learn.

coarse weather ~ rough weather.

coastal boat ~ a ship, owned or leased by the government, to carry passengers, freight and mail around the coast of Newfoundland and Labrador. Going down on the wharf when the coastal boat came in was a highly anticipated experience for people in many outports.

coastal wharf ~ a public wharf erected and maintained by the provincial government especially to accommodate coastal boats.

coaster ~ 1. a ship in the coastal service as opposed to foreign-going ships. 2. a small

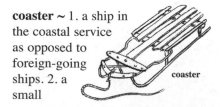

coaster

store-bought sled with metal runners and a steering device.

coasting ~ 1. plying the coastal trade in ships. 2. riding downhill on a sled. "Let's go coasting."

cob ~ to separate ore from rock in a mine yield.

cobby house also **coopy house**, **copy house** ~ a small house built by or for children to play in. Possibly from the word "copy," or possibly from the word " coopy," meaning "to crouch."

cock ~ See **cocky**.

cockabaloo ~ a bully.

cocket ~ See **pook**.

cock indian ~ a male Beothuk.

cockle ~ a mullosk, of the *Cardiidae* family, similar in appearance to a scallop.

cock of the walk ~ a leader. "Look at him strut – he thinks he's the cock of the walk."

cocks and hens ~ a variety of clams.

cocksidle ~ 1. to somersault. 2. a somersault.

cocky ~ a male person. "What are you at today, cocky?"

cod ~ to trick or fool. "You wouldn't cod me, would you?"

codfish ~ the common name for one member of the *Gadus* family of fishes *[Gadus morhua]*. Codfish grow to approximately 120 cm (48 in) in length, and to a weight of around 12 kg (26 lb); however, much larger fish have been recorded. For many years this fish, which actually started the British Empire, was king in Newfoundland and Labrador.

cod fishery ~ the main fishery in Newfoundland and Labrador.

cod jigger ~ a lead lure with two hooks for jigging codfish. The jigging motion emulates a wounded fish, which attracts the codfish. Cod are snagged on the upward motion of the jigger. Jiggers are now outlawed in Newfoundland and Labrador.

cod jigger

cod liver oil ~ the oil obtained from the processing of cod livers.

cod net ~ a gill net specially made to catch codfish.

cod piece ~ a knitted woolen sleeve worn on the penis by fishermen while fishing in the winter.

cod's head and mackerel tail ~ nickname for a round or bluff-bowed ship with a long tapering run.

cod socks also **cossocks** ~ long rubber boots cut off at the ankles.

cod trap ~ a box-like net with small mesh used for catching cod.

coffin ship ~ a very unseaworthy ship.

colcannon ~ a meal of vegetables and meat, usually served on October 31. Originated in Ireland.

Colcannon Night ~ Halowe'en night. See also **Colcannon Night** on page 198.

cold junk ~ unconscious. "Roy hit his head on the door facing and fell down, a cold junk."

collar ~ a device for mooring boats away from a wharf in open water in a harbour or cove. The collar consists of an anchor and a chain made to form a loop at the opposite end. This loop was placed down over the stem head of the boat and secured with lines. The anchor was left permanently in position, which was marked by a buoy. To prevent the chain from chafing the boat in rough weather, the loop was covered in canvas or some other material. This gave it the appearance of a collar on a garment, hence the name.

collar buoy ~ a float to mark the location of a mooring collar.

collop ~ a small group of sheep or goats.

combers {pronounced: *COMB - ers*} ~ large ocean waves.

come ~ came. "I don't know what come over me."

come-from-away also **CFA** ~ 1. a person from elsewhere now living in Newfoundland and Labrador. 2. a tourist.

comical ~ having a tendency to be humorous in speech and/or action. "She's so comical she could be on the 'I Love Lucy' show."

comical-looking ~ funny or strange-looking.

Commission of Government ~ the form of government in Newfoundland between 1934 and 1949. See also **Politics and Populations** on page 254.

community stage ~ the waterfront facilities available for use by the whole community.

companionway ~ stairs or ladder leading to a cabin aboard ship.

company ~ a group of wild birds or animals.

complected ~ having a dark complexion.

complete hand ~ an expert.

concert also **time** ~ an exposition of entertainment including songs, recitations, jokes and skits at a community venue.

concertina ~ a musical instrument,

similar to an accordion, but smaller, once popular in the province.

conch shell ~ a large, spiral shell, sometimes used as a horn.

condemn ~ to discontinue usage. "My schooner got so old she had to be condemned."

Confederation ~ the joining of Newfoundland and Canada in 1949.

confirmations ~ a button-up shirt and ankle-length drawers sewn together to make one garment. These were made of flour sacks. Some of these had a slit with a button at the back for using the toilet, while some had none and the shirt part had to be completely unbuttoned and removed so the drawers could be lowered to use the toilet.

conner also **sly conner** ~ the blue perch or sea bass *[Tautogolabrus adspersus]*, a bottom feeding fish of the family *Percidae*, often found around stage heads and wharves. "Mainlanders must have some stomachs on 'em – they calls conners ocean perch and eats 'em." See also **Catchin' Tomcods and Conners** on page 206.

cooch also **coochy, croochy** or **coopy, croodle** ~ to crouch or bend down. "Better cooch down behind the platform so your mother can't see you." probably from the word "crouch."

coochy ~ See **cooch**.

cookaloo ~ the ear. Possibly derived from the cockle shell which looks like an ear.

cookhouse ~ a sometimes roughly constructed building in the woods that serves as a kitchen for cook(s) and a dining area for loggers. See also **The Lumberwoods** on page 263.

coopy ~ See **coochy**.

coosh also **cush** ~ 1. a bed. 2. to nap. See also **alley-coosh**.

cooty also **booshy** ~ a louse.

copper fasten ~ 1. to come to a clear agreement. 2. to sign one's name on a written agreement.

copying pans also **gallying, jumping clampers, quabbering, step 'n' copy, tabby, tabbying, tally, tibby, tippy, tipsy** ~ jumping from icepan to icepan for fun. See also **Clampers and Youngsters** on page 207.

cordovan ~ a leather made from sealskin.

cork also **cark** ~ 1. oakum used to seal the seams between a boat's planks. 2. to fill in the seams between a boat's planks to make the boat waterproof. From the word "caulk," meaning "to stop up cracks or crevices with a filler." 3. the filter tip of a cigarette. "I lit the cork of my cigarette by mistake and couldn't get a whiff through it."

corker ~ the American bittern *[Botaurus lentiginosus]*, a medium-sized heron having a stout body and neck, short legs and a white neck. They grow to 58-86 cm (23-34 in) in length. These birds are seldom seen as they hide in the reeds and tall grasses, sometimes swaying to the movements of these reeds and grasses on a windy day to further conceal themselves.

corned ~ intoxicated.

cossocks ~ See **cod socks**.

cosy egg ~ See **whore's egg.**

cotched ~ caught.

cottage hospital ~ an outport hospital offering only the medical services of general practitioners.

cottage range ~ small, cheap row houses, especially in St. John's.

cotterall also **cottle** ~ a metal pot hook for a fireplace, with notches at different heights to control the heat while cooking.

cottle ~ See **cotterall.**

cotton ~ a thread used for sewing.

couldn's ~ leftovers. from the word "couldn't," ie. food that couldn't be eaten the day before.

country man ~ a hunter or trapper.

country tea ~ Labrador tea *[Ledum groenlandicum]*. This plant has been used to make a very palatable beverage. It has also been used as a medicine in the treatment of coughs, dyspepsia, and irritation of the membranes of the lungs. An infusion has been used to soothe irritation in infectious, feverish eruptions; in dysentery; leprosy; itch etc. Strong versions of this tea has also been used as a wash to kill lice.

coup ~ 1. a hen. 2. a call to hens. "Here coup, coup, coup, coup."

cove ~ a small bay or inlet.

covel ~ 1. a wooden tub with rope handles. 2. a covered water barrel.

covel

covel staff ~ a pole put through the handles of a covel so it can be carried by two men.

covey ~ a person from an outport.

cow bee ~ a flying insect that attaches itself to large domestic and wild animals.

cow belly ~ a bogland.

cowed out ~ tired.

cow flock ~ the marsh marigold *[Caltha pulustris]*. This plant of the buttercup family grows in swamps and stream edges to a height of 20-61 cm (8-24 in) with yellow flowers that measure 2-4 cm (1 - 1-1/2 in) in diameter.

cow patty also **cow platter** ~ cow dung.

cow platter ~ See **cow patty**.

cow's arse ~ an undependable person. "He's such a cow's arse he could frig up a two-car funeral."

cow's milk ~ milk fresh from the cow as opposed to store-bought milk.

crab ~ Any number of species of crab but especially the three species caught commercially. These include the Atlantic snow crab [*Chionoecetes opilio*], and two species of toad crab, [*Hyas araneus* and *Hyas coarctatus*]. The snow crab is the most important commercial crab species in eastern Canada. Only

snow crab

the male snow crab is kept as the female is too small to have any commercial value. Males may reach a maximum shell width of 16.5 cm (6.5 in), a leg span of 90 cm (37 in) and a weight of 1.35 kg (3 lb). The female grows to a maximum shell width of 9.5 cm (3.75 in), with a leg span of 38 cm (15 in) and a weight of 0.45 kg (1 lb). Toad crabs can be distinguished from snow crabs by differences in their shell proportions. In toad crabs the shell is longer than it is wide and its walking legs are tubular, not flat.

crab pot ~ a trap made of a metal frame with sides and bottom made of netting. The pot is baited and crabs crawl up the sloped sides and fall into the trap to get at the bait and are trapped.

crab pot

cracked ~ See **half-cracked**.

crackerberry also **pigeon berry** ~ the dwarf cornel [*Cornus canadensis*], an orange-red berry that grows in clusters and has many seeds that crack when eaten.

crackie ~ a small dog of mixed breed. A crackie was a pet and not used as a working dog.

crackie

cram ~ to squeeze or stuff. "Don't cram too much food in your mouth or you'll choke."

cramp ~ a humorous person. "I haves a good laugh when I goes fishing with Joe because he's a real cramp."

cramps ~ laughs heartily. "I cramps at him." From getting a cramp in one's stomach because one is laughing so hard.

cranky ~ tippy. "That rowboat was so cranky you couldn't stand up in her."

crannick also **cronnick, crunnock**

~ weathered root, branch or stump of a tree used for fuel or kindling.

craper ~ See **creeper**.

craw also **crawl, crop** ~ the upper chest and throat. "Button up your craw before you catch cold."

crawl ~ See **craw**.

crease ~ the parting of the hair when combed.

creep ~ to drag the bottom of the ocean or lake in an effort to snag a lost line or net or the clothing of a drowned person.

creeper also **craper** {pronounced: *CRAY - per*} ~ 1. a metal device with sharp points similar to a grapnel, used to drag the bottom. 2. a metal device fastened to the bottom of a boot to enable one to walk on slippery ice.

crewdle ~ to crouch together.

cribby ~ 1 a crowded and cheaply built part of St. John's. 2. a resident of such an area.

cripsy ~ brittle and easily broken. "When a chocolate bar gets cold it gets right cripsy."

crit ~ 1. cramped from being in one position too long. "I was knitting so long my back got in a crit." 2. a hump on one's back. 3. a bent or crooked back.

critch ~ a china jar.

cronnick ~ See **crannick**.

croochy ~ See **coochy**.

croodle ~ See **cooch**.

crooked ~ ill-tempered, contrary and cranky. "If he don't get his chew of baccy he gets right crooked."

croost ~ to throw stones at.

crop ~ 1. the items a sealer or fisherman can take on credit against his share of the voyage. 2. to clip the wings of domestic fowl. 3. See **craw**.

crop note ~ a merchant's note entitling a sealer to his supplies and equipment.

crossackle ~ 1. to make one angry by disagreeing with him or her, to vex by contrary argument. 2 to confront. "Don't crossackle me today."

cross bar also **bunk** ~ a plank atop and at right angles to the runners of a sled. 2. the top bar running between the seat and handlebars of a man's bicycle.

cross fox ~ the red fox *[Vulpes fulvus]*.

cross handed ~ 1. working alone. "It's hard to put a plank in a boat cross-handed." 2. rowing a boat with the hands crossed at the chest.

cross heckle ~ See **crossackle**.

cross patch ~ a disagreeable child.

cross pile ~ to pile logs or other items with each layer at right angles to the previous one to keep them from falling over. "Make sure you cross pile the fish on the flake because they'll fall over if they get too high.

cross wind ~ a wind blowing across a vessel's course.

crouch ~ to bend the body. "You can crouch down behind that table if you like but I can still see you."

crousty ~ ill-tempered and contrary. "If Grandmother haven't got Grandfather's supper cooked when he gets home, he gets right crousty."

crowdy ~ oatmeal and milk.

crown ~ to strike someone on the top of the head. "If I gets a hold of ye youngsters I'll crown ye."

crubeens ~ pickled pig's feet.

crud ~ coagulated milk. Probably from the word "curd."

cruddy ~ having a coagulated appearance. "That milk looks cruddy – it may be starting to go bad."

cruise ~ a trip of any kind on land or sea.

cruiser ~ a crewmember on a coastal vessel.

crump ~ in a hunched position. "The seats on the ferry were so small I was in a crump the whole time I was aboard of her."

crunnock ~ See **crannick**.

cubbagess ~ covetous.

cuckoo ~ a large sea snail.

cuddy ~ a compartment or house in the front of a boat.

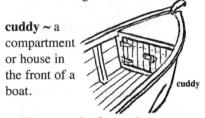

cuddy

cuddy oar ~ the forward oar.

cue ~ a piece of metal nailed to the heels of footwear to prevent them from wearing out too quickly.

cuff ~ 1. to strike. "Simmer down or you're going to get a cuff on the ears." 2. a mitten, especially one without fingers or thumb. 3. a tale or yarn.

cuffer ~ 1. a friendly chat between two or more people. 2. a lie.

cugger ~ to whisper.

cull ~ 1. to sort cured fish according to quality. 2. to choose or gather the best of something. 3. to reduce the size of a herd or flock by killing a certain number.

cullage ~ the most inferior grade of cured fish.

culling board ~ the table where cured fish are culled.

cund ~ to direct from a ship's barrel or crow's nest.

cunney ~ an offensive term referring to the female genitalia.

curbs ~ blankets.

cure ~ 1. to process fish by splitting, cleaning, salting and drying. 2. a humorous person.

curwibble ~ 1. a sudden change of direction. 2. a staggering movement. "He had a few drinks before he left and the last I saw him he was curwibbling down the cow path."

cush ~ See **coosh**.

custard cone ~ soft ice-cream.

cut ~ a number of sheep, goats or cattle taken from a flock or herd.

cute ~ keen and sharp.

cut the devil's throat ~ See **dead man's dive**.

cut-throat ~ 1. a fisherman who cuts the codfish's throat and splits the belly open. 2. the knife used for this operation.

cutwater

cutwater ~ 1. the lower front-projecting part

of a caribou antler. 2. the stem of a vessel.

cuverd ~ a cupboard.

dabber also **dapper** ~ a weighted hook that requires bait.

daddle ~ the hind paw or hind flipper of a seal.

dadyeens ~ settlers from County Cork, Ireland.

dagger ~ a whetstone.

dally ~ 1. a sudden slackening of the wind. 2. a wind coming from various directions.

damper ~ the round cover of a wood stove through which wood and coal is placed in stove. "Put that damper back on the stove before the kitchen fills with smoke."

damper

damper cake also **damper devil, damper dog, damper down, dolly bodger, gandy, goat's egg, flummy, fried dough, funnel bun, tiffin, toutin** ~ bread dough that is fried in a pan, directly on a stove top, around a stove funnel or on a stick over an open fire.

damper devil ~ See **damper cake**.

damper dog ~ See **damper cake**.

damper down ~ See **damper cake**.

dancing master ~ a wooden puppet with jointed arms, knees and legs, set on a board in a manner that when vibrated the puppet danced.

dander ~ temper. "Don't get his dander up."

danger bell ~ a bell rung on a ship at anchor to indicate danger in foggy weather.

danger flag ~ a flag raised on a sealing ship in an ice field warning sealers on the ice to return to the ship.

dank ~ moist or damp.

dapper ~ See **dabber**.

darby ~ 1. a fairy, 2. a disguised person or mummer.

darn ~ to repair a hole in knitted clothing. "I got to get Mother to darn my vamps."

darnback ~ See **thornback**.

darnbank ~ See **thornback**.

dart ~ 1. a quick, short blow. "If you don't stop mouzing me you're going to get a dart in the gob." 2. to go somewhere. "I'm going to take a dart down the road to see what is going on."

davit ~ one of two fittings which project out over a ship's side and used for raising or lowering lifeboats or other items.

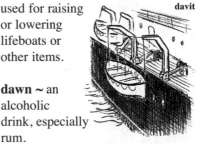

davit

dawn ~ an alcoholic drink, especially rum.

dawnies ~ realistic dreams or nightmares.

dawny ~ in poor health.

dawt also **tawt, thwart** ~ the cross seat in a small boat.

dawt

day bed ~ See **settle**.

dead-calm ~ perfectly calm.

dead cart ~ a hearse.

dead-eye ~ 1. a sore or callus on the hand. 2. a block made from hardwood through which a rope passes and is used in the rigging of a vessel. 3. a block made from hardwood which is part of a mooring device known as a "hail-off." The dead-eye is anchored to the ocean bottom a short distance from shore. A rope is passed through the eye (hole) in the dead-eye and used to haul boats into a mooring position and back to shore again. See also **haul-off**.

dead man's cap also **devil's cap** ~ a toadstool.

dead man's daisy ~ the common yarrow *[Achillea millefolium]*. This plant has been used as a poultice on inflammations, and a tea made from this plant was used to bath inflammations and was drunk to treat various conditions from colds and fevers to gastric distress and internal bleeding.

dead man's dive also **cut the devil's throat** ~ to throw a stone high in the air so it plunks into the water without making a splash.

dead man's flower ~ known elsewhere as the common meadow sweet, bridewort, meadow queen, meadow-wort, pride of the meadow, lady of the meadow or mountain spiraea *[Spiraea latifolia]*. This plant's flowery top contains methyl salicylate heteroside (monotropitoside) and salicylic aldehyde (used for its anti-inflammatory, analgesic and anti-blood clotting properties, common to all salicylic medication), as well as flavonoids (quercetol, kaempferol, etc.) responsible for diuretic action associated with tannins and mineral salts (particularly calcium, iron and sulphur), and vitamin C.

dead man's pinch ~ a small mark or bruise appearing without apparent cause.

dead man's share ~ a small portion.

dead moss ~ the beard moss *[Usnea barbata]*, a greenish grey pendulous lichen that grows on trees.

dead reckoning ~ calculation of ship's position by consideration of distance logged, courses steered and estimated leeway.

dead wood ~ the pieces of wood that join the stem of a boat to the keel, as well as the stern post to the keel for reinforcement purposes.

dean ~ a valley.

dear ~ expensive.

deck engine ~ a mechanical device used to raise a ship's sails or to raise and lower freight.

deck hand ~ an ordinary seaman who serves on the deck of a vessel.

deep ~ keeps one's inner feelings to one's self.

deer fence ~ a barrier in the woods used to direct caribou to a narrow opening where they could be taken.

deer path ~ the usual migrating route of caribou.

deese also **theese** {rhymes with *peace*} ~ you. "Deese knows, ol' man, that the schooner is on her way in." Originated in West Country England, from the word "thee."

delco ~ a gasoline generator of any make.

devil ~ a seam at a vessel's waterline.

devil-may-care ~ having a careless attitude.

devil's birthday ~ Saturday.

devil's blanket ~ a snowfall that hinders work.

devil-ma-click ~ a versatile worker, a jack of all trades.

devil's cap ~ See **dead man's cap**.

devil's clay ~ a grapnel used to fasten a vessel to an ice floe.

devilskin ~ See **devil's pelt**.

devil's match ~ a plant of the bulrush family *[Scripus cespitosus]*. Possibly got its name from the fact that it resembles a large match stick.

devil's pelt also **devilskin** ~ a mischievous child.

devil's pipe also **indian cup, indian pipe** ~ the pitcher plant *[Sarracenia purpurea]*, a greenish-brown, carnivorous plant, having an upside down, wineglass-shaped cup that traps water and insects. This plant is the floral emblem of Newfoundland and Labrador.

devil's pipe

devil's thumb prints ~ the black marks on a haddock's back.

dewberry ~ the dwarf raspberry *[Rubus arcticus]*. These berries are edible but are smaller and less succulent than raspberries.

dickey ~ a heavy, usually woolen, bib worn to keep warm, especially by children. See also **adickey**.

dickey bird ~ 1. a rooster. 2. the penis.

diddle ~ to make music with the mouth using unintelligible sounds so others can dance.

didoes {pronounced: *DIE - doughs*} ~ a fuss, or boisterous behavior.

diet ~ the food and keep of a servant or shareman.

dieter ~ one who works for board and keep.

dildo ~ See **thole pin**.

dill ~ 1. a duck. 2. a call to ducks. "Here dill, dill, dill." 3. the space in the bottom of a boat from whence bilge water may be bailed. See also **dill room.**

dill board ~ the cover over a dill room.

dill room ~ 1. a compartment in the lowest portion of a vessel under the floorboards. 2. an area in the bottom of a boat. from whence bilge water may be dipped out. "When you're finished bailing, put the punt's piggin back in the dill room."

dinner ~ a big cooked meal served around noon.

dip net ~ a circu-
lar net framed by a
metal ring at the end of a
pole, used for handling
fish.

dip net

dipper ~ a pot with a long handle, a saucepan.

dipping time ~ the period in March and April when young seals take to the water.

dipping tub ~ a wooden tub used to wash codfish that have been gutted.

directly ~ right away, soon. "I'll be over to see you directly."

dirty ~ 1. resentful. "She gave me some dirty look." 2. an adjective to describe bad weather. "We've been having some dirty weather lately."

dirty water ~ water in the ocean full of miniature marine organisms which make the water murky, hindering fishing.

dish ~ 1. to hand out the cards in a card game. 2. to shuffle playing cards.

dishy ~ pale or sickly-looking.

ditties ~ a fit of shivering brought on by a scare or a nightmare.

ditty ~ a fast tune sung or played to dance a jig.

ditty box ~ a small container for holding a seaman's valuables.

divet ~ a piece of sod or turf.

dock ~ 1. the cow-parsnip plant that has edible green leaves which are boiled with other vegetables. 2. the area of water on which a vessel floats when it is tied up to a wharf.

doddle ~ See **dodge**.

dodge also **doddle** ~ walk slowly, to stroll. "I think I'll dodge down the road to see if any of the b'ys are around."

dog ~ 1. a male animal. "I was scared to death when I saw the size of that old dog hood." 2. to follow in secret. "We saw John and Mary holding hands and walking in the lane last night so we dogged them." 3. to follow another sealing vessel thought to have knowledge of the main herd of seals. 4. an iron hook used to haul seal pelts aboard a vessel. 5. to secure the hatch on a vessel. "Make sure you dog down the hatches."

dogberry ~ the berry of the mountain ash tree [*Sorbus aucuparia*], also called the sorb apple, witchen and rowan tree berry. This tart berry is a popular ingredient in marmalades, jams, jellies, fruit sauces, liqueur, vodka and vinegar (particularly in eastern Europe and the former Soviet Union). Although there is no evidence that this berry has any medicinal effect, it has been used in various parts of the world in the treatment of kidney disease, diabetes, rheumatism, gout and constipation. It is also a folk remedy for sinus and throat inflammations, lung infections, internal inflammations, menstrual complaints, excess acid in the blood, poor metabolism, diarrhea, and vitamin C deficiency. In Newfoundland and Labrador dogberries are usually picked after the first frost. They were eaten right off the tree at one time, usually by children. They are also fermented to make a tart wine, and several local wineries produce a dogberry wine.

dogberry tree ~ the mountain ash tree.

dog-cat ~ a catamaran sled pulled by dogs.

dogfish ~ a name applied to several smaller members of the shark family, especially the *Scyliorhinidae* and *Squalidae* families.

dogfish

dog rose ~ two similar varieties of wild rose *[Rosa nitida* and *Rosa virginiana]*.

dogs ~ the last supports knocked away at the launching of a ship.

dole ~ pre-Confederation welfare.

dole boots ~ See **lumps**.

dole bread ~ bread made from unrefined flour containing bran (brown flour), and distributed to the needy.

dole days ~ the time of the Great Depression.

dole pin ~ See **thole pin**.

dolly bodger ~ See **damper cake**.

dolphin ~ the name given to a number of
dolphin

smaller species of the whale family. Dolphins are similar to porpoises but have a smaller and more slender snout.

donkey ~ 1. a wooden barrel in which salt cod was packed for export. 2. a home-made wooden clothes chest.

don't ~ doesn't. "He don't know which side of his bread is buttered."

doolamaun ~ seaweed, especially kelp or dulce.

doonee ~ the name applied to Newfoundland settlers from Kilkenny, Ireland.

door place ~ the area in front of the usual entrance to the house. "Father made us rake up all the wood chips, sawdust and bark around the door place."

doos {rhymes with *snooze*} ~ does. "He doos what he wants no matter what you say to him."

dory ~ a flat-bottomed boat with flaring sides and a small
dory
stern. Dorys were rowed but, in spite of the fact they had no keel, they could also be sailed. Some had make-and-break engines and were called motor dories, and sometimes outboard motors were used to power them.

dotard also **doter** ~ an older seal.

doter ~ See **dotard**.

dotterel ~ 1. a feeble-minded person. 2. refers to two long-legged shore birds, the marbled godwit *[Limosa fedoa]* and the hudsonian godwit *[Limosa haemastica]*.

double ball mitt ~ a heavy mitten knitted using two strands of wool.

double bitted axe ~ See **double bitter**.

double bitter also **double bitted axe** ~ a two-edged axe with one edge keenly sharpened to fell trees and the other, blunter edge used to "knock" off the branches.

double sled ~ 1. a wide, heavy sled using a team of two horses. 2. two bob sleds in tandem.

doughball also **doughboy**, **dumpling** ~ flour, water and baking powder made into balls and boiled, usually with boiled dinner or pea-soup.

dough boy ~ See **dough ball**.

douse {rhymes with *louse*} ~ 1. a quick blow. "You mind your manners or I'll give you a douse up side the head." 2. to throw something overboard. 3. to throw water onto something or somebody.

dout ~ to put out a fire or a light. This word probably came from England as it was used in the Shakespearian play *King Henry V*.

down house ~ on the floor. "The youngsters come in out of the snow and just throw their wet clothes down house."

down north ~ toward the north.

down punt ~ in the punt. "Throw your gear down punt."

dowsing rod ~ a Y-shaped stick believed to be able to find underground water. See also **Witch Hazel** on page 288.

dowsy poll ~ a moth.

doxy ~ a man's sweetheart.

draft

draft ~ dried codfish weighing 224 pounds or

two quintals, the amount two men normally carried on a handbar.

drag ~ 1. a caulk for a wheel. 2. a device for slowing the movement of a sled.

drain ~ to hold the note of a song for a long time while singing.

drang also **drong**, **drung** ~ a narrow road or lane.

draught {pronounced: *DRAFT*} ~ the depth of water a ship displaces.

draw ~ to secure a fishing berth by lot.

drawing bucket ~ a bucket with a long rope left at a well and used to draw water to fill the carrying buckets.

dray ~ 1. a two-wheeled cart with two long poles which can be pushed or pulled by one person. Larger drays were pulled by a single horse. 2. in the St. John's area, a dray was a wagon with four or more wheels.

dray

drenty ~ of tablecloths or bed linen, stained or streaked from improper drying.

dreshold also **threshold** ~ a door sill, a raised portion of the floor in a doorway. From the time when houses had dirt floors which were covered in thresh (straw, grain or corn

husks). The threshold was used to keep the thresh in.

dress ~ 1. to head, gut and split fish in preparation for salting and drying. 2. to remove the branches from a felled tree.

dresser ~ the kitchen cupboard.

dress up ~ 1. to put on a disguise to go mummering. 2. to go mummering. "Are you going to dress up this Christmas?"

drew ~ in knitting a fish net, the number of meshes formed in a single row.

dribs and drabs ~ sporadically.

drift of fish ~ a concentration of codfish.

drite ~ low humidity in the air – a good day for drying fish.

drive ~ 1. to drift rapidly. "If that anchor chain breaks your boat is going to drive ashore." 2. to insure pulpwood logs are afloat on the river and headed toward the paper mill.

driver ~ 1. a person engaged in driving pulpwood logs on a river. "There's none know the life of a driver, what he suffers with hardships and cold." 2. a square sail at the rear of a boat used for running before the wind.

driving shack ~ a cabin used by log drivers.

driving-works ~ See **carrying-on**.

drogue {rhymes with *rogue*} also **droke**, **drook** {rhymes with *brook*} ~ 1. a thicket or dense growth of small trees. 2. see **sea anchor**.

droke ~ See **drogue**.

droll ~ odd or unusual.

drong ~ See **drang**.

drook ~ See **drogue**.

drubbin ~ a mixture of oil and tallow, used to preserve boots.

drudge ~ a drag-net for taking bottom-feeding fish or shellfish, especially scallops.

drung ~ See **drang**.

dry diet ~ living on non-perishable items such as hard bread and salt fish.

dubbin ~ a compound of tallow and oil, used to seal leather.

duck ~ a canvas or strong, untwilled linen, used to make sails and as a waterproof covering for fish and other items.

duck berry ~ the bog bilberry *[Vaccinium uliginosum]*. This berry, which is about 6 mm in diameter and contains a reasonable source of vitamin C, is juicy and sweet and can be dried and used like raisins. A tea can be made from the leaves and dried berries.

duck gull ~ refers to two varieties of gull, the Iceland gull *[Larus glaucoides]* and the ivory gull *[Pagophilia eburnea]*.

duckish ~ starting to get dark. "It starts to get duckish a lot earlier in the fall." Probably from the word "dusk."

ducks and drakes ~ a stone-skipping game. See also **Ducks and Drakes** on page 213.

ducky ~ a friendly address to another. "How are you today, my ducky?"

dudeen ~ a short-stemmed tobacco pipe.

duds ~ clothing.

due note ~ a record of money owed by the merchant to the fishermen, as well as what was owed by the fishermen to the merchant.

duff ~ 1. a pudding made with flour and water and sometimes other ingredients, often boiled in a cloth bag. 2. a kick. "Behave yourself or you'll get a duff in the backside."

duff bag also **pudding bag** ~ a bag used to boil duff.

dulse ~ an edible seaweed.

dumbledore ~ the bumble bee.

dumb-tit ~ a baby's soother.

dumpling ~ See **dough balls**.

dun ~ 1. the mould or fungus which forms on improperly dried codfish. 2. cured codfish that has turned pink because of insufficient salt.

dunch ~ 1. without feeling in some part of the body, caused by a stoppage in blood circulation. "I was dunch from sitting in church on the hard pew." 2. dumplings made with flour and water only. 3. heavy and soggy. "My bread is right dunch."

dunderhead ~ a stupid person.

dung ~ manure.

dung bar ~ a wheelbarrow or handbar (fitted with a wooden tub or box) for transporting manure.

dung bird ~ the parasitic jaeger or Arctic skua *[Stercorarius parasiticus]*. Measuring 41-46 cm (16-18 in) in length, with a wingspan of 110-125 cm (43-49 in), this bird weighs 330-570 g (11-20 oz). It chases other birds, such as terns, in an attempt to get them to drop their food.

dung box ~ a box for holding manure.

dung cart ~ a two-wheeled cart for transporting manure.

dungeon ~ the below deck accommodation for sealers on a sealing vessel. These were frequently makeshift and poor as the vessel was often not meant to accommodate so many people.

dwall ~ 1. in a dazed, semi-conscious or unconscious condition. "When I struck my head on the door facing I was in a dwall." 2. the state of slumbering or being half asleep. 3. to slumber. "I dwalled for a few minutes there."

dwy also **snow dwy** ~ a snowflake. "There are only a few dwys falling tonight." 2. a short snow shower.

dwy

ean ~ the birthing of lambs.

earwig ~ a variety of centipede *[Lithicolus centipede]*.

easter ~ eastern. "I was fishing on the easter side of Gull Island all summer."

Easter water ~ Water obtained on Easter Sunday and used medicinally. See also **Aches, Pains and Ailments** on page 277.

eating ~ for home consumption. "We sold our fish and just kept a few eating fish for the winter."

eddy ~ of wind or water, moving in a circular motion.

Eddy ~ a brand of matches popular in the province. These matches could ignite if struck against anything.

egger ~ one who collects wild bird eggs.

egging ~ collecting wild bird eggs.

eiderdown ~ a bed covering which is stuffed with the down feathers of the eider duck or some other soft insulating material.

either ~ See **ar**.

elder ~ a cow's udder.

elevener also **levener** ~ a snack or alcoholic beverage at 11 am.

elsinor ~ a cap with ear flaps, especially one made of leather.

elsinor

elt ~ 1. a piglet. 2. a rogue.

emmet ~ an ant. Probably from the old English word "emete" meaning ant.

emper ~ See **empter**.

empt ~ to dump the contents from a container.

empter also **emper, picker** ~ a small berry-picking container that when full is dumped into a larger one.

en ~ {rhymes with the letter *n*} 1. it. "I got a new watch for Christmas but I can't get en to work." 2. him. "He's a hard worker but it's some hard getting en up in the morning."

engine house ~ a box built around a make-and-break engine to protect it from water and weather.

engine room ~ an enclosed area around the engine(s) on a larger vessel with space inside to maintain and operate the engine(s).

enter ~ the door to a cod trap.

entire ~ a young, ungelded stallion.

Eskimo boot also **mog, sealskin boot, sealskin mog** ~ a knee-length boot made of sealskin.

Eskimo boot

Eskimo curlew ~ See **mountain curlew**.

Eskimo dog ~ a powerful working dog, native to Labrador.

Eskimo dogs

Eskimo duck ~ the American common eider duck *[Somateria mollissima dresseri]*. American Common Eiders are the most abundant species of sea duck breeding along the East Coast of North America.

Eskimo fiddle ~ a stringed instrument made by Inuit.

Eskimo sled ~ a komatik.

evenin ~ an alcoholic beverage at the end of a day's work.

evening ~ any time between noon and dark.

excursion bread also **scursion bread**, **sweet bread** ~ a hard bread, similar to hard tack, but sweeter and softer, and eaten alone, or with butter or other spread.

face ~ nerve. "You've got some face to come around here after what you did."

face and eye berry ~ the juniper berry *[Juniperus horizontalis]*. This berry has been used to treat appetite loss, kidney and bladder stones, urinary tract infections, indigestion and digestive disorders such as belching, heartburn and bloating, as well as menstrual problems and diabetes.

faddle ~ a quantity of firewood, a bundle, back load or sled load.

faddle

fadge ~ 1. to manage, especially to manage household duties. "My wife is in the hospital having a baby so I have to fadge for myself." Possibly from the word "fetch." 2. a free meal. 3. a gift.

faffering also **farfaring** ~ 1. to blow in sudden gusts. 2. very cold.

fag ~ cigarette.

fagged out ~ exhausted.

faggot ~ 1. a small pile of fish on a flake. Fish were piled in faggots

and covered to protect them from the rain. 2. a roof-like covering shaped like an inverted V which was used to protect salt fish when it rained.

fair ~ almost, nearly, everything but. "Every time you say that my temper fair rises."

fair weather man ~ a man who is satisfactory when things are good but disappointing in adverse conditions.

fairy bread also **fairy cap** ~ a toadstool.

fairy breeze also **fairy squall** ~ a squall of wind on an otherwise calm day.

fairy bun ~ bread carried by lone travellers to keep the evil fairies away. See also **Fairylore** on page 283.

fairy cap ~ See **fairy bread**.

fairy handbar ~ a small piece of kelp shaped like a handbar.

fairy led ~ enticed away by fairies.

fairy lore ~ See **Fairylore** on page 285.

fairy man ~ a changeling.

fairy path ~ a little-used path through woods or undergrowth.

fairy squall ~ See **fairy breeze**.

fairy struck ~ mentally or physically harmed by fairies.

fairy tune ~ a tune thought to be learned by supernatural means.

fall fish ~ codfish, usually larger in size, caught by hand line in the autumn months up to December.

fall fishery ~ the hand lining fishery which takes place between September and December.

falling weather ~ a day with precipitation. "It's falling weather today so wear your oilskins."

fallish ~ the feeling of autumn in the air. "It's a bit fallish so wear your sweater."

fall of the year ~ autumn.

false face ~ any mask or face covering, especially when used by mummers.

fance ~ a female dog.

farbed up ~ confused and not in control.

fard ~ forward, toward the front part of a vessel.

farfaring ~ See **faffering**.

farforth ~ as far as, as much as. "The concert was good, as farforth as concerts go."

farl also **farrel**, **furl**, **varl** ~ the cover of a book. "Don't tear the farl off your scribbler."

farm ~ a farm, field or woodlot away from the ocean.

farrel ~ See **farl**.

fartnight ~ two weeks. From fortnight.

farty ~ forty.

fashion ~ a habit. "He's got a fashion of squinting when he talks to you."

fatback ~ a piece of fatty tissue from a pig.

father-giver ~ the man who gives the bride away.

fathom ~ six feet. "I just got me jigger about one fathom down."

fat oil ~ the oil obtained from the blubber of seals or whales.

fat pork ~ See **fatback**.

fat season ~ a prosperous sealing season.

fat soap ~ the soap obtained from the fatty tissue of animals.

feature ~ to bring to mind, to recall. "I feature the time we went rabbit catchin'."

features ~ the face. "Turn around so I can see your features."

feeder ~ 1. the pitcher in a game of rounders. 2. a small river or the tributary of a larger one, a brook.

feeler ~ one of the two tentacle-like appendages extending from the front end of a lobster. See also **smeller**.

feeler

fell a victim ~ went off to sleep quickly.

felt ~ a black sheeting material used to cover roofs, then tarred to make the roof waterproof.

fence-longer also **fence-lunger** ~ a horizontal rail to which pickets are fastened to make a fence.

fence-lunger ~ See **fence-longer**.

fender ~ the shelf under the door of a woodstove to keep embers from falling on the floor. "Put your feet up on the fender my son and warm your toes."

feraun ~ 1. the gypsywort, a weed with yellow flowers [*Lycopus europaeus*]. 2. the pineapple-weed [*Matricaria matricarioides*].

ferry ~ to use an icepan as a raft.

fese ~ to frighten. Possibly from the word "faze."

fess ~ 1. odd or abnormal. 2. overly enthusiastic and fussy.

fetch ~ 1. a ghost or token, especially of a person still alive. See also **Tokens, Fetches and Ghosts** on page 287. 2. a ghost ship. 3. to arrive at. "We should be able to fetch Carbonear by sundown."

fib ~ a type of dance.

fiddler ~ one who supplies music with a fiddle, accordion, harmonica or mouth music. "We can't have a dance without a fiddler of some kind."

fig ~ a raisin.

fig duff ~ See **figgy duff**.

figgy duff also **fig duff**, **fig pudding** ~ a boiled pudding made with flour, water and raisins.

figgy loaf ~ raisin bread.

figgy tit ~ raisins wrapped in a thin cloth and given to older babies to suck on as a soother.

fig pudding ~ See **figgy duff**.

file ~ a game in which players flick a knife in certain ways so it sticks in the ground.

fill ~ to weave in the leather strips on a snowshoe.

fill dyke ~ the month of February.

filling ~ the leather part of a snowshoe.

find ~ 1. to equip with provisions. 2. have trouble or pain with. "Ever since I fell down I find my knee."

finest kind ~ in great shape or condition. When asked, "How are you?" one might reply, "The finest kind, sir, how's yourself?"

finger ~ a unit of measure, a finger-width, especially in measuring the amount of shot and gunpowder in a muzzle-loading gun.

finger mitt ~ See **trigger mitt**.

finger stall ~ a sleeve used to cover an injured or sore finger.

fire rocks ~ to throw stones.

fire weed ~ the spotted touch-me-not plant *[Impatiens capensis]*.

firk ~ to scratch or dig gingerly. "The hen is firking in the ground for a bit of seed."

fish ~ 1. the codfish. When speaking of various species of fish each species was referred to by its name, but when

fish

the word "fish" was used it meant "codfish." 2. the female genitalia.

fish and brewis ~ a meal of fish accompanied by soaked hard bread served separately on the same plate and covered with scrunchins (fried

pork-fat cubes) and hot, rendered pork oil. See also **Meals** on page 240.

fish bar ~ See **fish barrow**.

fish barrel ~ a wooden barrel of a specific size to hold a specific quantity of fish.

fish barrow also **fish bar** ~ a hand-bar used to carry fish.

fish beam ~ a scale for weighing cured codfish.

fish beetle also **fish fly** ~ the rove beetle *[Staphylinus villosus]*, a large flying insect which feeds off and lay eggs on fish left out to dry.

fish-boil ~ a blister or sore on the wrists or hands from constant contact with saltwater and oilskin clothes.

fish book ~ the ledger a fish merchant used to record fish purchases.

fish box ~ 1. the humorous name given to vessels that were used to transport fish to foreign ports. 2. a wooden box in which fish are washed and salted.

fish breeches ~ See **britches**.

fisherman's anchor ~ See **banking anchor**.

fisherman's brewis ~ a meal of fish and hard bread, covered with scrunchins (fried pork-fat cubes) and hot, rendered pork oil, served mixed together on the same plate. See also **Meals** on page 240.

fish flake ~ See **flake**.

fish fly ~ See **fish beetle**.

fish fork ~ a device with a long wooden handle and one or two metal tines used for spearing fish and tossing them from a boat unto a wharf or stage head.

fish hawk ~ 1. the osprey *[Pandion haliaetus]*. With a length of 56 cm (22 in), and a wingspan of 137 cm (54 in), this large, narrow-winged hawk flies on flat wings with a distinct kink at the elbow. It is so called because of its ability to dive for fish. 2. a very capable and successful fisherman or fishing skipper.

fish hawk

fish house ~ 1. a building in which cured codfish are stored. 2. a large wooden box used to cover a pile of codfish.

fishing admiral ~ the captain of the first English fishing vessel to arrive in a Newfoundland harbour in the 1600s and 1700s, deemed to be the overseer and enforcer of the law in that harbour for the season.

fishing bank ~ See **bank**.

fishing boot ~ a high leather boot once worn by fishermen.

fishing ground ~ a shoal where fish gather to feed.

fishing jack ~ a fishing schooner between five and 25 tons.

fishing premises ~ the waterfront premises of a fish merchant.

fishing season ~ the time of the year (usually from spring until early autumn) in which codfish were mostly caught.

fish killer ~ a very capable and successful fisherman or fishing skipper.

fish merchant also **merchant** ~ a businessman engaged in the Newfoundland fish trade. Merchants procured fish from fishermen an, either resold it to St. John's Merchants to be exported or exported it themselves. They also supplied the fishermen and their families with provisions, including fishing gear, household items and groceries, usually on credit. See also **Merchants** on page 243.

fish pen also **fish pound** ~ a bin in a fishing stage were fish were salted.

fish pound ~ See **fish pen**.

fish scale ~ a silver five-cent coin smaller than a ten-cent coin, or dime.

fiss in ~ to eat hungrily.

fissog ~ face. "You got a fissog on you that even your own mother couldn't love." Probably from the word "facade," meaning a front or outer appearance.

fist ~ readily willing. "You got your water from the well but you weren't so fist when it came to chopping the ice out when it froze up."

fit ~ to equip a fisherman or vessel with supplies and gear for fishing or sealing.

fit-out ~ 1. the clothing, equipment and supplies used by a fisherman on a voyage. 2. any clothing. "What kind of a fit-out have you got on?" 3. the disguise worn by a mummer.

five-eight ~ a muzzle-loading gun with a 5/8 inch bore.

flake also **fish-flake** ~ a raised platform made of long poles, topped with boughs and used for drying salted codfish.

flake beam ~ a shore used to support a fish flake.

flake longers also **flake lungers** ~ long poles that form the top of a fish flake.

flake lungers ~ See **flake longers**.

flake room ~ the land on which a flake is constructed.

flake-work ~ all activity involved in curing fish on a fish flake.

flamer {pronounced: *FLAME - er*} ~ a pest. "If you don't stop tormenting, you young flamer, I'm telling your father."

flanker {rhymes with *banker*} also **blanker** ~ a spark from a fire. "The wind was blowing the flankers from the chimney clear across the harbour."

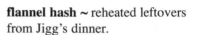

flankers

flannel hash ~ reheated leftovers from Jigg's dinner.

flapper jack ~ a cage-like trap for catching live birds.

flash ~ the twine-bound, leather end of a dog whip, flexible enough to make a snapping sound.

flashet ~ a water puddle, especially one on a bog. "Flashets are great places to find ducks on a windy day."

flat also **swamp** ~ 1. a small, flat-bottomed rowboat with a square stern. "Grandfather sawed his old dory in half and turned it into a flat." 2 the way people from the bay talk as observed by people from St. John's. "The crowd from Heart's Delight talks right flat."

flat

flat calm ~ not a ripple on the water.

flatform ~ See **bridge**.

flat iron ~ an iron heated on the top of a stove.

flat iron

flatty ~ a small flounder or flatfish.

fleece ~ a soft fabric used for lining in certain clothing.

fleece-lined underwear ~ warm longjohns that are soft on the inside.

flice ~ to make jerky movements with the body, legs or arms.

fllcer ~ a flexible sprig used to spring a snare.

flick ~ a short distance away. "Lewisporte is just a flick from here."

flicker also **flick stick** ~ the bat used in a game of piddely. See also **Piddely** on page 251.

flick stick ~ See **flicker**.

flincher {pronounced: *FLIN - sher*} ~ a type of carpenter's plane used in the coopering trade.

flinders ~ small pieces.

flint biscuit ~ hard tack.

flip-flops ~ sandals.

flipper ~ the front limb and shoulder of a seal. "We're having flipper pie for dinner today."

flirrup {rhymes with *syrup*} ~ a lamp, lantern or torch used when gutting, cleaning and salting codfish at night.

float ~ to shoot a seal in the throat so it doesn't sink. "Take a good aim at that seal and see if you can float it."

floater ~ 1. a Newfoundland fisherman, usually from the northeast coast, who fishes the Labrador coast from a schooner, as opposed to a stationer, who fishes from the shore. Fish were caught by floaters from trap skiffs and punts using cod traps and jiggers. The fish were heavy salted and brought back to their home port to be cured for export. 2. the schooner used by same. See also **stationer**.

floater crew ~ the crew of a fishing schooner on the Labrador coast.

floating jigger ~ a device for retrieving seals or birds that have been shot without using a boat. Made of wood, usually pine, the device has four barbless hooks attached. A strong line is attached to the device and it is thrown over the animals then drawn back to snag them and pull them in.

floating jigger

floating stage ~ a raft used to work on a ship's hull.

float line ~ a hand line that incorporates a weighted hook.

flockooly {pronounced: *FLOCK - who - lee*} also **flooholic** {pronounced: *FLEW - haul - LICK*} ~ foolish, especially with the way one spends money.

flooholic ~ See **flockooly**.

floor ~ the top of a fish flake consisting of long poles covered with tree branches.

floption {pronounced: *FLOP - shun*} ~ in a state of confusion,

flounce {rhymes with *bounce*} ~ let oneself fall into a lying position. "I was so tired when I came back from hunting that I just flounced on the bed."

flouse {rhymes with *cows*} ~ 1. thrash about in water. 2. fall in water. 3. throw water, 4. splash.

flowers {pronounced: *FLOE - ers*} ~ a rock over which the sea breaks.

fluke ~ either of the two lobes of the tail of a whale or related animal.

fluke

fluking ~ 1. twitching. "The horse was fluking her tail at the flies." 2. inebriated.

flummox {rhymes with *stomachs*}

~ 1. to discontinue or fail altogether. 2. be in a quandry.

flummy ~ See **damper cake**.

flunky ~ 1. a person who does odd jobs aboard a fishing vessel. 2. the anchor which holds an end of a trawl line in place.

flux ~ 1. to grab. 2. to steal.

fluxing ~ a beating or thrashing. "You're going to get a fluxing when your father comes home."

fly biscuits ~ thin, semi-hard biscuits containing raisins, that when viewed appear to be flies that got stuck in the dough.

fly catcher ~ 1. the round-leaved sundew *[Drosera rotundiflora]*, a carnivorous bog plant. 2. the red-breasted nuthatch, a characteristic bird of spruce and fir forests *[Sitta canadensus]*.

fly dope ~ insect repellent.

fob ~ foam.

fo'c'sle ~ See **forecastle**.

fodge {rhymes with *dodge*} ~ 1. a thick cake. 2. a large loaf of bread.

fog also **baker's fog** ~ bread from a bakery as opposed to homemade bread.

folly ~ to follow. "I knows the way to Codroy so why don't you folly me."

fond ~ simple-minded.

fong ~ a long bootlace.

foolish ~ feeble-minded. "Don't mind what he says, he's a bit foolish in the head."

footer ~ an idly, lazy person.

footins ~ animal tracks, especially in the snow.

foots ~ the bottom of a cod trap to which the lead weights are attached.

footy ~ mean-looking.

forecastle also **fo'c'sle** {pronounced: *FOLK - sull*} ~ the forewardmost cabin on a vessel.

foreign-going ~ refers to ships on oceanic voyages as opposed to those involved in the coastal trade.

forepeak ~ 1. the forecastle of a vessel. 2. the office of the foreman or manager in a lumberwoods' camp.

forinstead ~ in front of.

fork also **vark** ~ the crotch of one's trousers.

forestand room ~ the front part of a boat between the cuddy and the midship room where fishermen stood to haul their gear to keep the front of their boat up to the wind.

fornent ~ the opposite.

fortnight ~ two weeks.

forward reach ~ in a position ahead of another. "The *Arctic Sealer* just steamed past the *Algerine* and has the forward reach on her now."

foss ~ a kick. "If you don't stop tormenting you're going to get a foss in the starn."

fougere ~ edible roots. The word comes from France via Acadia.

found ~ equipped with provisions. "When you go to the ice with Skipper Guy, you're found in everything."

founder ~ 1. of a ship, to fill with water and sink. 2. to crumble or collapse. "That cliff is starting to founder."

fourer ~ an alcoholic beverage or snack at 4:00 p.m.

fousty ~ mouldy, and starting to smell bad. "If you don't eat that bun of bread soon it's going to get fousty." 2. having a foul-smelling odour. "That bologna is starting to smell fousty."

foxey ~ red headed.

fox eye ~ a circle around the moon indicative of bad weather to come.

foxey rum ~ amber coloured rum.

foxing ~ pretending. "You're not sleeping, you're just foxing."

frankum ~ the hardened sap of the spruce tree which is chewed like chewing gum. See also **Chewin' Frankum** on page 207.

frape {rhymes with *cape*} ~ 1. to drag the sea bottom with a hook or grapnel. 2. to haul a rope. 3. a pulley system used to moor off a boat.

frapse {rhymes with *capes*} ~ 1. to fasten a line carelessly. 2. to dress untidily. 3. to be in an untidy state of dress. "I'm in some frapse today."

freighter ~ a fisherman who travels to the Labrador coast via passenger vessel for a summer fishing.

French Shore ~ the portion of the Newfoundland coast where the French had fishing rights. From 1713 (Treaty of Utrect) until 1783 (Treaty of Versailles) this consisted of all the coast north from Cape Bonavista around the Northern Peninsula and south to Point Riche (near St. Barbe) on the west side of the peninsula. In 1783 the boundaries changed to become the coastline from Cape John in Notre Dame Bay around the Northern Peninsula to Cape Ray (near Port aux Basques). In 1904 the French gave up their fishing rights on this shore and were given total possession of St. Pierre and Miquelon.

frettin' frame ~ the bed.

frico ~ cubed vegetables, cooked in water (broth) with salt and pepper.

fried dough ~ See **damper cake**.

friend-girl ~ the female friend of another female.

frightish ~ easily frightened, timid. "Our horse is a bit frightish."

fritters ~ soaked hard bread fried with scrunchins.

froppish ~ cranky. "The baby is froppish lately."

frore {rhymes with *poor*} ~ very cold. "Put another junk of wood in the stove, I'm frore."

frostburn ~ frostbite.

frounge {rhymes with *lounge*} ~ to complain.

fudge ~ 1. to manage daily chores by oneself. 2. in wood working, to make a tight fit. "Fudge it in."

full chisel ~ at headlong speed. "When we got the boat around Western Head we gave her full chisel."

funk ~ to cause a bad smell.

funnel ~ 1. a stove pipe. 2. the smoke stack on a vessel with a steam engine.

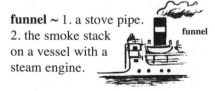

funnel

funnel bun ~ See **damper cake**.

furl ~ See **farl**.

fur path ~ the territory or trapline claimed by a fur trapper.

furrier ~ one who hunts or traps animals.

fur trade ~ the business of dealing in animal furs.

fur trapper ~ one who traps animals for their furs.

futter {rhymes with *butter*} ~ an idle fellow. From old English.

gad ~ 1. to wander aimlessly. 2. See **tinker**.

gaff ~ 1. a long wooden pole with a metal hook and often a spike at one end. 2. to snag a fish or something else with a gaff.

gaff

gaffer ~ 1. a fish so big that a gaff must be used to bring it aboard the boat. 2. a boy over the age of 10.

gaffle ~ to grab a hold of.

gaiter {rhymes with *later*} ~ a canvas winter boot with four metal fasteners between the instep and the top. One side of each fastener had four holes so the boot could be worn loosely or fastened tightly to accommodate different thicknesses of trousers.

gale bird ~ refers to two similar birds, the red phalarope

gale bird

[Phalaropus filicarius] and, the northern phalarope *[Lobipes lobatus]*.

galin' ~ See **rompsin'**.

gall {rhymes with *call*} ~ to chafe, usually on the hands, from doing some type of work that the person is not used to doing. "I'm going to have my hands galled from all this rowing." 2. nerve. "You've got some gall coming back here now."

gallery ~ a platform or veranda at the front of a house with steps leading to the street.

gallivanting {pronounced: *GAL - ah - VAN - ting*} ~ running around outside when expected to be at home.

gallon measuring can ~ a can used to measure liquid merchandise.

gallon measuring can

gally ~ to become exhausted during an endeavour.

gally beggar ~ a scarecrow.

gallying ~ See **copying pans**.

gally beggar

gam bird ~ the common eider *[Somateria mollissima]*. The largest duck in the northern hemisphere, these birds are famous for their down tail feathers that make great insulation when used in quilted bedding. They are known as well as for their taste.

gammett ~ rough horse-play.

Gander Bay boat ~ a long narrow boat, either rowed or powered by an outboard motor, made especially for navigating the Gander River.

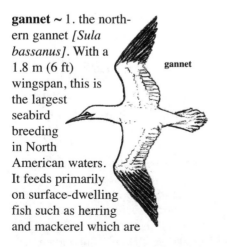
Gander Bay boat

gandy ~ See **damper cake**.

gang board ~ one of a number of boards used to cover the midship-room on a boat.

gange ~ to wrap fine wire around a fishing line to prevent the hook from being bitten off.

gang plank ~ the walkway between a ship and a wharf.

gannet ~ 1. the northern gannet *[Sula bassanus]*. With a 1.8 m (6 ft) wingspan, this is the largest seabird breeding in North American waters. It feeds primarily on surface-dwelling fish such as herring and mackerel which are

gannet

taken by diving from heights up to about 43 m and plummeting into the water at great speed and considerable force. The gannet's skull is especially strong, with a system of air sacs that also helps to absorb the shock of these plunges. 2. a young, misbehaving person. "If you don't listen, you young gannet, you won't be allowed down the road for a week!"

gansey ~ See **guernsey**.

garagee {pronounced: *GAR - ah - GEE*} ~ the act of scrambling to pick up items. "When we tossed the candy out for the youngsters at the birthday party there was a mad garagee for them."

garbits also **garpits** ~ the two bottom planks on a boat that are made into the keel.

garden party ~ a community party held outdoors. See also **Garden Parties** on page 197.

garnipper ~ a large, biting mosquito.

garnipper

garpits ~ See **garbets**.

gatch {rhymes with *catch*} ~ to show off.

gatcher ~ a person who shows off.

gauches {pronounced: *GOT - chess*} ~ funny words and tricks.

gave out ~ 1. died. "He's so old he just gave out." 2. stopped functioning.

gawmoge ~ to deceive.

gaze ~ 1. a hideaway or blind from which sea birds are shot. 2. a high piece of land.

gear ~ collectively all the items used in prosecuting the fishery.

genge ~ to fasten a fish hook permanently and securely to a line.

george martins ~ See **lumps**.

gert ~ See **girt**.

gerty ~ See **gurdy**.

get out! ~ an expression of surprise. "Get out? that can't be true!"

ghost flower ~ the ghost flower, ghost plant, ice plant, corpse plant or indian pipe plant *[Monotropa uniflora]*. A plant of the blueberry family, it requires no sunlight, is white and doesn't have any chlorophyl. Because of this it is sometimes mistaken as a fungus.

ghost net ~ a lost gill net that continues to snag and kill fish.

gib ~ herring offal.

giddy ~ dizzy. "I was swinging the youngster around and I got so giddy I almost fell down."

gig also **joog** ~ bit of strength. "I worked so hard I haven't got a gig left in me."

gill net ~ a net with various sized mesh to catch fish of various sizes. The mesh is too small for the fish to pass through and they usually only get through as far as the gills. Once this happens the fish get stuck in the net and can't back out. See also **Net Fishing** on page 247.

gilly ~ See **bull bird**.

gimlet ~ a small hand tool consisting of a pointed spiral metal tip attached at right angles to a wooden handle, used for boring small holes in wood.

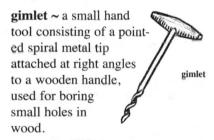

gimlet

girt also **gert** ~ great. "With a girt big stick I'll knock 'en down, blackbird I'll 'ave 'ee." Originated in West Country England.

give ~ gave. He got too close to me so I give him a shove.

give it out ~ to scold.

give out ~ 1. to break down. "My old engine is about ready to give out." 2. to collapse from age or sickness.

give us the breeze ~ to get married. "We're going to give us the breeze this fall, fish or no fish."

glab ~ 1. to become gummed up.

2. to apply a paste-like material in liberal quantities.

gladger {rhymes with *badger*} ~ a joker who pretends sincerity.

glams ~ 1 clams, especially soft-shelled clams.

glander ~ 1. a disease in horses. 2. a string of mucus hanging from one's nostril.

glass also **weather glass** ~ a barometer. "Is the glass rising or falling?"

glassells also **alleys** ~ marbles. See also **Alleys** on page 203.

glassen ~ made of glass. "Gram used to keep her money in a glassen jar."

glaum {pronounced: *GLOM*} ~ to snatch, grab or scoop. "Get the dip-net and we'll try to glaum some capelin for supper."

glauvaun {pronounced: *glah - VON*} ~ to whine or complain.

glean {rhymes with *seen*} ~ to jeer or laugh at someone behind their back.

glim ~ 1. the glow at the far end of an ice field. From "glimmer." 2. small. "They have a glim chance of surviving in this weather."

glitter also **silver thaw** ~ a freezing rain that puts a coating of ice on everything on which it lands.

glitter storm ~ a storm with freezing rain.

glockeen ~ a blade of straw.

glom ~ See **clom**.

glory ~ a euphoric feeling one gets at a church meeting.

glory hole ~ 1. a storeroom on a ship. 2. a broom closet under the staircase in a house.

glough {rhymes with *cow*} ~ to stare, ogle, glare. "When he gloughs at you he can see right through you." From "glower" which means to stare or look intently.

glut {rhymes with *cut*} ~ a large quantity, sometimes too much to handle. "Since the capelin came in there's been a big glut of codfish."

glutch {rhymes with *touch*} ~ to swallow. "Here take a sip of water to try and glutch the aspirin." 2. the act of swallowing. "She swallowed the chocolate in one glutch."

glutted ~ having a full stomach. "The fish are glutted – that's why they're not taking the jigger."

gly ~ a device with hooks and a float, baited to catch seabirds.

gnome ~ tame and gentle.

go ~ to take on in a competitive manner. "Do you think you can go your brother?"

goat's egg ~ See **damper cake**.

gob ~ 1. the mouth. "Shut your gob before I shut it for you!" 2. an unspecified amount of fish. 3. to remove a hook from a fish's gullet.

gobbet ~ a mouthful. "Have a gobbet of Mother's pie."

gobstick ~ a stick used to remove a hook from a fish's gullet.

go-devil ~ a horse sled.

God's cow ~ the lady-bird beetle *[Anatis ocellata malis]*.

God walkers ~ new shoes for Sunday church service.

goes ~ go. "I goes in the woods with Grandfather."

goin' ~ moving at great speed. "I know he wasn't goin' now, on his new motorcycle."

goldwithy ~ See **goowiddy**.

gollop ~ a large morsel of food.

gombecn ~ a merchant of small means.

gommer {rhymes with *bomber*} ~ 1. to grumble or complain. 2. one who grumbles or complains.

gommil {pronounced: *GOM - ull*} ~ a foolish person. "Even a gommil can make dumplings."

gomogues {pronounced: *gom - OGS*} ~ clownish tricks. "His gamogues are fun, but they get on your nerves after a while."

gone ~ aching or sore. "I was shoveling snow and my back is gone."

goolos ~ home or base in playing certain games; such a game.

go on ~ is that really true?

goose grass ~ a reedy plant of the *Sparganium* family, found around muddy freshwater shores.

goowiddy also **goldwithy** ~ the sheep laurel or lambskill plant, having sticky, pink flowers *[Kalmia angustifolia]*. This plant is poisonous to livestock, which probably earned it the name "lambskill."

gosset ~ See **gozzard**.

got ~ has. "She got some nerve."

goulds ~ open areas, suitable for farming.

government wharf ~ a community wharf erected and maintained by the provincial government.

gowdy {rhymes with *cloudy*} ~ awkward.

gozzard also **gosset** ~ the American common merganser *[Mergus merganzser americanus]*. Measuring 70 cm (27 in) in length, these sea ducks are carnivorous, feeding on mussels and shrimps, while young birds mainly eat aquatic insects.

Males have a dark green head, while the female's head is reddish-brown.

grain ~ a tine on a pitchfork.

grainted {rhymes with *tainted*} ~ ingrained. "Stop rolling around on the ground before you get your clothes grainted with dirt."

grand goose ~ the great skua, or catharacta skua *[Catharacta skua skus]*, a bird of the *Stercorariidae* family. Measuring 53-58 cm (21-23 in) in length and having a wingspan of 125-140 cm (49-55 in) this bird weighs 1.2-2 kg (2.6-4.4 lb). It chases and harasses larger birds such as gannets to get them to drop their food so they can steal it.

Grandy dory ~ a dory of a particular style, factory-built in Fortune, Newfoundland, by the Grandy family.

granny ~ a midwife.

grapnel also **grapple** {pronounced: *GREY - pull*} ~ a small iron anchor with three or more tines.

grapple ~ See **grapnel**.

grapnel

grass house also **hay house** ~ a small building in which hay is stored.

grassing ~ petting, necking or engaging in sex in a grassy area.

grass net ~ a small-meshed net used to carry hay.

great ~ large in size. This was sometimes used to differentiate between two localities. for example: "Great Harbour Deep and Little Harbour Deep."

great auk ~ a large (up to four feet, or 120 cm, tall), flightless bird of the penguin family *[Pinguinus impennis]*. The Funk Island, about 65 km east of Fogo Island, was the domain of the great auk. For years their only human enemy was the Beothuk indians who robbed their eggs for food, but when the Europeans arrived they killed the auks for food, and for fuel for their fires. The great auk is now extinct. The last one was seen in 1844.

great auk

great grey gull ~ the great black-backed gull *[Larus marinus]*.

green ~ 1. lawn, garden or meadow where Sunday school picnics were held. 2. uncured fish. 3. inexperienced. 4. a colour that was unlucky to wear. See also **Fairylore** on page 283.

green fish ~ uncured codfish.

green man ~ a man who was inexperienced in catching and curing fish and who signed on for a fishing voyage to Newfoundland.

grepe {pronounced: *GREEP*} ~ a diving bird, especially the eagle and osprey.

grey sole ~ the flounder *[Glyptocep-halus cynoglossus]*.

gripe ~ a rope used to secure a small boat aboard a larger vessel.

grist ~ sand and bits of sea shells given to hens to make the shells of their eggs hard and to keep them from eating their own eggs.

groaner ~ bell buoy.

grog ~ a mixture of rum and water. From the nickname, Old Grog, given to Admiral Edward Vernon who wore a grogram coat in bad weather and who introduced watered down rum to British sailors.

grog fish ~ the codfish caught at the beginning of the fishing season.

ground flake ~ long poles placed on the ground, especially on a beach, to make a fish flake.

ground pinning ~ a horizontal beam that forms the upper foundation of a house or other building.

grounds ~ hops which were used instead of yeast to bake bread when yeast was not available or not affordable. Grounds made the dough rise but was much slower working than yeast.

grounds' bottle ~ a bottle in which grounds were stored.

ground swell ~ a sea wave breaking from the bottom.

ground tier ~ the snowfall that stays all winter, as opposed to the earlier temporary ones.

grouse ~ See **brooker**.

grout ~ a small stick of firewood.

grouts ~ the sediment left after brewing beer, making coffee etc.

growl ~ the card game of Auction 120s. See also **Growl** on page 224.

growler ~ 1. a small iceberg. A growler was considered more dangerous than an iceberg because it sometimes became part of an ice floe and couldn't be differentiated from regular ice pans when navigating a vessel. 2. a large Labrador codfish.

growler

grub ~ 1. food. 2. the legless larva of certain insects. 3. to dig in the ground. 4. to search.

grub bag ~ a sack used to hold food during an outing.

grub box also **bread box** ~ a tub with a cover and rope handles for carrying food on outings.

gruel ~ oatmeal porridge. Originated in the British Isles.

grum ~ gloomy, morose, sullen. "For someone at a party you look pretty grum." Possibly from the word "glum," meaning the same.

grummet ~ a sleeve made of cloth, wool or leather which was worn over fingers, especially the index finger, to prevent chafing when hand-lining or jigging for fish.

grump also **gump** ~ a wharf post or similar device used to tether boats. Originally these were the upper extension of one of the wharf's up-rights, but later it became a steel device firmly attached to the wharf, often by cement.

guaranteed ~ definitely, I agree.

gud ~ See **tinker**.

guernsey also **gansey** ~ a pullover sweater. From Guernsey in the Channel Islands.

guggle ~ to swallow noisily. "I think I'll guggle down my tea and get going." Probably from the word, "gurgle."

gulch ~ a hollow or small valley with steep sides.

Gulf Stream ~ that part of equatorial current that has passed through the Gulf of Mexico and flows northward until it meets the Arctic Current off the south coast of Newfoundland. This meeting of a cold and warm currents causes much fog off Newfoundland's south coast.

gulvin ~ the stomach of a codfish.

gum ~ the sap or resin of evergreen trees.

gumbeems ~ cubes of chewing tobacco.

gum boots ~ See **lumps**.

gum bucket ~ a slop pail or garbage pail.

gump ~ See **grump**.

gun ball ~ a lead ball used in a muzzle loader.

gun cap also **beaver hat** ~ a percussion cap used to ignite gunpowder in a muzzleloader.

gun line ~ a piece of twine attached to the stock of a gun to prevent losing it overboard.

gunnel ~ See **gunwale**.

gunner ~ a seal hunter on a sealing vessel whose main job is to shoot seals.

gunner's cuff ~ See **finger mitt**.

gunny ~ to take a look.

gunshot away ~ a short distance away.

gunwale also **gunnel** ~ a side timber covering the timber heads of a vessel. This is where the breechings of upper deck guns were once mounted on ships.

gurdy also **gerty** ~ a winch on a boat or ship for hauling fish nets or seals aboard.

gurry ~ 1. the slime from fish offals. 2. the oil run-off from seal blubber or cod livers.

gussied up ~ well dressed and looking one's best. "He's like an atheist, all gussied up and nowhere to go."

gut ~ 1. a wide river's end where it meets the sea. 2. a narrow channel or inlet.

gut

gut-foundered ~ very hungry.

guttle ~ 1. drink quickly. "If you guttle the cod lover oil down it won't taste so bad." Possibly from the English word "guttural," mean-

ing "of or relating to the throat." 2. in a game of marbles, to win all the opponent's marbles. See also **Alleys** on page 203.

Guy Fawkes Night ~ November 5. See also **Bonfire Night** on page 199.

hacker ~ 1. to studder or stammer. 2. to chatter one's teeth with the cold.

had a like to ~ almost. "It snowed last night and when I left the house this morning I had a like to fall down."

haddock whale also **herring hog** ~ the harbour porpoise *[Phocoena phocoena]*, one of the world's smallest cetaceans (whales), growing to an average length of 1.55 m (5 ft) and weighing 55 kg (120 lb). Female porpoises are usually larger than males. It is believed that these porpoises can live as long as 20 years.

hagdown ~ See **bawk**.

hag-rode {pronounced: *HAG - rod*} also **ag-rode**, **old hag**, **hagorid** ~ a very realistic nightmare, where one is aware of his surroundings but is held to the bed by some unknown force and unable to move. Probably derived from the expression "hag ridden," which means "visited by the hag or witch." See also **Hag-Rode** on page 285.

hailed ~ reported the number of seal pelts aboard a vessel.

half a hand ~ half of the share from a voyage.

half-cracked also **cracked** ~ crazy.

halibut ~ the Atlantic halibut *[Hippoglossus hippoglossus]*. This giant member of the flatfish family has been recorded as large as 300 kg (660 lbs), although general commercial weights are from 2.3 to 56 kg (5 to 125 lb). Halibut range through the deeper waters of the western Atlantic from Labrador to the Gulf of Maine, seldom entering waters of less than 60 metres deep.

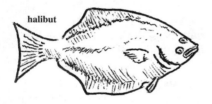

halibut

halifax job ~ personal work done on company time.

hamburg boot ~ a fisherman's long leather boot. Possibly from the days of trade with Hamburg, Germany.

hames {rhymes with *aims*} ~ curved pieces of wood on a horse's collar.

hand bar ~ a flat, rectangular carrying device, that incorporates two poles that stick out front and back so two people can lift and carry the load, usually cured codfish.

hand bar

hand barrel ~ a wooden tub with two poles attached to the side to enable it to be carried by two persons.

hand barrow ~ a large wooden tub, with handles made from poles attached to opposite sides so it could be carried by two people; one holding the front shafts, the other holding the shafts at the rear.

hand-car also **pump trolley** ~ a small, four-wheeled flat car, powered by hand, used by maintenance people on the railway line.

hand-car

hand-cart ~ a two-wheeled cart with two long poles which can be pushed or pulled by one person.

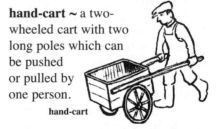

hand-cart

hand-lining ~ fishing, especially for codfish, with a single baited hook. See also **Hand-lining and Jigging** on page 226.

hand over hand ~ to haul a rope by putting one hand before the other on the rope, alternately, to keep a continuous movement going instead of a succession of pulls.

handsturn ~ assistance.

hand tight ~ as taut as a rope may be pulled, or as tight as a bottle lid or other item can be fastened by hand.

hand-wrist ~ the wrist.

handy about ~ See **handy on**.

handy jans ~ woolen wristlets worn for warmth.

handy on also **handy about** ~ nearly, just about. "The coastal boat is handy on getting in."

hanger ~ the handle of a bucket.

hangishore ~ See **angishore**.

hank ~ a quantity of wool yarn wrapped around one's arms that are held out in front about 45 cm (18 in) apart.

hansel ~ a gift given by a merchant.

hapse also **apse** ~ 1. a hasp or fastener. 2. to fasten with a hasp. "Don't forget to hapse the gate after you close it." 3. the slack in a pair of trousers. 4. the aspen tree.

harbour ice also **local ice** ~ the ice formed in a harbour or bay, as opposed to Arctic ice.

harbour rule ~ the method of selecting and allotting fishing berths for the season. "We uses the harbour rule in this community."

harbour seal ~ See **bay seal**.

harbour tom cod ~ an immature codfish. "He's got a gut on him like a harbour tom cod."

hard bread ~ a hard ship's biscuit, hard tack.

hardened ~ stubborn and disobedient.

hard hat ~ a top hat.

hard looking ~ ugly.

hard ticket ~ a hard case or impish person.

hark ~ listen.

harp seal ~ the Greenland seal *[Phoca groenlandica]*, found in abundance around the coast of Newfoundland and Labrador in late winter and early spring.

harp seal

harry ~ to torment.

harts ~ See **herts**.

hatch ~ 1. to fasten, especially a door or gate. 2. to become entangled in. "Don't hatch yourself in that linnet." Possibly from the word "hitch."

hatched ~ entangled or caught on something.

hat of trees ~ a clump of trees in the middle of a barren or on a hill.

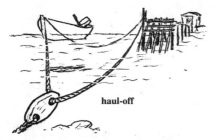

haul-off

haul-off ~ a mooring device that consists of an anchor, a dead-eye (wooden block with a hole through which the rope is passed) and a rope for hauling the boat to the mooring anchor from shore and back again when needed. See also **dead-eye**.

haul on ~ to physically assault. "I'm going to haul on you in a minute."

haul rope ~ the rope used to raise or lower a cod trap.

haul tub ~ a wooden tub with runners or barrel staves to be hauled over a wet, slippery wharf, or other surface.

have a mind to ~ to intend.

have half a mind to ~ to consider doing something.

hawk ~ 1. in a game of marbles, to win all the opponent's marbles. 2. the V at the end of a salmon net.

hay house ~ See **grass house**.

hay net ~ a fish net used to carrying hay.

hay pook ~ See **pook**.

hay prong ~ a pitchfork.

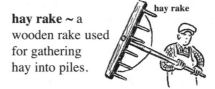

hay rake

hay rake ~ a wooden rake used for gathering hay into piles.

he ~ 1. it. "You got another shot bag, so give he to me." 2. him. "I gave he the loan of my punt." 3. you. "Your brother looks just like he."

head also **heed** ~ keenest. "The way you put that ship in the bottle is the head I've ever seen." 2. the seaward end of a wharf or stage. 3. netting that incorporates a hole formed by a piece of wood bent to form a circle at the end of a lobster trap. 3. to remove the head, especially the head of a codfish.

heading palm ~ a cloth sleeve worn on one hand for protection of the palm when snapping the heads off codfish.

heave also **heave away** ~ to lift or haul.

heave away ~ See **heave**.

heaving song ~ a sea shanty sung to co-ordinate the efforts when a number of men are hauling in unison.

heavy ~ stormy. "We have pretty heavy weather in the fall of the year."

hedge sparrow ~ See **rusty tom rooter**.

heed ~ See **head**.

heel also **heel-tap** ~ the end slice of a loaf of bread.

heel of the day ~ around sunset.

heels ~ the runners on a sled, especially the protruding back ends of the runners on which a person may stand.

heel-tap ~ See **heel**.

heft ~ 1. weight. 2. to weigh in the hand.

helf ~ the handle of an axe or hammer. From the word "heft" meaning the handle of any edged tool.

hemlock looper ~ *[Lambdina fiscellaria]*, an insect whose preferred diet in western Canada is the hemlock, but in Newfoundland it prefers the needles of the balsam fir tree. Outbreaks of large populations of these insects have devastated trees necessary to the province's logging industry.

hen ~ an adjective used to indicate the female of a species, ie: hen fox is a vixen or female fox.

hen and chicks ~ See **midsummer men**.

hermit beaver ~ a beaver that has lost its mate.

herring ~ the Atlantic herring *[Clupea harengus]*. Herring have been an important part of the wel-

fare of this province from the beginning,  both as a bait fish and a product for export. The ever-popular sardines are often small herring, although they are only one of 27 species of fish that end up being called sardines when they are canned.

herring barrel ~ a barrel specially made to ship herring in.

herring gull ~ the most common of all Newfoundland and Labrador gulls, these birds are carnivorous as well as being scavengers. They will eat anything from shellfish, to fish offal, to garbage. The herring gull will often steal the eggs of other birds and scare other birds into dropping their food so they can steal it from them.

herring jack ~ the Atlantic shad, American shad or white shad *[Alosa supidissima]*, a fish of the herring family. Like the salmon this fish only enters the freshwater river in which it was born to spawn.

herring net ~ a net especially made to catch herring.

herring trip ~ a fishing voyage when herring is used for bait.

herts also **harts**, **hirts**, **horts**, **hurts**, **whorts** ~ blueberries.

he's ~ his. "He has he's pants on hinder part afore."

hicker ~ a tangle in fishing gear. possibly from the word, "hitch."

hiding {pronounced: *HIDE - ing*} ~ a beating. "If you children don't behave you are going to get some hiding."

high flyer ~ a buoy that incorporates a vertical pole so it can be seen from a distance.

high-learned ~ referring to a highly-educated person.

high pear also **indian pear** ~ the juneberry *[Amelanchier alnifolia]*.

high water mark ~ the debris left on the beach by the ocean when tides reach their highest point.

hinder {rhymes with *finder*} ~ rear, back. "I could eat the hinder leg of a moose."

hinder daddle {rhymes with *finder - paddle*} ~ the rear flipper of a seal.

hinder part afore also **hinder part before** ~ backwards.

hinder part before ~ See **hinder part afore**.

hipped ~ melancholy and sad.

hippers ~ pins or nails used to attach the trousers to the shirt to hold the trousers up without a belt.

hirts ~ See **herts**.

his self ~ himself. "He can carry two sacks of flour by his self.

hit and run ~ See **rounders**.

hobble ~ a small, temporary job.

hobbler ~ a casual labourer.

hobbley high ~ a boy about 15.

hobby horse also **horse chop**, **horse chops** ~ the likeness of a horse carried by mummers, sometimes used to scare people.

hobby horse

hock also **ock** ~ to spit, especially to bring up spittle from the back of one's throat and spit. "Mom, John just hocked at me."

hog's nose ~ a waterspout or freak whirlwind at sea.

hoist ~ a tree or sapling used as a spring in an animal trap. 2. to put off or postpone. 3. a postponement.

hoist your sails and run ~ a children's game.

hold ~ 1. the cavity of a ship used to hold freight. 2. to maintain a ship's current position.

hold in ~ a command to a team of dogs to turn left.

holiday ~ a spot inadvertently missed with the paint brush while applying paint. "You've got some holidays left on that wall you just painted."

honey cart ~ See **jelly cart**.

hood ~ the hooded seal *[Cystophora cristata]*. Named for the cap-like bulge on its forehead and nose.

hoofish ~ referring to a horse that kicks.

hooking ~ to make a mat or rug. 2. to fish with a baited hook or dabber.

hoop ~ a device used to hold water buckets away from one's legs while carrying water from a well.

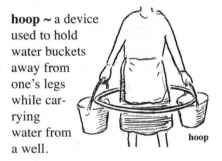

hoop

hooshing {rhymes with *pushing*} also **hoosing** {rhymes with *choosing*} ~ to yell at animals to drive them away.

hoosing ~ See **hooshing**.

hopped ~ bumped or bounced. "I hopped my knee off the coffee table and it still hurts."

hopper ~ 1. a seal in its second year. 2. a ceramic toilet bowl.

horn ~ 1. one of the four vertical sticks on a catamaran sled used to keep the load of logs from falling off. 2. one of the tentacles of a squid.

horn man ~ the devil.

horn slide ~ See **catamaran**.

horny whore ~ See **sculpin**.

horse cat ~ a heavy catamaran or sled, pulled by a horse.

horse chop ~ See **hobby horse**.

horse chops ~ See **hobby horse**.

horse fart ~ a puffball of the *fungi imperfecti* or *deuteromycetes* family *[Lycoperdon gemmatum]*. Having the consistency of a mushroom in the spring and early summer, horse farts can be found in long grass in many parts of Newfoundland. Later on they dry out and develop a thin skin on the outside while the inside turns to a dark powder-like substance. Children loved to find these items in the latter stage of development and squeeze them, sending the powder in the direction of a playmate and shouting, "Horse fart!" The powder was also used as a blood coagulant. See also **Home Remedies and Cures** on page 228.

horse haul ~ a small catch of fish.

horse it up ~ to make a bad job of

it, to render it unsatisfactory or use-less.

horse mackerel ~ a tuna fish.

horse stinger also **hosstinger** ~ the dragonfly *[Anisoptera]*.

horse tops ~ the swamp thistle *[Cirsium muticum]*.

horse work ~ hard manual labour.

horts ~ See **herts**.

hot ass ~ See **bibby**.

hotten ~ to heat.

hound ~ the old squaw duck *[Clangula hyemalis]*. From a dis-tance, these noisy ducks sometimes sound like a pack of yelping hounds on the trail of a fox, This is what earned them their local moniker. As a group these ducks can quickly zoom out of the water and just as quickly zoom down and settle in another part of the lake.

house ~ a business establishment.

house flag ~ the particular flag or pennant of a mercantile firm.

house-haul ~ the act of pulling a house from one location to another.

housemaid's knee ~ water on the kneecap.

house place ~ the kitchen.

house standard ~ the acceptable

quality of cured fish by a specific mercantile firm.

hove {rhymes with *stove*} ~
1. threw or tossed. From the word, "hove," a *nautical* past tense and past participle of heave. 2. {rhymes with *love*} same meaning, but this pronunciation is local to the St. John's area.

hove back ~ hindered or delayed. "We would have had our nets in the water yesterday, but the rats chewed up so much of the linnet and that hove us back."

hovel ~ an out-building of any kind.

hove to {rhymes with *cove to*} ~ refers to a ship that is attempting to ride out a storm by remaining sta-tionary with its bow into the wind. On ships powered by engines this was done by slowing down the engines just enough to keep the ship stationary. Sailing vessels used a sea anchor which slowed down the vessel's drift and kept her bow to the wind. Being broadside or stern on into the wind put the vessel in greater danger of being capsized or swamped.

howsomever ~ however.

hug ~ stay close to the shoreline. "In a leaky punt with a broken oar, 'tis always best to hug the shore."

hulder ~ to shield or protect some-one.

hum ~ a foul odour.

hummock ~ a small hill or mound.

hungry ~ a schooner returning from a poor fishing voyage.

hunk ~ to cut into large chunks.

hunting valentine ~ looking for a husband or wife.

hurts ~ See **herts**.

I ~ me. "Pass the jigger to I."

I allow also **I 'low** ~ I confirm. "Am I going to bring some tiddies to roast on Bonfire Night – well, I 'low I am."

I am ~ something that is excellent. "That new kitchen range is the real I am."

ice bird ~ See **bull bird**.

ice blind ~ 1. to become temporarily blinded because of the glare from an ice field.

ice candle also **clinkerbell** ~ an icicle. "Clinkerbell" originated in Somerset, England.

ice candle

ice gaze ~ a blind or hideaway constructed with pieces of ice from which birds could be shot.

ice-grips ~ heavy metal tongs used to hold and carry blocks of ice.

ice-grips

ice-master ~ 1. the captain of a sealing vessel. 2. the man in charge of a group of sealers on the ice.

ice pan ~ a flat piece of floating ice.

ice partridge ~ the ivory gull *[Pagophila eburnea]*.

ice party ~ a group of sealers on the ice floes.

ice pilot ~ a sailor skilled at navigating a vessel through ice-infested waters.

ice plant ~ the sea lungwort *[Mertensia maritima]*.

ice poker also **ice pole** ~ a pole used to clear a channel through the ice ahead of a smaller vessel.

ice pole ~ See **ice poker**.

ice quire ~ the ice formed from seeping water.

ice saw ~ a long saw used to cut chunks or blocks of from the ocean, a pond or a lake.

idden {rhymes with *hidden*} ~ 1. am not. "Some of you may be going to the Arts and Culture Centre, but I idden." 2. is not. "That boy idden paying attention in school."

idle ~ mischievous or naughty.

ignorant ~ showing bad manners.

imp ~ a mischievous child.

improve ~ to get bigger.

in ~ 1. at. "You talks just like me in certain times." 2. on. "If you looks sideways at him he's likely to give you a punch in the nose."

in a huff ~ to be angry or vexed.

in a tear ~ in a big hurry. "You are always in a tear to leave every time you come over to visit."

in collar ~ the getting ready of a fishing schooner for the Labrador fishery by the crew. "We're in collar now but we'll be leaving in two days."

indian cup ~ See **devil's pipe**.

indian meal ~ corn meal.

indian papoose ~ the porcupine [*Hystricognathi*].

indian pear ~ See **high pear**.

indian pipe ~ See **devil's pipe**.

injun ~ the way "indian" was sometimes pronounced.

in service also **out in service** ~ refers to a person hired by a well-to-do family to provide domestic services. "I was out in service when I met Eli."

inshore ~ as far to sea as a small boat might venture. "He fished the Labrador for years, but he's been fishing inshore for the last ten."

inshore fisherman ~ a small-boat fisherman who fishes relatively close to the shore.

inshore fishery ~ the business of prosecuting the fishery involving small boats closer to shore.

inside of ~ to the landward side of something. "When the two schooners came around Long Point, the *Grace Lorraine* was inside of the *Besse Marie*."

inside room ~ the parlour, or living room of a house.

in slings ~ 1. cluttered. 2. unfinished.

in the last going off ~ later, finally. "He moved away to Toronto in the last going off."

inuksuk ~ See **naked man**.

in wind ~ a wind that blows onshore. "With this in wind we're going to have to tack all day to get out of the harbour."

Irish chain ~ a type of pattern in knitting.

Irish toothache ~ pregnancy.

Irish youngster ~ an Irishman who was inexperienced in catching and curing fish and who signed on for a fishing voyage to Newfoundland.

iron last ~ an iron implement used to put taps and heels on boots and shoes.

iron last

is ~ 1. am. "I think I is going to the garden party. 2. are. "Them fellers is always throwing snowballs at the cat."

i-tally-o ~ boisterous fun. "We had i-tally-o the night my sister got married."

jackabaun ~ political reformer.

jackasses ~ heavy rough boats.

jackatar ~ a worker of the land (*Jacques terre*), referring to people of mixed M'kmaq and French extraction and once used as a derogatory term.

jack boat ~ a type of two-masted decked vessel.

jackeen ~ a mischievous boy.

jack-jump-up-and-kiss-me ~ the jewelweed or snapweed *[impatatiens capensis]*.

jack root ~ the avens or geum, a plant of the *Rosaceae* family *[Geum macrophyllum]*.

jack's curlew ~ the hudoniam whimbrel, a sea bird *[Numenius phaeopus hudsonicus]*.

jack's curlew

jaded ~ exhausted.

jader {pronounced: *JADE - er*} ~ nuisance. "He's such a jader he'll come and eat the blueberries I just picked."

jag ~ 1. drinking spree. 2. drunk. "I had such a jag on last night I had to hold onto the grass to keep from falling off the lawn."

jakey's gin ~ a hair tonic with a very high alcohol content, sold by Jake Somerton of St. John's in the 1950s and 1960s.

janney ~ See **mummer**. See also **Mummering** on page 244.

janneying ~ See **mummering**.

jar ~ 1. a small harbour seal. 2. a stone crock in which alcoholic beverages are kept. 3. to start something in motion. "I tried to haul me punt up by meself but I couldn't jar it." "The bottle stopper was on so tight I couldn't jar it."

jarred ~ nudged open or loosened.

jaw ~ 1. to scold or tell off. "Don't jaw me now, I'm not in the mood." 2. to chatter. "Myself and Elsie jawed for about an hour the other day."

jawbreakers ~ hard round candy. These were usually black when bought and were so hard they couldn't be bitten. They had to be enjoyed by sucking the coloured sugar coatings off them. This sugar coatings was multicoloured and lay-ered so that the candy changed colour as they disintegrated in one's mouth.

jaw lock ~ having cramped jaw muscles or a dislocated jaw.

jaw tooth ~ one of the back teeth, a molar.

jay also **robber bird** ~ the Canada jay or grey jay *[Perisoreus canadensis sanfordi]*.

jay killer also **silk jay** ~ the shrike, a bird of prey *[Lanius excubitor borealis]*.

jelly cart also **honey cart** ~ a horse-drawn, two-wheeled, enclosed vehicle used to carry excrement away from outhouses.

jenny ~ 1. a female dog. 2. a female harlequin duck. 3. a large jib sail.

jersey ~ a sweater which can be buttoned at the front.

Jersey fish ~ codfish caught and cured in Newfoundland by fisher-men from the Channel Islands.

Jersey house ~ a Channel Islands fish merchant operating in Newfoundland.

Jersey man ~ a Channel Islander who prosecutes the cod-fishery in Newfoundland.

Jersey room ~ fishing premises in

Newfoundland owned and operated by a Channel Islander.

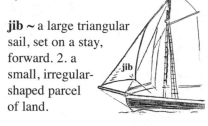

jib ~ a large triangular sail, set on a stay, forward. 2. a small, irregular-shaped parcel of land.

jib boom ~ a continuation forward of a schooner's bowsprit.

jig ~ 1. to fish in a jerking up and down motion using a single line attached to a weighted lure which has two or more hooks. 2. a lively step-dance. 3. a lively, rollicking tune, usually played on an instru-ment or mouthed to accompany a step-dance.

jigger ~ a weighted lure with two or more hooks, used to attract and snag codfish, squid and other fish.

jigging ~ using a jigger to catch codfish or squid. See also **Hand-lining and Jigging** on page 226.

Jigg's dinner ~ a boiled dinner comprised of salt beef, potatoes, carrots, turnip, cabbage and some-times parsnip, pease pudding and dumplings. Originated with American servicemen stationed in Newfoundland and Labrador during WWII who noticed the similarity between the boiled dinner served here and the favourite dinner of Jiggs, a character in the American comic strip series "Bringing Up Father."

jillik ~ to skip stones across the water.

jingle ~ a covered two-wheel cart.

jinker ~ a bringer of bad luck, a jinx.

jinny ~ a seal believed to be a look-out for the herd.

jit also **jut** ~ 1. to use the elbow to nudge a person. "She was telling me a story, and laughing and jitting me so often my ribs were sore." Possibly from the word "jolt." 2. to rock a cradle.

job's comforter {pronounced: *JOBE'S COM - for - ter*} ~ referring to one who sees only the negative side of situations. "After I broke my leg, she told me I'd have arthritis in it when I gets older. She's a real Job's comforter, she is." From Job in the Bible, on whom God sent disaster after disaster to test Job's faith.

jockey club ~ the one-flowered pyola plant or one-flowered wintergreen *[Moneses uniflora]*. The flowers of this plant arc reported to be good for treating rashes, bunions and corns.

jog ~ 1. to sail a vessel slowly. 2. to walk slowly. "I think I'll jog down the road and talk to everybody."

john bull ~ See **bull bird**.

john casey ~ a blueberry pudding.

johnny ~ See **mummer**.

johnny poker also **jolly poker** ~ a shanty, or chanty, sung to coordinate the efforts of a group of men hauling a heavy object, especially a house. "For it's to me Johnny Poker, we will haul this heavy joker, for it's to me Johnny Poker, haul."

jonah also **joner** ~ jinx.

joner ~ See **jonah**.

jonnick ~ 1. honest and fair. "He sold his motorboat to Uncle Jonas, when he promised it to me – that's not jonnick." 2. to vow, promise or pledge. "I'll be by to help with the house-haul, I jonnick." 3. To be fit and ready. "I'm jonnick enough to go back fishing."

joog ~ See **gig**.

jorum ~ a jug of liquor.

jostler ~ a big, crude person. "He's such a jostler, every time he comes here he breaks one of Mother's ornaments."

jowl ~ 1. the jaw bone of a pig. 2. the flesh, or meaty part of a pig's jaw bone. 3. the fleshy part of a cod's head. 4. to grasp someone by the throat.

jowler ~ an experienced and competent sealing skipper. "Captain Abraham Kean was one of the best jowlers ever born in Newfoundland."

Jubilee Guild ~ a women's organization, founded in 1935 to foster handicraft work and gardening.

jug ~ jigged. "I went out yesterday and jug a few fish."

juice ~ electricity. "If you keep too many lights on you'll burn too much juice and your light bill will go up."

July Drive ~ July 1. In the Great War (WWI), the July offensive opening the first battle of the Somme in 1916; especially the engagement of the Newfoundland Regiment at Beaumont Hamel. See also **Remembrance Day/Canada Day** on page 196.

Jumbo ~ a popular brand of chewing tobacco in Newfoundland and Labrador. The word J-U-M-B-O was formed across the length of the plug at the top. If someone wanted less than a full plug they bought it by the letter, each of which was equal to 1/5 of a plug.

jump aboard ~ get in. "Jump aboard the car and we'll go for a drive."

jumper ~ the name given to the tuna, porpoise and dolphin, as well as other similar sea-mammals and fish.

jumping clampers ~ See **copying pans**.

juniper ~ the larch or tamarack tree

[Larix europaea]. Growing extensively in Newfoundland and Labrador, this tree is the only conifer that loses its needles in winter.

juniper

junk ~ 1. a piece of firewood sawn off to fit a stove. 2. a piece of ice small enough to be handled by one person. 3. a piece of salt meat. 4. to cut firewood or salt meat into smaller pieces.

junky ~ thick. "If you cut that meat too junky it'll be too thick to fry."

justler ~ a big, rude person.

jut ~ See **jit**.

kamiks ~ sealskin boots.

kedgy ~ See **catchy**.

keekorn ~ See **kingcorn**.

keel out ~ 1. to lie down. "I'm so tired I think I'll keel out." 2. to faint. "Granny though she saw a ghost and she keeled out."

keel over ~ fall down. "The sun is so hot I could keel over."

keen ~ intelligent. "I allow he's keen enough to open Parliament."

keening ~ lamenting a dead person by speaking of his good deeds in a wailing sound at his wake.

keen queer thing ~ something that does not look good.

keep off ~ a command to a team of dogs to turn right.

keep on ~ to continually request or nag. "I'm not going to buy you a chocolate bar, no matter how much you keep on."

kegged ~ given up drinking alcohol. "I used to drink like a fish but now I've kegged."

kegged out ~ tired. "I had to walk to the top of O'Brien's Hill to pick them berries and now I'm kegged out."

kellep ~ kelp, a seaweed extensively found around the Newfoundland coast.

kenat ~ a contemptible young person.

kettle tea ~ tea with the sugar and milk added in the kettle.

khaki dodger ~ a bun or biscuit in which molasses is used as one of the ingredients.

kible ~ to joke or jest.

kick out ~ to dance.

kid ~ a young goat.

kilcorn ~ See **kingcorn**.

killick ~ an anchor made of wood and stone with wooden claws to

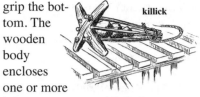

killick

grip the bottom. The wooden body encloses one or more heavy stones to weigh it down.

killick claw ~ one of the four protruding arms on the bottom of a killick that snag the ocean floor.

kindergarten outfit ~ poorly equipped.

king bird also **king drake, king duck, old king** ~ the king cider, a large sea duck (smaller than the common eider) which nests in tundra close to the sea *[Somateria spectabilis]*.

kingcorn also **kinkarn, keekorn, kilcorn** ~ the Adam's apple of the throat.

king corn

king drake ~ See **king bird**.

king duck ~ See **king bird**.

king hoop ~ in barrel making, the last hoop placed on a barrel.

kinkarn ~ See **kingcorn**.

kiss cat! ~ an utterance used to drive cats away from one's flower or vegetable garden or other place.

kit ~ a young beaver.

kitchen racket ~ a party in a kitchen.

kit kat - See **piddely**.

kitty kat ~ See **piddely**.

klick ~ 1. common sense. "He hasn't got a klick." 2. a brand of processed canned meat once popular. 3. the stiffening at the back of a shoe.

klit ~ a tangle or knot in one's hair.

klitty ~ regarding the condition of one's hair, tangled or matted. "My hair is so clitty I can't get a comb through it."

knap ~ a rise of ground.

knee-knocked ~ having legs bent inward so they touch when walking.

knit ~ to make or repair a fish net.

knob ~ 1. a round, usually isolated, hill. 2. the human head. "If you sauce me I'll knock your knob off."

knock off ~ to stop. "It's time to knock off work because I'm getting hungry."

knoll ~ a small rounded hill.

knotty ~ See **noddy**.

komatik {rhymes with *mom - a - tick*} ~ this name applies to a number of styles and shapes of sleds hauled by dogs. Some komatiks' runners are long enough at the back for a person to stand on and also has a handle at the back that comes up from the runners onto which a person can hold. Others are made by simply fasten-

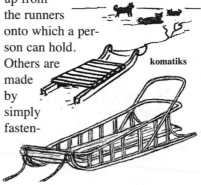

komatiks

ing boards directly across the runners. Sometimes this platform was made into a box to accommodate passengers and goods.

Labour Day ~ See **Labour Day** on page 198.

Labrador afloat ~ these were the words at the bottom of the address on the envelope containing a letter to someone prosecuting the Labrador fishery as a floater. These words were preceded by the name of the schooner aboard which the person was working.

Labrador Current ~ See **Arctic Current**.

Labrador dog ~ originating in Newfoundland, and once called the St. John's Water Dog, this dog is now often called the Labrador Retriever, now the most popular dog in the United States.

Labrador Dog

Labradorian ~ a native or resident of Labrador.

Labrador pine ~ the jack pine [*Pinus banksiana*].

Labrador slice ~ a thick slice of home-made bread.

Labrador slob ~ a poor grade of Labrador fish.

lacing {rhymes with *racing*} ~ 1. physical punishment dealt out with a belt or rope. "If you children don't come in to your supper you're going to get a lacing." 2. the leather webbing in snowshoes.

laddie-sucker ~ the sheep sorrel plant [*Rumex acetosella*].

laddio {pronounced: *LAD - ee - OH*} ~ a prankish fellow, a hard case, likely to get into trouble.

lady bird ~ See **lords and ladies**.

lallik ~ 1. a children's game of tag. 2. the "chaser" in a game of lallik.

lance ~ a sand eel.

lanch {rhymes with *branch*} ~ to put a boat in the water. "Can your crowd come over and give me a hand to lanch my boat?" From the word "launch."

land ~ 1. to go ashore.. "The water was so rough we had to land on Kitty's Beach." 2. to tie up at. "Every big ship that comes here got

to land at the Government Wharf." 3. to take someone somewhere. "Could you please land me over to Buchans?"

landing ~ one of the places where logs are piled on their way from the forest to the paper mill.

landsman ~ a person involved in the fishery on land.

land tacks ~ outdoor clothing, including coat and boots. "Get your land tacks on because we're leaving to go in the woods in a minute."

landwash ~ the shoreline or beach.

lanseer

lanseer ~ a black and white Newfoundland dog.

lap back ~ to answer saucily. "Don't you lap back at me, young lady!"

lapstone ~ 1. a beach stone used to soften leather. 2. a heated stone used as a bed warmer.

larch sawfly ~ an insect [*Pristiphora erichsonii*] that lives on the juniper (larch) tree. It damages the tree in two ways, initially by the female sawfly cutting slits in new shoots to deposit eggs. The worst devastation to trees, however, is by the larvae feeding on the tree's needles. After several years of having its needles stripped the tree could die.

lark ~ the American water pipit bird *[Anthus spinoletta rubescens]*.

lashing ~ a rope used to bind two items, or to secure an item in place. If one's sled was full of wood one would have to use a lashing to tie it down.

lashins ~ plenty. "I've got lashins on my plate so I'll have to say no to more potatoes." Probably from the word "lashing."

lassy ~ molasses. "Lassy, fat and doughboys, if you want some more, boys, come to the cookhouse door, boys."

lassy bug ~ the ladybird beetle. Children would hold these beetles in their hand and recite, "Lassy bug, lassy bug give me some lassy (molasses), or I'll chase your brother and sister and kill your mother and father behind the bedroom door." The beetle was expected to leave a brown spot on the child's hand.

lassy critch ~ a molasses jar.

lassy loaf ~ molasses bread.

lassy pop ~ molasses candy.

laths ~ See **lats**.

lats also **laths** {rhymes with *paths*} ~ 1. long narrow strips of wood, especially those used to make the housing of lobster traps. 2. long,

narrow strips of wood that are bent to form the ribs of small boats.

launch ~ put a vessel in the water.

lawnce {pronounced: *LONSE*} ~ a sand eel, a member of the *Ammodytidae* family of fishes, very similar to the capelin in appearance.

lawnya ~ a most-enjoyable time.

layers ~ young, debarked spruce trees used for fencing.

laying-room ~ an area where codfish are spread to dry.

lazy man's load ~ a too-heavy load carried by one who doesn't want to make extra trips.

leader ~ 1. the front dog in a team. 2. the part of a net stretching from the shore to a cod trap to guide fish into the trap entrance.

lean-in also **linny** ~ a building attached to and usually accessible from the house, usually the kitchen, in which provisions were kept and sometimes animals. See also **Houses and Other Buildings** on page 231.

leary also **leery** ~ faint, weak, dizzy. "Be sure to eat your breakfast so you don't feel leary in school."

lee ~ a sheltered area away from the wind.

lee-long ~ indefinitely.

leery ~ See **leary**.

leeward also **looard** {pronounced: *LURED*}, **looward** {pronounced: *LEW - erd*} ~ 1. toward the lee, 2. stormy weather. 3. signs of coming stormy weather. "The sky is pretty leeward today." 4. See **alee**.

leff ~ leave. "Leff him alone!"

leggings ~ snow pants.

leggy also **rounder** ~ unsplit codfish, salted and cured round.

lesser Newfoundland ~ the Labrador Retriever.

let drift ~ to throw. "As soon as her husband walked in through the door she let drift with the kettle."

let on ~ make known. "I didn't let on that I knew his grandfather."

letter of Jesus Christ ~ See **saviour's letter**.

levener ~ See **elevener**.

lew also **loo** ~ the common loon *[Gavia immer]*.

lickie ~ See **twirlie**.

lifter ~ a metal implement used to remove the dampers (covers) from wood, coal and oil stoves.

light cured fish ~ fish cured with a minimal amount of salt.

lighting plant ~ a gasoline or diesel powered generator.

light of firewood ~ a back load of firewood.

like ducks ~ under no circumstances. "You want me to loan you a hundred dollars – like ducks!"

limb ~ 1. cut the branches from a tree. 2. to beat someone. "If you make another face at me I'm going to limb you." 3. a practical joker.

link ~ See **lynx**.

linkum ~ See **cape ann**.

linnet {pronounced: *LYNN - ett*} ~ nets, traps, seines and the twine used to make them. "I walked out on the stage head and tripped up in the linnet."

linny ~ See **lean-in**.

liquor book ~ a ration book for those purchasing liquor.

lissom ~ pliable lumber.

little black diver ~ the American black scoter *[Oidemia nigra americana]*, a seaduck. The drakes are mostly black and the females are brown.

little crow ~ a small member of the bird family, *Corvidae*.

little curlew ~ the Eskimo or northern curlew *[Numenius borealis]*. Adults have long, dark, greyish legs and a long bill curved slightly downward.

live rock ~ a coral-like seaweed.

livyers ~ residents, settlers. "There used to be livyers on Trump Island one time but they all moved away."

loader ~ one who piles wood on a sled in the lumber woods.

loaf ~ bread. "I'd give anything for a slice of jam loaf."

lobscouse ~ a casserole composed of salt meat cubes, diced onion, rice, diced carrot, diced turnip, diced potato, diced parsnip and diced cabbage. This was a favourite meal on ships at sea so it possibly originated with cooks on ships.

lobster pot ~ See **lobster trap**.

lobster trap also **lobster pot** ~ a wooden trap with an entrance made from netting that forms a ramp up which a lobster may climb. Bait, in the form of capelin, flat fish or other fish, is placed inside the trap to entice the lobster inside. Once the lobster drops down from the ramp it has difficulty getting up to the entrance again and is usually trapped.

local ice ~ See **harbour ice**.

locker ~ See **bunker**.

lode stone ~ a magnet.

lodge ~ to place. "Lodge the teapot down on the stove while I get a cup."

loft ~ the upper story of a building, especially one where nets are made or mended or where hay is stored.

logans ~ shin-high lace-up boots with rubber bottoms and leather uppers. These were useful in deep snow and the bottoms were completely waterproof. See also **lumps**.

logy {rhymes with *stogie*} ~ lethargic, slow-moving, lazy. "When the weather gets hot I gets right logy."

lolly {rhymes with *jolly*} ~ soft ice beginning to form on the ocean, near the shore.

lollygagging ~ wasting time by horsing around. "Stop your lollygaggin' and make the hay."

long-billed mouse ~ the Labrador shrew. *[Sorex personatus miscix]*

long car ~ See **long cart**.

long cart also **long car** ~ a long horse-drawn, two-wheeled cart. This word is local to the St. John's area. In other areas it is known as a "dray."

longer also **lunger** ~ a long pole used to make the platform of a flake, as a fence rail or for some other purpose. "Be careful while walking on the flake, you may fall down between the longers."

long-liner ~ a decked fishing boat

long-liner

usually between 45 and 65 feet in length, used in various types of commercial fishing, including cod-netting, capelin-seining, crab-fishing, scallop-dragging and sealing.

long-lining ~ using a trawl (a long line with baited hooks) to catch fish from a smaller, open boat or a long-liner.

long rubbers

long rubbers ~ knee-high, slip-on rubber boots.

longshoreman ~ 1. a man who works in the fishery on land. Possibly originally "along-shore man." 2. a stevedore. 3. a permanent resident of coastal Labrador.

long side ~ beside, adjacent to. "I tied up my schooner long side the *Bessie Marie*."

long side a ~ toward. "Move closer long side a me."

long-tailed duck ~ the American pintail *[Anas acuta tzitzihoa]*.

long-tailed sugar ~ molasses.

long teeth ~ to swallow quickly without tasting. Alluding to a food one doesn't like. It isn't chewed, but swallowed quickly, barely touching the tips of the "long teeth" as it passes by them on the way past the taste buds. "I don't like canned spaghetti so I give it the long teeth."

long tom ~ a muzzleloader with a particularly long barrel. The barrel was made longer for trading purposes as at one time the value of a gun was the thickness of furs equal to the length of the gun.

loo ~ 1. the loon. 2. See **lew**.

lookout ~ a high point on land without trees or other objects that may obstruct a view of the ocean.

looper ~ See **mope**.

loose ice ~ ice that has broken into smaller pieces sufficient enough to allow vessels to pass through it.

looward ~ See **leeward**.

lopper ~ the Northern short-eared owl *[Asio flammeus]*.

loppy ~ rough water. "I wouldn't want to be on the water today, it's so loppy I think I'd get seasick."

lops ~ small white-capped waves on the water.

lords and ladies also **lord bird, lady bird** ~ the female and male harlequin duck *[Histrionicus histrionicus]*. With its dark purple colouring the male harlequin is regal in appearance, which earned the couple their name. These birds may be seen bobbing for invertebrate sea creatures in rough water near rugged cliffs. Oil spills and over-hunting have placed these ducks on the endangered list.

lord bird ~ See **lords and ladies**.

losing the moon ~ the period when the moon is waning.

lourd ~ dark and gloomy. "It's so lourd in this room with the drapes closed."

love child ~ a child born out of wedlock.

low-bush hert ~ a variety of blueberry *[Vaccinium]*.

low minded ~ in a state of depression. "Buddy's wife is so low minded that she won't speak to anyone, not even herself."

low pear ~ the purple chokeberry plant *[Aronia prunifolia]*.

lucksee ~ do you agree? "The codfish can't last if we catch too many, lucksee b'y."

luh ~ look. "Luh, there's a barquesailled schooner coming in the harbour."

lumberwoods ~ a wooded area where logs are cut to make timber or for pulp wood.

lume ~ a lighthouse.

lump ~ the lumpfish or lumpsucker *[Cyclopterus lumpus]*, a small fish harvested for its roe. On the underside of its body its ventral fins have been changed into a round sucker disc. The lumpfish is a bottom dwelling creature, preferring rocky areas where it can attach itself by this sucker. It also will sometimes attach itself to floating masses of seaweed. Adult lumpfish are usually 36-41 cm (14-16 in) long and weigh 1.36-272 kg (3- 6 lb).

lumper ~ a worker who loads and unloads ships' cargoes.

lumps also **cod's heads, george martins, rubber lumps, unemployment boots, dole boots, gum boots** ~ ankle-high, heavy-rubber boots that were laced up and, for the most part, waterproof. These were worn in the 1950s and earlier, and were often referred to as "unemployment boots." Leather uppers (often sealskin) were added to lumps to make logans. The name probably came from the lump fish which is a short, rounded fish.

lumps

lun ~ 1. an area sheltered from the wind. 2. calm. 3. of the wind, to abate.

lunch ~ a light snack eaten at a time other than breakfast, dinner or supper, especially before bedtime.

lunger ~ See **longer**.

lungy ~ clumsy and awkward. "He's so lungy he'd trip over a pencil mark."

lynx also **link** ~ the Canadian lynx *[Lynx canadensis]*.

lynx

machine ~ See **chummyjigger**.

mackerel ~ the Atlantic mackerel *[Scomber scombrus]*. Reaching sexual mature by age three, it measures about 47 cm (18.5 in) in length and weighs 1.3 kg (3 lb) in weight. There are two major groups of

mackerel

Atlantic mackerel: a southern group that spawns primarily in the Mid-Atlantic Bight during April and May, and a northern group that spawns in the Gulf of St. Lawrence in June and July. A member of the same family of fishes as the tuna, the mackerel is similar to the tuna in taste.

mackerel bird also **mackerel gull** ~ the Caspian tern *[Sterna caspia]*. At a length of up to 58 cm (23 in), making it the largest of all North American terns, the Caspian tern is less common than the Arctic tern or the common tern, as well as being more ferocious. Its diet consists almost entirely of small fish.

mackerel gull ~ See **mackerel bird**.

mackerel sky ~ high clouds which form in bands or stripes.

madeira ~ a grade of cured codfish.

mag also **meg** ~ a vertical stick at which an iron or rope ring is tossed in an attempt to encircle it in the game of quoits.

maggoty ~ 1. covered in maggots, or blowfly larvae, especially covering cured fish or fish that is curing. 2. in large numbers. "The people were maggoty at the garden party."

magna teaberry also **maidenhair teaberry**, **manna teaberry**, **maiden's tresses** ~ the creeping snowberry *[Gaultheria hispidula]*. A white berry measuring about 6 mm in diameter, having a mild wintergreen flavour and aroma. The leaves are also used to make medicinal tea.

mahone soldier ~ a lazy person.

maid ~ 1. a young unmarried woman. "She's a fine looking maid." 2. one's daughter. "My maid has been helping her mother since she was thigh-high to a tickleass."

maiden aunt ~ one's unmarried aunt.

maidenhair teaberry ~ See **magna teaberry**.

maiden ray ~ a small member of the skate family of fishes *[Raja radiata]*.

maiden ray

maiden's tresses ~ See **magna teaberry**.

maid teacher ~ an unmarried female schoolteacher.

mainland ~ continental North America. "There wasn't enough work here fer me youngsters so they all moved to the Mainland."

mainlander ~ one who lives in continental North America or its adjacent islands outside Newfoundland and Labrador.

mainso ~ the main sail on a sailing vessel.

make-and-break ~ a one cylinder, two-cycle, gasoline engine that had a small battery and a coil to generate enough spark to ignite the gaseous mixture in the chamber. The engine had a built-in timing device that made spark when it was needed and broke spark when it was not. Dry cell batteries were used to provide the spark as well as rechargeable wet cells that looked like a small car battery. This engine

make and break

had no electric starter but was started by hand, by spinning the heavy flywheel at the front of the engine. The flywheel had a hole into which a "handle" could be inserted to help turn the engine over. This required some effort as the gaseous mixture had to be compressed in the piston chamber while the engine was being advanced enough for the timing device to make spark.

make away with ~ to kill. "If buddy finds out you've been seeing his wife he'll make away with you."

make away with yourself ~ to commit suicide.

make fish ~ to cure codfish by salting and drying.

make out ~ pretend. "Let's make out we're pirates." Originated in England.

make strange ~ to be shy. "She always makes strange when there's grown-ups around."

making old bones ~ staying up late.

making your soul ~ getting your spiritual affairs in order.

mall dow ~ See **maw dow**.

mamateek

mamateek ~ the winter wigwam or dwelling of the

Beothuk, in which several families lived.

mampus ~ a large number. "There was a mampus of fish in the trap this morning."

man-cat ~ a smaller catamaran or sled, hauled by one or more men.

maneen ~ a boy who fancies himself a man. "Them maneens is always hangin' around the street."

mang ~ 1. a mixture of different foods. 2. to mix different foods together.

manna teaberry ~ See **magna teaberry**.

manus ~ 1. a mutiny. 2. to mutiny. "The captain aboard the *Maiden Ray* was so cruel that the crew wanted to manus."

mare-browed ~ referring to a person whose eyebrows meet.

mare's tails ~ cirrus clouds. These clouds appear after a cloudless and windless night when a light air springs up from a little north of east. They may be seen to be moving from the southwest or northwest at great velocity. See also **Clouds** on page 291.

marked ground ~ a fishing ground located by observing landmarks and using triangulation to determine the location.

marks ~ land features that when observed from the sea allow one to pinpoint his location by triangulation.

marl ~ to meander apparently aimlessly. "I think I'll marl down the road fer a spurt."

marlin also **marline** ~ small rope.

marline ~ See **marlin**.

marning ~ morning. "It's a fine marning this marning."

marry too far ~ to wed someone from a far-away community.

marsh berry ~ the small cranberry, bog cranberry, wild cranberry and swamp cranberry and cranberry *[Vaccinium oxycoccos]*. Found in marshes, this berry is rich in vitamin C and was used by early explorers to cure scurvy. In modern medicine its juice is sometimes prescribed for urinary infections and hypoglycemia.

marsh birch ~ a white birch tree found in marshy areas *[Betula papyrifera]*.

marsh blackbird ~ the rusty blackbird, a medium-sized blackbird, having a pointed bill and pale yellow eyes *[Euphagus carolinus]*.

marsh lily also **meadow sweet** ~ the Canadian burnet, a member of the rose family with white leaves *[Sanguisorba canadensis]*.

mash also **meesh, mish** ~ a marsh or bog.

master ~ 1. the supervisor of a group of men. 2. the captain of a vessel. Originated in the British Isles.

master of watch ~ See **master watch**.

master watch also **master of watch** ~ the person in charge of a group of men who hunt seals on the ice from a sealing vessel.

mathers also **mazzard** ~ the oval-leaf blueberry [*Vaccinium ovalifolium*].

matting needle ~ a tool used to hook rugs.

matting party ~ a group of women gathered to hook rugs.

maugre {rhymes with *logger*} ~ in spite of.

mauzy {pronounced: *MAH - zee*} ~ an overcast, foggy day with little or no wind, sometimes accompanied by misty rain.

maw dow also **mall dow, moldow, old man's beard** ~ a whisker-like lichen plant which grows on trees.

mawk ~ a silly person.

maw mouth ~ 1. any large-mouthed fish. 2. a gossiper or a person who talks a lot.

mayflower ~ refers to a number of plants that flower in May, including the cuckoo flower [*Cardamine pratensis*]; the ground laurel [*Epigaea repens*]; the alpine azalea [*Loiseleuria procumbens*]; the saxifrage [*Saxifraga oppositifolia*] and the violet [*Viola pallens*].

May pole also **May tree** ~ a tree with branches removed, used in May as a decoration near the entrance to property in May.

May tree ~ See **May pole**.

May water ~ the water obtained by melting snow that falls in May, used for medicinal purposes. Some Protestants believed this was how Roman Catholics got their holy water.

maze ~ to confuse someone.

maze-headed ~ confused.

mazzard ~ See **mathers**.

me ~ my. "I got me long rubbers on."

meadow sweet ~ See **marsh lily**.

meal of tongues ~ 1. a bawling-out. 2. to have a very passionate necking session with someone of the opposite sex.

me ducky also **my ducky** ~ a friendly way to address someone.

meesh ~ See **mash**.

meg ~ See **mag**.

merchant ~ See **fish merchant**.

merry-begot ~ illegitimate child, or bastard, often used as a curse word. "You come down from that hay loft, you merry-begot, before I come up and bring you down." Originated in the British Isles.

merry dancers ~ the aurora borealis or northern lights.

Methodist bread ~ raisin bread.

Mi-Careme ~ a celebration over several days in the middle of Lent by French-Acadian residents of the province. This was similar to mummering, as people disguised themselves and visited homes to have the occupants guess their identity.

mick also **mickey** ~ a term used by Protestants to refer to Roman Catholics.

mickey ~ See **mick**.

Micmac ~ See **Mi'kmaq**.

middler ~ a beaver in its second and third years.

midshiproom ~ the storage area somewhere between the fore and aft of a small boat in which fish is stored.

midship room

midsummer men also **hen and chicks** ~ a plant of the stonecrop or sedum family *[Crassulaceae]*.

Mi'kmaq {pronounced: *MIG - maw*} also **Micmac** ~ an Indian of the Algonkian people, who traditionally lived in what is now Nova Scotia, New Brunswick, Prince Edward Island, eastern Quebec and northern Maine. One group of Mi'Kmaq (whose home territory was what is now Cape Breton Island) often travelled to Newfoundland in large canoes to fish and to trap animals on land. 2. the language spoken by same.

mile-a-minute ~ the Japanese knotweed plant *[Polygonum cuspidatum]*.

milk slide ~ a sleigh pulled by dogs to deliver milk door to door.

milk slide

mill blanket ~ a heavy blanket, used in the making of paper and sometimes used as a bed cover.

miller ~ 1. moth. "If you kill a miller you'll have bad luck." 2. a member of the ray family of fishes, the thorny skate *[Raja radiata]*.

miller

millyer ~ the pitcher in certain ball games.

mind ~ 1. be careful, pay attention to. "The sidewalk is very icy so mind you don't fall down." 2. to remember. "Do you mind the time we went moose hunting up Buchan's way?"

mind like a sieve ~ a poor memory.

mind out I don't also **mind out now** ~ I'm certainly not going to do that. "You want me to do all the work while you sit and watch - mind out I don't."

mind out now ~ See **mind out I don't**.

minister ~ See **smelt**.

minister gull ~ the eastern glaucous gull *[Larus hyperborus]*.

minister gull

mish ~ See **mash**.

misky ~ misty. "There's a bit of misky rain falling today."

missus ~ 1. Mrs. 2. a term of respect for a mature or older woman. 3. wife.

mitt ~ a mitten.

mitten flower ~ cotton grass *[Eriophorum]*.

mockbeggar ~ an impressive-looking house without hospitality.

mog ~ See **Eskimo boot**.

molasses ~ a thick, syrupy derivative of the juice of the sugarcane or sugar beet plants, imported from the Caribbean and often used as a sweetener in baking, as a spread on bread and in other applications.

molasses beer ~ a beer made from the fermentation of molasses.

moldow ~ See **maw dow**.

mole of the skull ~ top of the head.

mollyfodge ~ lichens, or symbiotic organisms, used to make dye.

money purse ~ a pouch with a flap found on the underside of crabs. See also **Catchin' Tomcods and Conners** on page 206.

monge ~ to eat. Possibly from the French "manger," meaning "to eat."

Monk dory ~ a dory of a particular style factory-made in Monkstown, Newfoundland, by the Monk family.

Montagnais ~ an indian of the Algonkian people who reside in southern Labrador.

month of Sundays ~ a number of years, a long time.

mooch also **pip** ~ to skip school.

moonlight child ~ a child born out of wedlock.

moonshine can ~ 1. a can used in

the making of moonshine. 2. a can in which moonshine is kept.

moot ~ 1. a pin feather, or the root of same, which must be plucked from birds in the cleaning process. 2. a human hair. "I haven't got a moot left on my head."

mooty hen ~ 1. a hen that is shedding its feathers. 2. a hen that might attack and bite humans while mooting.

mop ~ See **mott**.

mope also **stunned whooper, looper** ~ the pine grosbeak *[Pinicola enucleator eschatosus].* One of the largest members of the finch family of birds, its tameness and slow-moving behavior earned it the names "mope' and "stunned whooper." Although it feeds insects and spiders to its young (often mixed with plant food), 99 per cent of its diet is vegetable matter, especially the fruit, seeds and buds of spruce, pine, juniper, maple, dogberry (mountain ash) and crabapple trees. It measures 20-25 cm (8-10 in) in length, and has a wingspan of 33 cm (13 in).

mop head ~ See **choby**.

moppsed ~ messy, messed. "The wind got my hair all moppsed up."

more ~ 1. to dig up the root of a tree in search of one suitably shaped to form a vessel's timber. 2. other. "Sometimes I like to go rabbit catching and more times I don't." 3. others. "Some people go to church every Sunday while more don't care if they see the inside of a church door."

moryeen ~ fertilizer made by combining peat with fish offal.

moss berry ~ See **blackberry**.

moss lily ~ a low evergreen plant *[Diaspensia lapponica].*

mot ~ flammable items used to light a fire.

mother carey's chicken ~ See **carey's chicken**.

mother fish ~ a large codfish of breeding age.

mother-in-law door ~ the front door of a house. Most homes were built in this province by degrees as people could afford it, leaving the least important projects for last. Since front doors were seldom used, access to this door was usually the last thing to be worked on. Some people never got

mother-in-law door

around to finishing them. Over the years they acquired the name, mother-in-law doors.

motion ~ a stretch of water, with turbulent movement caused by the meeting of heavy cross currents.

motorboat ~ a large punt fitted with a make-and-break engine and a rudder.

mott also **mop** ~ the hole in a game of alleys (marbles). See also **Alleys** on page 203.

mountain curlew also **Eskimo curlew** ~ the northern curlew *[Numenius borealis]*. Adults have long, dark greyish legs and a long bill curved slightly downward. With populations in the millions, this was once one of the largest species of birds in North America. But many were killed over the years, particularly in the late 1800s, when as many as two million were killed each year. There have been sightings of this bird in recent years, but it is very much an endangered species and may already be extinct.

mountaineer ~ a name sometimes applied to the Montagnais Indians.

mountaineer sled ~ a type of sled used by the Montagnais Indians.

mountain hare ~ the Arctic hare *[Lepus arcticus]*. Adult hares have few enemies beside human hunters – and in Labrador, the wolf – while young hares are taken by snowy owls, foxes and lynx. When alarmed these hares rise up on their hind legs to look for danger, then, like kangaroos, they bound off on their hind legs at speeds estimated to be more than 50 kilometres (30 miles) per hour.

mountain partridge also **rock partridge** ~ the Welch's rock ptarmigan *[Lagopus mutus welchi]*. This partridge strictly confines itself to the bleak sides and summits of mountains and rocky hills of Newfoundland. Unlike some of its cousins, who travel some distance, mountain partridges never stray far from their place of birth in their lifetime. They grow to 33-40 cm (13-16 in) in length.

mountain turnip ~ the gall-of-the-earth plant *[Prenanthes trifloiolata]*.

mouth ~ See **mouze**.

mouth music ~ See **cheek music**.

mouth organ ~ harmonica.

mouze {rhymes with *cows*} also **mouth** ~ 1. to imitate mockingly. "If you mouze me one more time I'll make you wish you were spending Easter on Calvary." 2. to make faces at.

mucker ~ in a state of confusion.

muckle ~ 1. to pull strenuously. 2. to hug.

mud fish ~ codfish caught too late in the season to be properly cured, so they are kept in salt until the following season.

mud rubbers ~ short rubber overshoes.

mud sucker ~ 1. a bog hole. 2. See **devil's pipe**.

mud trout also **speckled trout, sea trout** ~ the eastern brook trout *[Salvelinus fontinalis]*. Found in ponds lakes, mud holes, brooks and rivers, as well as in the ocean all over and around Newfoundland and Labrador, technically the eastern brook is not a trout but a char. The flesh of this char is very tasty and is often white. In cases where it has to resort to cannibalism during the winter when food is scarce it eats the young of its species, in which case the flesh is pink. The average size is 10 to 12 inches but are sometimes much bigger. They sometimes measure up to 53 cm (21 in) and weigh up to 3 kg (6.6 lb). The largest eastern brook trout on record weighed 6.6 kg (14.5 lb).

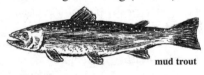

mud trout

mug up ~ a snack or lunch which usually includes the making of tea.

mullygrubs ~ cranky and cross. "No one looked at Mother's new hat at the church service last night and she's in the mullygrubs today."

mummer also **janney**, **johnny** ~ a disguised person who goes door-to-door during the 12 days of Christmas to have fun

mummer

and merriment. Originated in England and Ireland.

mummering also **janneying**, **mumming** ~ to visit houses during the 12 days of Christmas disguised as a mummer. See also **Mummering** on page 244.

mumming ~ See **mummering**.

mundel ~ a stirring stick or wooden spoon, especially used for stirring soup.

munge ~ to chew or munch. Probably from the word "munch," or the French "manger," to chew.

mungey {rhymes with *spungy*} ~ the stomach.

murre ~ See **turr**.

muskrat ~ a large aquatic rodent, between 25 and 40 cm (10 and 16 in) in length, hunted for its fur and sometimes for food. *[Ondatra zibethicus]* The name comes from the musky secretion it uses to mark its territory.

muskrat flower ~ the round-leaved sundew plant *[Drosera rotundifolia]*. Derivatives of this plant are used to alleviate asthma, bronchitis, whooping cough and other respiratory conditions marked by viscid mucous.

mussel ~ the female genitalia.

must go ~ leftovers. "We're having must go for dinner today."

muzzle-loader ~ a long-barreled gun which fires a single lead ball or a quantity of shot, propelled by igniting loose gunpowder, all of which is loaded through the muzzle, or barrel-end, a musket. The gunpowder is ignited by the hammer striking a percussion cap placed on the gun's nipple.

muzzle-loader

myrrh also **turpentine** ~ the sap of the balsam fir tree, used to help heal cuts on the human body.

nag ~ 1. chip away with a blunt axe. 2. a small stick stuck vertically in the ground and used as the target in the game of pitching buttons. 3. an old horse past its prime.

nagger ~ tooth, especially the tooth of a child or baby.

naggle ~ to grumble or fuss.

nail ~ 1. to set a vessel's course. "Nail her on west, sou'west for the next three hours, then swing her to the nor'west." 2. to strike someone. "I sometimes feels like nailing him right between the two eyes."

nair ~ See **nar**.

naked man also **American man, cairn, inuksuk** {pronounced: *in - NUK - SHUK*} ~ a man-made landmark for navigation, usually made by piling stones on top of each other to make the shape of a

naked man

human. These were once prevalent along the Labrador coast. They were very useful in determining one's location at sea.

naluyuk ~ the Inuit word for a Christmas mummer.

nanny ~ 1. a sheep or goat. 2. a call to sheep or goats. "Here nanny, nanny, nanny."

nanny goat ~ a female goat. The following rhyme was recited by children:
"The nanny goat
Chased the billy goat
Over the hill
And tore her petticoat."

nansarey ~ a small sled that uses barrel staves for runners.

nape ~ the fleshy part of a codfish behind the head.

nar also **neither, ne'er, nair** ~ none, not any. "I got nar cent of money to me name."

narder ~ ready. "I'll pick you up when I gets narder." Derived from "in order."

narn ~ never a one, not a single one. "I was hoping to get a moose for the winter but I never got narn."

narrows ~ 1. a constricted part of a water feature. 2. a confined entrance to a harbour.

narrows

nary a one ~ hardly any.

Naskapi {pronounced: *na - SCOP - ee*} ~ 1. a member of a group of nomadic Algonkian people living in Labrador. 2. the language spoken by same.

Naskapi sled ~ a type of sled, used by the Naskapi of Labrador.

native ~ 1. the Beothuk of Newfoundland, now extinct. 2. the Innu and Inuit of Labrador. 3. animals, birds or fish that breed in Newfoundland and Labrador, or in the waters around same. 4. plants that grow in Newfoundland and Labrador, excluding those introduced in more recent years. 5. anyone born in Newfoundland and Labrador.

nature ~ sexual drive. "After I turned 80, I started to lose me nature."

nawpoll ~ a stupid person.

neck also **strand** ~ a narrow peninsula or isthmus.

neither ~ See **nar**.

ne'r ~ nor. "The schooner got no sail ne'r spar."

ne'er ~ See **nar**.

nesh ~ See **nish**.

nest ~ to store dories, one inside the other.

net-bag ~ a small-mesh net shaped into a large bag, used to temporarily moor surplus codfish to be retrieved later and brought ashore.

net gallows ~ a frame made with long poles on which nets are hung to dry.

net loft ~ a loft above the fisherman's store (storage shed) where nets were made and mended, and many stories told.

net loft

net-mender ~ the person responsible for insuring fishing nets are in good repair and making any repairs necessary.

net needle ~ a device carved from a piece of wood, used to make and repair the meshes in fish nets.

net needle

never ~ didn't, was not the one who. "I never stole Aunt Martha's sheep, that was Ellis Coles and Dick Nolan who did that."

Newfie ~ a jocular term for a Newfoundlander, sometimes used in a derogatory sense.

Newfoundland banks ~ any fishing banks in close proximity to Newfoundland and Labrador.

Newfoundland coffin ~ sea-going vessels that were locally-made in the early days of settlement.

Newfoundland company ~ a company chartered by England to establish a fishing plantation in Newfoundland.

Newfoundland dog ~ a large black, brown or black-and-white dog with a waterproof coat and webbed feet. This dog is noted for its bravery, in the water and out.

Newfoundland dog

Newfoundland dwarf birch ~ a small birch tree *[Betula michauxii]*.

Newfoundland fishery ~ the fishing industry in Newfoundland.

Newfoundland hardwood ~ the wood of the paper birch, or American white birch *[Betula papyrifera]* or yellow birch *[Betula lutea]* tree.

Newfoundlandia ~ all things that pertain to Newfoundland and Labrador.

Newfoundland man also **newlander** ~ 1. a crew member on an English West Country vessel involved in the Newfoundland fishery. 2. the vessel used by same.

Newfoundland pony ~ a hardy animal that is the product of 300 years of interbreeding of the Exmoor, Dartmoor, New Forest, Galloway, Welsh, Connemara and Highlands ponies brought by the early settlers. The pony stands approximately 11 to 14.2 hands high, and weighs between 180 and 360 kg (400 and 800 lb). It has a thick dark mane, tail and lower legs. It is usually brownish in colour though other colorus are not uncommon. It has short, hairy ears, small flint-hard hooves, and a low set tail. Its thick coat, which helps it survive during harsh winters, and its ability to survive on relatively small amounts of most available grasses and foods made it an ideal workhorse.

Newfoundland pony

Newfoundland Regiment ~ See **Remembrance Day** on page 196 and **War Heroes** on page 270.

newlander ~ See **Newfoundland man**.

nib also **nip** ~ in the game of rounders, to nick the ball and send it foul.

nice ~ considerable. "St. George's is a nice distance from Cape St. George."

nickel ~ a motion picture. From The Nickel Theatre in St. John's, which originally charged a nickel for admission.

Nicodemus {pronounced: *NICK - oh - DEE - mus*} ~ 1. a turncoat. 2. one who changes religions. In the New Testament, Nicodemus was a ruler of the Jews who came to Jesus by night to find salvation.

nigger head ~ 1. a drum-shaped device which is part of a ship's winch and which turns to haul the ropes or cables wound around it. 2. a home-made winch on a motor boat powered by the gasoline engine from a washing machine.

nip ~ See **nib**.

nipper ~ 1. a biting mosquito or fly of the family *Culicidae*. The female has needle-like mouth-parts and sucks blood before laying eggs. Males feed on plant juices. "The nippers is so plentiful and viscous in Black Tickle, Labrador, that last year they stripped the sails from Grandfather's schooner and this year they came back wearing canvas jackets." 2. a thick band of cloth, used to protect a fisherman's hands or fingers while jigging or hand-lining.

nippy ~ 1. tight, miserly. "He's so nippy he'd want the grub from his own wake put away for the next day." 2. cold weather. "It's a bit nippy out tonight."

nish also **nesh** ~ 1. of the human flesh, soft and tender, easily injured. "I haven't worked all winter and my hands are gone nish." 2. of ice, brittle and easily broken.

nobble ~ to drag something along the ground, especially a heavy object.

noddy also **knotty** ~ the Alantic Fulmar *[Sterna solida]*, a dark web-footed sea-bird, often seen in the company of the Greater Shearwater. This, the most common of offshore birds, gets its name from the fact that it has a habit of nodding its head, which is larger than that of gulls.

noddy

noggin ~ 1. a small cup 2. a person's head. See also **nopper**. 3. a small tub used in the galley of sealing vessels for transporting food. 4. a small cask.

nog head ~ 1. a small piece of wood. 2. one who is thick-headed. 3. an under-nourished seal pup.

nointer ~ a mischievous child. "Don't be throwing rocks at the hens, you young nointer." Possibly the sarcastic use of "anointer." This word is also used in Australia.

nokes ~ a simple-minded person.

nonia ~ 1. an acronym for Newfoundland Outport Nursing and Industrial Association, a not-for-profit cottage industry that was started to assist outport women in becoming cottage-industry business people by producing hand-made clothing and goods. The profits were initially used to pay the salaries of nurses in the province. 2. the name of one of Newfoundland's coastal vessels.

noody nawdy ~ 1. lackadaisical, lazy. "He's so noody nawdy that he'd sooner turn his underwear inside out than wash them." 2. one who is lackadaisical or lazy.

nopper ~ the head.

nor'ard ~ toward the north.

norther ~ 1. a strong, cold wind from the north. 2. the more northerly of two places.

northern cod ~ the codfish found off the northeast coast of Labrador.

northern fishery ~ the fishery prosecuted by Newfoundland fishermen off the northeast coast of Labrador.

northern turr ~ the Brunich's guillemot, or thick-billed murre *[Uria lomvia]*, a member of the auk family of seabirds, measuring up to 17 inches in length, with a 24-inch wingspan.

north shore pork eaters ~ people who lived on the north shore of Conception Bay. Possibly from the fact that a lot of pigs were raised in parts of the area.

Norway ~ a fine-grained, tapered whetstone, used to sharpen knives.

Norwegian jigger ~ a heavy silver-coloured lure with three hooks, used to jig codfish.

Norwegian jigger

nor'wester ~ a heavy hooded oilskin coat.

nose ~ 1. a promontory extending seaward. 2. the front end of something. "Uncle Billy's schooner could just get her nose into the end of the wharf."

Nose and Tail of the Grand Bank ~ two portions of the Grand Banks' fishing grounds that extend into international waters.

nosey parker ~ applied to a very inquisitive person.

not bad like him/her ~ a strong resemblance.

not caribou ~ a male caribou without antlers.

notch ~ a pronounced break in cliffs or headlands. 2. a gash in a log, or piece of wood. 3. to cut a gash in something.

notch the beam ~ to show surprise.

notchy ~ having sharp indentations, serrated.

not cow ~ a cow without horns.

not easy ~ qualified, successful, competent. "You built your house all by yourself – you're not easy."

not hurt ~ in good condition, without a stain or mark, hardly worn, like new. "You can have these shoes, they're old but they're not hurt."

novie ~ a fishing vessel out of Nova Scotia.

now, the once ~ shortly. "I'll come over and see you now, the once."

nuddick ~ a small, flat-topped hill that can accommodate a house and garden.

nug ~ a chunk of wood cut to fit a stove.

nugget ~ a black pig.

number ~ a prefix used with the numbers one, two or three that indicates a grade of cured codfish. "That's number two fish."

number nineteen ~ a number given to public outhouses in St. John's.

nunch ~ a snack or light lunch.

nunchie ~ See **bullbird**.

nunny bag ~ a small bag used for carrying provisions while travelling.

nunnyfudger ~ an idler or slacker. "He's such a nunnyfunger, you wouldn't want to go on the halves with him."

nuzzletripe also **nuzzletrite** ~ the runt of the litter.

nuzzletrite ~ See **nuzzletripe**.

oakum ~ a hemp or hemp-like fibre, used especially for caulking seams between planks in wooden vessels. This was sometimes obtained by unravelling old rope.

oar's egg ~ See **whore's egg**.

oaths ~ swear words or cuss words.

ock ~ Sec **hock**.

ockie {rhymes with *hockey*} ~ 1. human waste. 2. something not fit to be put in one's mouth.

ochre ~ a natural earth containing ferric oxide, silica and alumina, used by the Beothuk to colour their skin, clothing and other possessions.

offal ~ the remains of fish after splitting and cleaning, often used as fertilizer.

off-and-on boat ~ a small boat used for transportation to where a bigger boat is on collar, or moored.

offer ~ 1. to try. "I'm going to offer at building a boat this winter." 2. farther away from the land. "People used to live on the Offer Wadham Islands one time."

off in water ~ swimming or playing in the ocean or a lake, pond or river. "Every time we goes to Black Bank the youngsters goes off in water."

offshore ~ some distance from the land, especially on a fishing bank.

ogous {pronounced: *OH - jiss*} ~ very big.

oil range ~ a stove fuelled by oil. See also **range**.

oil-skins

oilskins ~ any outer clothing worn by fishermen that has been treated with oil to make it waterproof.

Old Christmas Day ~ January 6, which marks the 12th day of Christmas. This was Christmas Day before the adoption of the Gregorian calendar.

old cock ~ See **old trout**.

old dooman ~ wife. This appears to be nothing more than a bastardization of "old woman."

old hag ~ See **hag-rode**.

old harry ~ the name given to a number of locations having rocks or sunkers that are dangerous to navigation.

old king ~ See **king bird**.

old lord ~ a mature male harlequin duck *[Histrionicus histrionicus]*.

old man ~ husband. "The old man t'inks he runs t'ings and most of the time I let's 'en believe it."

old man's beard ~ a lichen which grows on evergreen trees and is beard-like in appearance.

old man's cap ~ a type of mushroom.

old saddler ~ See **saddleback**.

old soldier ~ 1. squid that are too spoiled to be used for bait. 2. chewing tobacco with the flavour chewed out.

old tom ~ common rum from the West Indies.

old trout also **old cock** ~ a friendly way to address a male. "How are ya gettin' on, me old trout?"

old woman ~ 1. wife. "One trouble never comes alone, last night the old woman died and this marnin' the hen didn't lay." 2. the inedible part of a lobster located inside the lobster near the eyes. So called because it resembles an old woman sitting in a rocking chair.

omadawn ~ 1. a clownish person. 2. a foolish person.

omaloor ~ a half-wit.

omigon ~ a big, stupid, lumbering person.

on collar ~ referring to a boat at anchor. See also **collar**.

on collar

one lunger ~ 1. a single-piston

engine. 2. a motorboat with such an engine.

on hand ~ to have something close by, ready for use.

on her beam ends ~ said of a vessel when she has rolled over so far on her side that her deck beams are almost vertical.

only ~ as well. "Our house is only a small place."

on my own hooks ~ an independent fisherman.

onshook ~ See **oonchuk**.

on the halves ~ to give half of one's catch, to provide cut logs, or other product in return for services rendered. "I got my lumber cut on the halves at the sawmill, so it didn't cost me that much to build my house."

on the hand of ~ nearly or close by.

on the hoof ~ walking.

on the ree-raw ~ quickly.

onto ~ on. "As soon as the train gets here I'm going to get onto it."

oonchuk also **oonshook, oonshick, ownchuk, onshook** ~ 1. a male Christmas reveller, wearing a disguise, usually that of a female. 2. a fool or person of low intelligence.

oonshick ~ See **oonchuk**.

oonshook ~ See **oonchuk**.

operas ~ binoculars.

oreweed ~ kelp.

orphan ~ the dough left over after bread is baked that is too small to make another.

ose egg ~ See **whore's egg**.

osy egg ~ See **whore's egg**.

otter rub ~ an incline where otters slide down to water.

ouannaniche {pronounced: *WAUN - ah - NISH*} also **winnish** ~ landlocked Atlantic salmon.

ourn ~ ours. From the contraction of "our one."

out ~ outside. "It snowing out today."

outer ~ away from the land.

out-field ~ the position of the players in a game of piddely not at bat. See also **Piddely** on page 251.

outfit ~ to supply with necessities for a fishing or sealing voyage.

outharbour ~ See **outport**.

out in service ~ See **in service**.

outport also **outharbour** ~ a coastal village in Newfoundland and Labrador.

outporter ~ one who lives in an outport.

outport motor ~ an outboard motor. "Outport," not "outboard," was used in Newfoundland and Labrador to refer to things attached to and outside the vessel.

outside door ~ 1. the seaward entrance to a cod trap. 2. a storm door in a dwelling.

over ~ by. "Why don't you come over to visit?"

overfall ~ a waterfall.

overhead ~ a storage space in the beams and rafters of a building. 2. a loft or attic. 3. to be in a loft or attic. "Father is overhead getting the Christmas decorations."

over-right ~ adjacent to.

overshoes ~ rubber footwear worn over the shoes to protect them from rain and snow.

over-top ~ to pile too high, to make top-heavy.

owing to ~ because of. "The picnic was cancelled owing to rain."

ownchuk ~ See **oonchuk**.

ownded {pronounced: *OWN - did*} ~ owned. This pronunciation is mostly limited to the St. John's area, especially the west end, and is still in use today.

oxters ~ the armpits.

pack ~ a package of cured caribou meat.

package ~ a fish barrel of any size.

packet ~ a mail boat that also carries passengers and freight.

pack ice ~ icepans that have come together and are in contact and usually packed tight to the land at some point.

paddle ~ an one-handed oar, used to row a boat, as well as a two-handed paddle.

paddler ~ a young seal, about two-weeks-old. At that age the seal is just learning to swim, or paddle with its flippers.

Paddy ~ an Irishman.

Paddy Keefe ~ pretty close. "I didn't win the race but I went Paddy Keefe to it."

painter ~ the forward rope on a boat which is used for tying the boat to a wharf.

palaver ~ to coax using flattery. "You can palaver all you want, but I'm not lettin' you take me home this night."

palens {pronounced: *PALE - ens*} also **palings** {pronounced: *PALE - ings*} ~ vertical poles or pickets nailed or tied to horizontal rails to make a fence. Possibly from the word "peelings," since the bark was peeled from trees to make palens.

palter ~ to hesitate.

pan ~ to pile seal pelts on an ice-pan.

Pancake Day ~ Shrove Tuesday. See also **Pancake Day** on page 193.

pancake ice ~ thin sheets of ice that do not impede navigation.

pan flag ~ a flag from a sealing vessel, used to show ownership of the seal pelts on that pan, and to help in later locating that pan.

panshard ~ broken glass or crockery.

pantry stall ~ a place where home-made preserves are sold.

pap ~ biscuits or bread soaked in milk to be fed to infants.

papoose ~ a beaver in its first year.

parish boat ~ a vessel used to transport clergymen to and from coastal parishes.

parlour ~ 1. the living room in the houses of yesteryear, rooms which saw more dying than living as it was the room where the dead were laid out while awaiting burial. Apart from wakes, the room was only used to entertain special guests, or to celebrate Christmas. 2. the inner-most part of a lobster trap. See also **Lobster Catching** on page 236.

parlour door ~ the entrance to the innermost section of a lobster trap.

parson ~ the Atlantic common puffin *[Fratercula arctica]*. From the bird's black back which gives it the appearance of a clergyman.

parson harvey ~ a touton or a slice of bread well covered with molasses.

partined off ~ divided by a wall or partition, partitioned.

partridge ~ one of several types of ptarmigan, including Allen's willow ptarmigan *[Lagopus lagopus alleni]* and Welch's rock ptarmigan *[Lagopus mutus welchi]*.

partridge berry ~ the mountain cranberry or lingonberry *[Vaccinium vitis-idaea]*. These berries are very popular because of their abundance and have been made into jams for many years, although the jams required a large amount of sugar to make it palatable.

partridge bird ~ the fox sparrow *[Passerella iliaca]*. Preferring bushy habitats, the fox sparrow is most conspicuous during spring migration, when its melodious song may be heard coming from brushy areas. Measuring 16 cm (6.25 in), the fox sparrow is much larger than other sparrows and is sometimes mistaken for a larger species of bird, such as a ptarmigan.

partridge hawk ~ the eastern goshawk *[Accipiter gentilis atricapillus]*, a medium-large member of the hawk family that preys on starlings, pigeons, grouse, rats and young rabbits, young hares and even young foxes. In Newfoundland, the only animal that preys upon this hawk is the pine marten.

passage ~ 1. water transportation. "I booked passage to St. John's on the *Glencoe*." 2. a narrow stretch of navigable water. "It took us two hours to come down the eastern passage."

patch ~ a group of wild animals, especially seals.

patch bag ~ a small bag to carry personal effects.

patch fox ~ the red fox *[Vulpus fulvus]*.

patience ~ klondike solitaire.

Patrick ~ a fisherman, especially an Irish fisheries indentured servant.

Patrick and Sheila ~ a winter storm just before St. Patrick's day. See also **Sheila's Brush** on page 194.

pawn ~ to give an unwanted item. "My sister tried to pawn me off with her old dress."

pay out ~ to slack off on and let out a rope as needed.

peach ~ to inform on. "One of the moonshiner's neighbours peached him."

pear tree ~ the juneberry tree, a flowering shrub.

peas ~ fish roe.

pease ~ to seep or ooze.

pease duff ~ See **pease pudding**.

pease pudding also **pease duff** ~ split yellow peas boiled in a cloth bag along with Jigg's dinner. Butter and pepper is added before it is served. This fare, or similar versions, originated in the British Isles where it is also known as mushy peas and pease porridge.

pea-shooter also **rubber gun** ~ a sling shot.

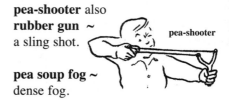
pea-shooter

pea soup fog ~ dense fog.

peck also **pick** ~ a very small amount, a bit.

pecking ~ starting to rain. "It's pecking out, I think we're in for a shower."

peddle house ~ a brothel.

pee wee ~ a miniature marble.

pelt ~ 1. the hide of a seal with the blubber attached. 2. to remove the hide and blubber from a seal.

pen ~ a bin where fish are washed and salted.

peppermint knob ~ a hard, peppermint flavoured candy produced in Newfoundland.

pepper tops ~ the sweet gale, or bog myrtle plant *[Myrica gale]*. This plant or its derivatives have been used over the years as a mosquito repellent.

perfume willow also **willow perfume** ~ the bog candle plant of the orchid family *[Platanthera dilatata]*.

perishing ~ very cold. "I was perishing so I put my sweater on."

periwinkle also **wrinkle** ~ a snail-like saltwater mullosk, having conical, spiral shells, mostly referred to in this province as the wrinkle. See also **Catchin' Tomcods and Conners** on page 206.

perney ~ immediately.

pet day ~ an extremely nice day.

petticoat ~ a lady's undergarment. This word was at one time extensively used. The following rhyme was recited by children:
"Mother dear, may I go swimming
Yes, my darling daughter
Hang your petticoat on the line
And don't go near the water"

petticoat merchant ~ a female fish merchant.

pew ~ 1. a sealer's bunk or berth. 2. a prong with only one tine, used to throw fish from the boat to the stage head.

philandy {pronounced: *fill - AND - dee*} ~ 1. to jump about. 2. to laze around.

pick ~ See peck.

picker ~ See empter.

picket fence ~ a fence made with pickets or palings.

pickets ~ vertical boards or sticks nailed to horizontal rails to make a fence, palings.

pickle ~ brine used to preserve food.

pick off ~ surprise. "He thought she was going to marry him but he got some pick off."

pick-ups ~ a children's game. See also **Pick-ups** on page 251.

piddely also **tiddely, pippy, kit kat, kitty kat, flick stick, snig, puss in the hole** ~ a game played with a bat and a second stick. See also **Piddely** on page 251.

pied duck ~ the Labrador duck (now extinct) *[Camptorhynchus labradorius]*.

pig-a-wee ~ the Newfoundland black-capped chickadee *[Parus atricapillus bartletti]*. Found only on the island of Newfoundland and

Miquelon, this bird is larger and has darker colouring than the eastern chickadee.

pig berry ~ the dogberry, or berry of the mountain ash tree.

pigeon also **saltwater pigeon, sea pigeon, wild pigeon** ~ the black guillemot *[Cepphus grylle atlantis]*. With a length of 30-32 cm (about 1 ft), a wingspan of 52-58 cm (20-23 in) and weighing 300-460 g (10-16 oz), this seabird is similar in appearance to landbirds such as the pigeon and dove. It is silvery white in winter, while in summer it is mostly black with white patches on its wings. These birds live on small fish and sea worms. They were once hunted but are now a protected species.

pigeon

pigeon berry ~ See **crackerberry**.

pigeon diver ~ See **bull bird**.

pig fish ~ See **sculpin**.

piggin also **punt's piggin, punch piggin** ~ a square or four-sided (usuallty wooden) bailing utensil having one side extended to form the handle.

piggin

pike pole ~ a wooden pole with a sharp nail on the end, used on river drives.

piles ~ hemorrhoids.

pin boughs ~ the needles of evergreen trees, especially when dried in heaps on the ground.

pinchgut ~ 1. a narrow body of water. 2. a miserly purser on board a ship.

pinfish ~ See **thornback**.

pink bells also **canterbury bells** ~ the twinflower *[Linnaea borealis]*, a shrubby, creeping evergreen plant, having roundish, opposite leaves and paired, bell-shaped, pinkish flowers. This plant grows to 122-183 cm (4-6 ft) in height.

pink fish ~ a lesser quality cured codfish, having a pinkish colour from improper curing.

pink tops also **rock flower** ~ the fireweed *[Epilobium angustifolium]*, a perennial plant of the willow herb family. When properly prepared soon after picking they are a good source of vitamin C and pro-vitamin A.

pinky ~ 1. cheap port wine. 2. Old Niagara Port Wine mixed with Dominion Ale and consumed by winos in St. John's.

pinnacle ~ 1. a jutting point on the top of an iceberg. 2. rafted-up ice in an ice floe.

pinnacle tank ~ a water tank aboard a vessel in which fresh water is obtained by melting iceberg ice.

pinnacle tea ~ tea made at sea from melted iceberg water.

pinny ~ an apron. From the word "pinafore."

pinnyole ~ See **tickle-ace**.

pinny owl ~ See **tickle-ace**.

pinover ~ a cloth covering on the lower part of the face to protect it from the cold.

pip ~ 1. the entrails of a squid, herring or other fish. 2. to remove the entrails of a squid, herring or other fish. 3. to skip school, to become truant. "I'm going on the pip."

piper ~ See **bibby**.

pipkin ~ a small cooking pot, made of iron, bronze, ceramic or tinned copper, used for cooking in a fireplace.

pippy ~ See **piddely**.

pipsi {pronounced: *PIP - see*} ~ fish cured in the sun and wind without the aid of salt. From the Inuit language.

pishogue {pronounced: *PISH - hog*} ~ 1. a superstition or a story generally discredited. 2. witchcraft.

pismer ~ ant.

pissabed ~ the dandelion flower. Children were told that if they played with these flowers they would wet their beds.

piss pot ~ an impolite term for a chamber pot. See also **chamber pot**.

pissquicks ~ slippers, especially slippers made by cutting the tops off old rubber boots.

pisswig ~ a mildly contemptible name for a small child.

pitch ~ 1. to land, touch down, make contact with from above. "I watched the plane pitch on the runway." 2. a dark-coloured solid obtained from the distillation of tar. 3. of a swelling, to reduce in size and height. "That bunch on your arm is starting to pitch down."

pitcher ~ a rib in the fore and after sections of a boat's frame.

pitchypaw ~ a type of butterfly.

pitnagen ~ the purple-stemmed aster plant *[Aster puniceus]*. The roots of this plant have been chewed and placed on an aching tooth to ease the pain and an extract from the root has been used in the treatment of colds, tuberculosis, typhoid, pneumonia and fevers.

pitty-hole ~ the grave.

plabbery ~ overly decorated. "She looked so plabbery at the Christmas concert that I didn't want to let on she was my cousin."

plait ~ a length of hair that has been braided.

planch ~ to put down flooring.

planchin' ~ the floor of a boat.

plank boat ~ See **carvel built**.

plantation ~ the land and buildings, used by a planter to prosecute the fishery.

planter ~ early settler who built fishing stores, stages, etc., to prosecute the fishery, as opposed to the migratory fishermen from West Country England.

plastered ~ drunk. "When me and the missus got married we were just like a brand new house – she was painted up and I was plastered."

platform ~ See **bridge**.

plaumaush ~ soft talk, flattery.

plim ~ to expand with the absorption of water, especially wood. "My punt was so dried out that when I launched her she filled with water, now I have to wait for her to plim up. Possibly from the word "plumb."

plover curlew also **sand plover** ~ the black-bellied plover [Squatarola squatarola]. Adults are 25-33 cm (10-13 in) in length. This bird is shy and usually the first to take flight when a flock of shorebirds is approached. Its chief foods are small crabs and sandworms.

plug ~ 1. a wooden peg, used to drain water from a small boat. 2. to

strike. "If you don't watch it I'll plug you."

plug eye ~ See **sculpin**.

plumboy ~ the dewberry, a fruit of the dwarf raspberry plant [Rubus pubescens].

ply ~ to bend. "One of the hardest things about making snowshoes is trying to ply the wood into shape."

pod auger days also **pot auger days** ~ a long time ago. From the era when fireplaces were used for cooking. A pot auger was an adjustable pot hanger which could raise and lower the pot over the fire to control the cooking temperature.

pogey ~ employment insurance benefits.

poisoned ~ fed up. "I'm poisoned with this."

poison eel ~ the conger eel [Conger oceanicus].

poison snake ~ refers to two member of the eelpout family of fishes which are eel-like in appearance [Lycodes reticulatus and Lycodes vahlii].

poison turnip ~ the cow-parsnip or hogweed [Heracleum maximuum], this plant is part of the Apiaceae (or Umbelliferae) family which includes anise, carrot, celery, coriander, dill, fennel, parsley and parsnip, as well as the highly toxic hemlocks. The blossoms of this plant have been steeped in oil and rubbed on the body to keep off flies and mosquitoes.

poke fun ~ to joke about or make light about someone.

poker ~ a long metal implement used to stir the fire in wood and coal stoves.

pole birch ~ a tall, straight birch tree, suitable for building purposes.

poleman ~ one who uses a pole to propel a small boat.

poll {pronounced: *POLE*} ~ 1. the back of the neck. 2. the top and back of the head.

pollard ~ See **rampike**.

polly peach ~ See **polly pitchum**.

polly pitchum also **polly peach**, **polypudjum** ~ the sweet fern *[Polypodium vulgare]*. The fresh root of this plant has been boiled or made into a powder to treat such ailments as melancholia, rheumatic swelling of the joints, jaundice, dropsy and scurvy.

poltogue also **fall tucker** ~ a smack or kick.

polypudjum ~ See **polly pitchum**.

pompey ~ See **bibby**.

pond ~ a body of fresh water, including bigger ones that would be called lakes elsewhere.

pond diver ~ the broadbill, spoon-bill, shovelbill, and maiden duck *[Spatula clypeata]*, a river duck with a large bill, broadest toward the tip.

pond gull ~ the ring-billed gull *[Larus delawarensis]*. A medium sized gull, measuring 41-54 cm (16-21 in) in length, with a wingspan of 105-117 cm (41-46 in), this gull builds its nests and breeds mostly in fresh, inland waters, as well as around the coast. These birds are scavengers and are at home as much in a McDonald's or KFC parking lot as they are fol-lowing a fishing vessel in the act of cleaning fish.

pond poppy ~ the pond lilly, bull-head lily *[Nuphar variegatum]*, found in lakes, ponds and slow-moving streams all over Newfoundland and Labrador.

pondy ~ See **saddleback**.

poodler ~ the ocean pout *[Macrozoarces americanus]*. A bot-tom-dwelling, eel-like species of saltwater fish with a dorsal fin that starts just behind the head and extends almost to the tail, and rang-ing from Labrador to Delaware that attains lengths of up to 98 cm (39 in.) and weights of 5.3 kg (14.2 lb).

poojy ~ a seal. From Inuit lan-guage, "puijik."

pook also **hay-pook**, **save cock**, **cocket** ~ hay piled up in a teepee-like shape.

pooked off ~ sticking out, especially when referring to ears that stick out. "His ears are so pooked off that he looks like a Volkswagen going down the road with the doors open."

pooking rod ~ one of the two poles that are attached to a piece of netting as handles and create a device used by two people to carry hay.

pooky ~ puffed up, or sticking up in a certain place. "Your hair is all pooky."

poole gun ~ a muzzleloader, or musket. These originally came from Poole, England, from where most goods and provisions came.

pooler ~ a salmon that has been in a river for some time and not yet spawned,

poor ~ used when referring to someone deceased. "I remember going berry-picking with poor Aunt Bessy before she died."

poor jack also **poor john** ~ cured codfish.

poor john ~ See **poor jack**.

poor man's cows ~ goats.

porch ~ a room on the main level of a house, usually at the rear, through which people enter and leave, and used for storage of items, including a water barrel, firewood, overshoes and winter footwear.

porcupine racket ~ a type of Labrador snowshoe.

pork bun ~ a bun, made of bread dough and fried in pork fat.

pork rind ~ the hide of a pig attached to pork fat.

pork slut ~ a large chunk of salt pork skewered on a stick and lit. This was used to replace candles or lamps when none were available.

porringer ~ a tin porridge bowl.

port ~ 1. the left side of the ship when facing forward. The light on the port side of the ship is red. 2. a harbour with facilities for ships to load, unload or obtain supplies.

port hole ~ a small window, usually circular, in the side of a ship, used for lighting, ventilation and other purposes.

portmantle ~ a travel bag.

potato garden also **potato ground** ~ ground enclosed with a fence for keeping animals out, used to grow vegetables, especially potatoes.

potato ground ~ See **potato garden**.

potato prong ~ a four-tined prong used for cultivating soil and for digging potatoes.

pot auger days ~ See **pod auger days**.

pot belly stove ~ a cast iron stove that burned wood and coal, used for heating an area, especially a classroom.

pot belly stove

pot day ~ the day of the week on which a boiled dinner of vegetables and salt beef is prepared and served.

pothead also **blackfish** ~ the northern pilot whale *[Globicephala melaena]*. Up until 1972 potheads were hunted in Newfoundland and Labrador for their meat, which was mostly exported to fur farms. The most common method of taking potheads was to drive them ashore in groups. Almost always found in groups, potheads are very playful and vocal. Adult males measure up to 6.1 m (20 ft) in length and weigh up to 2,722 kg (6,000 lbs). Adult females measure up to 4.9 m (16 ft) in length and weigh up to 1,361 kg (3,000 lbs).

pothead

potlids ~ round snowshoes made by nailing two pieces of board to a frame of birch, which has been bent to shape.

pot liquor ~ the water that a boiled or Jigg's dinner is cooked in. This was sometimes drunk from a cup by people, and was sometimes kept as a base for soup.

pound ~ an enclosure, or bin, used for storage.

powder gun ~ a muzzle-loading gun.

powder horn ~ the horn of an animal, especially a cow, which was plugged at the large end and a small opening made at the tip. It was used to hold gunpowder.

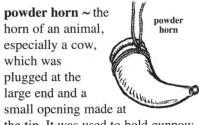

powder horn

prate {rhymes with *late*} ~ 1. talk, chatter. "Stop your prate, you're getting on my nerves." 2. mouth. Shut your prate!"

pratie {pronounced: *PRAY - tee*} ~ a potato. "I met her in the garden where the praties grow." Originated in Ireland.

press ~ to place drying codfish in a pile.

press gang ~ a party of Royal Navy seamen with the authority to compel men to serve on Royal Navy ships.

prickle back ~ See **thornback**.

prickles ~ the needles of spruce or balsam fir trees.

prickly ~ See **thornback**.

prig ~ to steal.

prime berth ~ the best fishing

ground close enough to shore for trap fishing.

primer {rhymes with *simmer*} ~ 1. kindergarten. 2. a book used to teach kindergarten children to read.

prime seal ~ a seal with good fur and having a large quantity of fat.

prior also **pryor** ~ a pole buoy attached to fishing gear in the water.

prise ~ 1. a lever. 2. to raise with a lever.

pritchet ~ a prop under the shaft of a cart or dray.

privateer ~ 1. a civilian ship's master given the authority to plunder ships of enemy nations in times of war. 2. a seaman who serves under such a master.

prog ~ 1. a store of food and supplies. 2. to provide food and supplies. 3. to poke.

prong ~ 1. a tool with several tines, used for digging potatoes and other purposes. 2. pierce or stab with same.

proper t'ing ~ the right thing to be doing.

prosecute ~ to engage in, to carry on the business of, especially the business of fishing or sealing.

protestant ~ salt herring.

protestant tea ~ strong tea.

protestant whisker ~ whiskers growing from the throat.

proud ~ pleased. "I was proud as punch with the gift you gave me for my birthday."

pryor ~ See **prior**.

public school ~ a non-denominational school.

public wharf ~ a wharf erected and maintained by the provincial government for use by all.

puck ~ 1. to strike or bounce off from. "I just pucked my knee off the coffee table." From Ireland.

puckawn ~ a goat. From Ireland.

pucklin ~ a boy.

puddick also **puddock, puttick** ~ the stomach, especially the stomach of a codfish.

pudding bag ~ See **duff bag**.

puddock ~ See **puddick**.

puds ~ the hands. "With the size of the puds on him he could cover up the scuppers on the *Titanic* with one of 'em."

puffin ~ the Atlantic common puffin *[Fratercula arctica]*. An auk (or alcid) with a brightly coloured beak in the breeding season. These are pelagic seabirds that feed mainly by diving. They breed in large colonies, nesting in burrows or crevices. Puffins are about 30 cm (12 in) in length, With its colourful orange and yellow beak, the puffin is often called the parrot of the sea. Its black cape has also earned it the name "parson bird."

puffin

puffin pig ~ See **puff pig**.

puff pig also **puffin pig** ~ 1. the harbour porpoise *[Phocaena phocaena]*. One of the smallest member of the cetacean or whale family, the harbour porpoise grows to an average length of 1.55 (5 ft) metres and and weighs an average of 55 kgs (121 lbs). It feeds on herring, capelin, pollack, hake and squid. The harbour porpoise is a deep diver, and can reach depths in excess of 200 metres (650 ft). 2. the northern pilot whale *[Globicephala melaena]*. See also **pothead**.

pull-up box ~ a wooden frame or box that holds the propeller in a motor dory.

pull-up dory ~ a type of motor dory which allows the back section of the propeller shaft to be raised and lowered easily. This allowed the dory to be rowed in shallow water or if the engine broke down.

pummy ~ something in a pulpy mass.

pump ~ 1. to urinate. 2. the act of urinating.

pump house ~ a men's urinal.

pump trolley ~ See **hand car**.

puncheon (pronounced: *PUNCH - in}* ~ the largest wooden barrel used in the Newfoundland and Labrador fish trade.

puncheon tub ~ one of two tubs obtained by cutting a puncheon barrel in half.

punishment ~ pain. "I'm in punishment with my bad back."

punt ~ a round-bottomed boat of between 20 and 25 feet in length that could be rowed, sailed or sculled. From the English "punt," meaning "a flat-bottomed boat." The same shape as a rodney, but bigger.

punt's piggin ~ See **piggin**.

puny ~ sick.

pup ~ See **water pup**.

purdle ~ to stumble and fall.

pure ~ 1. real,. actual, absolute. "That Mecca Ointment is the pure thing for healing cuts." 2. definitely. "My mouth was pure watering for a piece of blueberry pie."

purser ~ 1. on a passenger vessel, the person responsible for collecting the fares. 2. on any vessel, the person responsible for the vessel's disbursements, money transactions and stores.

purse squid ~ a small squid shaped like a pouch *[Rossia palpebrosa]*.

pussel {rhymes with *muscle*}~ 1. a scallop. 2. the giant or deep sea scallop *[Placopecten magellanicus]*. Found in deeper waters of the cintinenrtal shelf, this is the largest American scallop, usually measuring 13-16 cm (5-6 in), and sometimes up to 20 cm (8 in) in diameter.

puss in the hole ~ See **piddely**.

put ~ 1. the amount of fish brought in after one placement of a net, trap or trawl. "That last put was nine quintals." 2. to throw or pitch. "As soon as he came out of school I put the snowballs at him." 3. to assault another. "That bully put the boots to him as soon as he fell down."

put away ~ get rid of. "The seventh son of a seventh son can put away warts."

put down ~ to sow or plant. "I'm going to put down some coady red potatoes this year."

put in ~ to apply for. "I put in for a job at the fish plant."

put off ~ 1. to provide entertainment. "The Ladies' Home League

put off a concert last Saturday night." 2. to be made unhappy. "I was some put off when I didn't get to go to St. John's."

puts me in mind of ~ reminds me of. "That story you told me about the bear puts me in mind of the time a bear came into our cabin."

puttick ~ See **puddick**.

put to rights ~ to organize or prepare. "If we can't get the meeting put to rights there's no sense in calling one."

quabbering ~ See **copying pans**.

qualmish ~ See **quamish**.

quamish {pronounced: *KWAM - ish*} also **qualmish, squalmish, squamish** ~ queasy or nauseated. "My stomach feels right quamish this marnin'."

quarter ~ of a human, the upper thigh, hip and lower back. "I feels the rheumatism in me right quarter this marnin'."

quat {rhymes with *not*} ~ to crouch down. "You'd better quat down before someone sees you."

quay {pronounced: *KEY*} ~ a place where vessels tie up, a wharf.

queak ~ a squeek, only slighter.

queen bird ~ the white-crested cormorant, farallon cormorant, northern double-crested cormorant and

Florida cormorant *[Phalacrocorax auritus]*, this large dark bird with its long body and long neck has the appearance of a vulture. Measuring between 75 and 90 cm (29 and 36 in) from bill to tail, the queen bird has a wing span of up to 137 cm (54 in). Flying in V-shaped flocks, the cormorant alternately flaps and glides. While perched or swimming, it usually tilts its bill upward.

Queen's Birthday ~ May 24. See also **Victoria Day** on page 195.

queen's fettle ~ the garden monkshood plant *[Aconitum napellus]*.

queer hand ~ person with an odd personality.

quickie ~ See **bibby.**

quicknie ~ See **bibby**.

quid ~ a chew of tobacco.

quidlin ~ fussy, picky. "My aunt was very quidlin' because I didn't put the dishes away properly."

quiff hat ~ a type of man's hat similar to the type of hat Humphrey Bogart often wore in the movies.

quiff hat

quintal {pronounced: *CANT - ull*} ~ 112 pounds of uncured codfish. When cured the fish weighed approximately 100 pounds.

quintering ~ killing the occasional seal while the ship is moving

through loose ice.

quire ice ~ ice that was formed from dribbling or seeping water.

quism ~ an odd or witty remark.

quoit ~ a Newfoundland two-penny piece.

quoits ~ a game, similar to horseshoes, in which iron or rope rings are tossed at a vertical stick in an attempt to encircle it.

race ~ See **run**.

rack ~ 1. comb one's hair. 2. to be in company with. 3. wreck.

racket ~ 1. a type of employment. "I'm going at the lumberwoods racket this fall." 2. a fight, altercation or disturbance.

rackets also **skin rackets** ~ snowshoes made by using moose hide or the hide of some other animal.

rackets

rafter ~ to pile up in layers, especially ice pans.

rafting ~ piling up.

ragged ~ jagged, especially jagged cliffs.

ragged jacket ~ a young harp seal in the process of changing from a whitecoat to a beater, which is the stage before bedlamer.

rag moll ~ an untidily dressed person.

rail ~ a long pole.

rail's length of fence ~ the section of fence between fence posts. During winter people didn't have to worry about animals getting into their garden so often a rail's lengths of fence was removed to allow access to horses and slides.

rain spider ~ a certain species of spider, which, when killed, was thought to cause rain.

raise ~ to lead off a group in singing, especially to start a hymn.

ral ~ a rowdy person or rioter.

rally ~ a run after seals on the ice by a group of sealers.

ram cat ~ a tom cat.

rames ~ skinny. "Since he got sick he is nothing but the rames."

ramlatch ~ to talk using meaningless words.

rampike also **pollard**, **whiten** {pronounced: *WHITE - en*} ~ a dead tree that is dried out but still standing.

rand ~ a strip or piece of animal meat or fat.

randy ~ 1. to play boisterously, to have fun. 2. to slide down a snow-covered hill on a sled. "The youngsters are kicking up some racket out randying on the hill tonight." 3. a short journey. 4. a boisterous party. 5. sexually aroused. 6. sexual intercourse.

range

range ~ a stove with enamel sides, fuelled by wood, coal and sometimes oil, and used for cooking and heating.

ranger ~ 1. a seal in its third year. 2. a member of the Newfoundland Ranger Force, which served as police officers and performed other duties in Newfoundland and Labrador from 1935 to 1950.

rangette ~ an electric kitchen stove that ran on 117 volts and plugged directly into an outlet. These were usually white enamel, with four burners and an upper and lower burner in the oven.

rank around with ~ to be in the company of.

rat's tail ~ the mountain club moss, fir clubmoss or little club moss *[Lycopodium selago]*. For centuries traditional healers in China have claimed that drinking tea brewed from this plant would improve memory and failing mental capacity.

rattle ~ the rushing and noisy part of a river.

rattle

ravel {rhymes with *gravel*} ~ 1. a loose thread. 2. a piece of thread or lint clinging to one's clothing.

rawny ~ 1. thin. "He's as rawny as a weasel." 2. of cloth, threadbare, flimsy.

razorback {pronounced: *RAZZ - zer - BACK*} ~ a domestic pig. From the word "razorback," meaning a wild or semi-wild pig of the southeastern U.S., having a narrow body, long legs and a ridged back.

reach ~ a straight section of a navigable waterway.

reach of the year ~ the high point of the year.

read cups ~ to tell fortunes from the silhouette images left by tea leaves around the sides and bottom of one's teacup.

reap hook ~ an implement with a long, curved blade and a wooden handle, used with one hand to mow hay, a sickle.

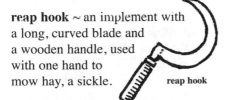

reap hook

rear ~ to shout. "You don't have to rear at me, I can hear you."

red belly ~ a term used by Roman Catholics to refer to Protestants.

red cod ~ a reddish-coloured variation of the common cod.

redd ~ a salmon nest.

reddening box ~ a box in which ochre and water is mixed to make dye.

red indian ~ a Beothuk Indian.

red jack ~ a knee-length leather boot, worn by fishermen.

red raw ~ a curse word.

reel ~ a wooden device around which jigger-lines and hand-lines are wound for storing purposes.

ree raw ~ untidy, in a state of disorder. "This house is in a ree raw."

reeve ~ to wander about.

reeves ~ snow or rain falling heavily in great swirls and drifts.

reeving rope ~ a draw-string for a clothes-bag or other similar item.

refuse fish ~ cured fish of a quality too inferior to be marketable. This was sometimes eaten by the fisherman's family or fed to their sled dogs.

Regatta Day ~ See **Regatta Day** on page 197.

relieving officer ~ a government employee charged with administering relief to the poor.

republic flag ~ the old pink, white and green flag from 1843, recently revived and used as a symbolic gesture of discontent with the Canadian Government. See also **Flags and Emblems** on page 217.

rhyme ~ 1. to utter a string of successive curse words, swear words and oaths. "When he gets mad he can sure rhyme 'em off." 2. to recite poetry or rhymes.

ribband ~ a large, flexible timber, used in ship-building to secure a ship's frame while the planking is in progress.

ribbon ~ one of several boards placed length-wise on a catamaran sled, resting across the two cross-seats, thereby creating a platform for transporting certain items. The main use of the catamaran was to haul logs, but sometimes it was handy to haul a few sacks of flour or a barrel of water.

riddle also **riddling, riggle, riggling, roddle, wriggle, wriggling** ~ 1. a thin, flexible piece of wood that is sometimes inter-woven with others, or with rails to make a fence. 2. the act of making such a fence. 3. to shake or shiver.

riddling ~ See **riddle**.

rig also **rig out, rig up** ~ 1. to out-fit for a voyage or a venture. 2. clothing. "That's some rig you got on there."

rigged out ~ dressed in the best clothing. "I was rigged out for Grandfather's funeral."

riggle, riggling, roddle, wriggle, wriggling ~ See **riddle**.

riggling ~ See **riddle**.

right ~ very, excessively, absolutely. "That feller from Tilting was right cute." "Right on!"

rightify {pronounced: *RIGHT - a - FI*} ~ to correct or rectify.

rig out ~ See **rig**.

rig up ~ See **rig**.

rind ~ 1. the bark of a tree. 2. to remove bark from a tree. "If you rind a tree and then flatten the rind and dry it you can use it to cover the fish on the flake when it rains."

rinder ~ one who debarks trees.

rinding time ~ the time in spring, usually in May, when the tree sap is running and the bark can be removed most easily.

ring-billed diver ~ the ring-necked duck *[Aythya collaris]*. Because it doesn't gather in large flock this duck is not hunted as extensively as other ducks. This fast-flying duck prefers ponds and lakes in wooded areas where its favourite foods are the seeds of aquatic plants as well as snails and insects. Adults measure between 36 and 46 cm (14 and 18 in).

ringer also **ringing table** ~ a circular wooden table, used to form birch barrel-hoops.

ringing table ~ See **ringer**.

ring me up ~ call me on the telephone.

rip ~ to remove the intestines and gills from herring or mackerel before marketing them.

rip for run ~ in a state of disarray, untidy.

rise ~ 1. cod net mesh. 2. the sheer, or low-rising-arc look of a a vessel, as viewed from a distance. A ship was identified by her rise.

rise end ~ the slight curved portion of a codfish's back near the tail.

rise line ~ a line used to close the door of a cod trap before it is hauled to the surface.

rising ~ a strip of wood that was attached to the timbers around the upward sheer of a boat's hull. Its main purpose was to hold up the thwarts of the boat but it also served other purposes, such a place on which to tie things and a place to keep spare thole pins etc. (wedged between the rising and the planks).

rising pan ~ a round pan used to hold bread dough while it rises, usually overnight.

rittick ~ See **sterrin**.

roach ~ 1. rough and coarse in appearance. 2. hoarse. "You must be getting a cold because your voice is right roach."

roaration ~ a loud, persisting sound.

robber bird ~ See **jay**.

robustic ~ strong and hardy.

rock cod ~ a darker coloured codfish found on a rocky bottom.

rocker-tail lark ~ the spotted sandpiper [Actitis macularia]. Measuring 18-20 cm (7-8 in) and having a 37-40 cm (15-15 in) wingspan, the female is larger than the male and it is the female who establishes and defends the territory. The male takes the primary role in parental care, incubating the eggs and taking care of the young. One female may lay eggs for up to four different males at a time. She may store sperm for up to one month, and the eggs she lays for one male may be fathered by a different male in a previous mating. The rocker-tail constantly bobs its tail and rear end up and down as it walks.

rock flower ~ See **pink tops**.

rock partridge ~ See **mountain partridge**.

roddle ~ See **riddle**.

rode {rhymes with *toad*} ~ anchor or grapnel rope.

rode-laid ~ the size and number of strands in a piece of rope.

rodney ~ a small rowboat with a sleek, rounded hull and a small flat stern.

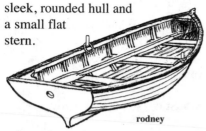

rodney

roke ~ 1. smoke steam or vapour. 2. perspiration.

roller ~ a roll of carded wool ready to go on the spinning wheel.

rompsin' also **rampsin', galin'** {pronounced: *GAIL - in*} ~ horse-play, wrestling, or boisterous behavior by children, including impermissible acts, like jumping on furniture. Parents in some communities would admonish children with the following rhyme:
"Timothy Thompson
Fell out of bed, rompsin'
And banged his head on the floor
Now Timothy Thompson
Don't go rompsin'
Anymore

rookery ~ 1. in a state of disorder or confusion. 2. in a state of untidiness, or mess.

room also **rooms** ~ the land and buildings that comprise a planter's fishing operation.

room berth ~ See **berth**.

roomer ~ a Newfoundland fisher-man who prosecutes the Labrador fishery from premises on shore.

rooms ~ See **room**.

root ~ 1. a strong drink. 2. the high one gets from a strong drink.

rory-eyed ~ drunk. "I was so rory eyed the other night than when the policeman brought me home, the missus took one look at me and told him he should have locked me up."

rot ~ of ice, to melt.

rot oil ~ the oil obtained from the decomposition of cod livers.

rotted ~ very angry.

rotten ice ~ ice that has melted to the point of being unsafe to walk upon.

roughery {pronounced: *RUFF - ah - REE*} ~ heavy swells on the ocean.

rough-handle ~ to handle one in a rough manner.

rough ice ~ Arctic ice pans, as opposed to the ice that is frozen in local harbours etc.

rough-spun ~ uncultured and having poor manners.

roughstone ~ a whetstone.

rough weather ~ stormy weather, usually accompanied by blowing snow.

round ~ unsplit, especially of fish before the entrails are removed.

rounder ~ See **leggy**.

rounders also **hit and run** ~ a game similar to baseball. See also **Rounders** on page 259.

rouse {rhymes with *louse*} ~ to rush into an undertaking.

rowt ~ a repulsive, difficult and exhausting task, or endeavour.

rub ~ a very narrow wood path.

rubber ~ 1. a strip of wood which goes completely around the upper portion of a vessel's hull to protect it from a wharf or other marine structure. 2. a pencil eraser. "You paid five cents fer a pencil with nar rubber. You'm some foolish." 3. a condom. 4. See also **scrubber**.

rubber boot crowd ~ a loose-knit group of St. John's residents who were or are into the arts and music scene. Members could always be counted upon to be at the forefront at any protest or demonstration. They are looked-upon by some as being the ones who get preference when government grants are being decided. In the earlier days many members wore knee-length rubber boots, which earned them their name.

rubber gun ~ See **pea-shooter**.

rubber lumps ~ See **lumps**.

rubbers ~ one of two types of footwear: knee-length rubber boots, known as long rubbers; and rubber overshoes, known as short rubbers.

rubbish ~ any fish not caught to be consumed or marketed, now called under-utilized species.

ruckle ~ 1. to rotate. 2. to push or pull a wheeled toy.

ruckler ~ a wheeled toy.

ruckshins ~ commotions or hullabaloos. "They had ruckshins the night of John's birthday party."

rug ~ rigged. "The tent was rug up when I got to the campground."

rummage ~ 1. to search. "You rummage through those trunks and you might find something to wear to the dance." 2. to forage for wild game. "I had to rummage through the woods for a while before I found a place to tail a rabbit snare."

rumper ~ a small turnip.

run ~ 1. a voyage between two ports. "It's only a short run from Norris Arm to Botwood." 2. a group of animals or fish in motion. "There is some run of seals out to the wester." 3. passage on a vessel or on a road vehicle. "Give us a run into St. John's in your new car."

running line ~ one of the draw strings on a cast net to pull the net's bottom shut.

running mark ~ one of the land-marks used in line with another behind it to guide a vessel straight through the safest part of a channel, such as a narrow entrance to a har-bour.

running tap ~ a stiff, leather sole placed on the bottom of a sealskin moccasin.

rusty-jacket ~ a seal in the stage of maturity between whitecoat and bedlamer.

rusty tom rooter also **bobby root-er, hedge sparrow** ~ the eastern fox sparrow *[Passerella iliaca]*. Measuring about 18 cm (7 in) these birds breed in brushy wooded areas, especially those with stunted trees and streamside thickets, where they forage for millipedes, spiders and insects on the ground. They also feed on tiny crustaceans in coastal areas.

sabine ~ See **saffron**.

sack ~ the scrotum of a male animal.

saddleback also **old saddler, pondy** ~ 1. the great black-backed gull *[Larus marinus]*. The saddleback gull is not only very fierce, it is the largest gull found near Newfoundland and Labrador waters. Although mostly inac-cessible, the saddle-back's nests can be seen

saddleback

on cliffs throughout the province. 2. a mature male harp seal *[Phoca groenlandica]*.

saddle-dog also **saddler** ~ a mature male harp seal *[Phoca groenlandica]*.

sadogue ~ 1. soggy, as in dough that didn't rise. 2. a soggy cake or loaf of bread. 3. a fat, easy going person.

saffron also **sabine** ~ 1. the liquid from sheep manure, used to cure measles and other ailments. 2. the creeping juniper *[Juniperus sabine]*, a dwarf juniper.

sagger ~ a boat full of fish.

St. George's Cross ~ the flag of England in 1497, the year of John Cabot's sailing. See also **Flags and Emblems** on page 217.

St. John's Water Dog ~ old name for the Labrador Retriever.

St. Peter's ~ a qualifier for differ-ent kinds of alcoholic beverages from St. Pierre; ie: St. Peter's rum, whiskey etc.

St. Peter's line ~ a type of strong twine.

sally ~ 1. a branch from a willow tree. 2. the willow tree itself. 3. to rock or tip a boat from side to side. 4. to weave from from side to side while running.

sally saucers also **sally sours, sally suckers** ~ the common sorrel *[Rumex acetosella]*. This weed was sometimes chewed by children for their sour taste.

sally sours ~ See **sally saucers**.

sally suckers ~ See **sally saucers**.

sallywood ~ the mountain holly tree *[Nemopanthus mucronatus]*.

salmon ~ the Atlantic salmon *[Salmo salar]*. The Atlantic salmon is an anadromous fish – one that spawns in fresh water but spends much of its life at sea, travelling extensively. The salmon begins its life as a pea-sized egg which is deposited in riverbeds in autumn. Early the next spring they emerge as alevin, which are about 2 cm long. These subsist off the attached yolk sac while hiding in the gravel

salmon

on the bottom. When the sac is almost gone they enter the "fry" stage and make their way up into the water, where they grow to a length of about 5 to 8 cm (2 to 3 in), at which time they become "parr." These are identifiable by the bars (between 9 and 11) along the side, which serve as camouflage in the river, where they remain for two to six years depending on temperatures and food supply. By this time they have reached a length of 12 to 24 cm (5 to 10 in) and they enter

the smolt stage. Their internal systems adapt for saltwater life and the parr camouflage is replaced by a silvery coat, its sea camouflage. At sea, on a diet of small crustaceans and fish, they grow rapidly into adults. After one or more years at sea, following a hereditary route and timetable, Atlantic salmon return to their home rivers between April and November on a journey that may span more than 4,000 km. of open ocean. They then fight their way upstream, sometimes injuring or killing themselves while leaping high falls to start the cycle all over again.

salmon catcher ~ See **salmonier**.

salmon flower ~ the birdeye primrose *[Primula laurentiana]*, a plant of the primrose family.

salmonier {pronounced: *SAM - in - EAR*} also **salmon catcher** ~ a commercial salmon fisherman.

salmon leap ~ the part in a river's waterfalls up which migrating salmon "leap."

salmon leap

salmon peel ~ a young salmon.

salmon plantation ~ an area ashore on which a salmon fishery is prosecuted.

salt and pepper cap ~ a peaked hat that is wedge-shaped, being slightly taller at the back and lowering at the peak. Speckled black and white in appearance, these were popular among Newfoundlanders in the early part of the 20th

salt and pepper cap

century, but dropped out of vogue with the young people of the late 1930s through 1950s. They made a comeback when singer and accordion player Harry Hibbs, of Bell Island, Newfoundland (who continually wore one) became internationally well known and a Newfoundland star in the 1960s.

salt box house ~ a wooden house of one-and-a-half or two stories, with a steep saddle roof. See also **Houses and Other Buildings** on page 231.

salt bulk ~ salted but uncured codfish for bulk sale.

salt burn ~ 1. to spoil fish by applying too much salt. 2. an adjective describing fish so spoiled.

salt cart ~ a two-wheeled wooden cart, enclosed at the front and sides, used to move salt about in an area where fish is being processed.

salt fish ~ codfish that has been cured by removing the water with salt and by drying in the sun.

salting scoop ~ a wooden tool used to apply salt to split codfish.

salt pen ~ a bin in which salt is stored.

salt shovel ~ a hand-made wooden shovel, scooped-out specifically to handle salt, which caused rust in metal implements.

salt water bird ~ any species of bird hunted on the ocean.

salt water duck ~ a wild duck hunted at sea.

salt water ice ~ the ice frozen from the salt water of inshore waters.

salt water pigeon ~ See **pigeon**.

salt water snake ~ See **tanzy**.

salt water soap ~ a type of soap using lye as an ingredient.

salt water trout ~ 1. a trout which spends some or all of its time in the ocean. 2. the Arctic char *[Salvelinus alpinus]*.

salt water worm ~ a sea-worm of the *Nereis* family.

salvationer ~ a member of the Salvation Army church.

sand dollar ~ a shelled mollusk having a five-petalled floral pattern on one side of its shell.

sand dollar

sand hill grass ~ a member of the sand-sedge family of grasses *[Carex arenaria]*.

sand peep ~ the least sandpiper *[Erolia minutilla]*. This relatively tame, small, shore bird measures 12 cm (4.75 in) and has a thin, slightly downward-curving bill. It is one of several sandpipers known as "peeps." It likes inland mudflats and wet grassy areas where it feeds heavily on insects. It also feeds along the coast on crustaceans, mollusks and marine worms.

sand plover ~ See **plover curlew**.

sapper ~ a boat-load of codfish. "Uncle Ben pulled his skiff up the front of the stage head last evenin' with a sapper."

sapping ~ very wet. "It rained so hard my clothes are sapping."

sauce box ~ an insolent person.

savage ~ angry. "When I mooched from school Mom was savage at me."

save cock ~ See **pook**.

saving trip also **saving voyage** ~ a fishing or sealing venture that turns a modest profit.

saving voyage ~ See **saving trip**.

saviour's letter also **letter of Jesus Christ** ~ written words, purported to be by Jesus Christ, kept and used as a charm.

sawboo ~ an old boot cut off at the ankle.

saw horse ~ See **wood horse**.

sawn ~ sent. "I sawn you a letter last week."

scad ~ a small amount, especially a small amount of rain or snow. "The weather has been so good we haven't had a scad in weeks."

scalded {pronounced: *SCAWLED*} ~ made, overcome, licked, beat. "You won the lottery; sure, you got it scalded."

scaley ~ mean and stingy.

scalp ~ See **sculp**.

scantlin ~ a piece of plank.

scarffed ~ haphazardly joined together. From the English word, "scarph," meaning "a joint used when uniting ends of two strakes or planks."

scarlet ~ the creeping Charlie or creeping Jenny plant *[Glechoma hederacea]*. The early Saxons used this plant to clarify their beers, before hops had been introduced. It has also been used for medicinal purposes to remove phlegm from the sinuses and chest, and in the treatment of bronchitis and coughs.

scattered ~ 1. not many. "I went out fishing yesterday but I only caught a scattered one."

scattered time ~ not often. "The youngsters comes back from the

Mainland to visit us a scattered time."

scent bottle ~ the leafy white orchid plant *[Platanthera dilatata].*

schooner-rigged ~ the only clothes in one's possession which one is now wearing.

scoff ~ a big meal, especially an impromptu or unexpected one.

scolping ~ See **sculpin**.

scoop ~ a boat-bailing container.

scoopy ~ referring to an object that has sharp angles and sides that arc inward.

scooter ~ a type of clay pipe.

scopin ~ See **sculpin**.

scopy ~ See **sculpin**.

scotch apple ~ the juneberry plant, a plant of the *Amelanchier* family.

scotch cure ~ a method of curing herring developed in Scotland, in which herring was gutted and immediately salted and packed in casks.

scotch dumpling ~ a type of Scottish haggis, made with cod livers.

scotch poke ~ when dealing cards, to poke out a number of cards in the centre of the deck to change one's luck.

scote ~ See **skote**.

scow-ways {rhymes with *cow - ways*} ~ slanted, crooked, askew. "My son, the wind got your hat gone skow-ways."

scrabble also **scravel** ~ hurry or move fast. "If you keep working at it you won't have to scravel to finish on time." Possibly originated from the word "scramble."

scrad ~ See **scrod**.

scraggley ~ 1. a small, mis-shapen tree. "We tried to find a Christmas tree but all we could find were scraggleys." 2. an untidy person. "If you don't stop looking so scraggley someone is likely to take a whisk to you."

scram also **scrammed**, **scram handed** {pronounced: *SCRAM - hand - did*} ~ a condition of the hands that has rendered them ineffective or uncoordinated. "I'm so scram-handed from the cold that I can't hold on to my fishing pole."

scram handed ~ See **scram**.

scrammed ~ See **scram**.

scrape ~ 1. a bare, rocky section on the side of a hill.

scraper ~ 1. a device made of stiff wire to propel a barrel hoop forward by children at play. 2. a stick used to propel the wheel or rim of a bicycle forward by children at play.

3. a person who makes too long a stroke when flicking a marble toward a mott. See also **Alleys** on page 203.

scraping his wing ~ looking for a wife.

scratch ~ chicken feed.

scratch box ~ a box in which hen's feed is kept.

scraub also **scrob** ~ 1. to scratch or claw. "If you don't stop throwing rocks at me I'm going to scraub the face off you." 2. a scratch on one's body. Possibly from the word "scrub.'

scravel ~ See **scrabble**.

scrawn ~ 1. to grope, grab or snatch. "If you don't give me a piece of your apple I'll scrawn it from you." 2. food. "Without a bit of scrawn we won't survive the winter."

scrawn bag ~ a lunch bag.

scrawn box ~ a lunch box.

scrawny ~ skinny. "He is so scrawny that if the door opens and no one comes in, it's him."

Screech ~ the brand name for a Jamaican rum bottled in St. John's, Newfoundland.

screecher ~ a storm in which the wind is quite audible.

screed ~ a piece of cloth, especially one used to make clothing.

screedless ~ 1. without possessions. 2. without any clothing. "Poor Shirley, when her husband died she was left screedless."

screwing room ~ See **screw store**.

screw press ~ a large rotating screw-like device, turned by a number of men to force a quantity of salt fish into a shipping container such as a wooden box or barrel.

screw store also **screwing room** ~ the part of a merchant's fishing premises in which salt fish is pressed into boxes or barrels for shipping.

scribbler ~ a covered notebook made with lined, newsprint-quality paper.

scrimshank ~ 1. to hesitate. 2. to avoid an issue.

scrimshaw ~ the art of carving, etching or decorating pieces of animal antlers, horns and bones, or sea shells.

script ~ a doctor's prescription, especially one that entitles the bearer to alcohol for medicinal purposes.

scrob ~ See **scraub**.

scrod also **scrad** ~ 1. a small cod-fish, usually kept for home consumption. 2. a child who is small for his or her age.

scroop ~ to squeak, scrape or make a grating sound. "When I wrote on the blackboard the chalk made a scroopy sound."

scroopy boots ~ boots, so new they squeak when the owner walks.

scrouge ~ to push one against another in a crowd.

scrub ~ an ad hoc baseball game. See also **Scrub** on page 260.

scrubbing board ~ See **washboard**.

scrubber also **rubber** ~ a strip of wood which goes completely around the upper portion of a vessel's hull to protect it from a wharf or other marine structure, a fender.

scruff ~ 1. back of the neck. 2. an inferior grade of codfish with no commercial value.

scrumpshy ~ See **scumpshy**.

scrumpsion ~ See **scumpshy**.

scrump up ~ to overbake.

scrunch ~ 1. to crunch or make a grating sound while chewing. "Stop scrunching on that apple, you're getting on my nerves." 2. to burn to a useless state. "The steak I was frying is burnt to a scrunch."

scrunchins ~ small, fried, pork-fat cubes, often used as a garnish, especially on fish and brewis.

scrunchins

scuddy also **scutty** ~ of the weather, misty and damp, accompanied by gusts of wind.

scuff ~ dance. "Would you like to get out on the floor for a scuff?"

scuff and scoff ~ a dance that includes a meal.

scull ~ 1. to propel a small boat by alternating the pitch, or angle, of an oar's blade as one alternates a back and forth motion of the oar. 2. the action of schools of capelin coming ashore to spawn. 3. a school of fish, especially capelin.

sculling ~ propelling a small boat with a single oar through a hole in the stern. The oar is inserted through the sculling hole and is turned at an angle so that when a sideways motion of the oar is made it propels the boat forward. The oar is then turned at the opposite angle so

sculling

that the return stroke also propels the boat forward. This action is similar to the way a propeller works.

sculling hole ~ the hole in the stern of a small boat through which a sculling oar is utilized to scull a small boat forward. The diameter of this hole was smaller than the width of the blade on the oar, so the oar had to be brought in from the outside. Sometimes a notch was cut in the hole to allow the oar to be inserted from inside the boat.

sculling oar ~ a single oar used to propel a small boat from the stern.

scully ~ See **sculpin**.

sculp also **scalp** ~ 1. the skin of a seal with the blubber attached. 2. to remove the skin and blubber of a seal.

sculpin also **horny whore, pig fish, plug eye, scolping, scopin, scopy, scully, scummy, scumpy, scushie** ~ refers to several species of big-mouthed scavenger fish of the family *Cottidae,* including the shorthorn sculpin *[Myoxocephalus scorpius]* and the longhorn sculpin *[Myoxocephalus octodecimspinosus terranovae]* found in inshore waters, especially around fishing stages where much fish offal was discarded.

sculpin

sculping knife ~ a heavy knife with a broad, thin, rounded blade, about six inches long, used to remove the pelt and blubber from a seal.

scummy ~ See **sculpin**.

scumpshy {pronounced: *SKUMP - she*} also **scrumpshy, scumpsion, scrumpsion** ~ a clumsy, awkward or incompetent person.

scumpsion ~ See **scumpshy**.

scumpy ~ See **sculpin**.

scun ~ 1. to direct a vessel through ice floes. 2. to keep a look-out for fish or seals. 3. to perform some action quickly. "Scun up to the shop before it closes." 3. to make a temporary repair job. "Let me scun up that hole in your sweater." 4. to stitch the edges of netting together with twine.

scuppers ~ holes in a vessel's bulwarks to allow water to run off the deck.

scurryfunging {pronounced: *SKUR - ee - FUN - jing*} ~ scrubbing vigorously.

scursion bread ~ See **excursion bread**.

scushie ~ See **sculpin**.

scut ~ 1. a dirty, mean person. 2. to remove build-up or dirt from the hull of a vessel.

scuts ~ See **scutters**.

scutter ~ 1. the rear flipper of a seal. 2. to move away quickly. 3. to sail before the wind.

scutters also **scuts** ~ diarrhea.

scuttle ~ 1. thrash or beat severely. "If you hits your sister one more time I'm going to scuttle you." 2. to sink.

scutty ~ 1. angry, contrary, ill-tempered. 2. miserly.

sea anchor also **drogue** ~ a device usually made of a large piece of canvas attached to an iron hoop that holds a vessel's bow to the wind in stormy weather.

sea cherry ~ a variety of sea-cucumber.

sea dab ~ a variety of jelly fish.

Seadog ~ 1. a brand of matches popular in the province. Advertised as safety matches, these matches would only ignite if struck against the special edge of the box in which they came. 2. an old sailor.

sea duck also **shore duck** ~ the common eider duck *[Somateria mollissima borealis]*. Weighing between 850 g and 3.025 kg (1 lb 14 oz and 6 lb 10 oz) this is the largest duck in the northern hemisphere. And with a life span of 20 years, this the longest lived of all sea ducks. Young birds are often cared for by "aunts" or non-breeding females in the flock, which may be as many as 10,000.

They feed during the day by diving to the bottom in waters from 3 to 20 m (10 to 65 ft) deep to take mussels, clams, scallops, sea urchins, starfish and crabs. These are swallowed whole and crushed in the large gizzard.

sea hen ~ a name referring to three members of the jaeger family of birds: the long-tailed jaeger *[Stercorarius longicaudus]*, the parasitic jaeger *[Stercorarius parasiticus]* and the pomarine jaeger *[Stercorarius pomarinus]*. All three are hawk-like in appearance and chase gulls, terns and other seabirds to steal their food. Although prevalent around the shores of Newfoundland and Labrador in summer, these birds winter in the southern hemisphere, especially in Australia.

seal ~ any seal found in the waters off Newfoundland and Labrador, especially the harp seal *[Phoca groenlandica]* and the hooded seal *[Cystophora cristata]*.

seal cat ~ a newly born seal.

seal catcher ~ a person who uses seal nets to trap seals inshore.

seal finger also **seal hand** ~ an infection of the finger or hand, causing inflammation and swelling, from handling seal carcasses.

seal fishery ~ the business of being involved in the hunting and taking of seals, whether in the inshore or offshore hunt.

seal head ~ a type of plant with a mint flavour *[Prunella vulgaris]*. A salve made from this plant is used to treat herpes simplex one (the common cold sore) and herpes simplex two (genital herpes).

seal hole ~ See **blow hole**.

seal hunt ~ the hunting and taking of seals from vessels on the ice floes offshore.

seal hunting ~ the pursuit of seals.

sealing also **swiling** ~ the hunting and taking of seals.

sealing capstan ~ a winch used to haul seal nets ashore.

sealing captain ~ the master of a sealing vessel.

sealing plane ~ an aircraft used to spot seals on the ice floes.

sealing vessel ~ a vessel adapted or used to prosecute the seal fishery.

seal killer ~ a sealing captain who is continually successful.

seal net ~ a net with the proper size of mesh (sometimes attached to other nets of the same mesh) used to trap seals.

seal oil ~ the oil obtained from rendering seal fat, which was exported and used locally to fuel lamps, make soap and for medicinal purposes.

seal pan ~ an ice pan containing a quantity of seal pelts.

seal pass ~ the route often used by seals migrating near the shore.

seal shot ~ a lead shot of a size large enough to kill seals.

sealskin ~ the pelt of a seal with the blubber removed, used for export as well as for making clothing, footwear and snowshoes.

sealskin boot ~ See **Eskimo boot**.

sealskin mog ~ See **Eskimo boot**.

seam boat ~ See **carvel built**.

sea parrot ~ the Atlantic puffin. See also **puffin**.

sea pea ~ the beach pea, a variety of wild pea *[Lathyrus japonicus]*. Found on the coast as well as on the shores of inland waterways, this plant has alternate leaves that are divided into several segments and has clusters of purple to blue pea-like blossoms.

sea pheasant ~ the pintail duck *[Anas acuta]*. Found in wet meadows, mud flats and the edges of reedy, grassy waters, this duck feeds largely upon bulbous roots, tender shoots, insects and their larvae, worms and snails, as well as various seeds, water plants and grain.

sea pigeon ~ See **pigeon**.

sea stock ~ rum carried on a vessel for medicinal purposes.

second joint ~ the thigh portion of the leg of a turkey, chicken or other bird.

seed ~ See **zeed**.

seeny-sawny ~ a mentally retarded person.

seine {pronounced: *SANE*} ~ a fish net usually dragged behind a vessel to catch fish.

send in ~ to complain to the government by mail. "The road across the neck is almost washed out. "I'm going to send in about that."

sennet hat ~ a fisherman's hat made of birch bark.

septembers ~ slip-on, rubber workshoes that were made by cutting the tops off the knee-high rubber boots worn by fishermen. After a season of fishing the rubber uppers were often worn to the point that only the bottoms could be salvaged. Sometimes these were worn inside the house as slippers. For many fishermen, the fishing season ended in September, which is likely where the name originated.

servant ~ a person indentured to a planter for a period of time to perform various tasks.

servant girl also **serving girl** ~ a young woman who hires herself out to provide domestic service to a

family who can afford to pay her for her services.

serving girl ~ See **servant girl**.

set ~ 1. the placing of a trawl or net in the water to catch fish. 2. to place a trawl or net in the water. 3. to become solidified from a liquefied state. "I put me jelly in the cellar a few hours ago, so it should soon be set."

setee ~ See **settle**.

settle also **setee**, **day bed** ~ a couch kept in the parlour or kitchen on which people sat or lay down. They came in a number of styles, some without backs or arms.

settle

settling time ~ the time of year when a fisherman settled his account with the fish merchant.

seven ~ a blessed and holy number, the Lord's number.

seven-eight ~ a muzzle-loading gun with a 7/8 inch bore.

sevenses ~ a children's game in which a ball is thrown against a wall. See also **Ball-Bouncing Games** on page 204.

sewell {pronounced: *SUE - ull*} ~ to erect a caribou fence which herds caribou in a direction where they may be shot.

shack yourself ~ to live alone and tend to all the chores of everyday living. "Since your wife went in the hospital you've had to shack yourself."

shag ~ a member of the cormorant family of birds, especially the common or great cormorant *[Phalacrocorax carbo]*. This dark member of the pelican family has all four of its toes webbed, which helps it swim after fish underwater. It will sometimes take salmon and trout, but its chief food is flatfish and eels. It also eats mollusks and crustaceans. Adults measure 80-100 cm (31-39 in) in length, have a wingspan of 130-160 cm (51-63 in) and weigh 1.7-3 kg (3.75-6.6 lb).

shag

shallop ~ a small, light fishing vessel.

shalloway ~ 1. a smaller boat used to transport fish. 2. a dragonfly.

shanks mare ~ on foot.

shanty ~ 1. a shack. 2. a chanty or song sung by sailors to co-ordinate their efforts when hauling ropes or other such endeavors aboard ship. See also **Hauling Houses** on page 227.

shard ~ a blunted portion on the edge of an axe or other cutting tool. "Don't try to chop tree roots with your good axe or you'll get shards in it."

share ~ the portion of the profit allotted to an individual involved in a fishing or sealing venture.

shareman ~ a man who shares in the profits of a fishing venture.

sharoosed ~ disgusted.

shaugraun ~ 1. a drinking spree. "He's been on a shaugraun for so long he's afraid to come home to the wife." 2. a vagabond frame of mind. "He has such a shaugraun that he'll never get married."

shaves ~ See **sheaves**.

shavings ~ wood chips that are the leftovers from wood that has been planed.

shears ~ a lifting device consisting of two or more poles joined at the top.

sheath {rhymes with *teeth*} ~ a case to hold a hunting knife or other knife.

sheathe {rhymes with *breathe*} ~ 1. to cover with a tarpaulin or other such covering. 2. to reinforce the hull of a sealing vessel with hard wood or metal.

sheath knife ~ a heavy knife with a broad, thin blade.

sheating paper ~ a heavy paper pasted to the walls of a room and painted.

sheave {rhymes with *sleeve*} also **backpaddle**, **backwater** ~ to row backwards with an oar. "Sheave with your left oar and row with your right and the boat will turn around."

sheaves also **shaves** ~ the shafts of a horse-drawn cart, wagon or sled.

sheebeen ~ an unlicensed premises where liquor is sold.

sheebeener ~ a boot-legger.

sheer ~ use a rope to swing a boat into a desired position.

sheeter ~ a young seal on the ice.

Sheila ~ in Irish folk legend, the wife, sister, housekeeper or acquaintance of St. Patrick.

Sheila's Brush ~ a fierce storm after St. Patrick's Day. See also **Sheila's Brush** on page 194.

shell bird ~ the red-breasted merganser duck *[Mergus serrator]*. The tuft of feathers that projects from the back of the shell bird gives it the appearance of hair that needs combing. These birds, which frequent isolated coves are easily startled and fly away at the least provocation.

shift ~ move or relocate. "Our family shifted to Arnold's Cove during the resettlement program." 2. to change clothing. 3. a change of clothing.

shim ~ a thin piece of some kind of material used to fill an empty space.

shimm ~ a spoon-shaped tree-bark removing-tool.

shimmick ~ a highly despised person.

ship ~ the act of delivering fish (or other sea product) to a merchant, fish plant or fish collector for payment or credit to one's account. "I got $400 dollars when I shipped my lobsters this morning."

ship's room ~ the land from which settlers prosecuted the fishery.

shive ~ to remove the limbs of an evergreen tree.

shoal ~ 1. an area of shallow water. 2. a large number of codfish or seals migrating together.

shoby ~ See **choby**.

shocking ~ extremely. "It's shocking cold."

shoe ~ a long, narrow, flat strip of metal attached to a sled-runner to protect the runners from wearing and to reduce friction. 2. the same type of device used on the keel of a vessel.

shooneen ~ a coward.

shoot ~ 1. a narrow, inclined street. 2. a narrow drop in a river.

shoot a net ~ to place a gill net in the water in a position to catch fish.

shoot a trawl ~ to place a trawl in the water in a position to catch fish.

shore ~ a vertical pole used as a foundation for a house or other building. It required a number of shores to support one building. "I have to replace several shores under the house because the floor is starting to sag."

shore duck ~ See **sea duck**.

shore fast ~ a rope or cable fastened to rocks or shore to anchor one end of a herring or salmon net.

shoreman ~ a member of a fishing crew who works at processing the fish on shore.

shore work ~ all the work involved in curing codfish.

short rubbers ~ rubber overshoes worn in rain or snow.

shot bag ~ a leather bag, especially made to hold shot.

shoulder spell ~ the distance a person can carry a load on his shoulder without resting.

shove ~ a sharp tool for making the grove in the barrel staves which holds the barrel's head.

shrew ~ the masked shrew *[Sorex cinereus]*. A very tiny mouselike insectivore with a sharply pointed muzzle, tiny eyes and a long tail. This animal was introduced to the island of Newfoundland in 1958 to combat the larch sawfly, a forest pest.

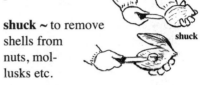

shuck ~ to remove shells from nuts, mollusks etc.

shucks ~ larger mittens worn outside regular mittens or gloves.

shuff ~ to shove. "Why don't you shuff your wallet in your arse pocket before you loses it.?"

shule {pronounced: *SHOOL*} ~ to move away backwards.

sidelights ~ facial hair left to grow some distance below the earlobes, sideburns.

side sleigh ~ a walled-in sleigh drawn by a horse with an opening on one side for passengers and driver to enter. A seat runs the length of the sleigh against the side opposite the opening.

sidle ~ to move sideways rather than in the intended forward direction, especially a sled.

silk jay ~ See **jay killer**.

silver thaw ~ See **glitter**.

simon saw ~ a long cross-cut saw for use by two people.

sin ~ shame. "It's a sin the way that poor baby was treated."

single-handed ~ with only one person involved.

singlet ~ undershirt with no arms or shoulders and a deep neck and open back.

sing out ~ yell loudly.

sish ~ fine ice floating on a water surface.

sithers ~ scissors.

sive ~ See **sythe**.

skeg also **skig** ~ 1. the portion of a boat's keel that extends out past the boat's bottom and on which the rudder pivots. "When we haul up our skiff we have to be careful not to break off the skig." 2. the tail bone.

skein ~ 1. a long line of seals on the ice. 2. a flock of birds.

skerries ~ underwater shoals that break in rough seas.

skerry ~ to haul a load on a sled.

sketch ~ hint. "I don't know everything that's going on but I heard a little sketch of it.".

skidders ~ scissors.

skiff {pronounced as written or as *SKEEF*} ~ a large motorboat, often with a forecastle where fishermen could cook and sometimes sleep.

skiff-load ~ the amount of fish carried by a particular sized skiff.

skiff oars ~ a set of oars large enough to row a skiff.

skig ~ see **skeg**.

skimmer ~ a man who ogles women.

skin boot ~ a knee-length boot made of sealskin.

skinnywopper ~ a knee-length sealskin boot.

skin rackets ~ See **rackets**.

skint ~ great, wonderful, excellent. nice, fine, good. Sentences: "We had a skint time the other night ol' man!" or "That's a skint outfit you're wearing my maid."

skipper ~ 1. the master or captain of a vessel. 2. the boss in a logging operation. 3. a term of respect for an older person or a person of higher status. 4. to act as master of a vessel.

skip stones ~ to throw stones at the ocean in such a manner that they bounce a number of times.

skirr ~ to hurry around in search of something.

skirting board ~ a baseboard in a house.

skitter ~ a sudden movement across the water.

skivver ~ 1. a skewer or wooden net-knitting needle, or a stringer for holding trout. 2. the act of skewering. "The bullbirds were so thick I skivvered twenty of them by the eyeballs on a hand gaff."

skoat also **scoat** ~ 1. to push or pull hard, to strain. 2. the act of skoating. "The boys had some skoat getting the skiff hauled up."

skoat shore ~ a pole or log propped against another pole or log at an angle to keep the second one vertical.

skrob ~ See **scraub**.

skully ~ a sun hat worn by women for working outdoors.

skunk duck ~ the Labrador duck *[Camptorhynchus labradorius]*, now extinct.

skutty ~ stingy. "She's so scutty she'd rather frostburn her feet than light the fire."

slab ~ See bunker.

slack ~ 1. scarce. "The fish are pretty slack today." 2. foolish.

slack-fisted ~ lazy.

slack-twisted ~ careless, especially about the way one wears one's clothes.

slamdown ~ an untidy person.

slane ~ a type of shovel used to remove sods.

slatterly ~ slovenly.

slatter to sling ~ slovenly.

sleeveen {pronounced: *slee - VEE*N} ~ a sly and despicable person. From the Irish word "sleamhain," meaning "sly."

slew ~ turn or pivot.

slewed ~ turned, twisted, crooked or bent. "You got your cap slewed around backwards."

slice ~ a wooden stir stick.

slide ~ a sled.

slide load ~ a quantity of wood carried on a sled.

slide path ~ a path made in the snow by the continuous use of sleds.

slinge ~ 1. to avoid work. "If you're going to make something of your life you can't slinge around all day." 2. one who avoids work. "He's such a slinge that he'd rather have someone bury him than to have to plant potatoes himself."

slink ~ a buttermilk cake, similar to buns but baked all as one large bun. 2. a salmon in spent or poor condition after spawning upriver.

slinky ~ very thin.

slip ~ a piece of paper, bill, note of entitlement or doctor's prescription. "I can't get me drugs without a slip."

slob hauler ~ a long pole with a board attached to one end and used to drag boats through slob (freshly frozen ice).

slob ice ~ 1. slushy, densly-packed ice fragments 2. newly frozen ice.

slommocky ~ having an untidy appearance.

slop pail ~ a bucket, usually made of enamel, with a cover and used indoors as a toilet. This was usually kept in an upstairs hallway for use by everyone. In most homes the slop pail was only used in the winter, when getting dressed to go through the snow in sub-zero weather to get partially undressed again in an outdoor toilet was not a pleasant prospect. Considering that the parts of the body that seemed to feel the cold most were exposed to a cold seat over a drafty hole was motivation to own a slop pail. Yet there were some homes that didn't have one.

slovenly also **slubny** ~ messy and unkempt. "Harry might have bought a new hat but he's still slovenly looking."

slub ~ the slimy substance on codfish.

slubbin ~ a wagon with four or more wheels.

slub bucket ~ a large wooden barrel in which cod livers were kept to make cod liver oil.

slubby ~ slimy and slippery.

slubny ~ See **slovenly**.

slut ~ See **bibby**.

sly conner ~ See **conner**.

smack ~ a small one-masted wooden sailing vessel, used chiefly in the coastal trade.

smallagen {pronounced: *SMALL - ah - JEN*} ~ a male adult seal.

smarnin' ~ this morning.

smatchy ~ stale. "I think you should throw out that bologna, it's a bit smatchy."

smeller ~ one of the whiskers on a cat or seal. 2. one of two tentacle-like feelers on a lobster.

smelt also **minister, whitefish** ~ the American smelt or rainbow smelt *[Osmerus mordax]*. Found as far north as Hamilton Inlet, Labrador, these smelts inhabit coastal waters as well as inland rivers, ponds and lakes. They are sometimes caught as they enter the mouths of rivers and through the ice in winter.

smert ~ sting or hurt. "My finger smerts where I cut it with the knife."

smidge ~ a stain.

smouch ~ to prowl idly.

smut ~ See **bibby**.

snake root also **yellow mores** ~ a bog plant of the *Coptis* family *[Coptis groenlandica]* used in home remedies. See also **Home Remedies and Cures** on page 228.

Snapapple Night ~ Hallowe'en Night. See also **Colcannon Night** on page 198.

snarbuckle ~ 1. a tangle in a line, rope or string. 2. a hard knot. 3. burnt to a cinder.

snarl ~ 1. to tangle up a line, rope or string. 2. a tangle in a line, rope or string.

snazzy ~ spiffy.

snig ~ 1. to cut off a small piece. "Snig off a piece of that fatback for me, will you?" 2. See **piddely**.

snoff ~ extinguish.

snop ~ to break into two pieces.

snotty southeaster ~ a southeast wind that brings with it rain and sleet, and snow in winter. This wind is sure to swing around from the northwest and blow twice as hard and twice as long.

snotty var also **snotty ver** ~ a balsam fir tree with many myrrh blisters.

snotty ver ~ See **snotty var**.

snow dwy ~ See **dwy**.

snowshoe rabbit ~ the snowshoe hare *[Lepus americanus]*, so named because of its large back paws which prevent it from sinking into the snow. They can reach a length of 61 cm (2 ft) including their 5 cm (2 in) tail, and they can weigh 1.4 to 1.8 kg (3 to 4 lbs). In summer it is reddish brown, except for its belly, which is white; while in winter it is completely white, except for the tips of its ears, which remain black. Completely vegetarian, it feeds on many plant species in summer, and bark and shoots in winter.

soaked ~ fined. "How much did he get soaked when he was caught with the poached moose?"

Soft Tuesday ~ Shrove Tuesday.

soiree ~ a social gathering or party.

Solomon Gosse also **Solomon Gosse's birthday** ~ a boiled dinner with pork and cabbage, usually on a Thursday.

Solomon Gosse's birthday ~ See **Solomon Gosse**.

some ~ 1. very many. 2. very much. "You've got some mess made on the kitchen floor."

son ~ a reference to any male person regardless of age or relationship.

sook ~ a cry-baby.

sookey ~ jealous and whiny.

sound ~ a large arm of the sea.

sound bone also **zounbone** ~ the backbone of a codfish.

souse ~ to drench with water.

soused ~ drunk.

southern shore ~ the stretch of coastline from Cape Spear to Cape Race.

sou'wester ~ a water-proof fisherman's hat made of oilskin or oilcloth and having a brim all the way around, with a longer brim at the back to keep the water off the fisherman's neck. See also **cape ann**.

sove ~ the past tense of save, saved. "We sove up enough money to get the foundation put down for our house."

spall ~ a nick or gouge.

spancel ~ 1. a device used to keep animals from getting through fences. A spancel is comprised of three sticks tied around the animal's neck in a triangular shape. "If you put a spancel on your sheep they won't get into your potato garden." 2. the act of applying the device.

spanney tickle ~ See **thornback**.

sparble ~ a shoemaker's nail, especially one which has worked its way inside the shoe to the point that it hurts the wearer's foot. Possible a corruption of "sparrow bill."

sparny tickle ~ See **thornback**.

spawn ~ 1. fish roe. 2. to eject same for procreation.

speed boat ~ a small, open boat, usually less than 6 metres (20 ft) in length, with a wide transom to accommodate an outboard motor.

speed boat

speeder ~ a motorized, small, open, four-wheeled vehicle, similar to a hand car, used by maintenance people on the railway line.

spell ~ 1. a rest from work. "You've got half the wood sawed up,m so why don't you take a spell?" 2. a while. "I was in Port Saunders for a spell last year." 3. a turn. "I've been digging this hole for a while. Would you take a spell at it?"

spile ~ a peg for a hole in a cask.

spillar ~ a mackerel net.

spit ~ fly eggs.

spit jack also **spit maggot** ~ the rove beetle *[Creophillus maxillosus]*.

spit maggot ~ See **spit jack**.

splayer ~ a tool used to draw barrel staves together.

Splinter Fleet ~ a fleet of nine wooden diesel-powered vessels built in Clarenville and launched in 1944 and 1945. These ships were 135 feet in length with a gross weight of 322 tons. They were managed by the Newfoundland Railway to serve as coastal boats, as well as in the foreign trade. Each was named after a Newfoundland community. Alphabetically they were the MVs *Bonne Bay*, *Burin*, *Clarenville*, *Codroy*, *Exploits*, *Ferryland*, *Glenwood*, *Placentia* and *Twillingate*.

splits ~ kindling wood for starting fire.

splitter ~ one who cuts around the backbone of a codfish.

splitter's mitt ~ a mitten worn on one hand of a person who splits fish.

splitting table ~ a wooden table with a notch cut in it,

splitting table

used for splitting codfish.

splitting tub ~ a wooden tub, kept beside a splitting table and used to hold split codfish.

sport ~ sexual activity. "Having a brew with the b'ys is alright, but a bit of sport under the covers is not too bad either."

spotted dick ~ partridgeberry pudding served with sauce.

sprayed ~ sore and tender from exposure to the weather.

spring weakness ~ malnutrition caused by insufficient winter food supplies.

sprong ~ a manure fork.

spruce beer ~ a beer made by fermenting spruce buds and boughs.

spruce budworm ~ the eastern spruce budworm *[Choristoneura fumiferana]*. Native to North America, this insect is considered the most destructive pest of fir and spruce forests, causing serious damage to the majority of Newfoundland's mature balsam fir stands for 30 years, beginning in the 1970s.

spruce partridge ~ the spruce grouse *[Canachites canadensis]*. Measuring 33 cm (13 in) this bird is similar in appearance to the domestic chicken. The male has a red comb over its eye, a black throat with a white border, a black breast with white barring and grey plumage. The female is grey-brown or reddish-brown with white barring on its underparts, and a black tail with a brown terminal band.

spruce tea ~ a tea made from spruce boughs.

spruce up ~ to dress up and look spiffy. "The missus was all spruced up the day we got married."

spruce yeast ~ a fermenting mixture made from black spruce boughs.

spudgel {pronounced: *SPUD - jull*} ~ a small wooden bucket with a long handle, used to get a drink from a well or to bail a boat with a deep dill.

spuds ~ potatoes.

spurt ~ a short period of time. "I'll row for a spurt now to give you a rest."

spy glass ~ a telescope.

spy glasses ~ binoculars.

squabby ~ soft as jelly. "Your stomach feels right squabby."

squalled over ~ turned outward. "My shoes are all squalled over."

squalmish ~ See **quamish**.

squamish ~ See **quamish**.

square flipper ~ the bearded seal *[Erignathus barbatus]*.

squat ~ to dent or crush. "Uncle Dorm ran over Bobby's tricycle with his car and squat it."

squatum ~ berry wine.

squid ~ refers to two species of squid: the short-finned squid *[Illex illecebrosus]* and the long-finned squid *[Loligo pealiei]*. Only the short-finned squid has been of major com-

short-finned squid

mercial importance to the fishery in Atlantic Canada. Originally caught only for bait, the squid is now exported to such places as Japan and Russia, as well as consumed locally.

squid jigger ~ a weighted lure with between 20 and 40 barbless hooks, used to attract and snag squid.

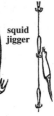

squid jigger

squid juice ~ an inky secretion given off by squids to drive away their enemies. When squid are hauled from the ocean on a jigger their defense mechanism is activated and squid juice flies in all directions. "With spots of the squid juice that's flyin' around."

squid roller ~ a device made of reels around which are wound a number of squid lines, with each line containing up to 20 or more hooks. The handle of the device is

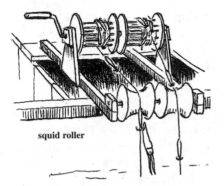

squid roller

rocked back and forth in a jigging manner. This motion causes the jiggers themselves to emulate the action of a wounded fish, which attracts the squid and snags them.

squid squall also **squid squaw** ~ jelly fish.

squid squaw ~ See **squid squall**.

squish ~ not straight. "The picture on the wall is squish."

stage ~ a building on or near a fisherman's wharf in which split and salted fish were kept until they were ready to be spread on a flake.

stage head ~ the portion of a fisherman's wharf on the seaward end of his stage. This area usually has a splitting table where fish are gutted, cleaned and salted before being placed in the stage.

stage head clerk ~ a person who knows how to do everything except work.

stain ~ a small amount, especially of liquid. "I'd give you a drink of home brew but I haven't got a stain."

stairn ~ See **sterrin**.

stall ~ a sheath to cover a thumb or finger.

stall fed ~ fed to capacity.

stalligans also **starrigans** ~ Slender trees and alders used for firewood when larger trees are unavailable.

stamps ~ credit from employment toward receiving benefit while unemployed. These were originally actual stamps which were pasted in a book.

standing room ~ the space between the thwarts of a boat.

staneen ~ a water kettle made from a scooped-out log. A part of one limb was left on to form the spout.

starboard ~ the right side of a ship when facing forward. The light on the starboard side is green.

starkley ~ ugly.

starky ~ stiff and hard to bend.

starn also **stern** ~ 1. the back end of a boat. 2. a person's behind.

starrigans ~ See **stalligans**.

start ~ a scare. "When the gun went off I got a bad start."

state ~ 1. a mess. "I've been working on the outboard motor and I'm in an awful state." 2 upset or depressed. "Her husband drowned the other day and she's in an awful state."

stationer ~ a Newfoundland fisherman, usually from the Avalon area of the province, who fished from the shore in Labrador during the summer. Stationers cured their fish on shore, which was shipped directly to European markets from there. See also **floater**.

stave slide ~ a sled which uses barrel staves as runners.

steady ~ a calm portion in a river.

steam ~ to subject wood to steam in order to shape it.

steamer ~ a vessel owned or chartered by the government to provide a passenger, freight and mail service to Newfoundland and Labrador

steamer

outports. These vessels were often powered by steam but were sometimes powered by an engine that used diesel or bunker C oil as fuel.

steerage ~ the lowest class of travel on a passenger vessel, usually below deck. The accommodations for steerage passengers were at one time near the rudder, which steers the ship.

stearn ~ See **steerin**.

steerin also **stearn, rittick** ~ 1. the Arctic tern *[Sterna paradisaea]*. Measuring 33-35 cm (13-14 in) in length, with a wingspan of 75-85 cm (29-34 in), and weighing 95-120 g (3-5 oz), this little bird is the world's most accomplished long-distance flier, flying 35,000 km (21,750 mi) between the northern and southern hemispheres each year. It eats mostly small fish and, to a lesser degree, small invertebrates like insects, shrimp and krill. 2. the common tern *[Sterna hirundo]*. Like the Arctic tern, this tern migrates from the northern hemisphere in the fall and back in the spring, but doesn't travel as far. The common tern is bigger than the Arctic turn, weighing 257-290 g (9-10 oz), and having a slightly longer wingspan.

stem head ~ the continuation of the forward end of a boat's keel, up above its upper hull, or gunnels. This "post" was sturdy enough to accommodate an anchor. Anchoring a boat by the stem head also insured that the bow was kept to the wind.

step-ins ~ female underwear.

stepmother's breath ~ a cold draught.

step 'n' copy ~ See **copying pans**.

stern ~ See **starn**.

stick ~ log. "I'll saw off a few sticks of wood if you'll cleave it."

stickle ~ See **thornback**.

stile ~ the steps that go up one side of a fence and down the other to allow people easy access to a field but keep the animals inside (or outside).

still and all ~ nevertheless.

stinger needles ~ a plant with small thorns that cause a stinging sensation when touched. Possibly from the English word "nettle," meaning "any weedy plant having serrated leaves with stinging hairs and greenish flowers."

stog ~ See **chinch**.

stogged up ~ clogged. "I threw some grease down the sink and it got stogged up."

stogger ~ a large steamed pudding.

stomach sick ~ nauseous.

stomachy ~ irritable.

stone curlew ~ the greater yellowlegs bird [*Totanus melanoleucus*].

stookawn {pronounced *STUKE - on*} ~ a simpleton.

stop ~ to stay.

stopper ~ 1. bottle cap. 2. drain plug for a sink.

stopwater ~ a wooden dowel inserted between two pieces of wood on a boat, especially where the stem joins the keel, to prevent leaking.

store ~ a fisherman's outbuilding that was used to store winter provisions, as well as fishing gear and other items, and was also used as a workshop and sometimes a barn. See also **Houses and Other Buildings** on page 231.

stories ~ lies. "Don't believe him, he tells stories."

storyteller ~ a liar.

stout ~ the deerfly [*Chrysops excitans*].

strad ~ to wind protective material around a cable.

stradding ~ the protective material used on cables.

straight ~ a stretch of coast without inlets.

straightened out ~ to have one's account settled with the merchant at the end of the fishing season.

Straight Shore ~ 1. the stretch of coast from Cape Freels to Farewell Head. 2. the stretch of coast from Bonne Bay to Port Saunders.

strait ~ a narrower body of water connecting two larger ones.

straits ~ the Strait of Belle Isle.

strand ~ See **neck**.

strapped ~ penniless, broke.

strapping ~ strong and healthy. "He's grown into a strapping young man."

streel ~ untidy person. "Button up your coat my son, you're starting to look like a streel."

stribbens ~ strippings from a tree, dried and used as kindling for a fire.

strifebreeder ~ one who is always trying to cause conflict between people.

striped head ~ the white-throated sparrow [*Zonotrichia albicollis*].

strouters ~ the vertical posts set into the sea bottom at the head of a fisherman's wharf. Horizontal poles were  nailed across the strouters to make a ladder for getting into and out of a boat.

strusset ~ desolate and bleak. "It's a strusset morning."

studder ~ to stammer.

studdle ~ one of the vertical timbers in the frame of a boat.

study ~ to ponder. "I'll have to study what you said and let you know."

stuffing box ~ a bearing fastened to the outside of a boat to keep it from leaking where the propeller shaft runs through.

stunned ~ stupid. The difference between stunned and stupid, according to the comedy group, Buddy Wasisname and the Other Fellers, is that there is a cure for stupid, but being stunned is incurable.

stunned whooper ~ See **mope**.

suant {pronounced: *SUE - ent*} ~ straight, or graceful in appearance.

sud line ~ one of a number of secondary lines with hooks that are attached to the main trawl line.

sugar daddy ~ a caramel candy on a stick, which was very popular in this province at one time.

sugawn ~ a rope made of twisted hay.

summer moles ~ freckles.

summer people ~ the name applied to Newfoundlanders who fish the Labrador coast.

Sunday man ~ a sealer or fisherman who refuses to work on the sabbath.

sun dogs also **sun dwys** ~ the rays

of the sun meeting the ocean, said by some to be "the sun drawing water" – which it was, since the water was evaporating into the warm air at the time, and thereby refracting the sun's rays in the mist so they can be seen.

sun dwys ~ See **sun dogs**.

sunker also **stag** ~ a rock which is close to the surface of the water. On rough days water breaks over the rock, which makes sailors aware of it, but on calm days it is very dangerous.

sure shot ~ a medicine in a capsule form shot down a horse's throat to cure it of bots. See also **bots**.

sure shot gun ~ a spring-loaded device used to shoot a shure shot capsule down a horse's throat.

swab ~ a burlap mop.

swamp ~ See **flat**.

swamper ~ one who takes out the stumps and finishes roads in the lumberwoods.

swank ~ to carry with great effort. "That big suitcase was as much as I could swank."

swanking ~ high-class goods.

swanskin ~ a fine, thick flannel material.

swarbin' {rhymes with *carbon*} also **swarvin'** ~ walking around without any apparent purpose or destination. "My grandmother was continuously telling me to sit still and stop swarbin around the house."

swarvin' ~ See **swarbin'**.

swatch {pronounced: *SWOTCH*} ~ 1. a group of seals close together in the water. 2. a small patch of open water left in an ice floe, or an ice-field. 3. to shoot seals in pools amid ice floes.

swatching {pronounced: *SWOTCH - ing*} ~ the act of taking seals by waiting for them when they come up for air in a patch of open water in an ice floe.

sweet bread ~ See **excursion bread**.

swig ~ 1. to take a drink from a bottle or cup. 2. a drink from a bottle or cup.

swile also **swoil** ~ a seal.

swiling ~ See **sealing**.

swinge ~ to burn the down from seabirds.

switchell ~ 1. black, unsweetened tea. 2. cold tea. 3. a drink of molasses and water.

swoil ~ See **swile**.

syrup ~ a fruit-flavoured beverage made from concentrate.

sythe also **sive** ~ an implement for mowing hay with a long metal blade adjoined at right angles to a crooked shaft which, has two handles at right angles to the shaft and which requires both hands to use.

tabanask ~ a toboggan. From the Labrador Inuit language.

tabby ~ See **copying pans**.

tack ~ 1. clothing. "I don't have a tack to put on my back." 2. money.

tacker ~ waxed hemp thread used by shoemakers.

tackle ~ 1. the act of harnessing a horse or dog. 2. to fish with a net.

taffety ~ particular about food.

tail a slip ~ to set a rabbit snare.

tail stick ~ the crossbar behind a horse to which the traces are fastened.

taint ~ to store animal pelts in a warm, moist place to make the removal of hair easier.

take a turn ~ to have a dizzy spell or to faint.

Talamh an Eisc ~ meaning "land of fish," the name for Newfoundland in the Irish language.

tally ~ 1. to count. 2. to add numbers together. "I tallied up the fish me husband caught and we should be able to pay off the merchant and have some left over for next year." 3. to jump from ice pan to ice pan.

tally-man ~ a fish merchant employee who keeps a record of the amount of fish, seal pelts etc, being traded.

tallywack ~ a rascal.

tallywacking ~ corporal punishment.

talqual ~ the good with the bad.

tanned ~ moved fast. "Our boat was only small so we tanned her across the tickle before the wind picked up."

tannel also **tanner** ~ an animal's claw, a talon. "The cat just scraubed me with her tannel."

tanner ~ See **tannel**.

tant ~ tall and slender, as in masts and trees.

tanzy also **tissy, salt water snake** ~ the rock gunnel [Pholis gunnellus], a small, black, eel-like saltwater fish. See also **Catchin' Darnbanks** on page 206.

tap also **tack** ~ 1. a small amount, any. "I haven't done a tap this month." 2. a small amount of money. "I haven't got a tap to me name."

taps ~ soles of shoes.

tareway ~ loud commotion.

tatie {pronounced: *TAIT - ee*} also **tiddie** {rhymes with *giddy*} ~ a potato.

tattle-tongue ~ a snitch, a gossiper. "Marina is such a tattle tongue that you can't tell her anything."

tawt ~ See **dawt**.

tayscaun ~ a small quantity.

tea ~ supper.

tea doll ~ Made of cloth, wool and caribou hide by Innu men and women for their children, these innikueu (doll in the Innu language) were stuffed with tea which was used when the tea supply ran low. The doll was often a way to carry the family's tea supply while on excursions.

tea doll

tea flower ~ the purple-stemmed aster plant *[Aster puniceus]*.

Teak Day ~ January 6, Old Christmas Day.

teamer ~ a person who handled horses, especially in the lumberwoods; a teamster.

tear-all ~ a hard worker. "When Peter starts something he's a real tear all."

tea towel ~ a cup towel.

teetotal capsizement ~ to be totally surprised.

teetotalled ~ overly tired, beat out. "I've been planting spuds all morning and I'm teetotalled."

teeveen ~ a patch on a boot.

Terra Nova ~ the Latin name for Newfoundland.

terrible ~ 1. extremely. 2. remarkable.

the ~ this. "Are you going lobster-catchin' the year?"

the day ~ today. See also **the mar**.

the mar ~ tomorrow. "If the mar is either bit like the day it's going to be a good day the mar."

the once ~ in a while. "I'll be over to paint your kitchen the once."

there it is ~ that's the truth. "I know it's not what you expected, but there it is."

they ~ those. "They boots are too big for you."

they'm ~ they are. "They'm just like mine."

thine ~ your. "If thou don't keep thy sheep out of my garden I'll kick thine arse." Originated in West Country England.

thingamabobber ~ See **chummy-jigger**.

thingamajig ~ See **chummy-jigger**.

thole pin also **tole pin, dole pin, dildo** ~ a small round stick or dowel fastened to the gunwhale of a rowboat to hold the oar in place. Sometimes two

thole pin

thole pins were used and sometimes only one, which was fastened to the oar with a ring made of rope called a whet. "We usually keeps a few spare dole pins in the risin's of the rodney." The word thole is from the Scottish and Northern English dialect meaning "to bear."

thornback also **thornbank, thornyback, darnback, darnbank, barnystickle, prickle back, prickly, spannie tickle, sparny tickle, stickle, pinfish** ~ a small fish with thorn-like appendages; a stickleback, or fish of the family *Gasterosteidae*. See also **Catchin' Darnbanks** on page 206.

thornbank ~ See **thornback**.

thornyback ~ See **thornback**.

thou ~ you. Originated in West Country England.

thousands ~ plenty, lots. This is one of many hyperboles used in Newfoundland and Labrador. "I got thousands and thousands – damn near a dozen."

thrashberry also **thrasherwood berry, trash berry** ~ the northern wild raisin or withe-rod *[Viburnum cassinoides]*.

thrasher ~ a length of chain or other device for scaring fish into a net.

thrasherwood berry ~ See **thrashberry**.

threaten ~ to intend. "I've been threatening to get a shore job for a long time."

three-handed punt ~ a punt with capacity for three sets of oars.

three-quarter ~ a muzzle-loading gun with a 3/4 inch bore.

thumb glutton ~ See **trigger mitt**.

thumby ~ a heavy mitten.

thunder mug ~ a jocular term for a chamber pot on the Southern Shore of Newfoundland.

thwart ~ See **dawt**.

thy ~ your. "Thy mother is the salt of the earth." Originated in West Country England.

tibby ~ See **copying pans**.

Tib's Eve also **Tip's Eve, Tipsy Eve** ~ December 23rd. See also **Tipsy Eve** on page 200.

ticket ~ 1. a trouble maker. "He was quite the ticket when he was growing up." 2. a certificate of competency. "I got my mate's ticket and now I'm going for my captain's ticket."

ticklass ~ See **tickleace**.

tickle ~ a narrow body of water between two islands, or between an island and a mainland. Probably got its name because with the tides that sometimes sweep through between the landfalls, crossing this body of water is sometimes a ticklish proposition.

tickleace {pronounced: *TICK - ah - ACE*} also **tickle-ass**, **ticklass**, **pinnyole**, **pinny owl** ~ the kitti-wake *[Rissa tridactyla]* , a gull with a fairly large head and short

tickleace

legs in comparison with the rest of its body. It probably got its name because of its flying ability which made it the ace of the tickle. This bird breeds in large colonies during the summer and spends months at sea without touching land. It is the most numerous gull in the world.

tickle-ass ~ See **tickle-ace**.

tiddely ~ See **piddely**.

tiddie ~ See **tatie**.

tierce ~ a 35-gallon barrel used to ship fish, particularly salmon.

tiffin ~ See **damper cake**.

tighten ~ to make a vessel water tight. "If you tighten the seams with oakum your new punt won't sink on you."

tiller ~ the helm or horizontal stick which turns the rudder of a vessel.

tiller lines ~ two lines that run from the tiller, one up the starboard side and the other up the port side of a motorboat, on pulleys so the boat could be steered from the engine house of the boat.

tilly ~ a small amount more than the amount paid for.

tilly lamp ~ a lamp with a special mantel and an oil container that was pressurized by a pump, which was part of the lamp. This gave off much more light than conventional oil lamps with a wick.

tilt ~ a cabin or temporary shelter in the woods.

time ~ a social gathering or party. "At our last time we raised $120 for charity."

time piece ~ a clock.

tin ~ a tin can. "Hand me that tin of milk."

tinker also **gad, gud**, **tinker duck** ~ the northern razorbill *[Alca Torda]*. Measuring 37-39 cm (about 15 in) in length, and having a wingspan of 63-67 cm (25-26 in), this bird weighs 590-730 g (1.25-1.61 lbs).

tinker duck ~ See **tinker**.

tinnen ~ made of tin.

tintacks ~ tin washers used with nails to hold roofing material in place.

tip cat also **cat, cat-stick** ~ a game played with a ball and sticks on the ice in which the goals were holes cut in the ice. This game was also played on land, with holes dug in the ground.

tippy ~ See **copying pans**.

Tip's Eve ~ See **Tib's Eve**.

tipsy ~ See **copying pans**.

Tipsy Eve ~ See **Tib's Eve**.

tiss ~ to fizz. "As soon as the baking soda started to tiss in the glass of water I glutched it."

tissed ~ made a hissing sound.

tissy ~ See **tanzy**.

titivate ~ to adorn exceedingly fine.

to ~ to shut. "Pull the door to on your way out."

to beat the band ~ very hard. "It was snowing to beat the band."

tod ~ a small quantity.

todger ~ a piece of wood with hooks and a long line attached for retrieving birds that have been shot and have fallen in the water.

toe ~ cotton wool. "A bit of toe with some olive oil on it is good for the earache."

togged down ~ dressed up. "I was togged down in me Sunday suit."

toggle ~ 1. a home-made latch for a door or gate. 2. the Atlantic common cormorant *[Phalacrocorax carbo carbo]*.

to hand ~ toward one's share. "Them five quintals of fish I just spread on the flake is going to be good to hand."

token ~ omen or ghost. "Old Mr. Snelgrove must have died because I saw his token last night." See also **Tokens, Fetches and Ghosts** on page 287.

tole pin ~ See **thole pin**.

toller {rhymes with *roller*} ~ an enticement, especially to game animals.

tom cod also **tommy cod** ~ a young codfish, especially one caught by youngsters off the stage head or wharf.

tommy cod ~ See **tom cod**.

tommy-sticker ~ a makeshift candle holder.

to my name ~ belonging to me. "I don't have a cent to my name."

tongue-banging also **tongue-lashing** ~ a scolding, or bawling out. "When I gets home tonight the wife is going to give me some tongue-banging."

tongue-lashing ~ See **tongue-banging**.

took a fright ~ bolted. "When the gun went off, the horse took a fright and didn't stop 'til she got to Drong's Hill."

toothache string ~ a charm worn around the neck to prevent toothache.

tooting owl ~ the American hawk owl *[Surnia ulula caparoch]*. Unlike other owls this owl may be considered strictly diurnal: seeking its prey, to a great extent at least, during daylight, usually during the early morning or evening hours. Its principal food consists of various species of rodents, insects and small birds. It grows to a length of 36-46 cm (14-18 in) and weighs 284-340 g (10-12 oz).

top-man ~ the person manning the upper handle of a pit saw.

tossle cap ~ a knitted wool hat, or toque, with a tassel on the top. "When we used to play hockey on the road everyone had a tossle cap."

tough as a gad ~ able to withstand very cold weather.

toutin ~ See **damper cake**.

townie ~ a native of St. John's.

towy {pronounced: *TOE - ee*} ~ soft and fluffy. "That new shampoo made your hair right towy."

traipse ~ walk. "This comin' Saturday we're going to traipse through the woods to see if there are any partridge on the go."

trampse ~ to walk heavily. "Don't trampse in the potato garden."

trap ~ a small-mesh, box-shaped fish net used in inshore waters.

trap berth ~ the fishing ground used by an inshore fisherman.

trap skiff ~ a skiff used for hauling cod traps. A second boat was towed behind the skiff, as two boats were needed to haul the trap.

trashberry ~ See **thrashberry**.

trawl ~ a long line with shorter lines, attached at intervals. The shorter lines (sud lines) have baited hooks for catching fish. "The only way to bait a trawl is to wind it inside a trawl tub and let the sud lines hang out over the edge."

trawl tub ~ a wooden tub with enough notches cut in the upper edge to accommodate all the sud lines of a trawl.

trenching ~ to create a trench by

shoveling soil onto a row of potato seedlings.

trigger finger mitt ~ See **trigger mitt**.

trigger mitt also **finger mitt, trigger finger mitt, thumb glutton** ~ a woolen mitten with a separate forefinger for pulling the trigger of a gun.

trigger mitt

trike ~ three or four wheeled all-terrain vehicle.

trike

trim ~ to move along close by something, especially a shoreline.

trimming ~ spanking or beating. "If you don't knock it off drivin' works you're going to get some trimming."

trip ~ 1. a venture to earn money. "I made enough money last trip to get married this fall." 2. to capsize a boat.

trounce ~ to scare fish in a particular direction.

trouncer ~ an implement used to thrash the water in order to drive the fish into a net etc.

Trouter's Special ~ 1. a train which would stop to discharge or take on people who were engaged in catching trout in ponds or streams in close proximity to the railway tracks. 2. the brand name of a rum brought from the Caribbean and bottled in St. John's.

truck ~ payment for fish in merchandise.

truck system ~ the system whereby fishermen were paid in goods from the merchant rather than cash. "We never got any money from the merchant, we took everything out in truck."

truckly-muck ~ 1. a small wagon. 2. a child's toy made by attaching a wheel to a stick and pushing it around.

trump hole also **trunk hole** ~ a square hole inside a stage over the water (not over ballast bed) which was used to dispose of fish offal. It was also used as a toilet.

trump hole

trunk hole ~ See **trump hole**.

trunnel ~ a wooden peg in a plank.

tuck ~ one of the lines used to draw a castnet opening shut. "One of me tuck lines got snagged on a rock and I lost all me capelin."

tuckamore ~ a balsam fir or white

spruce tree, whose branches only grow on the side away from the sea. Growth on the seaward side is prevented by salt water spray which kills the buds.

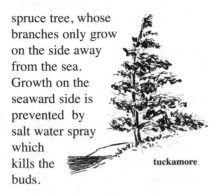

tuckamore

tumbler ~ a drinking glass.

turbot ~ one of the largest of the North Atlantic flatfishes, next to the halibut, this right-handed (that is to say, it lies on its left side, with its eyes on its right side, and its abdomen at its right edge) flatfish with slightly concave tail *[Reinhardtius hippoglossoides]*. This flatfish so closely resembles the halibut that it might easily be taken for one, were it not that its lateral line is nearly straight abreast of the pectoral fin. It grows to a length of about 102 cm (40 in) and to a weight of 9 to 11 kg (20 to 25 lb), although turbot caught on the Grand Banks weigh only from about 2.2 to 4.4 kg (5 to 10 lb). The turbot feeds on crustaceans, eelpouts, capelin, red-fishes, deep sea prawns and other bottom inverte-brates.

turbot

turn ~ 1. armful, shoulderful or as much wood etc. as can be carried in one trip. 2. a wooden log. 3. the wheel in a spinning wheel.

turn in ~ go to bed.

turn of water ~ one or two (usually two) buckets of water. "Go down to the well and bring a turn of water."

turn up ~ make a showing, return. "Wait a few days and I'm sure your dog will turn up."

turpentine ~ See **myrrh**.

turps ~ an oil used as a paint thin-ner. From the word "turpentine."

turr also **murre** ~ the Atlantic common murre *[Uria aalge]*. Turrs are much-sought-after saltwater game birds in this province in the fall. The meat of the turr, even the breast is dark and has a wonder-fully wild taste. Although many seabirds were hunted for food, the turr was a favourite. The cleaned and defeathered carcasses of turrs adorned the ceilings of many stores in the winter months; and many were salted and stored. Their black backs camouflage them when they are swimming from creatures above, while their white underbelly camouflages them from creatures below.

turr

turring ~ hunting turrs.

twack ~ to visit stores with no intention of buying anything. "I was twacking around all day Saturday."

twenty-cent piece ~ a
Newfoundland silver coin
equivalent in value to a British
shilling, used in pre-Confederation
Newfoundland.

twenty-sixer ~ a 26-oz bottle of an
alcoholic beverage. Since conversion to the metric system, alcohol is
sold in a similar-sized bottle – 750
ml, or 26.4 oz.

twig ~ to catch on to the meaning
of something.

twillick ~ 1. a person with little
comprehenson, a twit. 2. the greater
yellow-legs bird *[Totanus
melanoleucus]*.

twine needle ~ a wooden or bone
implement used to knit nets.

twirlie also **lickie** ~ soft ice cream
swirled into a cone.

twitchen ~ a path or narrow lane.

twite ~ to taunt or tease.

two-handed punt ~ a punt with
capacity for two sets of oars.

twooden {rhymes with *wooden*} ~
it wasn't. "I thought I saw a moose
on the bog but when I went back
twooden there."

tyler ~ the person responsible for
lighting the fire, making ready the
lamps, opening and closing the door

for the evening - particularly at
lodges for Orangemen and United
Fishermen.

ugly stick ~ a per-
cussion musical
instrument made
from an old broom
or mop handle
with beer caps or
felt nail heads
attached to make a
jingling sound. A
second stick is
carved with a serrat-
ed side which is
dragged along the
ugly stick like a fiddle bow
to make sound or is used to strike
the ugly stick to make sound.

ugly
stick

uncle ~ the title given any mature
man in Newfoundland and
Labrador, whether he is a blood
relative or not.

under-utilized species ~ any
species of fish not widely harvested
for market.

unemployment ~ monies given to
an unemployed person. "I got thirty
weeks' work this year, so I got
plenty stamps for me
unemployment."

unemployment boots ~ knee high,
green, rubber boots. See also
lumps.

unhandy ~ clumsy. "He's so
unhandy he could trip over a pencil
mark."

Upalong ~ mainland North America.

up sticks ~ a tied game.

urge ~ to gag or almost vomit. "When the boat started to roll I started to urge."

us ~ me. "Give us a piece of cake, I'm hungry."

vamp ~ to mend or put new soles in woolen socks.

vamps ~ short, thick woolen socks.

van ~ the credit run up by loggers for supplies obtained from the company store, such as saw blades, axe handles, tobacco etc. "The wood was so small that I didn't make enough to pay my van."

vandue ~ a sale by auction.

vang ~ melted porkfat served on codfish.

vark ~ See **fork**.

varl ~ See **farl**.

varr also **verr** ~ the balsam fir tree.

venemous ~ fiercely angry.

veranda ~ 1. a patio, or wooden (and sometimes concrete) structure outside the entrance to a house in St. John's. 2. the same structure in the outports with a roof to protect from rain, snow and sun. This roofed structure is known in St. John's as a gallery.

verr ~ See **varr**.

vessel ~ any size or shape of boat, but mostly used to refer to a larger boat or ship.

Victoria Day ~ May 24. See also **Victoria Day** on page 195.

vin ~ the fin of a fish.

virgin ~ new.

vitrid ~ vengeful.

vur ~ See **fur**.

wabble also **wobble** ~ the red-throated loon *[Gavia stellata]*, or the common loon *[Gavia immer]*. Although loons are very similar in appearance to ducks and geese, they are easily distinguishable in the water as they sit lower on the water than their cousins. The loon is very wary of danger and will dive at the slightest indication of a threat. Sometimes it will stay underwater for a period of time with only its periscoping head showing. There is also a culinary difference between these birds. While the meat of ducks and geese is not only tasty, but quite tender, loons are tough to eat.

wack ~ much, many, a lot. "I got a whole wack of hockey cards."

wad {rhymes with *nod*} ~ a large quantity or amount. "You don't have to worry about him paying you back, sure he got wads of money."

wagel {rhymes with *bagel*} ~ an immature black-backed gull *[Larus marinus]*.

wagtail ~ the spotted sandpiper *[Actitis macularia]*.

wake ~ See **backwash**.

waking ~ 1. to follow in the wake of another vessel. 2. partying in honour of a dead person before he or she is buried.

walk-about ~ to be between jobs.

warp ~ to throw.

wash basin ~ an earthen, ceramic or enamel bowl into which heated water was poured to wash one's face and hands.

wash board also **scrubbing board** ~ a laundry utensil made of ribbed glass or other material and used for scrubbing dirt out of laundry.

wash board

wash jug ~ an earthen, ceramic or enamel jug used to carry heated water to a wash basin.

wash stand ~ a small table which held a wash basin and sometimes a wash jug.

watch house ~ a concealment from which a seal hunter watches his seal nets.

water doctor ~ the water strider of the insect family *Gerridae*.

water gully ~ a wooden container used to store fresh drinking water.

water haul ~ a net, trawl, seine or trap that is empty when hauled. "The fish are so scarce all I got was a waterhaul."

waterhorse also **waterhoss** ~ split and salted fish that has not been dried.

waterhoss ~ See **waterhorse**.

water nipper ~ one who brings water to the workers at a worksite, usually a boy or an older man.

water pigeon ~ the southern black guillemot *[Cepphus grylle atlantis]*.

water pup also **pup, water whelp, fish-boil** ~ a blister or sore, common on fishermen's wrists, caused by the saltwater and the constant rubbing of the oilskin sleeve. Some fishermen wore copper chains around their wrists to prevent water pups.

water whelp ~ See **water pup**.

water witch ~ a divining rod. See also **Witch Hazel** on page 288.

wattle ~ a small, slim balsam fir tree.

we ~ with. "I didn't like the last man I went out we."

weasand ~ the throat.

weather ~ a bad storm with high winds and heavy precepitation.

weather glass ~ See **glass**.

weatherish ~ signs of an impending storm.

webber ~ ear.

weegee {pronounced: *WEE - jee*} ~ 1. a sudden change in movement. 2. to toss or throw.

weem ~ we are. "Weem all going to the Sunday School picnic."

weep ~ to leak slowly, to seep, to ooze.

weigh-de-buckety ~ see-saw. From the bucket on a weigh-scale device used to weigh fish. This was a fulcrum device, similar to a see-saw. It had a bucket on one end of the pivoting arm and a platform, on which various weights could be placed, on the other. The bucket was filled with fish unti the desired weight was reached, at which time the arm balanced.

welt ~ a large drink of an alcoholic beverage.

went to wing ~ died.

were you born on a raft? ~ close the door.

wert ~ wart.

wes'kit ~ a vest or waistcoat.

Wesleyan feet ~ refers to someone who can't dance.

West Country ~ the counties of Cornwall, Devon, Dorset, Gloucestershire, Somerset and Wiltshire in southwest England from where Newfoundland's English settlers mostly came.

wester ~ toward the west.

western boat ~ a schooner-rigged fishing vessel of 15 to 30 tons.

western coast ~ the south coast of Newfoundland west of the Burin Peninsula.

west indee ~ a lesser grade of cured, salt codfish shipped to the West Indies.

whabby ~ the red-throated loon *[Gavia stellata]*.

whale ~ any of a number of whales which frequent the waters of Newfoundland and Labrador, including the Atlantic pilot *[Globicephala melaena]*, beluga *[Delphinapterus leucas]*, blue *[Balaenoptera musculus]*, fin *[Balaenoptera physalus]*, humpback, *[Megaptera novaeangliae]* killer *[Orcinus orca]*, minke *[Balaenoptera acutorostrata]*, sei *[Balaenoptera borealis]*.

wharf {rhymes with *scarf*} ~ a platform built out from the shore into the water, supported by piles and providing access to vessels.

whatchamacallit ~ See **chummy-jigger**.

what odds ~ it makes no difference, who cares? "What odds if a man got nar cent a money?"

wheelbar ~ wheelbarrow.

whelp ~ 1. the act of a seal giving birth. 2. a newborn seal.

whelping bag ~ the placenta of a seal.

whet also **wit, whiff** ~ a rope spliced into a ring and used to keep the oar attached to the tholepin while rowing a boat. See also **tholepin**.

wheybelly ~ the name applied to Newfoundland residents from Waterford, Ireland.

whiff ~ a gulp of air. See also **whet**.

whiffen ~ See **bough whiffen**.

whig ~ a member of the Liberal Party.

whist ~ 1. be quiet! hush up! 2. to play a trump card in the games of 120s or 45s.

whistling diver ~ the American black scoter *[Oidemia nigra americana]*.

whitecoat ~ a young harp seal.

whitefish ~ See **smelt**.

whiten ~ See **rampike**.

white nose ~ an indentured servant after his first winter spent in Newfoundland.

white owl ~ the snowy owl *[Nyctea scandiaca]*. These owls are the largest bird species in the arctic, measuring 63-73 cm (25-29 in) in length with an average wingspan of 170 cm (67 in). White owls usually weigh about 1.5 kg (3.3 lb). they are predominantly white with dusky brown spots and bars. Females tend to have more markings than males, which may become nearly completely white as they age.

white pudding ~ a pudding containing pork meat, pork fat suet, bread and oatmeal formed into the shape of a large sausage.

white water ~ rain water used for drinking.

white wing diver ~ the eastern white-winged scoter *[Melanitta deglandi deglandi]*. Common to the Newfoundland and Labrador coastline year-round, this duck lives off shellfish and other bottom-dwellers that it finds in remote coves where it chooses to live.

white wing diver

Adult males are 53-58 (21-23 in) in length, and weigh 1.6 kg (3.5 lbs), while females are slightly smaller.

whittle ~ a heavy covering for a baby.

whizgigging ~ laughing and giggling sporadically over a period of time.

whore's egg also **oar's egg, cosy egg, ose egg, osy egg** ~ the sea urchin, a spiny sea creature of the class *Echinoidea*.

whore's egg

whorts ~ See **herts**.

wicked ~ great. "We had a wicked time at the party."

wild cat ~ the pine marten *[Martes americana]*.

wild pigeon ~ See **pigeon**.

willow bird ~ the Newfoundland or eastern pine grosbeak *[Pinicola enucleator eschatosus]*.

willow perfume ~ See **perfume willow**.

win'ard ~ See **windward**.

wincy ~ 1. to act in a promiscuous manner. 2. to play one's best card.

wind charger ~ an electrical generator powered by wind.

wind jack ~ 1. a propeller-shaped device which indicates wind velocity. 2. an electrical generator powered by wind. 3. a propeller-shaped child's toy.

windward ~ the direction from which the wind blows.

wing and wing also **winged out** ~ having sails swung out to both starboard and port when running before the wind.

winged out ~ See **wing and wing**.

wink ~ 1. the handle of a grindstone. 2. a winch.

winnish ~ See **ouannaniche**.

winter diet ~ winter provisions.

winterer ~ a permanent settler in Newfoundland.

winter houses ~ dwellings built in a more sheltered area away from the ocean and occupied during the winter months because, being sheltered from onshore winds, they were easier to heat.

wit ~ See **whet**.

witch hazel ~ the yellow birch tree *[Betula lutea]*. See also **Witch Hazel** on page 288.

without ~ unless. "You can't have a candy without you get one for me too."

withy ~ the shrubby cinquefoil plant *[Potentilla fructicosa]*.

witlow ~ an inflammation around a fingernail.

wizzle ~ the weasel.

wizzle-faced ~ having sharp facial features.

wobble ~ See **wabble**.

woman box ~ a wooden compartment on a sled for transporting sick people. See also **coach box**.

wonderful ~ extremely. "I had a wonderful good time at the Sunday School picnic."

wood cat ~ See **wild cat**.

wood horse also **saw horse** ~ a device for holding logs while they are being sawed into firewood-size junks.

wood horse

wool card ~ a device used to render wool into stringy fibres to be spun into yarn.

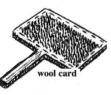

wool card

woostard ~ wool. Probably derived from the word "worsted," which means, "wool that has been combed to make it smooth and firm."

wop ~ 1. to strike. "If you don't behave I'm going to give you such a wop on the head, you'll have to turn down your socks to see out over them." 2. a wasp or similar stinging insect.

wrangle-gangle ~ to behave in a noisy and boisterous manner.

wren ~ the figure of a bird carried by children looking for handouts on St. Stephen's Day. See also **Mummering** on page 244.

wriggle ~ See **riddle**.

wriggling ~ See **riddle**.

wrinkle ~ See **periwrinkle**.

yaffle ~ armful, especially of fish. "There are only a few yaffles of fish left on the flake."

yankee slack ~ American soft coal.

yannies ~ wieners.

yarkin ~ lines to fasten a net to a head rope.

yarn ~ 1. to converse casually. 2. a story. 3. twisted wool fibres used in knitting.

yary ~ watchful and alert.

yawny ~ pale. "Since he had that operation he's right yawny."

ye ~ you. In some parts of Newfoundland and Labrador, "ye" is the plural of "you."

yean ~ of a sheep, to give birth.

yellow bellies ~ the name applied to Newfoundland residents from Wexford, Ireland. This name came from the yellow sashes worn across the bellies of former Wexford residents in support of their home football (soccer) team.

yellow hammer ~ a bird, the Newfoundland yellow warbler *[Dendroica petechia amnicola]*.

yellow mores ~ See **snakeroot**.

yer ~ 1. here. "Come yer I want's he." From West Country England. 2. your. "Fill yer boots."

yesses ~ worms.

yoke ~ 1. a dog's harness. 2. a team of two oxen.

yop ~ 1. to bite. "Paddy took a big yop out of an apple on Snap Apple Night." 2. to shout angrily. "I'm doing the best I can, you don't have to yop at me."

youm ~ you are. "You ordered a pair of mitts from the catalogue when your mother knows how to knit the best kind, youm some foolish." Originated in West Country, England, from the contraction of "you am."

youngster ~ 1. a child, 2. a man who was inexperienced in catching and curing fish and who signed on for a fishing voyage to Newfoundland.

yourn ~ yours. From the contraction of "your one."

your own self ~ yourself. "You knows that your own self."

you say ~ that's unbelievable.

zeed also **seed** ~ saw. "I zeed him with me own two eyes."

zever ~ sever. If you youngsters don't stop your wizgiggin' and laughin' I'll zever thine heads off." From West Country England.

zounbone ~ See **soundbone**.

Celebrations, Customs and Holidays

The source of the material for this section is the author's personal knowledge, as well as a number of publications and individuals. Although some of these are written in the past tense, many are still honoured today.

New Year's Day — January 1

If a friend leaves a coin in your house on New Year's Day you will have money all year.

If the first person to enter your house on New Year's day is someone with a dark complexion, you will have good luck all year.

In Newfoundland and Labrador, New Year's resolutions were originally made on New Year's Day, not New Year's Eve.

To work on New Year's Day will bring bad luck all year.

Old Christmas Eve — January 5

On January 5, the eve of Old Christmas Day, it was believed that the cows and other cattle fell to their knees and prayed.

Old Christmas Day — January 6

This is the day that would have been Christmas before the calendar changed in 1752. It is now the date that designates the end of the Christmas season, and the last night for mummering in Newfoundland and Labrador.

St. Brigid's Day — February 1

If you put a piece of string outside the house on January 31, the eve of St. Brigid's Day, the saint will walk on it. Tying that string around your ankle on St. Brigid's Day will guard against falls or accidents.

It was customary on St. Brigid's Day to make a cross, known as a "St. Brigid's Cross" out of rushes or reeds (other materials could be used if no rushes or reeds were available). Once the Cross was woven, it was blessed by a priest with holy water with the words, "May the blessing of God the Father, Son and Holy Ghost be on this Cross and on the place where it hangs and on everyone who looks on it." It was then hung on the front doors of homes and left in place all year, to be replaced on the next St. Brigid's Day. From Ireland, via the southern shore.

Candlemas Day — February 2

Once known as Midwinter Day, February 2 is observed as Candlemas Day, and is known in more recent years as Groundhog Day in Newfoundland and Labrador. If a hibernating bear came out of his sleeping place and the sun was shining on Candlemas Day, it was believed that wintery weather was almost over. This is the opposite to the predictions of the USA's Punxsutawney Phil and his Canadian counterpart, Wiarton Willy. These famous groundhogs claim that if they see their shadow on that day there will be six more weeks of winter. To date in this province, the groundhogs have been right about 40 per cent of the time and the bear about 60.

This rhyme from Newfoundland and Labrador agrees with the bear:
"If Candlemas Day is fair and fine,
half of the winter is left behind;
If Candlemas day is rough and grum,
half of the winter is yet to come."

Having a candle in your house that had been blessed by the priest in the parish church on Candlemas Day will protect it from fire for the rest of the year.

Coombs's Day — February 3

Coombs's Day commemorates the day when several members of the Coombs family died in a snow storm. It is still observed in the Upper Island Cove area of Conception Bay, nearly two centuries after the tragic death.

Pancake Day

Also called Shrove Tuesday here, and Fat Tuesday and Mardi Gras in other places, Pancake Day was the Tuesday preceding Ash Wednesday, which marked the beginning of Lent and was celebrated by serving pancakes. Pancakes contained eggs, which were forbidden during lent, and people got their fill of them on that day. Sometimes coins, buttons or other thin objects were placed in pancakes to surprise children. In some areas the item found in the pancake had special meaning; finding a coin meant that you would be rich, a button meant you would be a tailor or housewife, a nail meant you would be a carpenter or marry one, finding a holy item meant you would become a priest or a nun.

Pancake Day was observed by Protestants as well as Roman Catholics.

St. Blaise Day — February 3

On the Feast of St. Blaise Day, one could have a sore throat cured by having a priest hold two crossed candles over the heads of the ailing person or touch their throats with the unlit candles while he invoked the prayer of St. Blaise, "Through the intercession of St. Blaise, bishop and martyr, may God deliver you from every disease of the throat and from every other illness, in the name of the Father, and of the Son, and of the Holy Spirit." This practice originated in Ireland.

St. Valentines Day — February 14

On St. Valentine's Day, cards, often homemade, were delivered anonymously. The receivers had to guess who gave them each card. The number of cards received was indicative of the receiver's popularity. Because they were anonymous, it was also an opportunity to give a nasty card to someone you didn't like. It was believed that the first person of the opposite sex you meet on St. Valentine's Day would become your spouse.

Patrick and Sheila

A storm before St. Patrick's Day, right after a spell of reasonably good weather is called a Patrick and Sheila. See also **Sheila's Brush** below.

St. Patrick's Day — March 17

St. Patrick's Day is a big day in Newfoundland and Labrador, especially for those of Irish descent. In fact it is a provincial holiday. Since Roman Catholics were absolved of their Lenten fasting on that day, it was a day of feasting, imbibing in alcohol, concerts, parading, dancing and partying. Although not governed by the same religious rules, many Protestants also celebrated St. Patrick's Day.

Sheila's Brush

This was the last big storm of winter with a heavy snowfall, accompanied by high winds around St Patrick's Day. It came right after a spell of reasonably good weather. If it happened after St Patrick's Day it was called Sheila's Brush, which meant a good spring was on the way. If this storm came before St. Patrick's Day it was known as a Patrick and Sheila, which meant that a bad spring would follow. This storm could always be expected, and many fishermen would not venture out on the ice hunting seals until it had come and gone. Sheila's Brush comes from an Irish legend that Sheila was the saint's wife, sister or mother, and the snow is a result of her sweeping.

April Fool's Day — April 1

Many pranks and tricks were played on people on April Fool's Day, but in most parts of the province the tricks stopped at noon on April 1. This rule was adhered to by children as well as adults. If some child played a trick on another after noon, the tricked person might say, "April fool is gone apast, and you're the biggest fool at last."

The trickster might then reply, "Up the ladder, down the tree, you're a bigger fool than me."

The reply to this was often, "Skin the rabbit, pick the hen, you're the biggest fool again."

St. George's Day — April 23

St. George was a Roman soldier who protested the Romans' torture of Christians and was put to death because of his beliefs. During the Crusades, King Richard of England adopted George as the Patron Saint of England, and St. George's cross became part of the English flag. Although it is considered a national day in England, and is still celebrated there, as in Newfoundland and Labrador, St. Patrick's Day is a much-more celebrated day..

Victoria Day — May 24

Once known as the Queen's Birthday – the Queen being Victoria, who ruled England for 56 years until her death in 1901 – this is now a provincial holiday. A few years ago children could be heard chanting:
"On the 24th of May,
The Queen's birth day
If we don't get a holiday
We'll all run away."

Queen Victoria

Today in Newfoundland and Labrador the Victoria Day weekend, also called simply the May 24th Weekend, marks the opening of the trout season and the beginning of the camping season.

St. John's Day — June 24

At one time fires were lit on the headlands to celebrate St. John's Day, originally called Midsummer's Day and later Discovery Day. Today the celebrations are mostly limited to the St. John's. It was because John Cabot is believed to have sailed in through the narrows on this day in 1497, that the city of St. John's got its name. In the 1940s the Newfoundland Government instituted Discovery

Day, a holiday on June 24th to celebrate Newfoundland's history. The day was removed from the calendar by the provincial government in the late 1980s.

If a young woman boiled an egg in the morning on St. John's Day, removed half the egg from the shell, then filled it with salt and kept it next to her bed, her future husband would come to her that night in a dream. Sometimes a young woman would break an egg in a tumbler and place it on a window sill on St. John's Day, which would reveal her future husband in some other mysterious way. Another custom was for a young lady to break an egg in a tumbler and throw it out onto the street on the morning of St. John's Day. The first man to walk over the egg would become her husband or would have the same first and last initial in his name as in her future husband's name.

R emembrance Day/Canada Day — July 1

Although July 1 has been celebrated as Canada Day in Newfoundland and Labrador since 1949, it has been celebrated as Remembrance Day since the end of WWI. It was on that day in 1916, in what later became known as the July Drive, that the Newfoundland Regiment at Beaumont-Hamel was almost wiped out by German machine gun fire as the Regiment advanced through holes in the barbed wire across an open field. For many years forget-me-not flowers were worn on this day to remember those who gave their lives for freedom.

O rangemen's Day — July 12

Orangemen's Day commemorates the Battle of the Boyne and was once much celebrated by Protestants in this province. There were dinners, parades and parties to mark the event.

There were also fights between Irish Catholics and English Protestants.

The animosity between the two groups goes back to the late 1600s when James II, the last Catholic monarch of England, was in power. The king not only refused to work with parliament but appointed many of his Catholic supporters to high positions and continually tampered with private property and historic rights. He also had Archbishop Sancroft and six other bishops arrested for failing to proclaim the Catholic faith. Then James produced a male heir, which dashed parliament's hopes for a future Protestant heir to the throne.

At the time, Mary, James' Protestant daughter from a previous marriage was married to James' Dutch-speaking nephew, William, Prince of Orange in the Netherlands. Parliament appealed to William of Orange, urging him to save England from a Catholic takeover. William gathered his forces and landed in England in November 1688. His professional troops and the welcome they received from the English landholders intimidated James, who was captured while fleeing London. The new king gave his rival (and uncle) safe passage to France, and William and his wife ruled jointly as King William III and Queen Mary II.

In France in the meantime, James sought and got the support of Louis IX of France, an old enemy of England, who supplied troops to enhance the Irish troops James had garnered. What ensued was the most important battle in Irish history. Although King William had the blessing of the Pope and the army on each side had equal numbers of Protestants and Catholics, the battle of the Boyne, in which William's forces soundly defeated James' troops, put an even larger rift between the two Christian religions. It was a day that signified the loss of certain freedoms for Irish Catholics, especially religious freedoms, and one that caused many clashes between the two factions for many years.

G arden Parties

For many years churches throughout the province have held Garden Parties to raise funds for local parishes or for special projects. These day-long events were often held on a Sunday, when fewer people were working. If the weather was bad the events were moved into the church hall. There were races, wheels-of-fortune and other events during the day, followed by a meal in the evening and a dance at night. Sometimes these "times" went on 'til the wee small hours. In recent years, garden parties have been replaced by festivals, especially come-home-year festivals. They often last a weekend and sometimes a week.

R egatta Day

The first Wednesday in August – weather permitting – marks the celebration of North America's oldest regatta, the Royal St. John's Regatta. This shell-rowing event on Quidi Vidi Lake is visited by thousands of people every year; in some years more than 50,000 have visited.

On the eve of the event, while booths are being set up by charitable groups and small business, hundreds of St. John's residents and former residents walk around the area, meeting and chatting with old friends and acquaintances. Early the next morning, if it appears that the day is going to be too windy or too rainy for the races, a decision is made to postpone the event until the next good day. Most businesses are closed for Regatta Day.

Lady Day — August 15

Lady Day was a holy day for Roman Catholics and it was usually the day that marked the return of fishermen from the Labrador coast. For some it was the day that the first batch of new potatoes could be dug.

Labour Day

As in the rest of Canada, Labour Day is celebrated on the first Monday in September with parades and other entertainment. This day often marks the end of trouting season and the end of summer vacation for school children.

Colcannon Night — October 31

Halloween Night was once known as Colcannon Night or Snap Apple Night. Colcannon is a dinner with a number of vegetables (often seven types of vegetables) boiled together in one pot and served on that day. One of the ways of celebrating the event was with a game of tying an apple to a string and suspending it, then swinging the apple while trying to get a bite from it. This earned it the name Snap Apple Night. The custom of trick or treating was brought to Newfoundland from the United States by American soldiers stationed in this province during WWII.

On Colcannon Night, if two lovers placed a pair of walnuts side by side in the fire and they stayed together as they burned, it meant that the couple would have a happy future. If the nuts separated, the couple was in for a rocky relationship. This custom came from Ireland

If a young woman took an apple and a lighted candle into a dark room on Colcannon Night and looked into a mirror while eating the apple she would see the face of her lover reflected in the mirror over her shoulder. This also came from Ireland, via the Southern Shore.

All Saints Day — November 1

All Saints Day was once considered a holy day of obligation for Roman Catholics, and still is by some.

All Soul's Day — November 2

All Soul's Day was a day in which Roman Catholics remembered the souls of the dead. Three masses were held on that day and prayers were said for dead relatives.

Bonfire Night — November 5

Bonfire Night was once a big event in Newfoundland and Labrador. It celebrates the date in 1605, when 13 young men planned to blow up the English Houses of Parliament. Among them was Guy Fawkes, Britain's most notorious traitor. Bonfire Night is known as Guy Fox Night in Britain, where the likeness of Guy Fawkes is burned in effigy. Many of the boys who cut boughs and collected barrels, wooden boxes and many other items to burn in this province never heard the name Guy Fawkes, and the event was always called Bonfire Night.

Some of the items used to fuel this fire were taken without the owners' permission. Among these items were wooden boxes, barrels and sometimes even an old boat that the owner planned to repair. Although this was essentially stealing, it carried the kinder title of "bucking." The owners were never happy about losing these items, but seldom were charges laid. "Bucking" was considered one of the rites and rituals of Bonfire Night, but many a man stayed up late on the nights before to keep an eye on his old rodney. Sometimes old boats were given to boys to burn in their bonfires.

This was a fun night when boys and girls got together. There was singing and dancing, running through the smoke, frolicking and horse-play around the bonfire. Often young adults joined in the fun, and sometimes older adults as well. Since this was harvest time, often potatoes were brought to be baked in the fire. Sometimes a bunch were thrown right in the fire that often reached 12 feet in the air, or higher, and was so hot you had to throw on the potatoes and run to keep your eyebrows. The black balls that were once potatoes were dug out of the ashes after everything was finally burned. The burnt skin of the potato was cut away with a pocket knife by kids whose faces were sometimes as black as their hands. Bonfire Night was a fun night that at one time was second only to Christmas in Newfoundland and Labrador outports.

Armistice Day — November 11

Celebrated in Newfoundland and Labrador as Armistice Day, November 11 is a provincial holiday that marks the date the armistice was signed to end the First World war. Although this day was once celebrated by the lighting of bonfires and the firing of guns into the air, it is now mostly relegated to the marching of Canadian Legion members and the laying of wreaths at war monuments.

Tipsy Eve — December 23

Tipsy Eve was celebrated by men who went from house to house sampling the homebrew, moonshine, berry wine or other alcoholic beverages of their friends and neighbours. This was a night when the wife usually gave her blessing to her man to drink. Drinking too much on Christmas Eve or Christmas Day was frowned upon and forbidden by some wives. The Tib's Eve custom is local to residents of the southwest coast of Newfoundland. The name was most likely borrowed from St. Tib's Eve. There is no such saint as Saint Tib, so saying something would happen on St. Tib's Eve meant it was never going to happen. This saying didn't originate in Newfoundland, but like many others, was adopted. "You'll get a new pair of skates all right! On St. Tip's Eve!" Not to waste a saint's name, especially one that sounded so much like "tipsy," the people on the southwest corner of Newfoundland gave the good saint a permanent home. The person who originally applied the name to the event obviously saw the irony in giving the name of a day that never happened to one of drinking. Today "Tipsy Eve" is still celebrated in certain communities in the same way, while in others, such as Port aux Basques, it is also a fun night for both sexes at the local bar.

Christmas Eve — December 24

On Christmas Eve in Newfoundland and Labrador a meal of salt fish was usually served, the time for fresh fish being long past. In many outports a yule log was hauled through the community, but this practice is no longer in vogue. In some houses the Christmas tree was put up on Christmas Eve after the children were in bed, and the first time they saw it was on Christmas morning.

Christmas Day — December 25

Christmas Day in Newfoundland and Labrador, like everywhere in the Christian world, was the biggest day of the year. The "right tree" was sought in the woods, then the bottom was sawed off square and a wooden stand was nailed to it. The tree ornaments changed in product, appearance and price over the years, but the tree was always decorated with diligence and decorating it was always a fun part of a happy event. Christmas was an especially joyous time in Newfoundland and Labrador because it was one of the few occasions when the family could share hours of time together. Presents, which were often homemade items, were exchanged. In some parts of Newfoundland, children would visit neighbours during Christmas to look at their tree and tell them how nice it was. They knew they would get some kind of treat at most houses they visited, so each tree was "the best one." A big meal that consisted of boiled vegetables with salt beef, and either turrs, roast beef, mutton, goat or the hen that no longer laid eggs, was always served on Christmas Day. After the meal, in some communities, guns were fired to let the neighbours know they were welcome to visit.

St. Stephen's Day — December 26

Now celebrated as Boxing Day, which is really just another holiday from work during the Christmas season, December 26 was one time celebrated as St. Stephen's Day. St. Stephen was the first Christian martyr to be stoned to death after the crucifixion of Christ. At one time, when the fishery was big in Newfoundland and Labrador, the day was also used to celebrate Orangemen's Day by fishermen on the northeast coast of Newfoundland. Since the regular date, July 12, was in the peak of the fishing season, a holiday for fishermen on that day was out of the question.

Holy Innocents Day — December 28

The Holy Innocents were the children of Bethlehem under the age of two who were slain on the orders of King Herod in an attempt to kill baby Jesus, who was proclaimed to be the newborn King of the Jews. Holy Innocents Day was considered as the year's unluckiest day in some parts of the province. It was believed that any job started on that day would to come to a bad end.

New Year's Eve — December 31

In many Newfoundland and Labrador communities New Year's Eve was celebrated at the stroke of midnight by firing guns into the air to welcome the new year. The firing of guns was very popular at the time of the muzzle loader. Shot or musket balls weren't used, as powder alone was enough to get the desired "bang."

It was considered bad luck to let the fire go out during New Year's Eve.

In some outport communities people opened the back door to let the old year out and the front door to let the new year in.

Sweeping the floor on New Year's Eve meant you might sweep all your good luck out the door, and so it was frowned upon.

The birth of a child on New Year's Eve meant good luck. This was certainly true when it came to paying income tax because, although you only had to support the child for a few hours, you could claim that dependent as a tax exemption for the whole year.

Any unusual task you perform on New Year's Day you will have to perform often throughout the year.

A Way of Life

The source of the material for this section is the author's personal knowledge, as well as a number of publications and individuals.

Alleys

Alleys is a game played with marbles, which are also called "alleys," "glass alleys" and "glassells." This game can have a number of players, but always with each player competing singly, as the object of the game is to win and keep as many of your opponents' alleys as possible. The game is played by digging a hole in the ground, called the mott or mop. About 10 feet away a line is drawn to mark the starting point. Players may each use only as many marbles as is pre-chosen by the group. If five is the chosen number, then each player uses five marbles. Each player then tries to toss as many marbles as possible into the mott and gets to keep any of his or her marbles that makes it into the mott. The player with the most marbles in the mott, then gets first turn at trying to win the marbles outside the mott by flicking them into the mott with the forefinger, similar to a putt in golf. One has to curl his forefinger and place the second joint on the ground behind the alley, then flick it in the direction of the mott. Starting with the alley closest to the mott, the player continues flicking until he misses a shot. The person who tossed the second most alleys in the mott after the toss gets a turn, and so on.

If no one manages to get an alley in the mott during the toss, the person with

203

the alley closest to the mott goes first. Although this was sometimes played by a group of children, it was often a one-on-one game with spectators. If someone wins all the opponent's marbles in a single game, he was said to have "guttled" the other player.

If someone kept his finger on the alley too long, thereby dragging it closer to the mott before letting go, he was said to be a "scraper" and was considered to be cheating. In some areas of the province, the alley had to be flicked with the thumbnail after snapping it off the forefinger.

This game was played by both boys and girls, although mixed games were more the exception than the rule.

Ball-Bouncing Games

Games where a ball was bounced off the side of a building were very popular in Newfoundland at one time. These were especially popular among girls, although boys sometimes played them as well. The children would throw a ball, either a sponge ball or an air-filled rubber ball, at the side of a building and perform other movements before the ball came back so they could catch it. The movements included clapping their hands in front of and/or behind their backs; pivoting around; touching their head, elbows, knees or some other part of their body with their hands; or performing some other action one or more times. The game started out easy, with only one clap in front, but it got progressively harder, with more and more moves added. All through the game the children sang a song describing what they were doing.

"Eenie, clapsy, twirl around the batsy," meant throwing the ball, clapping once in front, then holding your two hands out in front of you and turning them around in a circular motion several times.

Berry-picking

Although picking berries was work and a means of survival, it was often a family outing that was made into a fun event. A number of different types of berries are picked for food. Partridgeberries and blueberries are the most popular. Raspberries, bakeapples, marshberries and blackberries (crowberries) were always plentiful and often gathered as well. To gather enough berries to last the family all winter required a full day or several days of picking by all members of the family. They started out for the berry patches early in the morning and picked until noon when a fire was lit and the kettle put on to boil. After the picnic everyone went back to picking. Each berrypicker had a small container, known as a picker or an empter, which were filled and then dumped into a larger container. This was sometimes a flour sack or an old pillow case. While this was going on, stories were often told and children talked of their day-to-day activities. Often there was a bit of fun and frolic on the berry hills.

Sometimes people picked berries to sell to the local merchant or to a hospital. For the people who had to do this to get money to survive, berrypicking was not an outing, it was hard work.

Partridgeberries, because they grow so plentiful and so close together, can be picked by the handful, as can blackberries. Blueberries can be picked by the handful as well, but because they are softer, one has to be more careful when picking them. When ripe, raspberries are picked individually, sometimes right off their core, taking only the edible part of the berry. Because they are fewer and farther apart, bakeapples are the hardest berries to pick, making them the most expensive. Bakeapples now sell for up to $80 per gallon.

B lind Buck and Davy

In this children's game, which is also called Bonna Winkie, all players are given their own number, except for one player, who is blindfolded. When the others form a ring about the blindfolded player, he or she calls out two numbers. The players having these numbers change places at once, while the player in the centre tries to catch one of them. If successful he takes the place and number of the person caught and that player goes in the centre and is in turn blindfolded.

B oilin' Wrinkles

One form of entertainment for boys in outport communities was boilin' wrinkles. Wrinkles or periwinkles are snail-like mollusks that can be found just underwater on rocks and wharf sticks at high tide, and often well above water at low tide. Their principal purpose, as far as most outport boys were concerned, was to be used as bait for catching conners, tomcods or flatfish.

They also served another purpose when outport children were looking for a new adventure – boilin' wrinkles. All one needed for boilin' wrinkles was a match to light the fire. A can that wasn't too rusty to serve as a pot could be easily found, and there was always plenty of firewood on the beach. It took about a minute to collect enough wrinkles to feed four or five boys, and another 20 minutes for them to cook in salt ocean water. Some outport boys have had a meal of escargot fit for kings, without going above the highwater mark on a beach. Although outport boys ate them, they were never cooked for consumption at home. However periwinkle harvesting for export has since been introduced to the province and has been expanding ever since.

B utton, Button

Button, button is a children's game that was often played at birthday parties. One person became the "button-holder" while the rest of the group formed a circle around him or her. Holding the button between the palms of the hands, the button-holder drew his hands down between the unclasped hands of the other players while pretending to drop the button in each pair of hands. Sometimes the same pair of hands would get visited more than once. In one pair of hands the button was left but the button-holder continued until he was sure he had deceived the players. He would then say, "Button, button, whose got the button?" then select someone to try and guess who had the button. The idea was for the button-holder to fool everyone into picking the wrong person. The person left holding the button would try to pretend that he didn't have it and if he was successful he would have a turn in the centre of the ring. If someone guessed correctly who had the button, that person took the centre-ring position.

Catchin' Darnbanks

Because of its rocky coastline, pools of saltwater are left in the craters in the rocks on almost every shore in this province when the tide goes out. All kinds of sea creatures are often found in these shallow pools of crystal clear water. For smaller children, this was an opportunity to go "catchin' darnbanks," one of many names used to refer to little stickle-back fish that were always plentiful. Darnbanks were scooped up with one's hands and placed in a tin can of saltwater. These fish are usually released after the fun of catching them and studying them was over. Some children tried to get them to survive in fresh water, but they never did.

Similar small fish can be found at the edge of freshwater ponds as well. These were sometimes called spanney tickles, and were caught by younger children in the same manner.

Besides darnbanks, children often caught small crabs, tanzies and other small sea dwellers in rock pools.

Catchin' Tomcods and Conners

Every wharf and stage head in a fishing community, where fish offal was continually dumped overboard, was a good place for an outport boy to catch tomcods and conners. Sometimes a pole or stick was used as a fishing rod, but it wasn't necessary as conners, tom cod and other sea creatures were always close to the wharf, or under the wharf between ballast beds. The bait of choice was the ever-plentiful wrinkle, a snail-like mollusk that clung to wharf sticks, rocks and other items. A big stone was necessary to crack the wrinkle shells open to get to the meat of the matter. With the amount of offal on the bottom, smaller fish were well-fed, but could often be enticed to make a snap at a juicy wrinkle that was dangled in front of their noses.

A flat fish, with its shape showing through the sand under which it was hiding could sometimes be enticed out by a tasty morsel of wrinkle as well. Crabs would sometimes hang onto a wrinkle or be entangled in the hook long enough to be brought onto the wharf. These were fun to catch because you could check their "money purse" to see how much money they had. The money purse was a triangular flap on the crabs' belly that could be opened. The inside had a number of dots that boys called the crab's money. Sculpins could always be caught off the stage head, but they were so ugly and spiny, that removing the hook from their huge mouths was not something that most boys favoured, so they tried hard not to catch them.

A starfish or two could usually be hooked on a bare hook and brought onto the wharf.

Chewin' Frankum

Spruce trees, which are plentiful in Newfoundland and Labrador, secrete a resin that when warmed by the interior of the mouth becomes as chewable and enduring as chewing gum. Although not sweet nor as tasty as the store-bought gum, many youngsters who couldn't afford gum often chewed frankum.

Chip, Chip

In this guessing game, children hid a number of marbles (or other items) in a closed hand and said, "Chip, chip, how many men aboard?" The other players then tried to guess the number of items in the hand. Sometimes pennies or other coins were used and it became a gambling game.

Clampers and Youngsters

The consistency of saltwater ice is softer and more easily broken than fresh water ice. This causes harbour ice to break into pans of various sizes in the spring, which were known as clampers as well as by other names. Often "lakes" of open water are left near shore, which provided a great venue for fun among outport youngsters. A clamper of a certain size made a great raft for one or more boys, who pushed the clamper around the open water with long poles. The clampers became fishing vessels,  pirate ships, battleships or merchant vessels travelling to exotic places around the world.

A more dangerous game has been played in harbours and coves throughout the province for many years. Called "Step 'n' Copy," and by many other names, this was essentially a "follow-the-leader" game. If the clampers stretched from one stage head to another, boys followed the leader by running across the ice pans. Some clampers weren't big enough to bear the youngster's weight so one had to run fast to keep from going down with the ice pan. This game was often forbidden by parents but that didn't stop the practice, even though the punishment for coming home soaking wet and freezing was often more severe than the wetting.

C oastal Boats

Because of its long coastline and the scattering of small settlements throughout Newfoundland and Labrador, providing freight, mail and passenger service to the outports was always expensive and often irregular. Coasting schooners originally  provided this service, motivated by profit and not service. Some of these vessels were schooners, originally used in the fishing business, that were utilized and sometimes converted to a certain degree to accommodate freight, mail and passengers traveling to and from St. John's and around the outport settlements. Governments sometimes subsidized the trips made by these vessels because of the service they rendered to the outports.

After self-government came to Newfoundland, attempts were made to provide a more regular service. This was done at the expense of taxpayers, as none of these services ever made a profit and mostly they lost large amounts of money over the years. In spite of the fact that the coastal service was a non-profit enterprise it provided a priceless service to the small-business fisherfolk trying to eke out a living in the outports.

The earlier vessels were known as "sailing packets," which plied the waters around Conception Bay as long ago as 1827. Because they relied on how often, how long, how hard and in which direction the wind blew, the service they provided was mostly irregular and unreliable.

The first government owned steam ship (which could offer a more regular service because it didn't rely on wind) was the *Victoria*. In 1860, she made alternate two-week trips from St. John's, north along the east coast and back, and along the south coast and back. The following year a number of Newfoundland companies chartered ships to the government to be used in the coastal service. In the late 1800s, Robert Gillespie Reid gained a contract to build the Newfoundland Railway across the province with branch lines connecting more important bays and areas of the province. Part of the contract was to provide a coastal boat service that would support and connect the rail lines to many outports. Vessels serving the Labrador coast, where settlements were fewer, less populated and farther apart, carried medical doctors to serve the sick and injured. The coastal boat sometimes also provided ambulance service to the nearest port with a hospital, both in Labrador and on the Island.

The Newfoundland Railway chose Port aux Basques to be its western terminus in 1893 and a new ferry intended for service to North Sydney, Nova Scotia, was built in Scotland. In October 1897, the new vessel named the SS *Bruce* arrived, but the docks at Port aux Basques had not been completed. As a result, from October until June 1898 (when it reverted to Port aux Basques), the *Bruce* operated from Little Placentia (later renamed Argentia) to North Sydney.

The Bruce was one of many ships the Newfoundland Railway had built in Scotland, but most of the others were used in the coastal service, beginning with the *Glenco*, which was put on the Notre Dame Bay run in 1899.

The tasks that the masters of these steamers had to undertake was phenomenal, as they had to navigate relatively large vessels into unknown waters with charts that were on too small a scale to show the rocks and shoals in most areas. Armed with a simple magnetic compass (their only onboard navigation device) and without local charts, they learned the rocks, shoals and landmarks. These ship's masters had to find their way into small harbours at night and tie up at wharves that were sometimes nothing more than stage heads, meant to accommodate much smaller craft. If there was no one on the wharf to take the mooring lines, the master had to maneuver the ship close enough for one of his crew to jump on the wharf to take the lines and secure the ship. This procedure, which would horrify deep sea masters, was carried out by these inshore navigators on a regular basis. Often the masters of these ships learned the route so well that it was said that in restricted visibility, if a point of land, tree or rock appeared out of the fog they knew their exact position. These vessels maintained fairly regular schedules, except when suddenly interrupted by a medical emergency, engine trouble, bad weather etc. Because of their local navigational knowledge many masters were kept on the same route for a long time. Captain Alfie Elliott, for instance, was on the Green Bay route for 40 years. He was a colourful character whose name was known in every settlement. On one occasion, because it was stormy, Captain Elliott passed by one scheduled port of call. When he arrived at the next port, about 20 miles away, he was met on the wharf by a man who told him that there was a telegram for him at the post office. The telegram was from a man who had been waiting to board the ship at the port which Alfie had passed. The message referred to the Sankey Song Book, the book of hymns with which Alfie was quite familiar. The message read, "Sankey, hymn number 63, 'While on others thou art calling, do not pass me by.'"

Captain Elliott's reply was, "Sankey, hymn number 1, "Hold the fort for I am coming,'" whereupon he went back to fetch the man.

Another valuable service provided by the coastal boats was taking fishermen (and often their families) to and from fishing grounds, especially those in

Labrador. Those fishermen operated small boats from the Labrador coast and were known as "stationers." After the vessel left St. John's and made ports of call in Conception Bay, Trinity Bay, Bonavista Bay and Notre Dame Bay, the vessel would gradually fill up with people and provisions, including hens, goats, pigs and other animals, as well as 30 - 33 foot trap skiffs tied up on the davits outside the life boats – all bound for a season of fishing on the Labrador coast. The cost of a ticket for fishermen from any Newfoundland community to the Labrador coast was $6. It remained that price until the cod moratorium in the 1990s. Some of the stationers found themselves at the end of the season without a means home or money for the tickets. The coastal boats always took these people aboard and transported them back, whether or not they ever collected the fare.

Known as "steamers," the coastal boats that visited Newfoundland and Labrador communities on a regular basis were always a welcome sight to outport residents. The "coastal" or "government" wharf at which the ship usually tied up was often filled with residents looking for a bit of news, a package, or to meet someone travelling on the boat. The hand-shaking and hugging, children running around and crackies barking, and shouts passed between people on the wharf and the boat made the event somewhat festive. Some communities had no government wharf or other suitable wharf and the steamers had to anchor in the harbour. In these instances, mail, freight, passengers and animals – including horses and cattle – had to be transported by local residents in their rowboats and motorboats.

In spite of the adverse conditions under which these coastal ships operated, accidents were few and usually minor, with never a loss of life. Though three ships, the SS *Invermore*, SS *Fife* and MV *William Carson*, were lost on the coastal service.

On the Gulf service, accidents and acts of God resulted in loss of vessels and the lives of both crewmembers and passengers. But these were few in number, considering the fog so prevalent in that area. The greatest loss involving a railway vessel on the Gulf service, however, was neither an accident nor an act of God. On October 14, 1942, German submarine U-69 was prowling the Cabot Strait when it came across the SS *Caribou* returning to Port aux Basques and torpedoed her. The shot blasted her out of the water and took the lives of 137 of her 239 passengers and crew.

The completion of the highway across Newfoundland in 1965, connecting nearly all communities on the Island saw the number of coastal boats decrease. Today the service is relegated to island communities and areas without roads, such as sections of the South Coast of Newfoundland, and parts of the Labrador coast.

Collecting Ballast

Ballast was needed in large quantities when government wharves, breakwaters or causeways had to be built. This was usually in the form of fallen cliff rocks that were collected by nearby residents, transported by small boat to the site and sold by weight. Although not lucrative enough for someone to make a living, collecting ballast did bring in extra money. When the causeway between Coley's Point North and Bay Roberts North was being built, collecting ballast was lucrative enough to have the locals call it a "Klondike," which the causeway is now called. Taking its name from the causeway, the annual festival in Bay Roberts is called the "Klondike Festival."

Contrabanding

Obtaining tax-free booze is prevalent in most societies and this province is no exception. In the early days of settlement, most of the alcohol consumed in this province came from Europe. Later on, rum from the Caribbean was imported. Duties were paid on this rum, but oftentimes some of it slipped past the excise officer and some people got a gallon or a bottle without paying any tax.

Most of the contrabanding in Newfoundland had to do with the foreign country of France, which is right next door with its colonial islands of St. Pierre et Miquelon. All kinds of scams were pulled to get tax-free liquor from those two islands over the years. If a revenue or police boat was bearing down on a vessel carrying cases of contraband liquor, the smugglers would sometimes tie sacks of salt to the wooden cases and throw them overboard. The heavy salt would take the liquor to the bottom. The contrabanders knew how long it would take for salt to dissolve, so they would be back at the same spot later when the cases of booze started popping up to the surface.

During prohibition in the United States a number of Newfoundland vessels, captains and crews were involved in the "rum-running" trade, especially the trade between St. Pierre et Miquelon and the States. Some captains had their schooners painted white on one side and black on the other, so that an excise boat would watch the white schooner it was keeping an eye on sail into a harbour then allow a black one to sail out unhampered. Some of these rum-runners were caught, tried and convicted, but many were not. For them it was a lucrative supplement to the legal ventures in which the schooner might be otherwise engaged, like coasting or fishing.

Dancing

The ever-popular step-dance is one of foot-work and leg-work. The best step-dancer is one who can keep his upper body erect and his arms at the side while light-footedly doing a series of heel and toe movements and other leg gyrations

and movements. This type of step-dancing is called "close to the floor." It is a very fast dance, usually done solo, but a number of dancers may be seen on the floor at one time doing their own interpretation of the music being played, not always in unison with anybody else.

Dancing a jig, also called step-dancing by some, requires a certain amount of foot stomping, as well as heel and toe and arm movements. As the dancers "plank 'er down" to the beat of a fast jig, their own foot-stomping becoming part of the music. At high points in the music they often shout "yahoo," "give 'er that, b'ys," or something else in keeping with the moment and the beat.

The old-fashioned waltz has long been a favourite for couples in this province. A man and woman would gracefully move around the floor to the 3/4-time beat of such favourites as "Harbour LeCou." Although participants move to the beat of the music in this dance, the movements aren't always structured. Sometimes, however, a waltz movement such as the three-step (three steps forward and one back) is utilized.

Square dancing in the form of quadrilles (involving four couples with about five movements) was common, and the most popular of these is a dance called the Lancers. This is a Newfoundland variation of the dance which was introduced in England in 1817. Among the movements of the Newfoundland Lancers is the star, basket and thread-the-needle. One of the most important people in a community was known as the "caller." This person knew all the square dance moves and directed the dancers in the intricate movements of the Lancers.

All the popular dances, such as the charleston, rock and roll, the twist and others have made their way to these shores in their time and new ones continue to do so.

Dole and the Depression

After government came to Newfoundland, fishermen who had a bad season because of the scarcity of fish, low market prices or the failure of their subsistence crops, could get some kind of government assistance to help their families survive. During the Great Depression this assistance was known as the dole and amounted to six cents per family per day. Even back then no family could survive on six cents a day, which made outport dwellers luckier than their St. John's counterparts. There was land in the outports on which to grow crops, and most families could fish for some of their own food in season, or salt their fish to put away for the winter. But in the outports money was still needed to buy such staples as flour, molasses, sugar, beans, peas, kerosene for lamps etc. and dole times were hard times.

In St. John's, where the livelihood of the working man depended almost solely on wages, the high unemployment made conditions much worse. There it was much harder to survive on six cents a day. At times this caused rioting, before and during the Depression.

Some men would refuse to take the dole unless they were given the opportunity to work on the roads or on some other government job to earn it. In fact, many of the province's earlier roads were built on what was known as "able-bodied relief."

Ducks and Drakes

In this game of skipping flat stones across a water surface, after the stone is thrown the following rhyme is chanted:
> "A duck and a drake
> And a double pancake
> And a penny to pay the old baker
> A hop and a scotch
> In another notch
> Slitherum, slitherum, take her."

"Duck" is chanted on the first bounce, "drake" on the second, and so on. The object is to make the stone bounce off the water surface enough times to finish the rhyme.

Another version of this rhyme is:
> "A duck and a drake
> A codfish cake
> And a bottle of brandy
> Ho, ho, ho, ho."

Education

Although there was some formal education in Newfoundland in the 1700s for people who could afford it, public education didn't start until the early 1800s. Because government revenue depended on customs and excise taxes, it could not totally support an education system. Education in this province was driven and supported by various churches, who made a very significant contribution to education for the times. Because of the lack of money to fund schools, teachers were underpaid.

In the years leading up to 1843, the many independent schools, (included St. John's Charity School, the Orphan Asylum School, various classical academies and the schools of the Newfoundland School Society) had been non-denominational. In that year the Protestant-sponsored Education Act was made law, which inaugurated the denominational system of education. The educational situation throughout the 1850s, '60s and early '70s was a continuing struggle to maintain adequate schooling on limited resources. Later in the century, government grants for education were increased and a system for the training of pupil-teachers in St. John's colleges was put into place. These grants were divided between Roman Catholic and Protestant schools; but in 1874 Bishop Feild persuaded the government to divide the Protestant portion of the grant between Anglicans and Methodists. The three denominations lost little time in opening new schools (with the Methodists in the lead), often at the expense of teachers' salaries, which declined in the following decades. By 1900 less than 50 per cent of the children aged five to 15 were attending elementary schools, the lowest participation rate since 1861. In 1893 the Council of Higher Education, an inter-denominational body, was formed with the primary purpose of setting examinations and devising appropriate curricula. In 1920, a national Department of Education with a Minister was established, and in 1925 Memorial University College (which was later given university status) was officially opened.

One of the devastating effects the 1929 Depression had on Newfoundland and Labrador was the cuts to education. The grants were cut from $1 million to $500,000, which saw further cuts in teachers' salaries and school closures. Yet the Depression did bring some good to Newfoundland education. In their wisdom, the seven men who made up the government at the time believed that education was one way to increase the Dominion's economic status, and they increased expenditure on education and opened more schools in the province. The seven Commissioners also tried to replace the school system at the time with a non-denominational one that would have allowed more flexibility and a better education for the Dominion's children without having to spend more money. Churches, who were afraid of losing control of the children they intended to be their future parishioners, were powerful enough to veto this plan.

When Newfoundland became part of Canada in 1949 and Commission of Government was replaced by the Liberal government under Joey Smallwood, the great majority of the schools were still small, wooden, one-room, one-teacher institutions, and the hold of the churches on education was as strong as ever. But with the transfer payments and social security benefits from the federal government, education at all levels was extended and upgraded. Large central high schools were built and great numbers of students entered the newly founded Memorial University. From this university more teachers received a better education to staff the expanding number of schools. Vocational Schools were also established in the province.

The Salvation Army had been granted the same educational rights guaranteed under the Constitution as the Roman Catholic Church, the Anglican Church of Canada and the United Church of Canada, to which the Pentecostal Assemblies was also added. The formation of a single consolidated board by these major Protestant denominations followed shortly afterwards, and in most respects the educational system had been brought up to national standards.

A decline in population and a large drop in the number of children being born saw the denominational system replaced by a more financially feasible system with the integration of students in the 1990s under Brian Tobin. In spite of rising costs and the struggling economy, which makes it hard for government to keep up with maintenance of school buildings, bus transportation etc, the education system in Newfoundland and Labrador is comparable with others in North America. Memorial University has grown to be the biggest post-secondary institution east of Montreal and has a reputation that attracts students from all over the world.

Farming

In the early days, farmers were also fishermen who grew crops to feed their own families. But in later years farms began producing crops for sale. By 1836, the agricultural lands covered 11,062 acres and expanded to 41,168 by 1855. In 1949 there were 4,000 people who did various types of farming out of a total population of 322,000 residents.

There have been a number of mink farms over the years and mink farming is still done in the province.

Today there are about 643 registered farms in the province and some 100 food processors. The agriculture industry employs about 6,200 people and total sales average about $500 million a year. The leading crops include vegetables (especially potatoes, turnips, cabbage, and carrots), greenhouse products and berries. In recent years cool climate crops, such as silage corn have been introduced to the province. Farms with a total acreage of 2,000 now produce this cattle feed, which increases milk production. The principal non-crop agricultural products are livestock, dairy and poultry products.

Fish Plants

The coming of electricity and modern technology in the mid-1900s changed the way fish would be processed forever. The demand for frozen fish increased, while the demand for salt fish declined. Fish plants, which hired and trained workers in new methods of processing were built in bigger Newfoundland outports. By 1972 there were around 50 of these plants operating around the province. Canada expanded its maritime economic zone to 200 miles in the 1970s and the number of plants quadrupled by the late 1980s. With the decline in codfish stocks there were often not enough fish to keep these plants going, and some went out of business. The decline of codfish, the biggest predator of crabs, saw an increase in the number of crabs that could be caught. There was a demand for crab at that time, so some fish plants changed production lines to accommodate this new product. Fish plants also began to accommodate other formerly under-utilized species, such as shrimp, lump roe, sole and others.But even with all the new species being processed, there was never enough product to keep the 140 or so fish plants going full-time. Workers could seldom get year-round work and sometimes not even enough work to qualify for unemployment insurance benefits. Now like the cod, the under-utilized species are on the decline and there are too many fish plants, too many plant workers and too many fishermen. To sustain the fish stocks, a renewable resource if maintained properly, many of these fish plants will have to cease operations.

Flying Kites

In some outport communities kites were slightly different than the conventional ones. These kites were made by crossing two sticks, the horizontal one being shorter than the vertical, and tying them together where they cross. A portion of a wooden barrel hoop was then fastened to the ends of the crossmember around the top of the vertical stick. A piece of string completed the perimeter of the kite. Brown paper was often used to finish the kite, but a favourite were pages torn from old magazines. There was usually someone in the community who subscribed to magazines who would give you old copies. These often had big pictures which could be pasted on the front for decoration.

Paste wasn't a problem. Some flour and water mixed together, with a bit of Gillette's Lye added to keep the mixture from getting mouldy, made great paste. Magazine pages were then glued on both sides around the perimeter formed by the string and the barrel hoop.

A piece of string, called the bridle, was attached to the top and bottom. The end of a reel of fishing line was attached to the bridle. The tail of the kite was made out of fishing line with rolled-up magazine pages tied at intervals of about a foot. The longer the tail, the more stable was the kite in the sky. A brown paper bag was blown up and attached to the bottom of the tail. The brisk spring breezes would carry the kite aloft and for a while you could still see the cigar in Winston Churchill's mouth. By the time the whole reel of line was let out you could no longer make out Churchill's magazine-cover features because the kite was just the silhouette of an ice cream in the sky.

Some youngsters made conventional kites, while box kites were sometimes made and flown. Box kites were made by crossing two sticks of equal length, in the form of the letter "X" and making a perimeter of string. As with conventional kites, paper (usually brown paper) was pasted to only one side. The box kite wasn't square, or even rectangular – it was taller than it was wide, and the two sticks crossed at a point closer to the top, making it narrower than the bottom. This kite had two bridles that diagonally criss-crossed the kite's front.

Youngsters would sometimes send a message up to their kite. This was done by writing the message on a piece of paper. A hole was punched in the paper and the end of the kite line was inserted through it. In a short while the wind would deliver the message.

Kite-flying was once popular all over the province, including the bigger centres such as St. John's.

Flags and Emblems

Emblems representing leadership, authority or dominance have been around for thousands of years. Flags have been around since cloth or similar material was invented. Some nations had two flags, one used at home and one to identify their ships at sea.

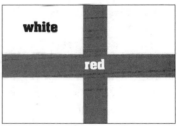

St. George's Cross
1277-1707

In 1497, when John Cabot made his historic voyage to the new world, he sailed under the flag of England and Wales, which at that time was the Cross of St. George. This was also the flag in 1583, when Sir Humphrey Gilbert proclaimed Newfoundland an English possession.

After King James VI of Scotland ascended to the English throne in 1603, thereby becoming James I of England, the national flags of England and Scotland on land continued to be, respectively, the red St. George's cross and the white St. Andrew's cross, which was a diagonal white cross against a blue background. Although, Scotland and England (which included Wales) were one kingdom, they were essentially two countries. Each having their own parliament, legal and religious systems, coinage, taxation and trade. The Scottish feared that union with England would see them swallowed up by the larger nation, as had happened with Wales four centuries earlier.

The British Flag
1606-1801

Confusion arose, however, as to what flag would be appropriate at sea. In 1606, the two flags were made into one by placing the red cross on top of the white cross. This was still the flag of England when John Guy established a settlement at Cupids in 1610; and in 1621, when George Calvert, aka Lord Baltimore after conversion to Catholicism, established a colony at Ferryland.

In 1707, at a poorly attended Scottish parliament, the MPs voted to unite with England. The Scottish parliament was dissolved and England and Scotland became one country. However, it was almost 100 years later that the present Union Flag came into being. England ceased to be a sovereign nation and became part of the larger Great Britain. The St. George's Cross retained England's identity as a distinct division of Great Britain and, indeed the St. George's Cross flag continues to represent the England of Great Britain.

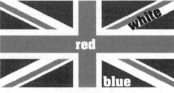

In 1801, Ireland united with England and the Cross of St. Patrick, a diagonal red cross on a white ground, was added to the new Union Flag. Although popularly called the Union Jack, it is officially the Union Flag. The Union Jack is merely a Union flag, not necessarily the same shape and usually smaller; "Union Jack" only applies when it is flown on the jackstaff of a ship.

The Union Flag
1801-1980

The Great Seal of the Colony of Newfoundland was given royal approval in 1827. It depicts Mercury, the god of commerce and merchandise, presenting to Britannia, a kneeling fisherman who offers her the harvest of the sea. Above them are the Latin words "Terra Nova," meaning Newfoundland; and below, the Latin "Haec Tibi Dona Fero," meaning "These gifts I bring thee." The shield held by Mercury is a circular depiction of the Union Flag.

The Great Seal
1827-Present

The first known native flag was created by the Native Society of Newfoundland, formed in 1840. The banner depicted two clasped hands extending to the elbows and a spruce tree in the centre. The tree rose from the joined palms, and underneath, running the length of the arms was the word "Philanthropy." The arms and the tree were green, the letters were white and the background was pink.

Native Society Flag
1840-1843

According to Fred Adams in his book, *Potpourri of Old St. John's*, "A great deal of ill feeling was engendered by the society until February 1843. During a big haul of wood for Bishop Fleming, a fight broke out between the *Bush Borns* (people of Irish descent) and the *Old Country* (Irish immigrants), as to who had the biggest haul of wood. The bishop called the ringleaders together and advised them to stop fighting and join the "Pink and Green" together. This they did, by inserting a piece of neutral white between then two colours, and the *Pink, White and Green flag* was born." The following song about the tri-colour flag was frequently sung during the early 20th century, and became an alternative national anthem. It was written by Archbishop Michael F. Howley in 1902.

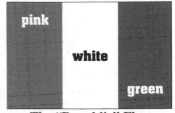

The "Republic" Flag
1843-Present

Government House Flag
1864-1870

"The pink the rose of England shows,
The green St. Patrick's emblem bright,
While in between the spotless sheen
St. Andrew.s Cross displays the white.

Then hail the pink, the white, the green;
Our patriot ring long may it stand,
Our sire lands twine their emblem trine
To form the flag of Newfoundland.

What e'er betide our ocean bride
That nestles midst the Atlantic foam,
Still far and wide we'll raise with pride
Our native flag, o'er hearth and home.

Should e'er the hand of fate demand
Some future change in our career,
We ne'er will yield on flood or field
The flag we honour and revere.

Fling out the flag o'er creek and crag;
Pink, white and green, so fair, so grand;
Long may it sway o'er bight and bay,
Around the shores of Newfoundland."

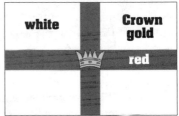

The Blue Ensign
1870-1904

The Governor's Flag
1870-1904

The Red Ensign
1904-1975

Although the flag was never given any royal or official sanction, it served well for some years. In recent times this flag has taken on the moniker, "Republican Flag," and is symbolic of unfair treatment of this province by the Government of Canada, under the Terms of Union.

**The Blue Ensign
1904-1975**

The official flags at the time were variations of the Union Flag, including the Government House Flag, in use from 1862 to 1870. It depicted a red St. George's Cross with a gold crown in the centre on a white background

Between 1870 and 1904, the Dominion was represented by two flags. The Blue Ensign had a royal blue background with the Union Flag

**The Governor's Flag
1904-1975**

in the top left corner and a gold and red crown inside a white circular background to the right. The words "Terra Nova" were written below the crown. Also in use from 1870 to 1904 was the "Governor's Flag," which featured a Union Flag with a gold and red crown inside a white circular background, surrounded by green and red laurel leaf. The words "Terra Nova" were written below the crown.

In 1904 the Dominion removed the crown emblem from its Blue Ensign and Governor's Flag and replaced it with the Great Seal. In that year the Red Ensign, a merchant ensign, was also introduced. This flag was only different from the Blue Ensign in that its background was red where the other was blue. This flag represented the Dominion's interests at sea. These three flags served in official capacity until 1975.

In 1928 the Dominion of Newfoundland adopted a coat of arms, which is still in official use today. Originally granted to David Kirke, Governor of Newfoundland from 1638 to 1651, by King Charles I of England, this coat arms consists of a red shield bearing a silver cross with lions and unicorns in the quarters. The supporters holding the shield are interpretations of Newfoundland's native Beothuk people. An elk, meant to represent Newfoundland's caribou herds, stands above the shield. The Latin motto, "Quaerite prime Regnum Dei," translates to "Seek ye first the kingdom of God," from the New Testament, Matthew 7:23.

**Coat of Arms,
1928-Present**

The British derived flags of Newfoundland differ from those of other Canadian provinces because Newfoundland did not join the Canadian Confederation until 1949. Thus the garland on the flag of the governor was laurel not maple, the badges also appeared on Blue Ensigns, and the Red Ensign was a merchant ensign and not a provincial land flag like those of other provinces.

The Union Flag, which symbolized Newfoundland's membership in the British Empire, was adopted as the Dominion's official flag by the National Flag Act of 1931, and was re-adopted as the provincial flag in 1952. It was originally intended that there should be three national flags, but this was amended to just one, the Union Jack. The circular badge on the governor's flag and ensigns was retained and not replaced by the shield of the arms.

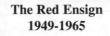

The Stars and Stripes 1940-1994.

In 1940, during WWII, The United States leased land in Newfoundland and Labrador for bases for their armed forces. For all intents and purposes, these land tracts became part of the United States. Babies born to American citizens on bases here were deemed to automatically be US citizens, and certain legal acts performed on the bases were deemed to have been performed in the United States. The "Stars and Stripes," although buffeted by the breezes on an alien shore, was as symbolic of Americanism here as it was in its home country. The Stars and Stripes flew in this province until the US base at Argentia was closed in 1994.

The Red Ensign 1949-1965

Confederation with Canada saw Newfoundland lose its Dominion status and become a province of another Dominion. The Dominion of Canada's flag at the time was also a Red Ensign, incorporating a Union Flag in the top left hand corner and the Coat of Arms of Canada on the fly. This flag was changed in 1965 when the current flag was adopted. The present Canadian Flag has a vertical red bar at each end and a white centre which is background to a red maple leaf.

The Canadian Flag 1965-Present

Having the Union Flag as our provincial symbol started to cause problems. Many people were mistaking residents as British. The problem

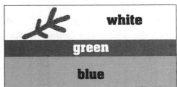

The Labrador Flag 1974-Present

was not only prevalent among people from the island, but those from Labrador as well.

In 1974 the Labrador Heritage Society had a flag designed to represent that part of the province. The flag they came up with is white in the upper portion and shows a green spruce twig in the left hand corner. Below this is a green horizontal bar and five horizontalbars of the same light blue colour. The spruce twig was chosen because this tree is common in all regions of Labrador. The three branches of the twig symbolize the three peoples of Labrador: the Inuit, the Innu, and the European settlers. The twig grows from one stalk, representing the common origin of all humanity. The shorter inner twig represents the past, while the larger outer twig represents a brighter future. The white represents snow, the green symbolizes the land, while the blue represents the waters of Labrador's rivers, lakes and the sea.

In 1980, the province as a whole adopted its own flag. Designed by Newfoundland artist Christopher Pratt, this flag symbolizes the past, present and future of Newfoundland and Labrador. The flag was first flown on Discovery Day, June 24, 1980. In this flag, the primary colours of red, gold and blue are placed against a background of white. The white represents snow and ice; the blue represents the sea; red represents human effort;

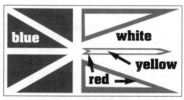

**The Newfoundland
and Labrador flag
1980-Present**

and gold, our confidence in ourselves. The blue triangles stand for our Commonwealth heritage in its similarity to Britain's Union Flag. The red triangles represent the island and mainland portions of the province. The gold arrow points toward our optimism for a bright future. When hung as a banner (vertically), the arrow closely resembles a sword – a reminder of the great sacrifice made by our province's war veterans. In this position the white centre incorporates the Christian cross, Beothuk and Naskapi ornamentation, and the maple leaf's outline. The trident emphasizes Newfoundland and Labrador's continued dependence on and connection to the fishery and marine resources.

Football

Football, or soccer as it is known in North America today, was a very popular game in Newfoundland and Labrador, played both in summer and winter. By the time Christmas rolled around the harbours were usually frozen over, which provided a great venue for the game. Christmas Day football games were very popular. Saltwater ice was level and not slippery, and it was soft enough to accommodate the securing of goal posts. Although goal posts were sometimes poles, they were often nothing more than frozen horse turds. Teams were chosen by captains, who often picked the youngest boys last. There was very little team organization in these games and sometimes all members of both teams, except for the goalies, could be seen chasing the ball in areas that would be considered "way out of bounds" in a formal game.

Football games were also played on land in winter. A snow-covered field or meadow was chosen and the boys ran back and forth over the selected area until the snow was sufficiently trampled. The surface of the playing area on land was often much more slippery than on saltwater ice, and often when someone made a kick at the ball he went arse over teakettle.

Before proper footballs made the scene, inflated pig bladders and cow bladders, both very durable, were used instead.

G rowing Vegetables

Many visitors to this province notice that most of the older homes and outbuildings are built over the top of a big rock. They immediately assume that the location was chosen to give the house a firmer foundation. Although there is some truth in this, that was not the real reason the site was chosen.

To survive in this part of the world required not only what the sea had to offer, but what could be gleaned from the land as well. Every fishing family in the outports kept vegetable gardens. Wherever there was a bit of soil, something was planted. No one would waste good soil by building a house over it.

The soil was tilled in the spring by a man (and sometimes a woman or older child) following a horse-drawn plough. If a fisherman didn't own a plough, he borrowed his neighbour's. If he didn't own a horse, he borrowed that too.

Like making fish on a flake, tending the vegetable garden was a family affair. From the planting and rowing, through the weeding to the harvesting, all family members big enough to take part dug in with the rest.

The big crop was potatoes, but most families also grew cabbages, turnips, carrots and sometimes parsnips and beets. At the end of one vegetable garden, a rhubarb patch could usually be found. This provided jam and relish for the winter.

Harvesting was the best part of gardening, especially for boys. They found joy in uncovering "potato balls" (small, green immature potatoes) that were soft enough to be fired at friends, sometimes with a sling shot. When dug, the vegetables were measured in barrels and were transported to the cellar in wheelbarrows or hand barrows, or in wooden barrels on horse-and-dray.

By spring the eyes of the potatoes were starting to sprout and a number were put aside to be used as seed potatoes. The seed potatoes were cut into chunks, with one sprouting eye left on each chunk. These chunks were planted in rows at regular intervals with the sprout facing up. Other vegetables were planted from seeds (usually store-bought), while the rhubarb patch flourished every year without much care and attention.

G rowl

The name "Growl" is popu-
larly used to refer to a card
game known as Auction
120s, or 120s. This is a team
game that was mostly played
in a very boisterous manner.
There was much shouting,
sometimes swearing, and
slamming of fists (often fists
holding a winning card) on
the table. There was often
growling at these games, particularly at an opponent who made
a good move or a partner who made a bad one.

The object of each team was to get 120 points before the other. Each player
was dealt five cards and each trick they won gave them five points. The person
with the highest card in each deal got 10 points for that trick, making it a total
of 30 points to be won each round. The best card won each trick and the best
cards were trumps. Trumps were the suite of cards chosen by the winning bidder. Players could make a bid between 15 and 30. If the highest bidder got the
number of points they bid or more they kept the points; if they didn't, they lost
the amount of their bid. If a player felt that with the help of his partners he had
enough cards to take all tricks, he would bid 30 for 60. If his team won all the
tricks they went up by 60 points, and if not they went down by 30 points. This
meant that sometimes a team would "go in the hole," or have less than zero. If
this happened, when the other team was within a hand of winning, the game got
more exciting, as the losing team often made impossible bids to keep the opponents from winning. The bid of "slam for the game" was often invoked at this
point. As in a 30 for 60 bid, in a "slam for the game" bid, all five tricks had to
be won. If the bidding team managed to do that they won. If not they went a further 60 points in the hole. This caused many a growl between the losing partners. The game of Growl came by its name honestly.

A variation of this game, known as 'railroad," was played if there were five
players. In this game the successful bidder called for a certain card he didn't
have. The person who had that card would become his partner for the round and
they both went up or down together.

The following poem, " A Good Newfoundland Game of Growl," by Tim
Brown describes the action:

Frank is pounding the table and shaking his fist
'Cause Aunt Anne just dragged out his trump with whist

Says Lorraine, "My cards are as black as the soot
And I'm sitting here holding a hand like a foot"

I cuts off with the Queen and comes back with the Jack
I allow that there's nar decent card in the pack
I picks up Anne's diamond and Uncle Ben's Ace
And that wipes the grin off Uncle Ben's face

A trump to the board to get home the five
We got two tricks in so we're still alive
But it don't take long for me high hopes to fall
Someone else got the five, not my partner at all

'Tis a good game of Newfoundland growl
'Tis a game of one-twenty
With arguments plenty
That's a good Newfoundland game of growl

Now Aunt Anne shouts as she jumps to her feet
"I'm poisoned 'cause trumps is as scarce as hen's teet'
'Tis just as well now to throw in the towel
But, my son, 'tis some fun with a good game of growl"

Now I opens the bid with a twenty or so
And says a quick prayer that they won't let me go
Well the next thing I knows me partner just roared
"T'irty fer sixty with a lay to the board!"

Now me partner just threw all his cards at the wall
And I'm cursin' him, and he's cursin' us all
As he stomps out the door he's wearing a scowl
But he'll be back next week for a good game of growl

For a good game of Newfoundland growl
A good game of auction
That comes down to boxin'
That's a good Newfoundland game of growl

Hand-clapping Games

Two children face each other and play a game, sometimes called "Clapsies." In synchronization the two (usually girls) clap their own hands, cross arms in front of chest, clap their own hands again, then clap hands with their partner three times, all the time reciting:

"Miss Mary Mack, Mack, Mack,
All dressed in black, black, black,
With silver buttons, buttons, buttons,
Down her back, back, back.
She could not read, read, read
She could not write, write, write,
But she could smoke, smoke, smoke,
Her father's pipe, pipe, pipe.
She asked her mother, mother, mother,
For fifty cents, cents, cents,
To see the elephant, elephant, elephant.
Jump over the fence, fence, fence.
He jumped so high, high, high,
He reached the sky, sky, sky,
And he never came back, back, back,
Till the end of July, 'ly, 'ly."

This chant is then sung a second time, this time at a quicker tempo. Each time through the lyrics the tempo gets faster and faster until the two can no longer keep up and the game ends with gales of laughter and at least two winners, as the game is as much fun to watch as it is to play. This game is still played today.

H and-Lining and Jigging

A hand-line is a single line with a weighted single hook called a dabber or dapper. The dabber is handmade by fishermen by placing a fish hook into a mould and pouring hot lead around it. Bait is then placed on the dabber and fish are hooked by the mouth. This method of fishing, used from the beginning, can catch fish only when they are hungry. It was used by inshore fishermen and by dories lowered over the sides of schooners fishing the offshore banks. Sometimes this was done between the time a trawl was set and when it was hauled. Like the trawl, the hand-line only catches fish when they are hungry. When fish were plentiful bait-fishing was a viable way to fish, but with time came new technology and ways to catch more fish, more quickly. As fish stocks decreased so did bait-fishing, until a living could no longer be made using a trawl, and one used a hand-line only to get a meal for dinner. For that "jigging" worked as well, if not better.

In jigging for fish the line has a jigger instead of a dabber. This device, which has two hooks facing away from each other, is handmade in a different mould. The end result resembles a silver-grey fish. The jigger is lowered to a fathom above bottom where codfish are known to feed, and the line is jerked up and down. The action of the jigger in the water has the appearance of a wounded fish. Numbers of codfish rush for this meal and one or sometimes two are snagged on the hooks by the upward action of the jigger. The fisherman, feeling the strike, then pulls the fish in, hand over hand.

Another jigger, known as the Japanese jigger, was introduced to Newfoundland. This factory-made, exact replica of the Newfoundland jigger was shinier and was made of steel alloy. Some fishermen said they were better, while others disagreed. Another jigger, factory-made in Norway but used locally was known as the "Norwegian jigger." Resembling a fish in only a very linear way, this good-quality steel alloy jigger was also shiny. Instead of two hooks, this device had three that were back-to-back at 120° angles to each other; and instead of being firmly fastened to the jigger, they swivelled on a ring. These worked well at times, and sometimes seemed to catch more fish than the other jiggers, while at other times only the other jiggers seemed to work. From my own personal experience, I found that when fish were in the mood to chase a jigger, it didn't much matter what jigger was used.

Because this method of fishing often killed fish, sometimes fish too small to be taken so they were left for the gulls, it is now against the law to use a jigger.

Hauling Houses

Sometimes families moved to get closer to a better fishing room, or for some other purpose. No one could afford to buy a house outright, mortgages were unheard of and the foundations were simply wooden

Hauling a House Across Land

shores anyway, so houses were hauled to the new location by the men of the community. If there was no snow on the ground, rollers, in the form of big poles, were placed under the house to be hauled. The majority of the volunteer house-haulers then manned the hauling rope while several men waited behind the house and as a pole became free they carried it to the front where it was placed to accommodate the moving house. They then went back to get the next pole at the rear of the house. One man was designated to sing "The Johnny Poker," a shanty (chanty) that coordinated the efforts of the men. This man would sing:

Hauling a House Over Ice

> "For it's to me Johnny Poker
> We will haul this heavy joker
> For it's to me Johnny Poker
> Haul!"

When the word "haul" was sung everyone pulled in unison and the house moved by the magic of music.

House hauling was always considered a bit of fun. During longer hauls that would sometimes take all day, the men were given a good meal provided by the lady who owned the house and prepared by herself with the help of other women in the community.

Floating a House

When a house had to be moved to a location across water it was some-times done in the win-ter, over ice; while in the summer it was floated using boats to tow it.

H ome Remedies and Cures

Without the availability of doctors and medical treatment, residents turned to home remedies that were either applied externally or taken orally to alleviate their medical problems. Among the external applications were hot or warm poultices, cold plasters and liniments.

Bread poultices made with a slice of bread and boiling water were often used in the treatment of abscesses, boils and carbuncles. Poultices made from combinations of ingredients that might include linseed, cod liver oil, oatmeal, onion, milk, salt, vinegar, soap, chickweed, juniper bark, fat pork, castor oil, molasses, sugar, mustard or flour were used to cure a wide variety of ailments. These could be asthma, bronchitis, colds, eczema, pneumonia, pleurisy, rheumatism, minor infections and sprains. Baking soda was used in poultice form to treat fly bites, hives and skin rashes. It is still taken internally to relieve heartburn and stomach gas, as well as for cleaning teeth. Cow dung was used to treat bruises sprains, and frostbite.

Human urine was used to cure skin conditions such as chapped hands, chilblains, freckles, pimples, sore hands and sunburn. Cloths were used to apply the urine, but sometimes direct application was utilized especially to the hands. Although this cure is no longer used, there is some scientific evidence that urine can be beneficial to certain skin conditions.

Pieces of flannel, sometimes made into items of clothing, were worn by sufferers of colds, bronchitis, pleurisy, pneumonia and rheumatism. Sometimes flannel, especially red flannel, was covered in goose grease, camphorated oil or turpentine (or combinations of these) before being applied to the body.

Myrrh from balsam fir and spruce trees, which has the styptic properties to curb bleeding, was often used on cuts. The powder from puff balls, known locally as "horses' farts" was also used to stop and control bleeding, as was flour and cobwebs. Camphorated oil was applied externally to the chest to fight colds and other lung ailments; it was also applied externally and taken internally to cure sore throats and rheumatism. Cold water or snow was applied to frostbitten areas to gently rewarm them until the sensation returned. The brain of the jaybird was also used to treat frostbite. To treat blisters sometimes a sewing needle was threaded with homespun wool, and the needle and wool were pulled through the blister and the ends cut off, leaving the wool to dry up the blister. Tea leaves, salt water and the intestines of rabbits were placed on closed eyelids to cure snow blindness. Brown paper was dipped in vinegar and applied to the head to cure headaches. Warm olive oil was used to cure an earache, as was cigarette or pipe smoke blown into the affected ear. A number of treatments were used for arthritis and rheumatism including external treatments such as the application of mustard plaster, liniments, eelskins, dissolved jellyfish and red flannel coverings. Butter, cod liver oil, kerosene, vaseline, olive oil, boiled willow bark, boiled alder roots, and soap were used to treat burns and scalds. Calamine lotion was and still is used on rashes, including those left by German measles (rubella). Goose grease, bear grease and pork fat were used to treat chest congestion, and steam from boiling kettles was used to treat bronchitis and other lung ailments. Blood from a black cat was sometimes used to treat stys. Ingrown toenails were treated by cutting a V-shaped notch in the nail. The roots of the water lily, sometimes called "beaver root," was used both as a tonic and an eye wash.

Soap enemas were sometimes used to treat constipation, as were concoctions that were taken internally. One such beverage made from black current roots; another was made from rhubarb roots, sugar and raisins.

There were various remedies taken internally to cure particular ailments. Among those was locally-produced cod liver oil which contains vitamins A and D and omega-3 fatty acids. Birds' hearts and rabbit livers, containing vitamin A were used to help with night blindness. Ginger wine was used for colds and upset stomachs. The cones or buds of two varieties of alders found in Newfoundland, *[Alnus crispa]* and *[Alnus rugosa]*, were used to steep a medicine taken orally to treat boils and rheumatism.

Concoctions taken orally to cure coughs included a mixture of turnip, sugar and wild cherry bark; and another of molasses mixed with kerosene, which was heated before it was drank. Sometimes this mixture was allowed to cool and form cough drops. Minard's Liniment was sometimes taken internally for colds and steeped blackberry roots were used for coughs.

Teas made from wild cherries, juniper berries, wild strawberries and the root of the raspberry bush were used to treat diarrhea. This tea was also put in the baby's bottle to fight colic. Teas made from the wild cherry tree and from dogberries were used to restore appetite. The tops and berries of the ground juniper plant were steeped and taken internally to treat bladder and kidney ailments, and stomach disorders.

Sheep manure was made into a drink and taken to get rid of ulcers and measles. A medicine made from the root of the pitcher plant was used as a treatment for smallpox. Cod liver oil; medicines made from alder buds, celery seeds, berries and roots of sarsaparilla; and gin mixed with sulphur were all taken internally as a cure for rheumatism and arthritis. A mixture of sulfur and molasses was taken internally to purify the blood. The snakeroot or yellow mores plant was made into tea and used to treat sores in the mouth and cold sores. Spruce beer, made by fermenting spruce buds, was used for coughs and also to treat scurvy. Squashberry jam and wine has been used for upset stomach. Toothache was and is treated by applying warm clove oil directly to the affected tooth.

The recipes for these remedies were often passed on from family to family, but sometimes people came up with medicines which they sold to others. The famous Newfoundland poet, E. J. Pratt, who would later become a professor at the University of Toronto and Poet Laureate of Canada, was first a Methodist minister in Newfoundland. Rev. Pratt peddled his "Universal Lung Healer," which contained spruce tops, wild cherry bark, fir bark and sarsaparilla.

Then there were cures that were almost superstitious in nature. A piece of green ribbon, a coloured string, a nutmeg or a flattened musket ball was worn around the neck to prevent a nosebleed. Passing a child through the limbs of a dogberry tree was believed to make the child immune to diseases such as measles, smallpox and rickets. A crustacean parasite found on codfish known as a fish doctor was sometimes worn around the neck as a charm against rheumatism and arthritis. Sometimes a pebble was placed under one's tongue, or a stone was put in one's pocket to cure a stitch (pain) in the side.

There were several "preventions" for rheumatism and arthritis. A haddock bone or fin was sometimes worn around the neck or carried in a pocket. Similarly a lodestone or a potato, especially one that had been stolen, was carried in a pocket or around the wrist or ankle. As well, copper and aluminum rings were worn for the same purpose.

A number of over-the-counter medicines have been used in Newfoundland and Labrador over the years, some of which actually served the purpose for which they were advertised. My grandfather, Jonas Cooper, strongly believed in Mecca Ointment, which he claimed, "could heal over a cat's arse overnight." Others had relatively little healing ability or worked only as a placebo cure. Some are still available in the province, while others are only available elsewhere. For instance, Scott's Emulsion is still available in countries in southeast Asia, such as Thailand. Included in the medicines manufactured for sale in this province are the following in alphabetical order: Absorbine Junior, Ayre's Cherry Cordial, Ayre's Sarsaparilla, Baby's Own Tablets, Beecham's Pills, Boracic Acid, Brick's Tasteless, Bromo Quinine Tablets, Buckley's Mixture, Carter's Little Liver Pills, Chafe's Spruce Beer, Dr. Agnew's Ointment, Dr. Bovel's Gum Salve, Dr. Chase's Cold Tablets, Dr. Chase's Kidney-Liver Pills,

Dr. Chase's Nerve Food, Dr. Chase's Ointment, Dr. Chase's Paradol, Dr. Chase's Syrup of Linseed and Turpentine, Dr. Hamilton's Pills, Dr. Nixon's Nixoderm, Dr. Pierce's Favourite Prescription, Dr. Pierce's Golden Medical Discovery, Dr. Strandgard's T. B. Medicine, Dr. Wilson's Herbine, Dr. Wistar's Balsam of Wild Cherry, Dodd's Kidney Pills, Fletcher's Castoria, Friar's Balsam, Gin Pills, Hoffman's Headache Powders, Kline's Extract of Wild Strawberry, Mecca Ointment, Melcalose, Methol and Camphor Cream, Minard's Liniment, Nerviline, Paine's Celery Compound, Pape's Diapepsin, Pazo Ointment, Philip's Milk of Magnesia, Radway's Liniment, Radway's Ready Relief, Scott's Emulsion, Sloan's Liniment, Stafford's Mandrake Bitters, Stafford's Prescription A, Steedman's Powders, Superb Ointment, Woodward's Gripe Water, Vapocresoline, Vicks Cough Drops, Vicks VapoRub, Wampole's Extract of C. L. O. and Zam-Buk Antiseptic Ointment.

Houses and Other Buildings

The first people to live in this province built and lived in sod huts. Later houses were built by these early settlers were small, one storey and usually had a kitchen, bedrooms, pantry and sometimes a porch. These were replaced by salt box houses, which were one-and-a-half or two storeys, with a steep saddle roof and often a parlour as well as a kitchen and bedrooms. The next house to make the scene was sometimes known as the biscuit box house. This house was a full two stories and was bigger than the salt box. It had a saddle roof that sloped gently and was almost flat. Most earlier houses had low ceilings to conserve heat. Row houses became popular in St. John's where building space was limited. Other styles of houses were also built in the 20th century, but many of the earlier style houses can still be seen around the province. Row houses that are painted in many vibrant and pastel colours are still very popular in St. John's.

Next to his house and possibly his outdoor toilet, the most important building to the outport fisherman was his store. This building was used to store winter provisions, including carcasses or partial carcasses of cows, pigs, sheep, goats, seabirds, rabbits, moose and other domestic animals and wild game. The cold winter weather usually preserved meat until spring in the unheated store, although a bout of warm winter weather sometimes required that the "fresh" meat be consumed prematurely. Preserved food, such as salt fish, salt capelin and pickled herring were sometimes also kept in the store, along with fishing gear and other items in the winter. It usually had a work bench and was a workshop for mending and making footwear and furniture, boat-building and other jobs at which a fisherman might be proficient.

Lobster traps were made and repaired in the store and fishing nets were made and mended there as well. Some stores had a loft, called the net loft, which was mostly dedicated to net-making and net-mending. Beasts of burden, such as dogs and horses were sometimes kept in the store. It was as well a meeting place for other men in the community to swap yarns and jokes and to generally converse. Some stores had a trump hole, which was a hatch that could be lifted to urinate on the ground below. Although the store was a part of most outport fishermen's property, many St. John's fishermen, some who didn't live close to the harbour, had stores which served the same purpose as those owned by outport fishermen. A building used as a retail outlet for merchandise was never called a store until recent years. It was always known as a shop.

Every family had an outdoor toilet which was often not far from the house. Some of these were simply a hole dug in the ground with a building mounted over it. These had a bench seat with one or two holes cut in them. The second hole was smaller to accommodate children. Because these smelled and sometimes posed a problem for nearby wells, some outhouses had no holes in the ground but instead had a large bucket which was placed underneath the hole in the bench.These buckets were dumped daily some distance from the house where the contents were covered with ashes from the kitchen stove.

Some families had separate wood sheds, and coal sheds and most had a cellar. The cellar was constructed of a combination of stones, cement and wood, which was then covered in sod. The floor inside was usually cement and often had a walkway down the middle, with a large bin for potatoes on one side and smaller bins for the other crops on the other. The insulation factor in these cellars was sufficient to keep the vegetables from spoiling on warm fall, spring and summer days, and from freezing on cold winter ones.

A lean-in, also called a linny, is a building attached to, and usually accessible from, the house, mostly the kitchen. This space was used to store pickle barrels, sacks of flour and other bulk foods. Animals, including horses, cows, pigs, sheep, goats and hens, were also kept in this building. The heat generated by the kitchen stove was usually enough to keep the foodstuff and the animals from freezing on cold winter nights. Animal carcasses were not usually kept in the lean-in but in the store, which had no heat.

The fisherman's stage was located near the end (and sometimes at the end) of his wharf. This building was uninsulated and usually nothing more than clapboard nailed on studs. They were often red because they were coated with a preservative that contained red ochre. Some stages had doorways but no doors, especially in the doorways that faces seaward. Besides the seaward doorway, many stages had open doorways on one or both sides. The doorway that lead to the beach or nearby road usually had doors, if only to keep the dust out. This was the building in which fish were gutted, cleaned, salted and stored before being placed on the flake to dry. The name may be derived from the fact that the stage head resembles a stage on which performers may appear, or because in this building a stage on the curing process was accomplished.

King William Was King George's Son

This is a children's kissing game in which boys and girls hold hands and form a circle. The child who is "up" stands in the centre while everyone else moves around him or her and chants,

"King William was King George's son
And from the royal race he run,
Upon his breast he wore a star,
To show to the world he's a man of war.
Go choose to the east. Go choose to the west.
But choose the very one that you love best."

If the person in the centre of the ring was a girl, she could choose a boy by holding her hands with her fingers interlocked and placing them behind his head. If he declined her selection, the group would then continue,

"If he's not there to take your part,
Choose another with all your heart."

When a boy accepted the challenge the group then sang,

"Down on this carpet you must kneel,
As the grass grows in the field."

The girl and boy would then kneel down in front of each other while the group chanted,

"Salute your bride and kiss her sweet,
Now you may rise upon your feet."

After the two stood, the group would then finish with,

"And now you're married, you must be good.
Hire a man to chop your wood.
Hire another to carry it in.
Now you may kiss your love again."

The boy and girl then kissed again and the game continued with the boy in the centre.

Kitchen Parties

Although most houses had parlours, they were generally used only at Christmas or on other important occasions, like waking the dead. For the most part, entertaining was done in the kitchen because that was usually the only heated room in the house. Music was supplied by a fiddle and maybe spoons. These instruments were joined in later years by accordions and guitars, but the most used musical instrument in the province was probably the mouth organ, or harmonica. Mouth organs were cheaper than accordions and many a Newfoundlander could charm "Mussels in the Corner," or another popular jig out of one. People sang and danced, and told jokes and stories at these parties. Many of the songs that were sung were made up by some of the partiers, or had been written by

other Newfoundlanders. Among the songs sung at kitchen parties were "The Old Polina," "Jack Was Every Inch a Sailor," "The Badger Drive," I'se the B'y," "The Squid Jigging Ground," "The Star of Logy Bay" and "Let Me Fish off Cape St. Mary's."

L istening to the Radio

Radio signals were available long before electricity in most outport communities, so the earlier radios were battery powered. Transistors had not been invented and tubes had to be heated in order for them to operate. The battery was actually two batteries in one. The bulk, or "A," portion of the battery provided a 1.5 volt source of power to heat the tubes, while a "B" outlet of a much higher voltage was used to operate the electronics of the radio. These batteries were very expensive, so radios were not kept on long. Often it was just a source for the news, weather and the Fishermen's Broadcast.

Because there were few telephones, radio was a means of communication between residents as well. The venue for this was usually the "Gerald S. Doyle Bulletin." Anyone who wanted to get a message to someone in another area of the province, could send a message to the "Bulletin" to be read on the air. Sometimes these messages were to husbands working in the lumber woods or on a ship at sea.

One humorous story about the "Bulletin" concerned a woman living on the Northern Peninsula, who had been ailing and who sent a message to her husband at sea. The message, which was supposed to have read, "Not getting any better, come home right away," arrived in the hands of broadcaster Aubrey Mack (MacDonald) without punctuation. The message intended for her husband and heard by all was, "Not getting any, better come home right away."

Sometimes women would turn on the radio during the day to listen to a favourite radio soap opera, such as "Laura Limited," and there were occasional

stories on for children. "The Chronicles of Uncle Mose," a night-time broadcast of stories written and narrated by Ted Russell, was a family favourite. The
"Irene B. Mellon" was a radio play in which actors played the part of crewmembers on the *Irene B. Mellon* as she sailed around the coast of Newfoundland and
Labrador.

The "Big Six" and "The Wilf Doyle Show" were popular musical shows out
of St. John's. Another extremely popular show out of St. John's was "The
Barrelman." In this 15-minute program, Joseph R. Smallwood told stories that
had been sent in to him by listeners. The show was so popular that it earned Joey
enough fame to later become the first Premier of Newfoundland and Labrador.

One of the stories he told on radio in 1928 follows:

It isn't so many years ago since the sealing fleet in St. John's could be divided roughly into two classes – those ships that were sailed by Newfoundland
captains, and those sailed by skippers from Dundee, Scotland.

Needless to say, there was the keenest possible rivalry between the
Newfoundland captains and the Dundee men. Those old Dundee skippers were
no slouches, and the struggle to be first to load and back in St. John's was very
keen every spring.

One of the Dundee men was a Captain Fairweather, an old Scotsman who
died only a few years ago in Scotland at the age of 90 or more. One spring
Captain Fairweather made up his mind that he was going to be the first to load
his ship and bring it home to St. John's.

The greatest of the Newfoundland captains at the time was the famous
Arthur Jackman. From the moment they started off through the narrows the
majority of the captains tried to keep Captain Jackman in sight. With equal
determination, Jackman tried to shake them off. All but one were left behind.
Captain Fairweather kept doggedly in his wake. This was the situation when
Captain Jackman spied the seals ahead late in the afternoon. He gave orders to
stop the ship and burn down for the night.

Up came Captain Fairweather, a quarter of a mile behind and sent word to
enquire what the trouble was.

Captain Arthur replied, "Dirty weather – no use going any farther tonight –
I'll wait 'til morning."

"I'll do the same," said the Scotsman. "What time will you start in the morning?"

"I'll tell you what," said Captain Jackman, "I'll hang a red lantern on the
stern so you can see me all night." And so they arranged it.

I don't suppose there's much need to tell you the rest. When daybreak came
you can imagine the Scotsman's disgust to find Jackman gone out of sight, and
the red lantern that he had seen all night still standing on the end of a pole that
Captain Arthur had propped up in the ice.

Captain Arthur arrived home first with a full load, and Captain Fairweather
got back clean.

Lobster Catching

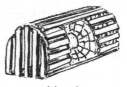

Lobsters were never plentiful enough and the season never long enough in Newfoundland and Labrador for any fisherman to make a full-time living catching lobsters. But it was lucrative enough to provide a good supplement to his other ventures. Fishermen still make their own traps, known as lobster pots or lobster traps. Flexible saplings are cut to make the top and upper framework for the trap. These are bent into semi-circles and the ends set in two holes, one at each end of a cross-member that determined the trap's width and formed one end of the trap. Thin lats that are about two inches wide are then nailed around the outside of two of these ends, with gaps between each lat so lobster can see the bait inside the trap. The ends of another small sapling are tied together to make a ring enough to allow a lobster to pass through. A small-mesh netting is then made around this ring, and together with the ring it forms one end of the lobster trap known as the head. After the outside part of this mesh is attached to the frame of the head, strings are used to pull the ring inside the trap so the mesh forms a ramp up which a lobster may crawl to get at the bait inside the trap. The bottom of the trap is comprised of a narrow compartment that is latted top and bottom and filled with flat rocks for ballast. If a trap should reach the bottom upside down, the rounded top and the weight of the ballast usually right it. Once a lobster makes its way up the mesh ramp and falls through the ring, it has little chance of making its way up to the ring from the inside, which has no mesh ramp. To insure they don't lose any of their catch some fishermen build traps with a second compartment called the parlour. This section also has a mesh and ring entrance called the parlour door. Some lobster pots have two mesh and ring heads, while others have three compartments, with the parlour in the centre. Lobster pots are lowered to the bottom on a rope which has a buoy. Fishermen paint their buoys a different colour than those of other fishermen for identification purposes.

Making Ice Cream

Often an ice cream maker was used to make home-made ice cream. This machine is a wooden tub with a cranking device attached to the top. A smaller container was attached to the crank, and this fits inside the tub and allows enough room for crushed ice to be added. A coarse salt was added to the ice to speed up the melting. The crank handle was turned, which rotated the can in which milk, sugar and vanilla had been placed. As the ice melted outside the can, its contents turned into delicious, soft ice cream. If an ice cream maker was unavailable, a wooden fish tub was used. The can with the ice cream was placed in it and the tub was filled with ice around the can. People took turns rotating the can by hand until the ice cream was ready. A pair of mitts was useful in doing this job.

Making Fish

Up until the mid-twentieth century, when electricity brought freezers, fish had to be preserved by curing it. There is a science involved in the proper curing of fish, one that can make a big difference in the final value of the product. The value of one's cured fish was decided by a culler. This was a person employed by the merchant to grade each fisherman's fish. He decided which was grade A, which was grade B, which was West Indie, and which was cullage. Cullage had no market value and was usually consumed by the fisherman's family or fed to his dogs. West Indie was traded in the Caribbean by merchants for molasses, sugar and rum, while grades A and B were sold to prime markets. Having mostly grade A or B fish was important to each family's survival over the coming winter, so every family member, as soon as he or she was old enough to understand, knew the importance of the proper curing of fish.

To cure a codfish is to dehydrate it, or remove the water which powers bacterial action causing the fish to spoil. The first step in the process is to clean the fish. This is usually done on a splitting table on the stage head, a portion of the wharf reaching beyond the stage. The splitting table, where codfish are beheaded, gutted, split down the back and their soundbone (backbone) removed, has a special notch cut in one side to assist in the beheading. This part of the process is done by division of labour, with each fisherman repeatedly performing the same operation before sliding the fish on to the next person around the table. Time was money and although you can't hurry the fish onto your hook or into your net, you can speed up the curing process, so most fishermen became very proficient at these individual tasks. Watching them perform was poetry in motion as they carved fish at speeds that were hard for the human eye to follow. The fish are then washed in a tub of saltwater before being covered in salt and laid flat in piles. The salting stage is the first step in dehydrating the fish, and is done in a building called the stage, an out-building near the end (and sometimes at the end) of a fisherman's wharf. From the stage the fish are taken by wheelbarrow or handbar to the flake and spread out to dry in the sun.

A flake is a raised platform made of long poles that aren't nailed down but simply laid in place, although the end poles are usually nailed down to keep the others from falling off. They were often built on a beach, hugging a rocky cliff. Since drying fish needs to be aerated, boughs were cut from trees and placed on the poles so the fish would have ventilation underneath. Fish were spread in a head-and-tails fashion to utilize all the space. Fish could not be left too long in the hot sun because they burned, which devalued them, so they had to be turned over regularly. If fish got wet during the drying process it could spoil them, so at the first sign of rain, which could be goats coming home in single file, everyone would scravel to the flake to pile the fish up and cover them with canvas. The job of tending the flake was often done by the fisherman's family, supervised and assisted by his wife. If a child wasn't big and strong enough to pick up the handles of a wheelbarrow full of fish or one end of a hand bar, he was big enough to turn a fish over.

Many a child learned the value and the meaning of life and survival on the fish flake.

Manufacturing and Industry

Fishing was always the biggest industry in Newfoundland and Labrador, and the settlers this attracted saw the development of other industries. Fishing created a need for boats and the boat-building industry in this province saw the making of all types of vessels, from small dories and rodneys to small schooners.

There were also a number of saw mills and several brick-making operations throughout the province. In 1940 there were 790 small sawmills in use, each producing an annual average of 35,000 board feet. Larger sawmilling operations, such as the one in Botwood owned by the French Company of Quebec exported lumber from that port between 1890 and 1900. From a nearby port, in 1900, Lewis Miller began exporting the lumber his company produced in the province's interior. This operation lasted a mere three years, but Lewis Miller left his name on the town where his woods operation started, Millertown, and on the port from which he shipped his product, Lewisporte. Both Miller's and the French Company's operations later became part of the newly-formed AND Company after it began making paper in Grand Falls.

Whaling, the new world's first industry, was started by the Basques in Red Bay Labrador in the late 1500s and later spread to other areas of Newfoundland and Labrador. With the declining number of whales, these operations began to decline and by 1946 only two whaling plants remained: one in Hawke's Harbour, Labrador, and one at Williamsport, White Bay. Today whaling is no longer done in this province.

Sealing, at one time the province's second-biggest industry next to fishing, is still carried on but on a smaller scale.

Farming was mostly done by fishermen to feed their own families, but there were also full-time farmers in the province. Today the province has about 725 farms (mostly on the island of Newfoundland), each averaging 65 hectares (161 acres) in size.

The first historical mineral discoveries were made in the late 1550s when ships sailing along the coast, charting the unknown and trading in fish, brought back reports and samples of "ore" to England. Incredible numbers of mining ventures were financed over the next 300 years, often based on great dreams but little evidence. Today the mining industry accounts for four per cent of the province's annual gross domestic product. By far the most important mineral is iron ore, found in the Schefferville area of Labrador. It accounts for more than 90 per cent of the value of the province's mineral output, and, by weight, constitutes more than half of the Canadian total. Other metals mined include silver and gold. The mining of nonmetallic minerals, such as asbestos and gypsum, also contributes to the economy. Crude oil from offshore wells and refined oil from the Come By Chance refinery make up a large percentage of the province's exports.

The province's largest utility industry is electric power. More than 70 per cent of the electricity generated is sold outside the province. The largest hydro-electric facility is located in Churchill Falls, Labrador, with a total installed capacity of 5,403 megawatts.

Prior to 1949 there were a number of manufacturing concerns in the province, including ship-building, sail-making, carriage-making, barrel-making, brick-making and the quarrying of stones for construction. Gadens Ltd. produced Keep Kool flavoured soft drinks and Coca Cola. Bavarian Brewing Ltd., Bennett Brewing Co., and Newfoundland Brewery Ltd. brewed beer for local consumption. The United Nail and Foundry Co. Ltd. and Trask's Foundry Ltd. produced such things as nails and stoves.

The Newfoundland Butter Company was established in 1925, which produced yellow coloured margarine for local sale. This was later exported to Canada where it sold for half the price of butter. When Newfoundland joined Canada in 1949, the Newfoundland Butter Company earned a special mention in the Terms of Union. It would become Canada's first margarine manufacturer, and the name changed to the Newfoundland Margarine Company shortly afterwards.

Following Confederation, Premier Smallwood's dream to industrialize Newfoundland suffered a blow from the onset, as a number of companies, particularly the foundries, were unable to compete with bigger Canadian companies and went out of business. Undeterred, Smallwood used a lot of his energy to bring about industrialization and a number of schemes were attempted at taxpayers' expense. Few of these ventures lasted for any length of time. Among these were the original Come By Chance oil refinery, United Cotton Mills in St. John's, a linerboard mill, a hockey stick factory and a company producing prefabricated homes in Stephenville. Terra Nova Shoes of Harbour Grace did survive and now sells high quality work and fashion boots to mainland and overseas markets. The oil refinery at Come By Chance has reopened, employing nearly 600 people and producing petroleum products for local sale and export.

Since then there have been other successful manufacturing ventures. Among those is Restwell Mattresses, which began manufacturing various types of box springs and mattresses in 1991 in Harbour Grace, and now also makes chesterfield sets, sofa beds, love seats and wing chairs. Superior Glove Works, which began producing gloves in 1988, now makes 10 million pairs of gloves a year and is Canada's leading manufacturer of gloves, which are sold primarily in Canada and the U.S. Abbyshot Custom Clothiers of Mount Pearl supplies custom fitted garments to more than 20 countries including the UK, Japan, Israel,

Poland and Slovenia. Highland Homes in Gander is building houses for families in Chile. Griffith's Guitars of St. John's produces quality guitars for the world market; and Newfoundland Styro, which began production in 1997, is a major manufacturer of building insulation, flotation blocks, styrofoam wall systems, insulated concrete forms and packaging for perishables.

Exports from the province were valued at over $11 billion in 2003. Goods account for well over 80 per cent of exports and services the remainder. Most of the goods exported are sold in foreign countries; the United States in particular accounts for about 53 per cent.

Tourism is the province's fastest-growing industry. In 1996 it generated $206 million. The surge in the tourism industry in recent years has seen an increase in the number of hotels and hotel rooms, and a large increase in the number of bed and breakfast facilities in the province. From 1998 to 2001, visitation increased 12 per cent and tourist expenditures increased 22 per cent, and in 2002 tourism attracted approximately 439,400 visitors and generated an estimated $304.5 million.

A large number of residents have been involved in cottage industries over the years. These include products knitted by women and sold to locals and tourists. The growing tourism industry has created a need for locally made products as gifts and souvenirs, and the demand is being met by talented men and women who produce these items for sale as an extension of their hobbies. Some of these have grown into small business, employing a number of people.

Apart from traditional industries, Newfoundland and Labrador also has a growing music industry, a fledgling movie-making industry and, because of its low cost of exporting, an expanding IT industry.

M eals

The big meal of the day in Newfoundland and Labrador was dinner, served around noon. A popular dinner meal was always fish and brewis: boiled fresh or salt codfish and boiled hard bread, served separately on the same plate and covered in scrunchins (small cubes of fried porkfat) and the rendered hot grease of these. A similar meal, known in some areas as fisherman's brewis, is made of boiled hard bread mixed together with shredded pieces of fish, over which the grease and scrunchins are poured. Codfish, salmon, flatfish, herring, mackerel and other species were sometimes cooked and served with potatoes, especially on Fridays and sometimes Wednesdays. Another meal, known as boiled dinner (more recently as Jigg's dinner), consisted of salt beef boiled in a pot to which all the vegetables grown in the garden (including potatoes, carrots, turnip, cabbage and sometime parsnip) are added. A bag of split peas was sometimes added to the pot to make pease pudding, and sometimes dough boys were included as well. On some occasions, fresh meat or fowl was baked in the oven to be eaten with the meal as well. This could be beef, pork, mutton, chicken, duck, goose, sea birds (especially turrs), seal, rabbits, partridge, caribou or moose. A duff (pudding made with flour) was sometimes baked in the oven along with the meat. This meal was usually only served on Sundays. Thick pea soup, which included salt beef or pork and sometimes dough boys, was often served on Saturday. Boiled beans, complete with chunks of potato, carrot and turnip, was often made for dinner. Beans were sometimes boiled without vegetables, and molasses was later added, after which they were baked. Rice soup, which contained meat, also made for a dinnertime meal. Bullbird soup was also another favourite, as was seal flipper pie.

For breakfast one could expect porridge, salt fish, herring, bacon and eggs, and sometimes simply toast and tea. Supper was a light meal which might be bread or tea biscuits and jam or cheese; salted capelin, roasted in the oven; or something from a can. On Sundays, on which the biggest meal of the week was served for dinner, supper might consist of nothing more than bread and jam or combinations of custard, jelly, canned fruit and cream.

Sometimes light snacks were served between meals, and very few people went to bed at night without having a lunch.

Medical Care

In the early days of settlement doctors were few and far between. Some vessels sent out from the old countries had doctors on board, as did Royal Navy ships; and in later years, with the coming of more settlers, doctors also came. Most of these set up practice in larger settlements, particularly St. John's. As newcomers settled in outlying, isolated areas – sometimes illegally – medical services were not available. Some of these people spent their whole lives never seeing a doctor, so devised their own medical cures and patched up accident victims the best way they could. Many went through life with a limp or a more serious disability because they didn't receive proper medical attention. Babies were brought into the world by midwives, These women, often with little or no training, sometimes travelled long distances to bring a child safely into the world. Travelling by boat, horse, dog team, or on foot, these women were often a welcome sight to a woman in labour and her worried husband and children.

Nurses, who had been enticed to come here, sometimes took the place of doctors in outports. One of these was Nurse Myra Bennett. After spending 10 years of her life as a nurse in her native England, in 1921 she was persuaded to move to Newfoundland by Lady Harris, the wife of Sir Alexander Harris, Governor of Newfoundland at that time. From her home in Daniel's Harbour, Nurse Bennett was for many years the only person with any medical training along a rugged 200-mile coastline. During this time she performed medical duties, including those normally performed by a doctor or dentist. She oversaw the birth of 5,000 babies and extracted 3,000 teeth. She also performed other medical operations, and at one time successfully reattached a man's severed foot.

Nurses and trained midwives were brought to the Dominion and sent to certain communities to provide medical services. Sometimes these services were underfunded by government, so in 1924 the Newfoundland Outport Nursing and Industrial Association (NONIA) was formed to support the work of these nurses and midwives. Committees were formed in rural communities to distribute materials to women who then made knitted goods for sale to cover the nurses' salaries and other expenses. NONIA no longer supports outport nursing, but it provides a valuable marketing service to craftspeople of the province.

A number of excellent, well-known and sometimes famous doctors have played a part in the history of this province. Not the least of which is William Carson, a Scottish doctor who, in addition to helping the sick, was partially responsible for bringing self-government to this colony. But the two doctor's who did the most for outport Newfoundland were the world-famous Wilfred Grenfell, and John M. Olds, who was famous in Notre Dame Bay and well-known in many parts of Newfoundland and Labrador.

Grenfell not only improved the health of the people of the Great Northern Peninsula and Southern Labrador, but their lifestyle as well. Grenfell was a very religious man who is on record as saying, "The service we render others is the rent we pay for our room on Earth." By a stroke of fate, Grenfell found himself in Newfoundland in 1892. After seeing the sad plight of the many fishing families around the coast, he returned to England where he pleaded passionately for funds to aid the more than 3,000 permanent settlers and the native people living on the coast, who had been serviced only by one government doctor on an annual visit from Newfoundland. Starting at Battle Harbour, Labrador, in 1893, the doctor built hospitals, orphanages, schools, nursing stations, industrial centres, agricultural stations and cooperative stores. The stores later expanded to other locations in Quebec. But most of all, he brought doctors to northern Newfoundland and southern Labrador.

Apart from his other talents and attributes, Grenfell was a charismatic person and a passionate speaker. The speeches he made in England, and especially the United States, brought not only funding for his projects, but also hundreds of doctors and nurses for his hospitals over the years. Many of them, inspired by Grenfell's charisma, came as part of their training before going on to large hospitals in the United States.

One of the doctors Grenfell's efforts attracted was a young Yale University student, a new graduate of the School of Medicine by the name of John Olds. Olds first visited the province in 1930, the summer before his last year of medical school. He returned two years later with his new bride, a nurse, to spend time in Twillingate before going on to bigger and better things. Instead the couple fell in love with the place and spent the rest of their lives here. Olds quickly picked up the way of life and before long he was using boats in summer to visit patients in all parts of Notre Dame Bay. He learned how to handle a team of dogs and, like Grenfell, travelled many miles over ice and snow behind a komatik to visit patients. Trained under world-famous neurosurgeon Walter Dandy, Olds was not only a good doctor but a good surgeon as well. At Twillingate he ran the hospital's emergency room where he performed complex surgeries. There were other doctors in the world more qualified to perform some of the surgeries he attempted, but they weren't around, so he did what he had to do. His fame brought people from other parts of the province for his medical advice and surgery. By the time he died in 1985 he was a legend in Notre Dame Bay and beyond.

Hospital boats, including a number of Grenfell Mission boats, brought medical services to Newfoundland outports as well. The best known of the hospital boats was the *Christmas Seal*. Her main objective was to combat the dreaded tuberculosis, which was rampant in this province by the 1950s. But in her 20 years the *Seal* provided other medical services and attended to many medical emergencies, sometimes providing ambulance service to the closest port with a hospital.

Better trained doctors, nurses and technical staff now provide much improved medical services to patients, but with the decline in outport populations the medical and hospital services are decreasing. In larger centres, such as Corner Brook, Gander and St. John's, medical services are more or less on a par with other cities and towns throughout North America with comparable populations.

Merchants

A well-known saying in this province is "A fisherman is one rogue, a merchant is many." This saying indicates the mistrust some fishermen had for merchants in general. Some merchants deserved this mistrust, as they took advantage of the mostly uneducated fishermen at every opportunity. One such Notre Dame Bay merchant, who among other things took the fishermen's cod livers as credit against their purchases, devised his own method of taking advantage. He had a "special can" made in St. John's that was somewhat larger than a gallon. Fishermen who sold their cod livers to him were given credit for a gallon, when in fact, the merchant was collecting more than a gallon. All through the season the merchant ripped off every fisherman he bought livers from before putting the can away for the next year. Then Lady Luck stepped in to even up the playing field somewhat. The following year when he went looking for his "special can" he couldn't find it. When he asked his employees about it, he found out they had been using it all winter to sell molasses, a much more valuable product than cod livers in Notre Dame Bay at the time.

Yet, not all merchants were dishonest, and many were caring people. But no matter the personality of the merchant, he was one of the most respected members of the community, and for good reasons. Without the merchant, the fisherman would have nowhere to market his product or get his provisions. Except for a very few highly successful fishermen, most depended on the merchant for credit. Although some of these merchants were stingy and uncaring, most were not. This can be attested to by the fact that most of them extended credit year after year, sometimes with no hope of ever getting it back and sometimes to the point of losing everything themselves rather than see someone go hungry.

Mining

The geology of this province brought and created prospectors over the years, resulting in a significant number of mineral finds. Some of these finds led to mining operations in such places as Baie Verte, Bell Island, Buchans, Little Bay and Tilt Cove. With the lack of sunlight and the presence of dust and fumes, going underground to work is not the most desirable way to make a living. Yet many Newfoundlanders became miners because it was a way to feed their families. Any who were claustrophobic soon got over it or learned to deal with it.

Unlike the fishery and forestry, mining involves a non-renewable resource, so mines have to cease operations at some point. Many lives have been uprooted and sometimes devastated by the closure of mines in this province. Yet in spite of their lack of longevity, mines provided a good way of life for families for many years, for some their whole lifetime.

Mining accounts for four per cent of the province's annual gross domestic product and still provides a living for many residents, as well as much-needed revenue for the government. The iron ore mines in Labrador West, which produce more than half of Canada's iron ore, have the potential of many more years of operation. Oil from under the ocean, although not proving the number of jobs originally anticipated, provides a good income for those involved and a source of revenue for the provincial coffers. The search for new mineral resources continues on land and below the ocean, with new finds still being made. Large nickel deposits found at Voisey's Bay, Labrador, about 10 years ago have the potential to provide jobs for many years, and recent gold finds on the Island are showing good potential. By far the most important mineral is currently iron ore, found in the Schefferville area of Labrador. Iron ore accounts for more than 90 per cent of the value of the province's mineral output and, by weight, constitutes more than half of the Canadian total. Other metals mined locally include silver and gold. The mining of nonmetallic minerals such as asbestos and gypsum also contributes to the economy. Although not the province's biggest employer, minerals are by far the most valuable commodity produced in the province.

Mummering

The way of life for most people in this province was very hard. survival meant getting up very early in the morning and working until dark every day but Sunday, for the whole year. In the winter there were nets to be made and mended, lobster pots to be made, wood to be gotten, clothing and footwear to be made, and many other maintenance jobs around the house to be done, such as making and repairing furniture. In the spring the real hard work began and lasted through the fall. There was fish to be caught and cured, ground to be ploughed, and vegetables to be planted, tended, harvested and stored. Hay had to be mowed, dried and stored because many households had animals, including horses. Some people had dogs for winter transportation that had to be fed and cared for all year. Goats and cows had to be tended and milked. Many families had sheep to be tended all year and sheared in the fall. Because these animals roamed, there was also fencing to be done to keep them out of the vegetable gardens. There were hens to be cared for and eggs to be gathered. There was wild game, such as seabirds and rabbits, to be hunted and cleaned. Daily there was water to be brought from the well and wood to be sawed, cleaved and brought in, and many other chores to be done. In all this, the woman worked as hard or harder than the man, and did most of the jobs he did, including making nets, curing fish and digging potatoes. Women also did some of the things men didn't do, like knitting and sewing clothing, doing laundry, cooking, cleaning and tending to children. As soon as they were old enough, the children were required to do their part in insuring the family's survival as well. For most families, life was serious work all year.

When fall rolled around and the winter provisions were stored, which usually took until Christmas, it was time to relax a little. Christmas was a time to doff the veil of toil and don a more leisurely apparel for the soul; a time for fun and merriment, when a little foolishness was in order. For many, the foolishness took the form of mummering.

The mummering tradition started out in Newfoundland as it was done in the British Isles. Starting sometime before Christmas Day, the Christmas Fools took over the Water Street district and made things lively for pedestrians. Wearing masks or thick veils and triangular hats made of cardboard and covered in wallpaper, as well as other gigantic cocked hats, they carried inflated pig's bladders which they used to strike passers-by about the head and shoulders. The costumes of these Fools were quite resplendent. Apart from the well-adorned hats, the Fools wore white starched shirts without a coat. These shirts were covered in ribbons and other adornments. Along with the Fools were a smaller number of Oonchuks. These were men dressed in women's apparel whose costumes were not as decorated as those of the Fools. The Oonchucks were usually a bit rougher on pedestrians than their counterparts. Both groups continued their boisterous frolicking until Old Christmas Day, January 6.

Boys in St. John's would visit houses on St. Stephen's Day, December 26, carrying a small tree decorated with ribbons and something to represent a bird on the top. They would knock on a door and when the occupant answered, they would shout, "Will ye have de wran (wren)?" If the occupant agreed, one of the group would recite:

"De wran, de wran, de king of all birds
St. Stephen's Day he was caught in the furds (evergreen trees)
And dough he is little, his honour is great,
Jump up landlady and give us a trate (treat)
A pocket full of money, a cellar full of beer
I wish ye a merry Christmas and a happy New Year.
Up wit de kettle and down with de pan
A penny or a tuppence to bury the wran."

The group moved from door to door collecting pennies or tuppences, which they used to buy candy.

This custom originated in Ireland, where groups of small boys would hunt for a wren. When they killed one, it was tied to the top of a pole or holly bush, that was decorated with ribbons or coloured paper. On St. Stephen's Day the wren was carried from house to house by the boys, who wore straw masks or blackened their faces with burnt cork and dressed in old clothes (often women's dresses). At each house, the boys would sing a variation of the Wren song.

From these earlier celebrations evolved the current custom of mummering. Groups of people wearing costumes and false faces (masks or veils of thin material) to disguise their features travel door to door, often carrying musical instruments to entertain occupants. The idea is to fool the people in the house as to their true identity. For this reason men often dress as women, and women as men. They knock on the door with a stick known as a "Johnny Stick." To disguise their voices they say something like, "Any mummers 'lowed in?" forming the words by inhaling their breath rather than exhaling. Once inside, the mummers entertain the occupants by singing, playing music and dancing. The mummers are often served food and refreshments, which in earlier years consisted of Christmas cake and syrup. In some houses, alcohol is also served. If a

mummer is correctly identified he has to remove his false face.

In some parts of Newfoundland and Labrador, mummers are called "john-nies," after the sticks they carried. This was later changed to "jannies" in some areas.

In earlier years mummers walked from door to door, but these days they travel by motor vehicle, often with a designated driver.

Navigation

Many fishermen didn't own a compass and the only schooling they got in nav-igation was what was passed down from their elders. One of the methods of navigation that every fisherman knew was "taking your marks," or triangula-tion. To mark a fishing ground or other spot at sea, from that spot one sights two objects in a line (one behind the other in one direction) then does the same thing with two other objects in a second direction. He is able to find the exact spot again by simply remembering the marks, which can be headlands, rocks, trees, church spires, the door to someone's house or any stationary object. The reason many churches were built on high ground was because their spires could be used as navigation marks at sea. Marks couldn't be used on foggy days, in which case fishermen used dead reckoning to find their net or trawl buoy. A compass is required for dead reckoning, which is calculated using the direction, speed and estimated drift of the boat. Dead reckoning in the fog to the fishing ground and back to the safety of the harbour is tricky business assisted only somewhat by lighthouses and fog horns on the headlands. Owners of make-and-break engines also made their own radar. A 90-degree elbow was placed on the exhaust pipe which could be directed toward both the starboard and port sides of the boat. In fog, the volume of the echo from unseen cliffs, and the length of time it took an echo to return was a great aid to navigating in foggy weather.

Net Fishing

Most of the nets used in this province were made by the fisherman or his wife. These had various sized meshes, depending on the species being caught and the method being utilized to catch them.

Gill Net

The age-old method for catching fish in a net is gill-netting. The gill net is a rectangular net with the diameter of the mesh slightly smaller than the size of the fish being netted. Cod nets are stretched close to the bottom in an area where fish migrate and move about. Unaware of the net the fish try to swim through the mesh and by the time the mesh is tightly around their bellies their gills have passed the mesh and they are trapped. Salmon nets and herring nets are set close to the surface to catch them as they migrate.

In 1876 the cod trap was invented by Captain William H. Whitely in the Strait of Belle Isle. This device is basically a large box, or a room with four walls and a bottom, constructed of netting. Most traps measure 75 - 150 metres (40 - 80 fathoms) in circumference and 15 - 28 metres (8 - 15 fathoms) in depth. In a typical trap the front wall is a fathom or more longer than the back wall. The trap is kept upright in the water by floats placed along the top of the walls and lead weights to anchor it at the bottom. These weights and the ropes to which they are attached are known as "foots."

Ropes are attached to each corner of the net at the top and these are anchored to the bottom away from the trap to act as guy ropes to hold the trap on location. The trap has an opening in the front wall and from one side of this opening a long rectangular net, known as the "leader," extends out for 38 - 183 metres (20 - 100 fathoms), and is made fast to the shore or to rocks not far from shore. The leader also has buoys, weights and guy ropes to hold it in place. Since codtraps are completely immersed in water, the length of the leader is determined by the angle of the sea bottom as it slopes away from shore. If the slope is steep and the water close to shore is deep, a shorter leader is required. More gradual slopes require longer leaders. Some fishermen custom-make their leaders to accommodate the slope of the shore so that it was wider (higher) at the trap and narrower near the shore so there was no wasted linnet lying on the bottom. Sometimes these traps reach the surface, while others are set as much as 10 metres (5 fathoms) below the surface.

The mesh size of the trap netting varies in different areas of the trap. Starting with the leader, which has a mesh of about 20 centimetres (eight inches), the mesh size gradually gets smaller toward the back of the net, where it can be as small as eight centimetres (three inches).

These traps are set in places where codfish are known to migrate to shore. Following the shoreline they come up against this "wall of linnet" where they generally follow it seaward into the opening of the trap. Once inside they swim around in circles until the fishermen arrive to haul the trap. Because of the way a trap is hauled, two boats are required for the job. It is also the reason for the different sized mesh. Hauling starts at the front and progresses toward the back, and the fish are brought up to the surface, where the smaller mesh at the back keeps them from escaping through the netting.

A dip net is used to scoop the fish into the midshiproom of the skiff. This is a storage area partitioned off for this purpose. In the days when trap-fishing was at its peak and the catch was large enough, the fish was also thrown in other areas of the skiff, and even in the rodney, sometimes loading both to the gunnels. If there was still fish in the trap it was handed off to other fishermen in the area to take what they could. If there weren't enough boats around to take all the fish, the trap was let go, allowing the fish to escape.

Although this method didn't catch the larger, deep water fish, trap fish were considered the best fish because, unlike trawl fish and gill-net fish, they were still alive when caught.

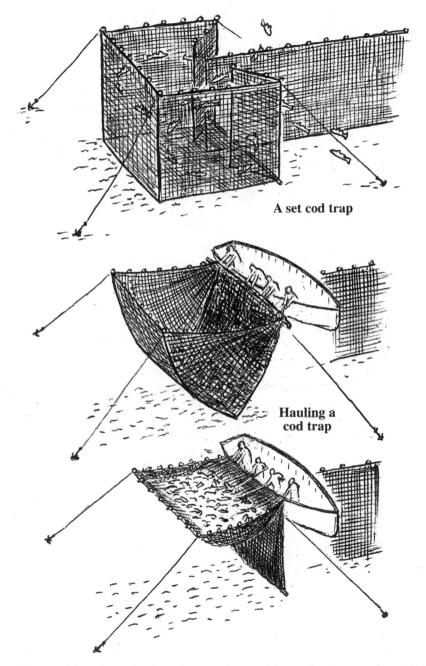

A set cod trap

**Hauling a
cod trap**

Traps with various sized mesh were also used to catch other species of fish such as capelin.

Seining also requires two boats, one at each end of the seine. The seine is a small-mesh, rectangular net with floats along the top edge and weights on the bottom. Schools of fish are encircled by this net and the bottom drawn in to trap them. The excess net is brought aboard the main boat, crowding the fish into a smaller area. When they are brought to the surface the fish are taken aboard the seiner with a dip net.

Dragging is using a net that is buoyant at the top and heavy at the bottom to catch fish. This net is dragged along the ocean bottom, scooping every living creature big enough to be trapped in the mesh from the bottom to the top of the net. The mesh of this net is of a size that will allow smaller fish to escape; but once this mesh fills with bigger fish, nothing can escape. Because this method of fishing catches all species of fish, not just the intended species, over the years the unwanted species were often dumped overboard where they died. Many believe that dragging also damages the sea bottom, the habitat and breeding grounds of many species. For these reasons, attempts to stop this method of fishing have been made in recent years.

Nicknames

In some Newfoundland and Labrador communities there were often a limited number of family names. The first names given to children were often taken from the names of kings, queens, saints or biblical characters. This often resulting in some communities, especially larger ones, having two or more people with the same first and last name. To alleviate this problem, nicknames were often used. One community might have a "John on the hill," Big John," "Big boat John," "Blacksmith John," or even "Stunned John." Married women with the same name were sometimes known as "John's Sarah," "Aunt Sarah down the lane," "Midwife Sarah," or other names associating with someone or something. In some parts of the province, particularly the Southern Shore, if there were a number of women with the same first name, her husband's name was sometimes used after her own. A community might have a Mary-Paul, a Mary-John etc.

Paddy McQuark Was Never Seen

In this game a finger ring called Paddy McQuark is strung on a piece of string. The string is then tied in a circle big enough to accommodate the number of players. All the players but one then grasp the string and form a circle outside the string, surrounding the one player who is "up." One player holding the string also holds the ring, hidden in one hand. As the game starts everybody starts sliding their hands along the string, at first touching the thumb side of their hands together, then touching the little finger side of their hands against the hands of the persons to their right and left. The ring is then passed hand to hand, while the person in the centre is looking the other way. Players try to give the impression that they have the ring when they don't, and that they don't have it when they do. While this is going on everyone is chanting in unison:

"Paddy McQuark was never seen,
never seen, never seen,
Paddy McQuark was never seen,
travelling around the railroad."

As the word "railroad" is sung, all movement ceases and the person in the centre has to guess who has the ring. If that person guesses right, he or she gets to stay in the centre of the ring. If not, the person who is wrongly chosen takes his or her place in the centre and the game continues. In a slightly different version of the game, the person who has the ring and is not picked becomes the person to occupy the centre spot for the next round.

Pick-ups

In the juggling game of pick-ups, five small, round stones, found on any beach are used. Two stones are used to start the game. One is placed on the ground, while the other is tossed in the air. A player has to catch the tossed stone, while first grabbing the stone on the ground and using the same hand to make the catch. In the next round three stones are used, two placed on the ground to be snatched up after the third is tossed. This continues until four are picked up, then the game gets more difficult. In this round, first two, then three and finally four stones are tossed and caught while the remaining stone(s) are picked up. This goes on until someone misses a catch or a grab, then his opponent gets a turn. Two or more players could play pick-ups, and it was played by both sexes.

Piddely

This game has a resemblance to modern day cricket and baseball. A short stick is used instead of a ball, and a second, longer stick (sometimes known as the "flicker") is used as a bat. There are no bases and no pitcher's mound in piddely. There are no teams and the game can be played with as few as two people. There is only one person up at bat at a time, while his opponents are all fielders. Two large stones are previously placed at the end of the field away from the fielders. These stones (or other objects) are placed close enough together to allow the short stick to rest across them. The batter then places the tip of the bat under the short stick and flicks it as far as he can, then places his flicker across the stones. The fielder closest to where the shorter stick lands then has one opportunity to knock the flicker off the rocks from where the shorter stick landed. If he succeeds he changes places with the batter. If not, the batter gets a chance to piddle. To piddle, one leans the shorter stick against one of the rocks so that one end protrudes above the rock. With a forceful downward blow the batter whacks the tip of the stick with the flicker and sends it spinning into the air. Then, taking a batting stance, he swings at the pirouetting projectile. If he strikes it he measures the distance in bat lengths from the rocks to where it lands. The number of lengths is added to his score. He then places the shorter stick across the rocks and goes through the procedure again. If he makes three attempts to strike the spinning stick and misses each time he is "out." If he connects on the first attempt but is not satisfied with the distance, he may try again. On the last attempt he has to accept the distance, even if it is a single bat length. If it is less than a bat length, he is out. He is also out if someone catches the short stick after he strikes it, and the person who catches it takes his place. In cases where the batter "strikes out," the person who takes his place is the person next in line according to a preselected priority. This is done the instant someone says, "Less have a game a piddely." The first person to say "First up!" is first up. If you aren't quick enough on the first try you immediately say "Next up!" After some heated discussion about who said what before whom, the game gets underway.

The shorter stick was often a piece of mop or broom handle about a foot (30 cm) long. The bat (flicker) was often a piece of mop or broom handle about two and a half feet (76 cm) in length.

In a variation of this game, instead of two stones, a hole is dug in the ground from which the shorter stick is propelled.

Playin' Hockey

Hockey followed Tip Cat as a popular ice game in this province. Instead of nets or goal posts, the goals in Tip Cat were holes dug in the saltwater ice, and it was played without skates. (See also **tip cat** on page 178). Skates were usually worn to play hockey, which was often played on freshwater ponds. If ponds froze over with no snow falling, they had slick surfaces ideal for skating and playing hockey. If while it was cold enough for ponds to freeze over, a strong wind to blow away the snow also made ponds ideal. Goal posts were often winter boots that had been doffed to put on skates, or other items such as stones or frozen horse turds. If a proper rubber puck was unavailable, one could be obtained by sawing off the end of a small log. Empty cans and even frozen horse turds were sometimes used as pucks when nothing else was available. The turd sometimes caused arguments when it broke into pieces and it had to be decided which of the larger pieces of the turd was actually the puck. If snow fell with no wind to clear the ponds, boys used shovels and homemade scrapers to clear a place on which to play hockey. If the pond was clear of snow, without boards to confine them. sometimes players fought for control of the puck in far parts of the pond.

Hockey sticks were often home-made by attaching the blade part of the stick to the handle and reinforcing it with two pieces of flat wood nailed or glued to the two parts to keep them together. These pieces of wood made stick-handling difficult but didn't deter from the fun of the game, as many players had similar sticks. Small trees with a curve near the bottom were often cut to carve out hockey sticks as well.

Hockey was sometimes played on skates on saltwater ice, which wasn't as slick as freshwater ice. This slowed the momentum of the game but never decreased the fun. Sometimes hockey was played on skates on ice-packed roads. Hockey was also played without skates on saltwater, on snow-packed roads and on fields in summer using a ball.

Playin' in the Hayloft

When the dry hay was stored in the hayloft, it was a great place for kids to frolic. Kids could dive or jump in the hay without getting hurt and it was great fun to hide away in the hay during hide-and-seek games. This was often done without the knowledge or permission of the hayloft owner. Many children got in trouble for beating down someone's hay and causing it to rot.

Policing a Colony, Dominion and Province

The Colony of Newfoundland had no civilian police force. This duty fell to the military until the early 1800s, when constables were assigned as part of an organized constabulary to St. John's, Harbour Grace and other populated towns. Originally called the Constabulary Force of Newfoundland, and later the Newfoundland Constabulary, the force reorganized when Britain withdrew the military garrison from the colony in 1869. A senior officer from the Royal Irish Constabulary was brought in to serve as Inspector General (Chief of Police). The Constabulary was the only police force serving in Newfoundland and Labrador until 1935 when Commission Government instituted the Newfoundland Ranger Force.

Ranger

The Rangers were assigned to policing duties in the more remote areas of Newfoundland and Labrador, while the Constabulary continued to provide policing services to St. John's and the larger towns across the island of Newfoundland. The Rangers were not only police officers, but representatives of the government, as such they served in other duties, such as welfare officers. These officers were very versatile and had to know such things as handling a team of dogs, as they often had to travel long distances in the large areas they served.

After Confederation in 1949, the Rangers were replaced by the Royal Canadian Mounted Police, and some Rangers joined the RCMP. The Newfoundland Constabulary was downsized as the RCMP assumed policing responsibilities for all areas of the Province outside the City of St. John's. In 1979, Her Majesty Queen Elizabeth II conferred the insignia "Royal" on the

Newfoundland Constabulary, and between 1981 and 1983, the Royal Newfoundland Constabulary's policing jurisdiction expanded to include all of the Northeast Avalon, namely St. John's, Mount Pearl and the communities from Seal Cove in the west to Cape St. Francis in the east. In July 1984, the RNC assumed responsibility for policing in Labrador West including the towns of Labrador City, Wabush and Churchill Falls. In 1986, the City of Corner Brook was also included in its jurisdiction.

The RCMP, under contract with the provincial government, continues to provide police services in all other areas of the province not included in the RNC's jurisdiction.

Politics and Populations

The politics of this province was mostly the politics of Great Britain, dictated to a large degree by West Country merchants who made fortunes from the fish caught in this part of the world. Newfoundland, whose population had reached 20,000 by 1804, was generally regarded by Great Britain as nothing more than a fishing base. Newfoundland had governors appointed by England over the years, starting with David Kirke, who was made Proprietary Governor in 1637. But the purpose of the governors was more to fulfill the needs of West Country merchants than to provide government to the settlers. Then in the early 1800s, Patrick Morris and Dr. William Carson led a movement towards self-government. In 1824, Great Britain authorized a civilian governor and an appointed legislative council, and in 1832 the British House of Commons granted a representative assembly to Newfoundland. The population of Newfoundland at that time had reached about 75,000, and in spite of the fact that outports weren't officially tolerated, the population continued to increase along with the number of outports.

In 1855, in spite of protests from West Country merchants, the colony was given Responsible Government status and outports were officially sanctioned. Phillip F. Little was elected as the first prime minister with a population of around 123,000 to serve. This was a challenge, since the revenue the government had for providing these people services consisted almost entirely of customs dues. As the population increased, the sources of revenue did not, which made governing even harder on subsequent governments.

A number of prime ministers were elected up until the time of Charles Fox Bennett, who was prime minister from 1870-1874. At that time the population of the Dominion of Newfoundland was 160,000, of whom 45,800 persons were engaged in curing and catching fish, and 26,000 were able-bodied seamen employed as fishermen. Besides these, the census returns of 1874 listed four bishops, 120 clergymen, 41 doctors, 589 merchants or traders and 1,004 farmers.

When the sun rose over Cape Spear to welcome Newfoundland into the 20th century on January 1, 1901, the population of Newfoundland was about

220,000, which was to increase considerably before the end of the century. In 1907 the status of Newfoundland changed to that of Dominion.

Successive governments saw the beginning and end of the Great War, which had an immense social impact on the Dominion. It not only robbed Newfoundland of many of its best in the battlefield, but also brought a war debt that the struggling Dominion could ill afford.

Richard Squires was elected prime minister in 1919, but in July 1923, he resigned after being arrested on corruption charges, which were later substantiated. Walter S. Monroe, who replaced Squires in 1924, was prime minister when the Quebec North Shore portion of the Labrador coast was given to Newfoundland in 1927. However, the unpopularity of Munroe's government saw Squires elected again in 1928. In 1932 corruption charges were again levelled against Squires, sparking a riot from which the Prime Minister barely escaped from a mob with his life.

By that time the effects of the Great Depression were much felt in Newfoundland and Frederick C. Alderdice, who replaced Squires, had to face what was left him by previous governments, including depleted coffers. Part of the reason for the Dominion's poor financial position was that previous governments had repaid Newfoundland's war debts, the only Dominion in the British Empire to do so. Even England hadn't repaid its war debts. The financial burden Newfoundland had incurred from repaying war loans, running the railway and the country, and the public relief to the destitute were more than the country could bear. Unable to borrow any more money, the only option for the bankrupt Alderdice government was to vote itself out of existence. This it did in 1933, ending 79 years of responsible government.

On February 16, 1934, the Commission of Government, consisting of a governor and six commissioners, was appointed by the British government. No elections took place and no legislature was convened for the next 15 years. Each of the six commissioners voted upon measures which the governor would sign into law. Although the Depression made it impossible to improve the poverty status, the commission did make significant improvements in public health services and education. It also tried to abolish the denominational school system and replace it with a more efficient and less costly one, but the opposition from churches was such that, even though the commissioners didn't have to worry about being re-elected, they were not able to bring this about. The Newfoundland Ranger Force was created to police the outlying areas of the province, as well as to serve other functions, including reporting directly to the commission to keep them apprised of the situation in their areas of the dominion. WWII brought prosperity to Newfoundland, and by the time it was over everyone knew that the end of Commission of Government was in sight. By the time it was replaced in 1949 the commission had payed off the dominion's debts and there was a surplus of money in the coffers.

With a population of around 300,000 at the time, there were three options open to replace the government: one was to return to self-government, another was to become a province of Canada, while Ches Crosbie fought to have Newfoundland enter an economic union with the United States. The pro-Confederation group, led by the flamboyant Joseph Smallwood, won out over Peter Cashin and self-government in a second referendum. Newfoundland became a province in 1949 by a small majority of votes. Smallwood had his work cut out for him because under the Terms of Union, costly health care, social services and education were left to the province, while revenue genera-tors, like customs and excise duties and income tax collection went to the fed-eral government. The province also lost control over its offshore resources, including fish and oil. To alleviate these burdens, the Terms allowed for a spe-cial transitional grant to the new province for the first eight years while it increased its taxable capacity. Also, the province would receive transfer pay-ments from the federal government according to the formula that applied across the country. Even with the implementation of sales tax, these were never enough to make up the difference, and served to make it look like Newfoundlanders were living on hand-outs from Canada.

By the time the Liberals were replaced by Frank Moores' Progressive Conservatives, the population had passed the half-million mark. Brian Peckford replaced Frank Moores as premier and leader of the provincial PC Party. Tom Rideout replaced Peckford just before an election, which was lost to Clyde Wells and the Liberals. After Wells, the Liberals remained in power, with Brian Tobin as premier, and then Roger Grimes. The election of 2003 saw the PCs again replace the Liberals with prominent lawyer and businessman, Danny Williams, as premier.

The population of Newfoundland and Labrador peaked before it reached the 600,000 mark and has been declining most years since. In 2003 the population was 520,170, which was up from the 512,930 it fell to in 2001.

R abbit Catching

In the middle of winter a brace of rabbits was a welcome change from salt fish and with more protein value than bread and tea, it was a needed part of the fish-ing family's winter diet. The two types of rabbits in this province are actually hares: the native Arctic hare and the snowshoe hare, introduced to the island from Nova Scotia between 1864 and 1876. Traditionally rabbits were snared in Newfoundland and Labrador, rather than shot. Anyone skilful and proficient enough to understand the rabbit signs in the woods and how to set a proper snare didn't need to waste money on shot and powder or time traipsing around the woods trying to flush out a rabbit.

A rabbit snare is made from wire, similar to picture hanger wire. One end is bent and twisted to form a small eye, while the other end of the wire is fed through this eye to make a slip knot. The earlier way of snaring rabbits was to cut a strong pole and fasten it across the rabbit path. The snare was attached to this pole in a position with the bottom of the loop above the ground a distance of a man's handwidth with the thumb extended. When the rabbit came down this bunny trail he hopped over the stick, not realizing his neck was going into a noose. This usually killed the rabbit quickly. Sometimes only one of his rear paws would get caught in the snare however, and some rabbits would chew the leg off rather than remain in captivity.

The "spring trap" is set on a flexible pole rather than a solid one. When caught in the noose, the animal is allowed some mobility and it is usually still alive when the snare is checked.

The "spring pole trap" utilizes a stiff, flexible pole called a "bender" that is bent over and hooked onto another pole on the other side of the rabbit path in a manner that it could be knocked free with a slight jolt. The rabbit jumping into the noose provides this jolt and the bent pole springs upward breaking the rabbit's neck or quickly strangling it. This kind of snare keeps the rabbit off the ground away from other animals, especially shrews, who enter the animal through an orifice and eat the rabbit from the inside out, leaving only the skin and bones.

Both types of hare may be taken in season in Labrador and its adjacent islands; while in Newfoundland it is illegal to hunt the Arctic hare, which is not nearly as abundant as the snowshoe hare on the island.

R ed Rover

In this children's game, two teams face each other with a distance of 10 or more feet between them. The members of the team selected to be "up" join hands to create a barrier. One member of the opposing team is then challenged to try and break through the human barrier by running fast and hard enough to cause a break in the clasped hands. The challenge was issued in the following manner: "Red rover, red rover, send Alice over." Alice would then take a zig-zagging run at the line trying not to reveal her intended contact point. If she was successful in breaking through the line she returned to her team, bringing one of the opposing players to join her team. If not she became a member of the opposing team. Her original team then offered the same challenge. The game went on until all the members of one team were "captured" by the other.

R eligion

There was little in the way of organized religion in Newfoundland during the first 300 years after its discovery, except for irregular and infrequent services held by the Anglican and Roman Catholic churches, mostly on the Avalon Peninsula. John Guy brought a Protestant minister to settle the colony at Cupids in 1610, there were two or three priests holding regular mass in Ferryland after it was settled in 1621, and the the French established a church at Placentia around 1650. But for the most part there was not much in the way of religion throughout the colony.

The Moravians established missions in Labrador in 1776 to serve the Inuit there. At that time Newfoundland was still under the jurisdiction of the Bishop of London. In 1787 the diocese of Nova Scotia was constituted, and Newfoundland was placed under the care of the Reverend Charles Inglis, the first bishop of that first colonial diocese. The first Anglican Bishop of Newfoundland, the Reverend Aubrey George Spencer, was consecrated in 1839, at which time Newfoundland ceased to be part of the diocese of Nova Scotia.

By 1800, Newfoundland had close to 20,000 Roman Catholic residents, most of whom were Irish, and a half a dozen or so priests including Bishop James Louis O'Donel. O'Donel returned to Ireland in 1806, but not before laying the groundwork for the Roman Catholic Church in Newfoundland. In 1829 Reverend Michael Anthony Fleming became the first episcopal consecration in Newfoundland. Bishop Fleming divided the Catholic population into regular parishes, increased the number of priests, introduced the order of Presentation Nuns in 1833, and the order of Sisters of Mercy in 1842.

Methodism, which was considered an evangelical religion when it was conceived by John Wesley, was brought to Newfoundland by an Anglican minister, Reverend Laurence Coughlan. He had worked with John Wesley before his coming to Newfoundland and, although he had temporarily withdrawn from the service of Methodism, he returned to it shortly after his arrival at Harbour Grace in 1765. Thus the Methodist Church, which would later be called the United Church came to this province

In 1843, under the influence of the growing number of people of Scottish descent in the province, the first Presbyterian Church was opened in St. John's. This was followed by the Salvation Army, which began in St. John's in 1886 and soon spread into the outports, and in 1895 Seventh-Day Adventism was introduced to Newfoundland. A Hebrew congregation was founded in St. John's in 1909, and several years later the Pentecostal Mission made its way to Newfoundland. First called the Mission, the Pentecostal Church grew rapidly, once it was established.

Besides the earlier religions, there are congregations of people of the Jehovah's Witness, Mormon and Apostolic faiths in Newfoundland and Labrador today, and there is a Mosque in St. John's serving local people of the Muslim faith.

Ring Around the Rosy

Ring Around the Rosy is a game in which a group of children hold hands and move around in a circle while chanting:

"Ring around the rosy
A pocketful of posies
Ashes, ashes
All fall down"

As the last line is recited the children fall to the ground.

This game is believed to have originated in London, England, at the time of the bubonic plague of 1665, which killed 60 per cent of the population. The symptoms of the plague included a rosy red rash in the shape of a ring on the skin. Because it was believed that the disease was transmitted by the bad smell, sweet smelling herbs (or posies) were often carried in pockets. The term "Ashes, ashes" is said to refer to the cremation of the dead bodies, and the falling down is said to represent death.

Rounders

The game of rounders was played in Newfoundland long before baseball became popular in the United States. The game has most of the aspects of modern day baseball except a softer sphere is used. In earlier years this sphere was a pig's bladder encased in hairy bull hide, but in later years an air-filled rubber ball or a sponge ball was used. Teams were picked by the two boys chosen to be captains. Who got first pick was decided by the captains, who tossed the bat (usually just a round stick) back and forth to each other nine times. On the last catch the catcher would hold his hand in position while his opponent grasped the bat right above the other's hand. The catcher then placed his other hand above that and the last one to get a hold on the bat had first pick. Sometimes the last person to grip the bat only had a small portion of his hand holding it. If he had enough grip on the bat to swing it around his head nine times, he was given first pick. Team members were chosen because of their known ability, their age or their size. Everyone wanted to be picked first and nobody wanted to be last choice, so choruses of "Pick me, pick me," could often be heard. The team of the captain who got first pick was usually also first at bat. There were pitchers, catchers, basemen and as many outfielders as were left over, none wearing baseball mitts. One was deemed "out" if someone from the opposing team caught a struck ball or were able to catch the ball on a bounce and tag the batter with it. If the person running for base was too far away to be tagged, the ball could be thrown at him and if the ball connected, he was out. Although there were a number of changes, modern day baseball evolved from this game.

Scrub

Often in Newfoundland and Labrador it was difficult to get enough players to make up two baseball teams, so scrub was played instead. There are no teams in scrub – everyone tries to get the most individual runs to win. A run consists of making it to first base and back. There are only two people "up at bat" at a time. If the first batter only makes it to first base the second batter has to bring him home by hitting the ball and making a run to first base, passing the first batter on the way home. Batters could be replaced several times before the man on base got home. When a batter was declared "out," he became the last outfielder. The catcher then got a turn at bat, while the pitcher became catcher, the first baseman, pitcher and so on. These games usually went on until the boys were called home to supper by their mothers, at which time the person with the most individual runs was declared the winner.

Skipping

As in most other places, skipping was a girl's game. Girls would get together and skip, using different steps and techniques while chanting such rhymes as:
> "The King of England went to France
> To teach the children how to dance
> This is how he taught them
> Heel, toe, over you go
> Bow to the Queen
> Salute to the King
> Turn your back to the Kaiser."

Social Differences

There was a very noticeable social difference between peoples of this province that to some degree exists to this day. There was a distinct difference between the well-to-do and the poorer class of people, which constituted a large majority of the population. The majority never travelled first-class on coastal boats, and on longer train journeys they slept in a seat and not in a berth. They seldom bought meals in the fancy dining car on the train, but ate what they carried with them. When travelling and had to stop over, they stayed with relatives, friends or friends of friends along the way, rather than at a hotel.

In outport communities the families of fishermen and others such as labourers never thought of themselves as well-to-do, nor were they thought of by others as such. Among those considered well-to-do were merchants, doctors, ship captains, and government workers, especially those who served social functions, such as relieving (relief or welfare) officers.

The earliest fishermen were indentured to a master to do his bidding for the length of the indenture. During that time the indentured man had to perform every task asked of him by his master, the same as a slave. This situation inspired such sayings as, "Jack is as good as his master," which was said when the man's indenture was up. Fishermen were often indebted to the merchant, which left him feeling inferior and bound to that merchant. Between the poorer fishing class and others there was a feeling of servitude not dissimilar to that of slave to owner. This social system was partly a leftover from the system that existed in the countries in which these people originated.

Teachers, clergy, welfare officers, police officers and certain others, although not considered well-to-do, were held in a certain esteem. Special care was given to the house when one of them visited, and one was careful about one's language when around them. Most fisherfolk had a certain feeling of inferiority to these people as well.

Then there were the rich. These were usually St. John's merchants, who were often the fish exporters, very successful outport merchants, or other business people. These were millionaires or near-millionaires. When Newfoundland became part of Canada in 1949, per capita there were more millionaires in this province than anywhere in the rest of Canada. This was no reflection of the wealth of the province, as at the same time there were more poor people per capita here as well.

Apart from economics, there were social differences in this province based on geography as well. There was a distinct social disparity between Townies (St. John's residents) and Baymen. A bayman was anybody living anywhere but St. John's. This difference is personified in the popular St. John's song, "Mussels in the Corner."

"Ask a bayman for a smoke,
He will say his pipe is broke;
Ask a bayman for a chew,
He will bite it off for you

"Here they was as thick as flies,
Dirty shirts and dirty ties
Dirty rings around their eyes
Dirty old Torbay men

"There they are as wild as goats,
Baymen in their little boats,
Women in their petticoats,
Bound for Petty Harbour."

This feeling toward baymen was shared by larger centres across the province including Grand Falls, Gander and Corner Brook. There was also a social difference between residents on the island and those in Labrador, many of whom were native.

There was a social distinction between those of European descent and native peoples also, both in Labrador and on the Island. For many years people with Mi'kmaq (Micmac) blood often kept it to themselves to avoid ridicule. As late as the 1960s (and probably later), the "Jackatars" of Bay St. George and Bay of Islands were often put down by others. The natives of Labrador were considered by some earlier settlers to be less than human.

Among outports themselves, including Labrador outports, there was a social difference between the more-populated settlements and the lesser-populated ones. Sometimes residents of a small outport had to visit a larger one to do business with the merchant, to visit a doctor or a hospital or just to visit friends or relatives. This was usually done in the family skiff or motorboat. It was a family affair, which sometimes included community members from other families, especially children who were friends of their own children. Although there was very little cultural difference between the smaller and larger communities, residents of the larger ones often made fun of the way the people from "up the bay" acted, spoke or dressed when they encountered them on the wharves where they tied up their boats. Yet all outport people were mostly humble people, yet still had a pride that showed through at any opportunity they got to one-up those who would put them down.

Within communities people were aware of social distinctions that could be discerned not only by the way one dressed and spoke, but by the clothes a woman had on her clothesline or what she was seen buying from the local merchant. Another way to tell a family's social status was in the clothes their children wore to school. Most children didn't wear store-bought clothes, only children of the better-off residents could do that. The others wore handmade and hand-me-down clothes, sometimes made-over into a completely different garment.

One interesting social difference observed between students by teachers some years ago in the province had to do with the food a student ate. Teachers and students could tell the richer kids from the poorer ones because the poorer kids were the ones with the lobster sandwiches.

Although there was a social stigma attached to the financially lesser-blessed families, very few children grew up feeling poor. After all, most families they knew were no better off than theirs. In spite of the hardship their way of life offered, and the hard work expected of these children to help the family survive, the freedoms they enjoyed made them richer than children in many parts of the world today.

Squattin' Cans

Carnation milk cans were great for squattin', because they still had both ends when they were empty. You placed one on its side, then stepped on it. If you applied the right amount of pressure to the right area and squat it properly, the ends would turn in and clamp onto your shoe. With one on the other foot you could be the Lone Ranger and his horse, Silver, all in one. Boys could often be seen clip-clopping down the gravel road chanting the William Tell Overture and shouting "Hi, ho, Silver!" Adults would sometimes get upset with youngsters who practiced this bit of fun, not just because of the racket and dust they kicked up, but because of the wear and tear it caused to their footwear.

The Great Outdoors

Traditionally most work in this province was done outdoors, yet it was the outdoors where many chose to spend their leisure time. Family picnics were often enjoyed on a secluded beach, which was reached by walking, by horse-and-cart or in the family rowboat or motorboat. These outings always included a boil-up and often a fresh fish caught on the way made part of the meal. These outings sometimes incorporated other activities such as picking mussels or berries. Motor vehicles have replaced the horse, but even today people enjoy picnicking in some secluded spot that can only be reached by boat. Overnight and weekend camping has for many years been popular. Trouting was often a part of these outings. Many residents own travel trailers or motorhomes, and although there are many parks to accommodate them, not all campers use them. Known as "gravel pit campers," many can be seen singly or in groups enjoying the great outdoors all over the province.

Quad-runners (all-terrain vehicles) and snowmobiles have made the outdoors more accessible to residents, and many have taking up downhill or cross-country skiing, as well as snowshoeing.

Sailing has made a comeback, with a number of residents owing their own sailboat for leisure cruising around the coast.

The Lumberwoods

Fishing alone wasn't always enough to support a family all year so some fishermen found other ways to supplement their income. One of the ways they did that was by working in the lumberwoods. Up until the 1900s this meant working for a lumbering operation. Few fishermen were involved in this, as there were not enough of these sawmill operations around.

After the Anglo-Newfoundland Development Company started a paper mill in Grand Falls, and Bowaters started one in Corner Brook, the woods workers they employed were still said to work "in the lumberwoods," even though the logs they cut were to make paper and not lumber.

Many workers were required to keep the two paper mills going, and these jobs were often filled by fishermen after they clewed up their fishing season. Especially if after they clewed up they were still in debt to the merchant. Sometimes they went further in debt to acquire the fare needed for the train that would take them part of the way to the logging camp. With their bag containing clothing, blankets, food and other items, these men walked many miles through woods and sometimes over saltwater ice to get to the nearest train terminal. Along the way they stayed with people they knew who would offer them a meal and a place to sleep, sometimes in a barn or other out-building. On the trains, which included the main line and branch line trains, they never ate in the dining car, as to do so would seriously cut into any money they might make in the woods. Instead they ate what they carried with them. At the end of the last branch line, which for AND Company loggers usually meant Millertown, loggers made their way to logging camps by various means: including on a gasoline-powered company train, by boat and on foot.

Logging camps had bunkhouses; a cookhouse, which included a dining area; a forepeak, which was the office and living accommodations for the foreman or manager; barns for horses; an outdoor toilet; storage sheds and a cellar. The roughly-made wooden bunks had no mattresses, and every man had to cut the tips of tree branches to make his bunk soft enough to sleep on. His big coat or clothes bag served as a pillow.

The food served by the cook was repetitious, and included such meals as beans and bread; salt fish and brewis; pea soup, with salt meat, potatoes and dough boys; steamed or boiled pudding, sometimes with fresh meat; porridge; fresh and salt meat, potatoes and green peas; rice soup and various combinations of these foods, served in the cook house for breakfasts and suppers, and packed as lunches to be taken in the woods by the loggers. Bread was baked by the cook at the rate of about a loaf per man per day, and he often made pies, cakes, rice pudding and other desserts to finish a meal.

Initially loggers were paid by the day, but later the company contracted with the men by the cord. This made more profit for the company and more money for the better loggers.

Double-bitted axes were originally used to fell trees; one edge was kept very sharp and used to fell the tree, while the duller blade was used to knock the branches from them. Various saws were later used in logging operations over the years. The first was the cross-cut or simon saw, which were four or more feet long had wide blades and a handle at each end so they could be operated by two men. Buck saws were later introduced and the first of these had wooden handles that were adjustable to apply tension to the blade, which was narrower than those on the crosscut saw. A buck saw, made in Sweden, with a tubular metal handle replaced the wooden version. These could be operated by one man and often were. Years later these were replaced by gasoline-powered chainsaws.

Logs were piled up over the winter and, although some were transported to the mill by train, most were set afloat in the Exploits River or one if its tributaries where they made their way to the mill at Grand Falls. Teams of horses handled by men known as "teamers' or "teamsters" were required to get the logs to the riverbank. Men known as "drivers" were necessary to insure these logs didn't get caught up along the river. The drivers had to be very agile as they often had to walk over a log jam and use pike poles to loosen the offending logs, then step lively back to safety over the moving and rolling logs.

Not all woods workers were also fishermen. Some worked full-time in the lumberwoods, often spending long periods of time away from their families. Part-time woodsmen were away from home for long periods and both groups often entertained themselves and each other in the bunkhouse by singing songs, playing a harmonica or squeezebox, reciting poems and telling stories. Arm-wrestling and other games tested one's strength or agility. Many tricks were played on fellow loggers, but all in all there was a camaraderie among them, which made times spent in the lumberwoods memorable ones.

At one time the logging industry employed 17,000 workers, but the coming of the chainsaw saw the numbers reduced to less than half that. Then heavy, mechanical, wood-cutting equipment known as harvesters, capable of cutting 50 cords of wood in 12 hours, reduced the number of men using chainsaws to less than 100. Trucks now haul the logs to the mill, and there is no longer a need for horses or the teamers who drove them. The quick-stepping river drivers have been replaced by truck drivers, and television has replaced the amateur entertainers so appreciated by the loggers. Apart from television, today's logging camps also have real beds and clean sheets, indoor toilets, showers and all the amenities of home.

The Newfoundland Railway

Affectionately and sarcastically called the Newfie Bullet, the train that ran the track between St. John's and Port aux Basques and branch lines along the way for more than a century got its name from American servicemen because of its slow speed and sometimes irregular service. That was partly because, for reasons of economy, the tracks were built on a narrow (3' 6") gauge, which required that the train slow down on sharp turns to keep from overturning. Its irregular schedule could be attributed somewhat to the fact that the train would stop to pick up or discharge trouters, hunters and berry pickers in wilderness areas along the track. Snow storms in winter, especially on the Gaff Topsails (high mountains in the centre of the island) could interrupt the service, sometimes for several days.

High winds blew trains off the track, This was particularly true at Wreckhouse, not far from Port aux Basques, where winds funnel down from the Long Range mountains with great force. A famous Newfoundlander by the name of Lauchie ({pronounced *LOCK - ee*} McDougal lived at Wreckhouse. It was believed that Lauchie had the ability to "smell" the wind before it came up. For this reason he was hired by the Newfoundland Railway, who installed a phone line in his house so he could call and warn the train master at Port aux Basques of any big blows that might be brewing. The one time they didn't heed Lauchie's warning because the weather was so fair in Port aux Basques, a total of 22 railway cars blew off the track at Wreckhouse.

The rail distance from St. John's to Port aux Basques is 882 kilometres (548 miles) which made it the longest such line (narrow gage) in North America. The company that built the line and operated the railway was begun by Robert Gillespie Reid, a Scottish bridge-builder who worked for the Canadian Pacific Railway in Montreal. Like the coastal boat service, the Reid Newfoundland Railway seldom made a profit and some years lost more than a million dollars. Nevertheless the railway provided a very essential service in the growth of this province. The freight and mail service began in 1882 and ended in 1988. The first passenger train across the island ran in June 1898 and regular passenger service ceased in July 1969. The railbed has since become a "linear" provincial park called the "T'Railway," a hiking and RVing trail that continues across the Canadian provinces and back around the northern territories.

The Seal Hunt

For at least 4,000 years, seals have been hunted in the spring of the year for food, fur and fat by the indigenous peoples of eastern North America. The seals arrive every year with the ice floes moving south on the same current that brings icebergs along our shores. When Spanish, Basques, Portuguese, French and British sailors began arriving in the 1600s for fish they, too, started harvesting seals for subsistence. But it was with the arrival of the English, who settled the northeast coast of Newfoundland in the early 1700s, that the global market for seal products began to surface.

English settlers first began taking seals when the ice brought the whelping herds to within walking distance from shore in the spring. These were usually taken in nets. Later in the season, seals were hunted from small boats using rifles. The meat and fur were in demand locally, while the oil was shipped back to Britain. There it was used as fuel for lamps, as lubricating and cooking oil, in the processing of leather and jute, and as a constituent in soap.

Schooners were later employed to hunt seals on the floes and before the century was out, large-scale commercial seal fishing had begun. This new catch became second in importance only to the cod fishery, accounting for up to one-third of Newfoundland's total exports.

Between 1818 and 1862 more than 18 million seals were landed, reaching a yearly average of more than 400,000 seals harvested by 1862. The industry peaked during this period, and in 1863 steam-powered vessels were introduced to the hunt. Although these ships were superior in size and strength to the small sailing schooners, the industry had started to decline because of previous over-harvesting.

The change from sail to steam dramatically increased the expense involved in the annual seal hunt, which meant that only the wealthy could afford to operate sealing vessels. So most commercial sealing ships were owned by large merchants, such as the Bowrings in St. John's. The driving force behind the seal hunt changed then from being one of survival to one of large profits for the ship owners.

With no local schooner to take them to the ice to share in the voyage's profits, the many fishermen wishing to go to the hunt had to compete with each other for a berth on the new steam vessels – sometimes they had to pay for their position. Fishermen lucky enough to secure a berth could expect less than favourable living conditions aboard a vessel intended to be used for other purposes than providing accommodations for several hundred sealers. The men's living accommodation below deck was so cramped that it was satirically called the "Ballroom." At the Front (the main sealing patch), sealers had to jump from the ship onto moving ice pans to rally after seals. Sometimes when the chase took the men a long distance away, the wind shifted and cut them off from their ship. When this happened they had to be found and picked up, sometimes in raging seas. It was a dangerous way to make a living and many lives were lost in the seal hunt over the years. Sometimes deaths came in large numbers at one time, like the 25 men of the SS *Greenland* who froze to death on the ice one night in 1898.

The worst sealing disaster in our history occurred in 1914, when the famous sealing captain Abram Kean was master of the *Stephano* and his son, Westbury, was in command of the *Newfoundland*. The younger Kean had sent his men over the ice to his father's ship, some distance away, to receive directions to a patch of seals. Despite the fact that a storm appeared to be brewing, Abram told the men where to find the seals and instructed them to return to their own ship when they were done. Over the course of the day, the storm became significantly worse and the crew of the *Newfoundland* lost their way on the ice. Unfortunately for them, each captain assumed all along that the men were safe on the other's ship. Because neither ship was equipped with a radio, there was no way for the captains to know a crew was still on the ice, and so no search party was sent out. The men spent 53 hours stranded on the ice without shelter, food or sufficiently protective clothing before being spotted by the *Bellaventure*. Of the men and boys left to the mercy of the blizzard, 78 died of either exposure or drowning, while 11 of the survivors were permanently disabled.

In spite of the poor living and working conditions, the hard work and the danger, men still competed for a berth to go to the ice. Their family's survival often depended on it. So sealing continued in much the same way for a number of years, although catches got fewer. The Royal Commission Report of 1933 stated "...the seal fishery has fallen off; in the present year only six ships with a complement of 1,122 men went to the seal fishery, as against 323 ships manned by over 10,000 men in 1851."

Conservation concerns led to quotas being placed on seals and by 1987, the commercial hunt of whitecoats was banned. That same year, the sealing policy prohibited the use of vessels over 65 feet (19.8 metres) long. This opened the door for longliners and smaller boats normally involved in other fisheries to participate in the hunt. With the biggest vessels out of the industry, the seal fishery was out of the hands of large corporations and back in the hands of ordinary fishermen. It was looking more like the subsistence hunt it once was.

The conservation measures seem to have worked well. In 1996, after a long decline in the number of seals taken, the catch jumped to 242,000 harp seals – making the Canadian harp seal hunt the largest commercial hunt of a marine mammal anywhere in the world. Today the seal hunt is still a viable operation, and will remain so as long as there is a demand for seal products and proper quotas are maintained to insure the survival of the seal herds in sustainable numbers.

Trawl Fishing

A trawl is a long line with secondary lines, called sud lines, attached at regular intervals. A hook is attached to the other end of the sud line. This line of hooks makes up one section of the trawl. Each section is coiled around a wooden tub, the edge of which is carved with notches, one to accommodate each hook. This is referred to as a "tub of gear." The hooks that dangle outside each tub are baited with a full capelin, pieces of squid or some other bait. These tubs are then loaded into the fisherman's boat.

At the fishing ground the first tub of gear is attached to the prior line. This is a rope with a grapnel at one end and a buoy at the other. The trawl line is attached about one fathom (2 metres or 6 feet), above the grapnel to help keep the baited hooks off the bottom. Once this is lowered into the water the boat then heads to the other end of the fishing ground with the trawl reeling out behind. This is called "shooting a trawl." The direction one shoots a trawl over a fishing ground is decided by which way the tide is sweeping. A second tub of gear is then attached to the first line and so on until all the lines of trawl are out. The end of the trawl is attached to a second rope with a grapnel and a buoy, and this is dropped overboard. With any luck the sweeping tide will keep the bait off the bottom. If not, there may be a crab or some other bottom dweller on one of your hooks when you haul your trawl later.

Sometimes fishermen would set their trawl in the morning and haul it in the afternoon and again next morning, while others hauled their trawls only once a day.

Hauling a trawl is hard work, especially if every hook has something on it, so many fishermen attached gerties (aka gurdies) to their motorboat engines to help with the haul. This was a pulley, similar that on the fan of an automobile engine, around which the trawl line was wrapped. There was a blocking device in front of the pulley which ripped the hook from the mouth of each codfish, and the fish fell down into the bottom of the boat. Unwanted bycatches didn't make it that far because one or two fishermen stood at the gunnel with a hand gaff and knocked off any crabs, sculpin, maiden ray (small skate), or dogfish (small shark) that had succumbed to the bait.

With trawl-fishing, the only time you can catch fish is when they are hungry. When codfish were plentiful, trawl-fishing was a viable way to make a living. Catching codfish only when they were hungry still gave fishermen enough of a catch to make a profit.

The long liner, which got its name from this type of fishing, gave the fishermen the ability to go further afield and the space to bring back bigger catches. Slowly the smaller skiffs and speedboats were replaced by these larger and more efficient vessels. But as fish stocks got more and more scarce, the longliner operators turned their attention to other methods of fishing and other species. Bigger and faster vessels also came on the scene, some of which dragged the ocean bottom and often destroyed the breeding grounds of many species of marine life.

Factory ships from other nations brought with them a fleet of smaller vessels, all of them much bigger than long liners, to the fishing grounds in offshore, and sometimes inshore, waters. These smaller vessels supply the factory workers on the mother ship with enough fish to make the voyage a paying one. These factory ships take enormous amounts in one voyage.

As a consequence, catching enough fish to make a living only when the fish are hungry is no longer viable. Yet, there are many, including scientists and fishermen, who believe that if trawling and hand-lining had been the only allowable methods of fishing, the stocks would not have been as devastated as they are today, and trawling would still be a viable way of fishing.

War Heroes

Men of this province were always quick to answer the call to arms in times of war. Among those were the men of the first Newfoundland Regiment, which was originally founded in 1780 and was disbanded and refounded several times under different names. Over the years it was known as His Majesty's Royal Newfoundland Regiment of Foot, The Royal Newfoundland Fencibles and The Royal Newfoundland Companies until being disbanded in 1862.

It was during the War of 1812 that the fighting men from this province earned a lot of gratitude from Canadians in the defense of Canada. On August 16, 1812, Newfoundlanders played a big role in the capture of Detroit, for which they won a special commendation from General Brock. In October of that year, longboats manned mainly by Newfoundlanders entered the mouth of the Genesee River and seized the schooner *Lady Murray* as well as several other vessels. In November a light company of 50 Newfoundlanders under the command of Captain John Whelan was responsible for holding Fort Erie against attack during the second major attempt by the Americans to cross the Niagara at Frenchman's Creek.

In January of the following year, 60 Newfoundlanders were among a British and Indian force which crossed the ice at the end of Lake Erie and engaged in a bitter fight to capture Frenchtown, Michigan. In February 40 Newfoundlanders were part of a bayonet assault which captured Ogdensburg, New York.

A party of 54 Newfoundlanders, along with native allies were successful in capturing two American ships, the *Tigress* and the *Scorpion*.

Soldiers and sailors from Newfoundland were in many engagements and operations during this war, including a daring operation to re-supply the starving garrison at Michilimackinac. Without supplies the garrison would have fallen to the Americans. The regiment, using the skill they learned at home as boat builders, felled trees and built 30 boats which they rowed some 360 miles across Lake Huron. Only one boat was lost when it was crushed in the ice-filled lake.

The part the Newfoundlanders played in the War of 1812 was very important to the defense of Canada. So much so that several Ontario towns still have daily reenactments of their efforts. In Midland, Ontario, actors in full uniform of the day play out the brave efforts of the soldiers from Newfoundland for the gathered tourists.

When the Great War (WWI) was declared on August 4, 1914, Newfoundlanders again volunteered to fight and by September 26, nearly 1,000 volunteers had signed up. About 500 of these, the first group in the newly formed 1st Newfoundland Regiment, passed the required medical examination. Since there were no uniforms for them yet, they marched down to the waiting ship *Florizel* in St. John's harbour wearing blue puttees (a bandage-like material which held the bottom of the pant leg tight at the ankles). As ill-equipped as they were at the start, this group went on to make themselves a reputation of being among the bravest and best before the end of that war. Some of them lived to see their regiment, the 1st Newfoundland Regiment, become the only regiment to earn the title "Royal" during that war. One of its members, Tommy Ricketts, became the youngest soldier to ever win the Victoria Cross.

Another courageous Newfoundlander, who was braver than many, was a young man from Fortune Harbour. In a battle with the enemy he was wounded in the neck, both legs and one arm and taken to a military hospital. While recovering from his wounds another soldier was brought in to the hospital who wasn't so lucky. Lieutenant-Colonel Goddard, 5780, Queens Own Rifles had serious wounds. By the time he arrived at the hospital a lot of blood had left his body. There was no hope for him. There were no blood banks back then and blood transfusions were virtually unheard of. In a feeble attempt to save the man's life one doctor decided to try getting blood from a volunteer patient, if they could find one who would be willing to try an experiment. The volunteer was 18-year-old Patrick Gillespie of Fortune Harbour. They inserted a needle in Gillespie's arm and another in Goddard's, with a tube in between. Gillespie's heart pumped 450 ccms of his blood into the officer's body and saved his life. I'm sure he had thoughts about his own life, but he still risked it to save another.

Another Newfoundlander saved many Allies from death and serious injury. The Germans ventured into chemical warfare in early 1915 by using a dreaded chlorine chemical known as mustard gas. This was a catastrophic problem on all fronts. It wreaked havoc among all the Allied troops. In one encounter alone, on April 22, 1915, at the village of Langemarck near Ypres, the Germans released a five-mile-wide cloud of chlorine gas from some 520 cylinders (168 tons of the chemical). The greenish-yellow cloud drifted over and into the French and Algerian trenches where it caused widespread panic and death.

Dr. Cluny MacPherson of The Royal Newfoundland Regiment was serving in Gallipoli in 1915 and decided to do something about the gas attacks. Using a helmet taken from a captured prisoner to fashion a canvas hood, he attached transparent eyepieces. He then treated the mask with chlorine-absorbing chemicals. The gas mask worked and many lives were saved.

Many other Newfoundlanders fought the good fight to the best of their ability. By war's end a total of 6,241 Newfoundland men had served in the regiment. Another 5,747 enlisted in the Royal Naval Reserve, the Forestry Corps, the Canadian Expeditionary Force, British Forces and the Merchant Navy.

The 1st Newfoundland Regiment first saw action in Egypt, and later in Belgium and France, where it was involved in fierce fighting with many casualties. The most-remembered battle of the Regiment took place at Beaumont-Hamel on July 1, 1916, where it was almost annihilated. The regiment of 790 men was ordered to attack a German trench through a gap in their own barbed wire. German machine gun fire mowed them down in the gap like sitting ducks as they advanced toward the enemy. Those who made it through the gap were gunned down before they reached the enemy's barbed wire, and only 68 answered roll call the following day. The rest were killed, seriously wounded or missing in action. Major General D.E. Cayley, Commander of the 88th Brigade, would later say the only reason the Regiment failed to reach its objective was because "dead men can advance no further."

Rebuilt with fresh recruits from Newfoundland, the Regiment went on to other battles until the end of the war, including a battle at Cambria in 1917, where their heroics earned them the "Royal" title. Their bravery in the line of fire throughout the war earned the Regiment a reputation of being a reliable fighting force. So much so that at the Battle of Ledeghem in September, 1918, upon learning the Royal Newfoundland Regiment held his left flank, Victoria Cross winner General Bernard Cyril Freyberg, Commander of the 88th Brigade at the time, said, "Thank God, my left flank is safe! Now for my right." General Sir Aylmer Hunter Weston called them "better than the best," which became the Regiment's unofficial motto.

World War II also saw a large number of volunteers (by comparison to population) from Newfoundland and Labrador sign up for the war effort. Among the areas they served were the Canadian and British armies, air forces and navies, as well as in the armed forces of other Allied countries. Newfoundland did not send local infantry units overseas. Instead, it raised two artillery regiments; the 59 Heavy (Newfoundland) Regiment and the 57 (later 166 Newfoundland) Field Artillery Regiment.

Their expertise at handling smaller boats, particularly during the evacuation of Dunkirk, caused Sir Winston Churchill to call them "the best small-boatmen in the world."

Many sailors from this dominion also served as merchant mariners on ships of a number of Allied nations. Their value during the Battle of the Atlantic, when German U-boats were sinking Allied ships at an alarming rate, was phenomenal. These mariners kept the supply lines to Britain open and prevented a successful German invasion of that country. Experts say the war was won on logistics, which means the supply of equipment and supplies to the forces in the field. We won the war because our logistics were better than those of the Germans. The major contributor to those logistics were the merchant mariners, many of whom gave their lives in the effort. Without the merchant navy we would have seen a different outcome to the war.

In 1950, Communist North Korea, aided by Communist China, went to war against South Korea. Many from this province also volunteered for that war in an effort to maintain world peace. A number of them gave their lives in that war as well.

The present day Royal Newfoundland Regiment is a militia reserve unit made up of men and women and is attached to the Canadian Military. These are everyday citizens with jobs, whose weekend training qualifies them as soldiers. Members of this regiment have been involved in many peacekeeping missions in world hot spots in the last 10 years, including Afghanistan, Bosnia, Croatia, Cyprus, East Timor, Rwanda and Yugoslavia.

A high percentage of the Canadian Forces is made up of men and women from Newfoundland and Labrador. They perform many brave and caring deeds for the citizens of these countries that are going through troubled times. But few people get to find out about their good deeds. This is probably because many Canadians don't know why they are there. Another Newfoundlander, General Rick Hillier, who is the commander-in-chief for the security of this country, knows why they are there. He understands the basic truth that if we don't stop the terrorists of the world on their soil we will have to try to stop them on ours. Many soldiers from this province have served in these peacekeeping missions.

Like the rest of this country's military they are doing an excellent job, risking their lives in parts of the world where the enemy is not distinguishable from the regular citizen. Some have paid the supreme sacrifice. One of those who gave his life for his country was Cpl. Jamie Murphy, a 26-year-old hero who was killed in a January 2004 suicide bomb attack near Kabul, Afghanistan.

Washing and Ironing

Having her family appear in public in clothes that were clean and neatly pressed was a matter of pride for most women of this province, although this required a lot of effort on her part. Large tubs, which were initially made of wood and later replaced by galvanized steel ones, were used to soak the clothes, towels and bed sheets. By rubbing one section of the cloth of these items against another, dirt and stains were removed. Rubbing the cloth over the glass ribs of scrub boards removed dirt more efficiently. Home-made lye soap assisted in this process until commercial laundry soap came on the scene. To insure winter whiteness in white clothing, a blue block of a substance called "blue" was often added to the wash. The excess water on these clothes was expelled by tightly twisting clothes before wringers were invented.

Wringers were hand-powered devices sometimes attached to the side of the wash tub. The woman fed the clothes between two rubber rollers with one hand, while turning the cranking handle with the other. The pressure from the rollers squeezed excess water out of the clothes.

Before electricity, people who could afford it had gasoline-powered washing machines to eliminate the hand-scrubbing of clothes. These required ventilation for the exhaust fumes, which meant that a hole had to be made in one side of the house to expel the fumes. For this reason gasoline-powered washing machines were sometimes kept in an out-building. Very few Newfoundland women could afford one of these.

With the coming of electricity, washing machines with an electrically-powered wringer lightened the load of housewives in this province. But after washing, clothes were still hung on the clothesline to dry in summer and winter, same as before. In winter frozen clothes were often removed from clotheslines by fingers that sometimes became almost as cold as the garments, sheets and towels.

Pressing these clothes was done with a flat iron heated on the kitchen stove. These flat irons were eventually replaced by modern. electrically-heated irons.

Modern day automatic washers and dryers replaced the washing tub and the need of drying clothes on a clothesline, but to this day some women prefer the fresh-smelling fragrance of clothes dried on the clothesline to those dried by a machine powered by electricity.

Wheelin' Hoops

A favourite bit of fun for youngsters in Newfoundland and Labrador was to shape a piece of stiff wire into a driving tool, sometimes called a "scraper," that would hold a barrel hoop in place while it was wheeled in front of the young-ster. Wooden barrel hoops worked well, but the metal hoops were tapered and it was hard to get the hoop to go where you wanted it to go, as it kept veering in the direction of the narrower side of the hoop. The Cadillac of hoops was actually the rim of an old bicycle wheel, especially if the spokes were missing. This "hoop" didn't require a piece of wire to propel it, instead a straight stick placed in the groove where the inner tube normally sat served the purpose of the scraper. Bicycle wheels were easier to control than metal hoops, and wheels without spokes were best because there were no spoke-ends in the groove of the rim to impede the scraper. A St. John's foundry produced a variation of this toy. This was a metal ring similar to a hula hoop, only smaller. The scraper had a loop at one end that was permanently welded around the ring.

Winter Fun

A drifting snowstorm often left snow drifts piled high. These drifts were a great place in which to dig snow tunnels. If the drift was big enough a labyrinth of tunnels was sometimes dug by children in which they played a game of tag. The youngster who was "it," or "the tagger," would scurry through the tunnels try-ing to tag the others who would then become the "tagger." Sometimes a young-ster had to scurry out of a tunnel to keep from being tagged. Then the game became a foot race with the tagger trying to get close enough to the pursued youngster to tag him as he entered one of the tunnel openings again. Sometimes the pursued person would run away from the tunnels to escape. This would beget cries of foul from the person who was "it." The word "foul" was never used. Instead one might hear, "If you goes past the corner of Uncle Ben's store, you're 'it'."

Snow forts provided hours of entertainment for children. A snow fort often consisted of only one wall built from large snowballs made from rolling small snowballs over the clammy snow. Sometimes a fort had two partial sides as well. Some forts had four walls and were entered by way of a tunnel-like open-ing in one of the walls. One half of a group of boys manned the fort to protect it from the other half who attacked it by throwing snowballs to keep the heads of boys in the fort down as they rushed. The defenders threw snowballs at the attackers to keep them from reaching the front of the fort. If the attackers were successful, the walls of the fort would be smashed and had to be rebuilt again for the next assault in which teams usually changed places.

Known as randying, sliding down snow-covered hills was very popular. If a home-made slide (sled) or a store-bought "coaster" was not available, youngsters often slid down a hill on a piece of cardboard or old kitchen canvas. Catamarans – sleds usually used for hauling wood – or other vehicles were often used in randying.

Outport families couldn't afford proper skis, so pieces of leather or rubber were often nailed to barrel staves to make them. These were hard to manoeuvre, and to make it to the bottom of a hill without falling down was a challenge.

Initially bob skates (skating blades fastened to winter boots) were used to go skating. Children whose family could afford it wore lace-up skates. These were often bought second-hand or passed down to younger children in the family. Because of this, sometimes a boy played hockey wearing girl's skates, earning him a certain amount of ridicule by other boys. Often girls suffered the same ridicule because they were wearing their older brother's hand-me-down skates.

After a fresh snowfall, making the first tracks in the field of newly fallen snow was a fun thing to do. Sometimes paths were made in a pattern that resembled a city block with roads (paths) running from one side of the perimeter to the other, intersecting other paths. A game of snow tag was sometimes played in these paths. Neither the tagger nor those he pursued were permitted to step outside a path, and if they did so to avoid being tagged they were considered tagged anyway.

After motor vehicles came on the scene, "hanging on cars" became a popular form of winter entertainment. Youngsters would hide behind a snow bank and wait for a slow-moving motor vehicle to pass. Then they would hang onto its bumper and be taken for a ride with their winter boots sliding over the hard-packed snow on the roads. Because this was dangerous, often drivers watched out for hangers-on and would stop their vehicle to chase the youngsters away. Youngsters would try to hang on as long as possible, but let go when a vehicle reached a place where it could pick up speed. Often a child's mitten was left clinging to the bumper as the car sped away.

On warm winter days when melting caused rivulets of water to run down hills and inclines, children would make dams from unmelted snow and back up large reservoirs of water, then smash the dam and let the water go cascading down the hill. In St. John's, where these dams were often built against a curb, this was called "making a flood."

Wishbone Wishes

Collin's English Dictionary describes a wishbone as "the V-shaped bone above the breastbone in most birds consisting of the fused clavicles." When a Newfoundland and Labrador home was having chicken, turr, turkey, goose, duck or bullbird soup for dinner, this bone was put aside to dry. When it was dry enough, after several days, two people would hold the alternate tips of the wishbone's V with their pinky fingers while each made a silent wish. One would then ask the other, "What goes up the chimley (chimney)?" The other would answer, "Smoke," and they would recite in unison, "Your wish and my wish will never be broke." They would then gently pull against each other until the wishbone broke into two pieces. It was believed that the person who got the bigger piece of the bone would have his or her wish come true as long as the wish was kept secret.

Sometimes wishbones were used to help one find a mate. After the wishbone was broken, the person with the smallest piece would place it above a doorway. The next person of the opposite sex who walked through that door would be the person he or she would marry.

Yarnin'

One of the favourite pastimes before modern technology came along was yarnin'. The venues for this activity were varied and included the galley on a fishing vessel, the smoking room on a passenger vessel, the fisherman's store, the netloft (while nets were being made or mended) and in the lamplight around the kitchen table. The stories told were sometimes true, but were often ghost stories, fairy stories or tales of impossible deeds. Sometimes yarnin' became a contest to see who could tell the biggest lie.

My grandfather, Pierce Young, often told about the time he was working as a carpenter on a skyscraper in New York City. He said that he fell off the top of one of these tall buildings one day and was headed for sure death when he remembered he had his hammer in his belt and four-inch nails in his pocket. He quickly drove a nail into the side of the skyscraper and held on until he was rescued.

Uncle Mose Butt of Twillingate claimed that he once had a pig that he had trained to help him build boats. He said he would nail one end of a plank to a timber and, using its shoulder, the pig would bend the plank into a curved position around the timbers while Uncle Mose nailed it in place.

Folklore, Cures and Omens

The material for this section was supplied by readers of *Downhome* magazine, from the author's recollections, as well as from a number of publications.

Aches, Pains and Ailments

A blade of grass from the grave of a member of the clergy can cure a toothache.

A bread poultice was often used to draw the core out of a boil. Other poultices were used for a number of ailments. These could be made from flour, molasses, tar, egg whites, mouldy bread, burnt cloth and many other ingredients.

A drink of boiled ground juniper can cure a stomach ache.

A haddock bone carried in the pocket alleviates the pain of rheumatism.

A jellyfish dissolved in a container until it became liquid, then applied to an affected area will cure rheumatism.

An extract from the dogberry was sometimes used to cure stomach problems.

A raisin placed on the affected tooth will cure a toothache.

Bee stings can be cured by applying mud to the affected area.

Cobwebs were sometimes used to stop the flow of blood from an open wound or cut.

Drinking vinegar or pickle juice will dry up your blood.

Easter water is a cure for all kinds of aches, pains and ailments. This could only be obtained from a stream before sunrise on Easter Sunday morning. When dipping up the water, the bucked must not be filled against the flow in the traditional way, but by holding the mouth of the bucket toward the flow.

For stomach trouble the buds of alder trees were often steeped and taken internally.

Headaches can be cured by walking backwards in a circle with a piece of brown paper soaked in vinegar on your forehead.

Hiccoughs can be cured by placing a saucer upside down and staring at it.

If you count your warts and tie a like number of knots in a piece of cotton and bury it, the warts will disappear.

If you count your warts then use a piece of chalk to make a mark on the top of the stove for each wart, as the marks burn away the warts will disappear.

If you wear a walnut on a string around your neck, it will cure boils.

May snow is good for sore eyes.

One cure for hiccoughs is to startle or frighten the afflicted person.

Pebbles from the grave of a pious person were once believed to cure toothache.

Pine tar was sometimes applied to hemorrhoids to shrink them.

Placing a pebble under your tongue will relieve a pain in the side.

Rubbing aspirin, oatmeal or baking soda paste on a bee sting will cure it.

Rubbing a potato on your wart, then throwing it away without looking where it lands will cure the warts.

Swallowing a mixture of kerosene oil and molasses was once thought to be able to cure a cough.

The core of a boil was once removed by using a small-necked bottle. The bottle was filled with hot water, then the water thrown out. The neck of the bottle was then placed over the boil and as the air cooled it would draw out the core of the boil.

The finbone of a live haddock worn in a bag around the neck will cure the toothache.

The fin of a haddock that didn't touch the side of the boat is good to cure the cramps.

The leaves of the snake root plant *[Coptis groenlandica]*, also known as canker-root was sometimes steeped and used as a cough remedy.

The scrapings of dust from a tombstone were believed to cure a toothache.

The seventh son of a seventh son was believed to have special healing powers and could charm away things like toothaches and warts.

To get rid of warts you rub a piece of meat on the warts, then bury the meat. As the meat decays your warts will wither and disappear.

To stop nosebleeds, wear a cross made out of lead around your neck. (This was before anyone realized the dangers of lead poisoning.)

Vinegar in the mouth relieves the pain of toothache.

When the sterrins (Arctic tern) return from the Arctic it is a sign that the herring have left the bays.

A nimals

If a calf was sick, a knot, called a worm knot, was placed around its neck and pulled clear nine times, if it got tangled it meant the calf would die.

To get rid of a rat in your house, write him a note telling of another house where there is lots of food and he will go away.

One cure for dog bite was to kill the dog that bit you and place his liver on the wound.

The arrival of the swallows is a sign that the salmon have arrived.

The water in your well will remain pure if you leave a live trout in it.

Throwing hairs from a horse's tail into a pond will grow eels.

B ad Luck

A bad Monday is a sure sign of a bad week.

A clock striking the hour after being stopped for a long time is a sure sign of a death in that house.

A dog moaning near a house is a sure sign that someone close to you is going to die.

A framed painting, drawing, print or photograph suddenly falling from a wall was a sign of death, not necessarily in the family. Some people believed that something about the subject matter of the painting was a clue to who the person might be.

A letter telling of a death is called "a letter edged in black."

A night wind that sounded different than the sounds usually made by wind, often a moaning-like sound, was a sign that someone close to you would die. In some parts of Newfoundland this was called a "Banshee Wind."

A ringing in your left ear means that you are going to get bad news

Breaking a mirror means that you will have seven years of bad luck.

Buy a new broom in May
And sweep your best friend away
Buying a new broom in the month of May is considered bad luck that will result in the death of someone close to you.

Having a woman, especially a nun, aboard a ship is considered bad luck.

Having 13 people at table is bad luck.

If a wild bird finds its way into your house a death in the house is forthcoming.

If a window blind suddenly snaps open for some unknown reason it is a sign of the death of a neighbour.

If rigor mortis does not appear in a corpse it is believed that another family member will die soon as well.

If someone from your house calls you back after you leave to go on a journey, you will have bad luck on that journey.

If two knives become crossed at a table, one of the people at the meal will have bad luck.

If you don't like someone, you can throw the dust from your shoes over your left shoulder in his or her direction and they will have bad luck.

If, while looking into a mirror, someone walks up behind you and looks at you in the mirror, you will have bad luck for seven years.

It is considered unlucky to count your fish while at sea.

It is unlucky while entering a dwelling to put your left foot in over the door threshold first.

Leaving a house by a door other than the one through which you entered will bring bad luck.

Lighting a candle and setting it adrift on a loaf of bread in a pond or other body of water where one has drowned will help locate the body.

Meeting a cross-eyed person is bad luck.

Opening an umbrella inside a house is bad luck.

Spilling salt was considered bad luck. To avoid the bad luck one would throw a pinch of salt over the left shoulder.

To kill a grey jay is bad luck.

To kill a weasel is bad luck. Some believed that the bad luck would be in the form of the weasel's mate coming to cut your throat while you slept.

To break a wine glass at a wedding is bad luck.

To place a hatch cover upside down on a vessel's deck was considered bad luck.

Wearing a grey sweater is bad luck.

Wearing the colour green, especially a green coat, was thought to upset the fairies and was considered bad luck. Wearing green at a wedding was considered to be very unlucky.

Cats

In spite of the fact that the people of this province had to kill animals for food, they always had a soft spot for animals, including the wild and domestic ones they had to kill. There was often much admiration, respect and affection for their beasts of burden. Some of these were sometimes treated as pets. They also kept cats, strictly as pets.

The black versions of these brought as many beliefs about their supernatural abilities here as they did elsewhere. For thousands of years, black cats have been regarded as mysterious creatures with supernatural powers and were associated with witches, the devil and death. One superstition here comes from the Irish, that "killing a black cat brings 17 years of bad luck." Having a black cat cross your path is bad luck in most parts of Newfoundland and Labrador, while in other areas seeing any cat is good luck.

Whether lucky or otherwise, cats are second only to dogs in popularity as pets in this province, where many people prefer black cats. If a cat of any colour starts washing its face it is believed to be a sure sign that visitors are coming. If a young woman kept a black cat under a pot all night it would delay the departure of the ship on which her sweetheart was a crew member.

Children

A gap in between a child's upper front teeth means the child will live far away from home.

If a child bites his fingernails it indicates that the child will be a thief.

If a child passes through the branches of a dogberry tree it will prevent such childhood diseases as measles, chicken pox and rickets.

If you step over a child on the floor you will stop its growth.

To split a green witch hazel tree and pass a child through the split will cure the child of a hernia.

Coins

The first time you see a newborn baby, if you put a silver coin in the baby's hand it will never be in want.

Crows

According to most experts, crows are the smartest of all birds. Birds are much less intelligent than most of the world's fauna, much less intelligent than pigs, and much less intelligent than apes, who are next in intelligence to humans. Yet research has shown that crows are so bright that they are more closely related to other creatures in intelligence than they are to other birds. A 1991 paper by Irene Pepperberg of the University of Arizona evidences the fact that crows may share "the cognitive capacities" of many primates. In several tests, the crow's performance was on par with gorillas and chimpanzees. Their intelligence was borne out in a recent theft investigation at a car wash where a lot of money, in the form of coins, was being stolen. A surveillance camera showed crows finding their way into the coin machine and coming out with coins in their beaks. Because of their great intelligence, people have always had an awe, respect, and even a fear of them.

Many people thought crows were bad. Consider this: a group of lions, even though they are killers, is called a "pride," while a group of crows is called a "murder." The Greeks thought crows were the devil himself. They have an expression. "Go to the crows," which means "Go to hell." The Romans had great respect for crows. Their expression, "To pierce a crow's eye," meant, "something impossible to do." In some parts of the British Isles people would tip their hats to ravens in order not to offend them, while in other parts they associated them with the devil. In Yorkshire children were threatened with the Great Black Bird, which would carry them off if they were bad. Legend has it that Alexander the Great was guided across the desert by two ravens sent from heaven, while the French had a saying that evil priests became crows. It seems that feelings were mixed about these intelligent birds everywhere down through history.

This is also true in Newfoundland and Labrador, which is home to several species of crows, including the largest crow, the raven, and that equally sly member of the *Corvidae* family of birds, the jay. However, it is only the black varieties of these birds that have gained notoriety. Depending on where you are in this province, seeing a single crow could mean either bad or good luck. Sometimes the luck went from bad to good, depending on the number of crows one saw. Seeing a single crow fly overhead was bad luck while seeing two was good luck. Finding a dead crow on the road is good luck while seeing a live one in a cemetery is bad luck. Crows also predicted weather and other things. This is borne out in some of the rhymes that were recited upon seeing a murder of crows:

"One, for wet; two for dry,
Three, for sorrow; four, to die,
Five, for silver; six, for gold,
Seven, for stories never told."

A variation of this rhyme is:

"One, for wet; two for dry,
Three, for a letter; and four, for a boy."

Curses

Widows were believed by some to be able to place a curse on you.

Dreams

If you dream of a wedding it means you will be going to a funeral.

To dream of your father means good luck.

Fairylore

Years ago, when walking was the main mode of travel in Newfoundland and Labrador, an encounter with fairies was not something that was sought out. Here fairies have generally been considered frightening and mean. Thousands of stories of unwanted encounters with fairies were told around the kitchen table. Sometimes when someone went missing and was never seen again, it was thought that they had been kidnapped by fairies. There are stories of people who went missing for long periods of time, then came back and claimed they had been kidnapped by the Little People.

Many people feared that their young children might be captured by fairies and made into "changelings." A changeling had the features of your child but the spirit of a fairy. These changelings would bring discord and grief to the family and wreak havoc in the community. To guard against their babies becoming changelings, these mothers would put the babies' socks on inside out when they put them in their beds at night. These changelings were called fairy men according to the Dictionary of Newfoundland English, which quotes the source as saying, "known to small boys as the fairy man or changeling who played incessantly on a tin whistle."

The Newfoundland dictionary has 14 references to fairies. Among them is fairy path, "a path which never becomes overgrown by shrubs or bushes, even though it is little used by humans." It is believed that such paths are used by the fairies."

The dictionary's definition of fairy-struck is, "mentally or physically harmed by the fairies; afflicted by paralysis."

In his latest book, *Wonderful Strange*, Dale Jarvis has a chapter dedicated to fairies. In one story he tells of a boy in Witless Bay who ventured across a marsh on a moonlit night and was shot in the leg with a fairy arrow. According to the tale, an elderly person, who knew about such things was able to surgically remove the "fairy poison," and although the boy got better he walked with a limp for the rest of his life.

There were a number of things which could help guard one against fairies according to local folk lore. Carrying such items as fairy buns was thought to ward off the fairies. Some people carried horseshoes and even coins to keep the evil little critters away.

While there were certain things that could protect one from the fairies, there was one thing that was a sure attraction to them. That was wearing an item of green clothing. In their book, *Fables, Fairies and Folklore*, Alice Lannon and Mike McCarthy tell the story of a Conception Bay man who was taken by fairies to an underground kingdom, where he was chained, taunted, attacked and beaten for seven days because he had been wearing a green sweater when he came upon the fairies. The man is alleged to have had chain marks around his ankles to back up his story.

The colour green was also the cause of major disasters, according to one of Lannon and McCarthy's stories: "...many Newfoundlanders of the time firmly believed that the St. John's fire of 1892, followed by the Bank Crash of 1894, were caused because in each of those years the Newfoundland government issued green postage stamps, and so aroused the ire of the Little People."

Another way to fall into the power of Fairies was to speak or acknowledge their presence if you came upon them, according to Lannon and McCarthy, who also talk about carrying bread in one's pocket as protection. They mention as well another favourite fairy protection used by Newfoundlanders.

"If night overtook you, or you lost your way, and you had no bread on your person, you could protect yourself from the fairies by turning your coat or jacket inside out."

Fishery

Catching small fish at the beginning of the season is a sign of a good fishery that year. However, if small fish are caught in the middle of the season it is a sign that the rest of the season will be bad.

If a fisherman inadvertently leaves a fish in the bottom of his boat it is a sign of bad luck.

The first salmon caught for the season should be eaten by the fisherman's family to bring a good fishing season.

Good Luck

A baby smiling in its sleep means good luck.

A ringing in your right ear means that you are going to get good news.

Having a bee come in through an open window or door is good luck.

If a rooster crows on your doorstep it is a sign of good luck.

Picking up a coin, pin or white button is good luck.

Placing an old sail on a new vessel before she was launched was believed to bring good luck to the vessel.

Putting on a garment inside out by mistake means good luck.

Wearing a hole in your shoe was once a sure sign of wealth in the future.

Hag-Rode

The old hag or witch made herself known to many people in this province while they were sleeping in their beds at night. I have had a number of encounters with her myself. The first, and most vivid, was when I was about 11 and visiting my grandparents in Twillingate for the summer months. My room was across the hall from my grandparents. One night I was awakened by a heavy weight on my chest. There was someone kneeling on me and trying to strangle me with the sheet. Although the moon was shining in through the window I couldn't make out the features of the person holding me. I tried to move my arms to push the person away, but I was unable to move them. I was never so terrified in my life. I started screaming out to Gram. After what seemed like about 10 or 15 minutes, Gram was suddenly beside my bed and the hag was gone. She didn't hear my screams but heard something and figured I was being hag-rode. I have had several visits from the hag since and talked to many who have had similar visits, some who claim to have actually seen the hag.

Since my first visit from the hag I have learned a few things about dreams. A dream occurs when someone is in the REM, or "rapid eye movement" state of being asleep. This is a state somewhere between being asleep and awake. The visit from the hag probably occurs when one is awake enough to be aware of his surroundings, but not enough to get his conscious mind away from the workings of the subconscious.

One of the beliefs surrounding the hag was that a person who was hag-rode shouldn't be aroused, instead one should say the afflicted person's name backwards to end the trance. Another belief was that if you were hag-rode and made the sign of the cross with your eyes the hag would leave you.

Horseshoes and Luck

When nailed above the door of a house, store, stage or ship's cabin in a position that made it look like the letter *U*, the horseshoe brought good luck. In that position it was believed that the good luck wouldn't run out. This was in reference the U's resemblance to a container for liquids. Nailed the other way around it was believed to keep witches, demons and fairies away. This belief is Irish in origin, where it was thought that you couldn't have both kinds of help from the horseshoe. You had to settle for one or the other before nailing the horseshoe in place. If it helped with one it wouldn't help with the other. Once a horseshoe was nailed in place it was bad luck to remove it. It is probably for this reason that horseshoes can still be seen on older buildings throughout the province.

A horseshoe placed in a chimney was believed to keep witches from flying in on their brooms, while placed on a nail above one's bed, a horseshoe will keep the nightmares, including the old hag, away.

Marriage

A piece of your friend's wedding cake placed under your pillow will bring you dreams of the person you will marry.

By placing your mother's wedding ring under your pillow you will dream about the person you will marry.

To drop the ring at the wedding ceremony means the couple can expect a bad marriage.

Two spoons accidentally placed in a sugar dish means a second marriage.

M oon

If the first time you see the new moon is over your left shoulder you will have good luck for the rest of the month.

**If you don't want your pork to ruin
Kill your pig at the full of the moon.**

Shellfish, both mollusks and crustaceans, are believed to be best and fullest during the full moon.

Timber cut on a losing moon will rot quickly. Timber should never be cut when the moon is on the wane.

T okens, Fetches and Ghosts

In this province a token and a fetch mean the same thing – a ghost, but not just the ghost of a dead person. It could be a vision of someone very much alive. When this happened it was considered an omen of future events. If someone saw the token or fetch of someone who was away at sea or some-place else, it usually meant that person had died or was soon to die. Seeing the token of someone entering his or her own dwelling was a sign of long life for that person. Seeing a token in other circumstances would indicate different foretellings. The word "fetch" was used predominately by people of Irish descent, while the word "token" was used mostly by those of English descent. Ghost means the same here as elsewhere.

V isitors

If a piece of cutlery falls to the floor from the table you will have a visitor before the meal is finished.

If you lift the damper off your wood stove and a flanker (spark) pops out and lands on the floor, it is a sign of company on the way.

When a group of people are visiting, the first one that the cat glares at will soon die.

W histling

**A whistling woman and a crowing hen
Will bring no luck to the house they're in**

At one time it was considered unladylike, improper and even bad luck for a woman to whistle. Hens seldom crowed, and when one did it was thought to be a bad sign. Crowning hens were considered such bad luck that they were killed as soon as they were discovered. These were never eaten, just simply disposed of. A variation of this rhyme is:

A whistling woman and a crowing hen
Is neither fit for God nor men

It is bad luck to whistle at the dinner table.

To whistle while at sea once signified a bad journey.

Witch Hazel

Known also as the spotted alder and the yellow birch tree, the witch hazel tree is believed to have medicinal value. The bark or leaves can be used to make a tea believed to be a cure for dysentery and internal hemorrhaging. This tea may be applied as a poultice to help heal burns, insect bites, contacts with stinger nettles and inflammation brought on by whatever means. In some houses an extract of witch hazel was kept in a bottle to use on scrapes, cuts and bruises.

The witch hazel also has another use, that of a dowsing rod or divining rod. "Dowsing" is using some item to find underground water in order to dig a well. Although often used in Newfoundland and Labrador, the practice is very old. It has been traced back to the Babylonian civilization 5,000 years ago. In this province the branch of a witch hazel tree is sometimes used to make the rod, which is sometimes called a "water witch." It is trimmed and cut into a "Y" shape. One holds one of the top parts of the "Y" loosely in each hand and lets the single part of the branch point in the direction he is walking. When the single end starts to point down on its own, that's the place to dig your well. Dowsing rods were made not only of witch hazel, but from other trees and other items as well. Metal ones were also used, sometimes in the form of a re-shaped wire coat hanger.

Weatherlore

The material for this section was supplied by readers of *Downhome* magazine, from the author's recollections, as well as from a number of publications.

Aches and Pains

Rheumatic pain
Is a sure sign of rain.
When the air got damp enough to cause one's rheumatism to act up it was a sign that rain was on the way.

Animals

Cats cleaning behind their ears or being extra playful are signs of impending bad weather.

Dogs sleeping all day is a sign of rain.

Goats going under the flake is a sign of rain.

Gulls flying at great height
Windy weather overnight.
When the sea gulls are flying high, expect windy weather the next day.
A variation of this rhyme is:
When gulls fly high over sea or land,
Stormy weather is close at hand.

If ducks do slide at Hollandtide (November 11)
At Christmas they will swim
If the weather is cold enough to freeze the ponds over by November 11, it will
warm up enough by Christmas to thaw the ice.

If small pebbles are found in the stomachs of codfish it is a sign of stormy
weather to come.

If the goats come home in files
Get your fish in covered piles.
Goats coming home in a single file is an indication of rain.

Old seals jumping into the water is a sign of wind and snow.

Seabirds keeping near the land
Tell a storm is near at hand
But flying seabirds out of sight
You may stay and fish all night.

Thick coats on wild animals indicates a cold winter.

When porpoises leap from the water in large schools it is a sign of a gale of
wind in the direction the porpoises are headed.

When seals whelp (give birth) it is a sign of a heavy snowfall.

B arometer

At sea with low and falling glass
Soundly sleeps a careless ass
Only when it's high and rising
Truly rests a careful wise one.
Only a fool would sleep at sea when when the weather glass (barometer) is
low and falling, indicating bad weather; a high and rising glass indicates fair
weather.

Long foretold, long last
Short notice, soon past.
Any upcoming type of weather which the barometer indicates well in advance
is weather that will last a long time; when a short warning is given, that
weather won't last long.

Quick rise after low
Sure sign of a stronger blow.
If the barometer rises quickly after windy weather, it will blow again, only
harder.

When the glass falls low, prepare for a blow
When it slowly rises high, lofty sails you may fly.
When the barometer indicates a drop in air pressure, expect strong winds; if
the air pressure increases slowly, expect fair winds (if it increases quickly,
expect strong winds.)

Candlemas Day (February 2)

If Candlemas Day is fair and fine
The worst of the winter's left behind.
If Candlemas Day is dark and grum,
The worst of the winter is yet to come.

Clouds

If clouds are gathering, thick and fast
Keep sharp lookout for sail and mast
If they slowly outward crawl
Shoot your lines, net and trawl.
If clouds gather fast, bad weather is on the way; if they spread slowly
outward, good weather is coming.

Mackerel sky and mare's tails
Makes lofty ships carry low sails.
When cirrus clouds (clouds made of ice particles) that are sometimes as high
as 20,000 feet, take on the shape of the bands on the side of a mackerel or the
shape of a mare's tail, expect stormy weather.

Dreams

Dreaming of horses is a sign of an impending storm.12

Fog

Mists in May, heat in June. A misty or foggy May means a warm June.

Frost

Hoar frost (crystallized frost) is a sign of south wind and rain.

Months

If March comes in like a lamb, it will go out like a lion. If the weather is good at the beginning of March it will be bad at the end.

The weather for the first 12 days of January indicates the weather for the next 12 months.

Moon

Clear moon
Frost soon.
A clear night in the fall indicates frost is on the way.

Saturday's change and Sunday's full
Never brought good and never will.
If the change in the moon is on a Saturday and it is full on Sunday, expect bad weather.

The closer the ring to the moon or sun
The further the weather yet to come.
A ring around the sun or moon indicates bad weather on the way. The smaller the ring, the longer it will take for the weather to arrive.

The old moon in the arms of the new
Bodes no good for me nor you.

When the moon rings round, the heavens will weep. A ring around the moon is a sign of rain.

Northern Lights

Bright Northern Lights above the hill,
A fine day, then a storm foretell.
Brilliant Northern Lights foretell a fine day followed by a storm.

Patrick and Sheila

A winter storm just before St. Patrick's Day, is a sign of a bad spring to come. See also **Sheila's Brush** on page 194.

Rain

A dripping June
Brings all things in tune
Rain in June is good for the growing of crops.

A wet Christmas means a poor harvest the following year.

If it rains on the day of the Feast of Corpus Christi (June 22), it will rain for 40 days and ruin the crop of bakeapples for that year.

If the 8th of June is wet there will be a wet harvest.

If the first days in April be foggy
Rain in June will make the grass boggy.
Foggy weather in early April indicates a rainy June.

Rain before seven
Fine before eleven.
If it rains early in the morning it will be clear before afternoon.

When distant hills appear near, rainy weather is coming.

Sheila's Brush

A winter storm just after St. Patrick's day, which is a sign of a good spring to come. See also **Sheila's Brush** on page 194.

Smoke and Soot

Smoke from a chimney falling to the ground is a sign of low air pressure, which indicates bad weather.

Soot falling from the sky is a sign of rain.

Snow

A peck of March dust is worth a king's ransom. It is good to see the ground bare of snow in March.

A warm Christmas means a cold Easter, while a green Christmas means a white Easter.

If February gives much snow,
A fine summer it doth foreshow.

If January is a warm and sunny month there will be snow in May.

St. Bartlemy Day (August 24)

If St. Bartlemy Day be fair and clear
Hopes for a prosperous autumn that year.

St. Matthew's Day (September 21)

If St. Matthew's Day is bright and clear
It means good weather for the coming year.

St. Swithin's Day (July 15)

St. Swithin's Day if we have rain
Forty days it will remain.
If it rains on St. Swithin's Day then it will rain a little for the
40 days following.

St. Vitus Day (June 15)

If St. Vitus Day is rainy weather
It will rain for thirty days together.

Sun

Evening red and morning grey
Double signs of one fine day.

If it is fair and sunny on March 17, St. Patrick's Day, the saint will take the
cold stone from the water and there will be an early and warm spring.

Red sky at night
A sailor's delight
Red sky in morning
A sailorman's warning.
When there is a red glow at sunset on the western horizon, expect fair weather
next day; when there is a red glow on the eastern horizon at sunrise, expect a
bad day with strong winds. A variation of this rhyme is:
The evening red, the morning grey
Are surely signs of a fine day
But the evening grey and the morning red
Makes the sailor shake his head.

Sunshine on St. Mary's Day (August 15) **brings good red wine.**

When the sun is setting in a bank
A westerly wind is on the hank.
If there is a cloud bank on the horizon into which the sun sets, the next day
will be a fine one with westerly winds.

When the wind shifts against the sun
Trust it not for back 'twill run.
If the wind turns against the direction of the sun it will change again shortly.

Thunder

Winter thunder
Summer hunger.

Trees

A lot of murr on evergreen trees means it is going to be a very cold winter.

The tops of alders turning red is a sign of rain.

Water

Water coming in over the ice is a sign of rain.

Wind

A lot of wind on Christmas Day indicates a good crop of berries next year.

A nor'wester is never in debt to a southeaster. A north-west wind is sure to follow a southwest wind, and blow twice as long and twice as hard.

A windy, frosty October means a mild January and February.

If the wind blows south on New Year's night a warm and sunny year
will follow.

If the wind blows west on New Year's Day it foretells a good fishery.

If the wind's in the east on Candlemas Day (February 20)
There it will stick 'til the end of May.

If you throw pennies overboard for the devil he will cause the wind to blow.

If you get wind before the rain
Hoist your topsails up again
Bur if it rains before the wind
Topsail halyards you must bind
If is starts to rain before the wind begins to blow, expect strong winds; but if the rain comes after the wind starts, the wind won't amount to much. A variation of this rhyme is:
When rain comes before the wind
Halyards sheets and braces mind
But when wind comes before the rain
Soon you may make sail again.

When the wind blows from the south
It blows the bait from the fish's mouth
When the wind blows from the north

The skillful fisher goes not forth
When the wind blows from the east
'Tis neither fit for man nor beast
When the wind blows from the west
Then 'tis at its very best.

When the winds of October won't make the leaves go,
There'll be a frosty winter with banks of snow.

When the wind is drawing water
Better bide home with wife and daughter.
When sun rays are visible down to the water, it was said that the sun was drawing water (causing water to evaporate). This was a sign of bad weather ahead.

Sayings and Expressions

Not all these sayings and expressions are exclusive to
Newfoundland and Labrador, but many are, and all were in
common usage in Newfoundland and Labrador at one time or
another. Many are in use today. The material for this section
was supplied by readers of *Downhome* magazine, from the author's
recollections, as well as from a number of publications.

Advice and Information

A narrow neck keeps the bottle from being emptied in one swig. ~
Everything in moderation.

A ship is often lost because of one man. ~ One man's mistake can often have
a dire effect on many. From Ireland.

Come in out of the wet. ~ Don't be stupid. "You're going to marry that
sleeveen? Come in out of the wet, my maid."

Crying is not far away from laughter. ~ Things may get bad but it won't last long.

Don't be breaking your shin on a stool that's not in your way. ~ Don't go out of your way to find trouble. From Ireland, via the Southern Shore.

Don't cut tails ~ Don't be too particular. Fish tails were occasionally cut to mark them. If a person on a fishing vessel wasn't a full shareman, he marked his fish by cutting their tails so he could later identify them when they were being shipped (sold to a merchant).

Don't get your pee hot. ~ Calm down.

Don't make little of your fish for it might be an ignorant man who judges it. ~ Don't undervalue your work because there is always someone who will appreciate it.

Don't mistake an old goat's beard for a fine stallion's tail. ~ Things are not always what they seem.

Don't see all you see and don't hear all you hear. ~ Things are not always as they seem. From Ireland.

Don't show all your teeth until you can bite. ~ Don't overestimate your abilities and start something before you are ready. From Ireland, via the Southern Shore.

Don't spit to win'ard (windward). ~ Don't be stupid.

Don't tell me, ask me! ~ I know more about it than you do.

Firelight will not let you read fine stories, but it's warm and you won't see the dust on the floor. ~ Count your blessings.

Get on outdoors and let that wind blow the stink off you. ~ Go out for some fresh air.

Go to grass and let the cows eat you. ~ There's nothing I can do to help you.

In a leaky punt with a broken oar, 'tis always best to hug the shore.

In the land of the blind, the man with one eye is king. ~ Despite what little nature gives us, we are all good at something. From Ireland, via the Southern Shore.

It's for her own good that the cat purrs. ~ When people do things they usually do it for themselves.

It's the jewel that can't be got that's the most beautiful. ~ It is the thing that we can't get that is the most sought after. From Ireland.

Let no man steal your lines. ~ Beware of competition.

Look at the river before you take the ferry. ~ Be aware of every aspect of a situation before you proceed. From Ireland.

Mourn the dead, but do everything else for the living.

Never bid the devil good morrow until you meet him. ~ From Ireland.

Never give cherries to a pig, or advice to a fool. ~ Don't waste time helping those who don't appreciate it.

Never scald your lips with another man's porridge. ~ The possession of another man that you desire may be more trouble than it's worth. From Ireland, via the Southern Shore.

Nofty was forty when he lost the pork. ~ Never be sure of anything. In the game of 45s, one can have 40 points and still lose the game.

One good pair of leather soles is worth two pairs of upper leather.

Say nothing and saw wood. ~ Mind your own business.

Shit or get off the pot. ~ If you're not going to do anything, get out of the way and let someone by who will.

Speak neither ill nor well of yourself. ~ Don't brag and don't put yourself down. From Ireland.

Take gifts with a sigh – most men give to be paid. ~ There's an ulterior motive to most things.

Tell the truth and shame the devil. ~ Be truthful.

The best way to keep loyalty in a man's heart is to keep money in his purse. ~ From Ireland.

The first sip of broth is always the hottest. ~ The first step in a task is always the hardest to take. From Ireland.

The friend who can be bought is not worth buying.

The herb that can't be got is the one that brings relief. ~ The things we need most in life are the ones that are usually out of reach. From Ireland.

The longest road out is the shortest road home. ~ Overcome obstacles and you'll reach your goals.

The man without eyes is no judge of beauty. ~ Some people don't see the true value in things. From Ireland, via the Southern Shore.

Them that gets their asses burned have to sit on their blisters. ~ Be prepared for consequences.

There's favour in hell if you bring your own splits (kindling wood). ~ You can make the best of any situation if you know the right way to do it.

Wait a fair wind and you'll get one. ~ Opportunity always comes along if you are patient.

Willful waste makes woeful want. ~ From Ireland.

A ffirmation

God strike me dead. ~ I'm telling the truth.

Is a frog's arse watertight? ~ That is absolutely correct.

Yes-sir-ee-bob ~ Yes, for sure. "Am I going to your wedding, Mary? Yes-sir-ee-bob!"

You got it blistered. ~ Things are going great for you.

You got it knocked. ~ Your life is going great.

You got it scalled (scalded). ~ Your life is going great.

You knows that your own self. ~ You are very aware of that.

A ge, Experience and Learning

A man of learning understands the half word. ~ An educated person can read between the lines. From Ireland.

An old broom knows the dirty corner best. ~ The experienced person can do the job better than the greenhorn.

A scholar's ink lasts longer than a martyr's blood. ~ The written word outlasts the unrecorded deeds of men. From Ireland.

The old dog for the hard road. ~ Experience is a big help in overcoming adversity.

The older the buck, the harder the horn. ~ A man's sexual virility improves with age.

The older the crab, the tougher its claws. ~ It is not easy to fool a sophisticated person.

The older the fiddler, the sweeter the tune. ~ Older folks can do things in a more comforting and competent way.

The oldest pipe gives the sweetest smoke. ~ Older people are more understanding than younger ones.

A lcohol

He'd drink it off dead Nelson, the one-eyed hero. ~ He'd never miss an opportunity to have an alcoholic beverage. Alluding to the death of Admiral

Nelson at sea, whose body was preserved in a barrel of rum for transportation back to England.

He would go to mass every Sunday if holy water was whiskey. ~ From Ireland, via the Southern Shore.

Just able to navigate ~ Intoxicated.

My head feels right logy. ~ I have a hangover.

Three sheets to the wind ~ Intoxicated, or nearly intoxicated.

A lienation

I felt like a Friday fish at a Saturday market. ~ I felt out of place.

A nger and Altercations

Ding dong for doughboys ~ Referring to a fight or argument. "When Fred called his brother a bad name they had ding dong for doughboys."

He's like the cat. ~ He'd claw your eyes out.

I'll haul off and let you have it. ~ I'll draw back my fist and strike you.

I'll put you in the middle of next week. ~ I'll hit you hard.

I'll send you to kingdom come. ~ I'll kill you.

I'll zever thine head off. ~ An expression of anger. *Zever* means *sever* and *thine* means *your*. Both words come from West Country England.

My blood was boiling. ~ I was very angry.

A nimals

A fine kettle of fish ~ Trouble.

Anything to help the lame horse over the stile. ~ A sarcastic remark one makes to a person who is hindering progress or attempting to put roadblocks in one's way.

A shut fist won't catch a fish hawk. ~ Be prepared for any eventuality.

As the old cock crows, the young cock learns. ~ The young learn from their elders.

A wild bird never laid a tame egg. ~ Children take after their parents.

A wink is as good as a nod to a blind horse. ~ If a person doesn't want to understand, no kind of communication will work.

Cattle are caught by their horns, and people by their tongues. ~ People know animals by their actions and other people by what they say. From Ireland, via the Southern Shore.

Every dog is brave on his own dungheap. ~ People act braver around their friends. From Ireland.

Everyone lays a burden on the willing horse. ~ It's the most generous person to whom everyone goes for help. From Ireland, via the Southern Shore.

Far off cows wear long horns. ~ Things are not always what they seem.

Feeding the gulls. ~ Vomiting from seasickness.

He eats like the gull. ~ He eats fast.

He's got eyes on him like a capelin goin' offshore. ~ His eyes are bloodshot.

He's got the appetite of a gull. ~ He's a big eater.

He's got the stomach of a gull. ~ He'd eat anything.

He's so ugly he would turn a dog from his own vomit.

I could eat the arse out of a low-flying duck. ~ I'm very hungry.

I don't have a chick nor a child. ~ I'm a free person with no worries.

If you catch a pig, catch it by the leg. ~ Choose the easiest and best way to complete a task. From Ireland.

It's not every day that Morris kills the cow. ~ Good opportunities are rare.

It's not for the want of a tongue that a horse can't talk. ~ I know as much about your past as you know about mine.

It's no use going to the goat's house to look for wool. ~ Don't go in a direction in which there is no hope.

It would knock a buzzard off a shit wagon. ~ It smells awful.

Just when you think you're on the pig's back you're up his arse. ~ Just when things start to look good they all go bad. The expression *on the pig's back*, means *living well*, or *living high on the hog*.

Lazy as a cut dog ~ Very lazy. A cut dog is one that has been castrated. Castration causes dogs to eat more and become less aggressive and less active.

Many a shabby foal made a fine horse. ~ Don't be fooled by appearances.

Nervous as the cats ~ Very nervous.

On the pig's back ~ Prosperous, living high on the hog.

Out dogs and in dieters. ~ Prepare for the summer fishery. In the spring it was not only warm enough for the dogs to be outside, but it was also the time for dieters (workers who had to be housed and fed) to take up residence.

Pigs may fly but they are very unlikely birds. ~ To hope in vain.

Sending a goose on a message to a fox's den. ~ A fool's mission.

Skin the cow. ~ When cold March weather persists into April the cow dies of hunger.

Sleep in the puppy's parlour. ~ To sleep on the floor in one's clothes.

There never was a shabby sheep that didn't like to have a comrade. ~ No matter our station in life we all like companionship.

To a raven, even her own chick is white. ~ People see what they want to see.

When the snipe bawls, the lobster crawls. ~ After sunset.

When your hand is in the dog's mouth, withdraw it gently. ~ If you find yourself in a ticklish situation, withdraw with caution. From Ireland.

You can't tell the mind of a squid. ~ Refers to an unpredictable or unreliable person. Probably derived from the fact that a squid can move backward as well as forward.

You might as well be hung for a sheep as for a lamb. ~ One sin is as bad as another, so if you're going to do something wrong, turn it to your best advantage.

You can get only one shot at a shellbird. ~ A shrewd person can only be fooled once. A shellbird (red-breasted merganser duck) is a type of duck that startles easily.

Appearance

All mops and brooms ~ Unkempt hair.

Done up like a stick of gum ~ Neatly dressed, spiffy looking.

He's wearing his pants half mast. ~ His pants are too short. From American servicemen stationed in Newfoundland whose trousers were somewhat shorter than those worn by local men.

Rake for run ~ In a state of disarray, untidy.

Appearances

Empty vessels loom largest. ~ Don't be fooled by appearances; the ship looks biggest when it's empty of cargo.

Even a tin knocker will shine on a dirty door. ~ Everything is better when compared to something worse.

A ttention

Look at what he went and done. ~ Look at what he did.

B ad language

You so and so. ~ This was said instead of using bad language toward another person.

B ehind

Sucking hind tit ~ Way behind. "We only got 15 points in this game of growl while they got 105 – we're certainly sucking hind tit."

B etter

It's better than a pointed stick in the eye. ~ It's great.

B orrowing

The borrowed horse has hard hooves. ~ From Ireland.

The law of borrowing is to break the borrower. ~ From Ireland.

B ragging

Too big for your boots ~ Bragging about something one is incapable of doing.

Too big for your britches ~ As above.

B usiness

Go on the halves with ~ To share in the products or the profits of labour. Sometimes a man who was planning to build a house would cut twice as many logs as was required to make the lumber. He would then make a deal with a sawmill owner to cut all the logs and keep half the lumber to sell for a profit.

C apability

The best kind ~ In the most capable manner. "Mother can row a punt the best kind."

Carefree

Beating the streets ~ Out on the go. "She'd rather be out beating the streets than home learning how to sew."

Come day, go day, God send Sunday. ~ Refers to a lazy, unorganized, careless person.

He don't care where night overtakes him. ~ He has a carefree attitude.

The carefree mother's daughter makes a bad wife. ~ Daughters take after their mothers.

What would frighten you would make the devil run his country. ~ Said to a carefree and stubborn child.

Cheap

Cheap enough to take the coppers off his mother's eyes ~ Very miserly. From the days when copper coins were used to hide a dead person's eyes.

He who is bad to give the loan is good for directing you. ~ Some people won't loan you money, but they'll tell you what to do with it if you have it. From Ireland, via the Southern Shore.

Tight as a bull's arse in fly time ~ Very cheap and stingy.

Clergy

If there is a hen or a goose, it's surely on the priest's table. ~ The clergy is always well-looked-after. From Ireland, via the Southern Shore.

Close

If I didn't knock it down, I staggered it. ~ I may not have gotten it perfect but I came close.

Common Sense

A block of common sense ~ Refers to one who has his or her life in order.

Companionship

Get in go with ~ 1. To team up with. 2. To date someone of the opposite sex on a regular basis, to court.

Rack around with ~ Be associated with. "I used to rank around with them when we were youngsters."

Rank around with ~ Be associated with.

Tangled up with ~ Associated with. "When your daughter married my son, you didn't know what kind of crowd you were getting tangled up with."

There never was an old slipper but there was an old sock to match it. ~ There's someone for everyone.

Concern

It's no odds to me. ~ It's not my concern. "The kettle is boiling but it's no odds to me."

What a sin. ~ That's too bad.

Condition

Still in the same ice ~ The condition hasn't changed.

Conversation

A silent mouth is sweet to hear. ~ Silence is sometimes better than chatter.

A tongue like a beggar's clapdish ~ Talks too much. A clap dish was a wooden dish carried by beggars. When there were coins inside, the beggars constantly rattled the dish to entice others to give. From Great Britain.

Chewing the fat ~ Involved in a conversation. The consistency of fat is such that it requires a lot of chewing.

Chewing the rag ~ Gossiping.

Did 'er now? ~ Did he do that?

Don't let your tongue cut your throat. ~ Don't say something you'll regret.

Every man is smart 'til he says something. ~ It is only when one speaks that his lack of knowledge shows. From Ireland, via the Southern Shore.

He could talk the legs off the table. ~ 1. He talks a lot. 2. He is a smooth talker.

He got more in his cheek than he got to eat. ~ He says more than he knows.

More lip than a coal bucket ~ Talks too much

More tongue than a logan ~ Talks too much.

Never came over it ~ Didn't mention it. "Aunt Sarah was looking at the snaps of Christine the other day, and even though she knows Christine is dead she never came over it."

She got a record in her as big as a 45-gallon drum. ~ Referring to a woman who talks a lot.

The person with the least knowledge talks the most. ~ It's the person with the least knowledge of a subject that has the most to say about it.

To praise God is proper, but a wise man won't blackguard the devil either. ~ Don't say anything bad about anybody because you never know when it will cause you problems.

What's 'er say? ~ 1. What did you say? 2. What did he (or she) say?

Dancing

How are you fixed for a few steps? ~ Do you want to dance?

Debt

Tom Long's account ~ To pay the merchant what you owe and have nothing left.

Difficulty

A noggin to scrape ~ A very difficult task to be done.

Direction

Up the bottom ~ Toward the bottom or head of the bay.

Doubt

Get out and push! ~ That's unbelievable!

Go away with ya! ~ That's unbelievable!

Good morrow to you. ~ You are mistaken.

Dressing

Get to rights ~ To get dressed or get ready.

Easier Way

Hold on to the bone and the dog will follow you. ~ There is usually an easier way to do everything. From Ireland.

It is no delay to stop and sharpen the axe. ~ Doing things the right way makes the job go faster.

Eating and Drinking

Down the shute! ~ Drink it up!

He's digging his grave with his fork. ~ His overeating is going to kill him.

I allow there's tins of corned beef in his puddick not opened yet. ~ 1. He eats a lot.

I gotta clink in me tinker and I can't glutch. ~ I have trouble swallowing.

I'm so hungry I could eat the lamb of God.

I'm so hungry my stomach thinks my throat is cut.

Last time I ate that I had to wipe me arse with an oven mitt. ~ That food is too spicy for me.

Put the kettle on, the boys are working. ~ We can afford to eat, so let's eat.

What butter and whiskey won't cure, there's no cure for. ~ Food and strong drink is all a person needs.

Effort

Face and eyes into it ~ Working at something with full effort.

Give her that! ~ Put all effort into it!

Gave her all she could suffer ~ Made something work as hard and as fast as it can. "When we came around Wester Head in me old skiff, I gave her all she could suffer."

Entertaining and Entertainment

Any mummers 'lowed in? ~ Is this house open to mummers?

A scoff and a scuff ~ A meal followed by a dance.

He'd charm the heart of a grindstone and make a wheelbar laugh. ~ He is a very entertaining fellow.

Play with the devil ~ To play solitaire.

Expectations

A watched pot never boils.

Don't bless the fish 'til it gets to the land. ~ The sea is unpredictable, so don't expect to profit from your catch until it is safely ashore.

It's on boil-on. ~ The situation hasn't come to a head yet.

Keep a scattered eye out. ~ To casually keep a lookout for someone or something. "I don't know what time you'll get here, but I'll keep a scattered eye out."

Facial Features

A face like a can of worms

A face like a smacked baby's arse ~ Having rosy cheeks or a ruddy complexion.

Beauty knows no pain. ~ From Ireland.

Beauty won't make the pot boil. ~ Because one's wife is good looking doesn't mean she's good in the kitchen. From Ireland, via the Southern Shore.

He was the goalie for the dart team. ~ He has a bad complexion.

Homely as sin ~ Very ugly.

If I had a face the likes of yours, I'd walk backwards. ~ You are ugly.

You got a face only a mother could love.

You got a face that would stop a clock.

Fairies

A man can lose his hat in a fairy wind.

Family

A wise son makes a father glad, but a foolish son is a mother's sorrow. ~ Fathers are proud of a wise son, but if the son has problems it's the mother who suffers the most worry about him. From Ireland.

Often the fool's son is a wise man. ~ Children don't always take after their parents in every way. From Ireland.

Street angel, house devil ~ Referring to a man or woman who treats everyone good except his or her own family.

Your nose is broken. ~ Said to a first-born child (usually by someone outside the family) when a second child is born, to indicate that he is no longer the only child in the family.

Your son is your son today, but your daughter is your daughter forever. ~ From Ireland.

Feeling Good

Some shockin' good ~ Wonderful, great, the best. This expression presently in jocular use in the province.

Fishery, Fishermen and Fish

A fisherman is one rogue – a merchant is many. ~ Merchants are not to be trusted.

Cape St. Mary's pays for all. ~ Referring to the once lucrative fishery at Cape St. Mary's.

Fish or no fish ~ Regardless of the outcome. "I'm getting married in the fall, fish or no fish."

If you lose your grapnel, you'll find it in the fall. ~ Your grapnel {pronounced *GRAPE - ull*} may be lost overboard in the summer, but it will still be on the merchant's books when you clew up in the fall and be deducted from your profits.

Not fit for a cuckoo pot ~ A very inferior salt fish. A cuckoo pot is a trap once used to trap large saltwater mollusks that resemble snails and are known as cuckoos.

Poor men take to the sea; the rich to the mountains. ~ From Ireland, via the Southern Shore.

The fish is eating the rocks. ~ The fish are plentiful.

Flattery

You are taking a rise out of me. ~ Your flattery is only intended to make a fool of me.

Flight

Took to wing ~ Flew away. "I tried to get a shot off at the turrs before they took to wing."

Foresight and Preparedness

A look in front is better than two behind. ~ Foresight is more necessary than hindsight.

A bad reaper never got a good reap hook. ~ Nothing good comes from bad.

A single line can have two hooks. ~ Things are not always as they appear.

Be afraid and you'll never meet danger. ~ If you have enough fear you will always avoid dangerous situations.

Be first in the woods but last in the bog. ~ Be quick to do the smart thing but slow to do something stupid. From Ireland, via the Southern Shore.

Every patient is a doctor after he's cured. ~ Everyone knows what the problem was once it's solved.

Every way is likely. ~ Anything can happen.

French Origin

Me, I come from the Crossing on a dog team, me. God damn, no snow." I just came from Stephenville Crossing, but there wasn't much snow for my dog sled. This is typical of an expression that might be made by resident of the Port au Port area with a French background, and is still jocularly bantered about by people in the Port au Port, St. George's Bay area today.

Throw the horse, over the fence, some oats. ~ Throw some oats over the fence for the horse. From the residents of Newfoundland whose first language was French. The structure of sentences in French is different than it is in English, making this statement in French quite acceptable and understandable.

Throw the kids, down the stairs, some candy. ~ Throw some candy to the kids downstairs.

Gratitude

God bless your cotton socks. ~ Said if someone does something special for you.

Good Qualities

As fine a man as ever broke a cake of the world's bread. ~ A good man.

Good as gold ~ Referring to a friendly, nice and kind-hearted person.

Greetings and Farewells

Best kind, b'y, how's yerself? ~ The answer usually given when one asks, "How are you getting on?"

Fair weather to you and snow to your heels. ~ A wish for a safe journey, especially a journey made by dog team. Heels refer to the runners on the dog sled.

How's she cuttin'? ~ How are things with you?

How's she gettin' on b'y? ~ How are things with you?

Long may your big jib draw. ~ Good luck. The jib sail is at the front of the ship and is not used if winds are unfavourable. When this sail draws (is filled with) wind it makes for a speedier journey, especially if it draws wind for a long period of time.

May God bless three times and three spits for luck. ~ A saying used at the birthing of a calf. From Ireland, via the Southern Shore.

May I see you grey and combing your children's hair. ~ Long life, strength, good health and happiness to you and yours. From Ireland.

May the face of every good news and the back of every bad news be toward you. ~ May your good news be coming and your bad news be going. From Ireland.

May the strength of three be on your journey. ~ From Ireland.

May you have a feather bed in heaven. ~ You are a very deserving person.

May you live to be a hundred years, with one extra year to repent. ~ May you have a long life, filled with all the fun things it has to offer, and still go to heaven after you die.

See you the week. ~ I'll see you before the week is out.

Snakeshit ~ Everything is great. Said when someone asks how another is doing, or as a greeting when meeting a friend. This expression is local to the Port au Port area of the province.

What are ya at? ~ How are you doing?

Heart-breaker

He'd break the heart of a grindstone. ~ He's a heartbreaker.

Honesty and Dishonesty

A liar wants a good memory. ~ When one tells lies he has to remember every lie he told so as not to get caught.

A lie looks the better for having a witness. ~ We tell the second lie to cover up the first.

An honest man when there are no anchors around ~ He is honest when there is nothing to steal; but if there is something around, even something as heavy as an anchor, he'll take it.

Bribe the rogue and you need have no fear of the honest man. ~ From Ireland.

He'd steal the eyes out of your head and come back for the sockets. ~ 1. He is a big thief. 2. He has a lot of nerve.

He'd steal the milk out of your tea. ~ He's a sly thief.

He handles the truth very carelessly. ~ 1. He sometimes tells lies. 2. He stretches the truth.

He tells more lies than Tom Pepper and he was turned out of hell.

Not a word of a lie ~ The absolute truth.

The lying man's witness is his wife. ~ Don't put much faith in what he says. From Ireland.

There's no back doors about him. ~ He speaks his mind.

What comes in over the devil's back goes out under his belly. ~ Ill-gotten gains don't last long.

Horsing around

Knock off drivin' works! ~ Stop horsing around.

House

Put the wood in the hole! ~ Close the door!

Housekeeping

Everything to her finger's end. ~ Everything needed to perform housekeeping.

Humour

I dies at he. ~ He makes me laugh so hard I could die.

Snark out laughing ~ Make a single laughing sound, but hold back so as not to offend or embarrass someone.

Idleness

Helping Larry ~ Doing nothing. "Me old man said he was going to be busy down in the stage all day, but I daresay he's helping Larry."

He never does a tap. ~ He never works.

Ill-equipped

How can I do ar t'ing when I got nar t'ing to do ar t'ing wit'? ~ How can I do anything when I have nothing to work with?

The soles of my shoes are so thin I can stand on a dime and tell if it's heads or tails.

Illness, Injury, Pain and Death

Brew a cold ~ Develop a cold.

Death is the poor man's best physician. ~ A poor person can't afford a doctor so the best cure for his pain is death. From Ireland, via the Southern Shore.

I'm only fit to be prayed for. ~ I'm not feeling very well.

I'm sick enough to be in three hospitals.

She put away two men. ~ She buried two husbands.

Someone just walked over my grave. ~ A phrase used when one shivers unexpectantly.

Split your straddle ~ Injure your pelvic area.

There is hope from the mouth of the sea but none from the mouth of the grave. ~ You may survive the sea but there is a grave waiting at the end.

There'll be many a dry eye at his death. ~ He is not very well liked. From Ireland.

What do you find? ~ In which part of your body is the pain?

What would shame him would turn back a funeral. ~ Not very much shames him. From Ireland.

Immature Berries

They'm red 'cause they'm green, that's why they'm not blue. ~ The explanation as to why blueberries are red in colour before they ripen. This expression is in present jocular use in the province.

Insult

A kick in the arse ~ Adding insult to injury. "Losing me old motorboat after I put a new engine in her was a kick in the arse."

Irish

An Irish youngster for the bow oar ~ A youngster was an inexperienced fisherman. Because he was inexperienced he was given the bow oar, which meant that he was more likely to be splashed with water than the other oarsmen.

Put an Irishman on the spit and you'll find two more to turn him. ~ Irishmen don't look after each other. From Ireland.

The Irish forgive their great men when they are safely buried. ~ From Ireland.

Kitchen

Done it brown ~ Overdid it. Alluding to burnt brown or overdone bread.

Just show it to the pan. ~ Don't cook it too long.

Storm the kettle. ~ Put the kettle on to boil.

Turn out the dinner. ~ Set the table and serve the food.

Labrador

Down on the Labrador ~ In Labrador. The original expression was "Down on the Labrador coast," but the word "coast" was later dropped.

God made Labrador in six days; on the seventh day he threw rocks at it. ~ Referring to the rocky coastline of Labrador.

The land God gave to Cain ~ A reference to Labrador made by Jacques Cartier upon seeing the rugged coastline of the Big Land for the first time.

Language

Got a straw up your nose ~ To speak using one of several American accents. Sometimes young local women who lived for a while in the United States, especially the Southern States, would return for a visit. Conversing in their acquired accent, it wouldn't be long before someone would say to them, "You talk like you got a straw up your nose."

Lazy

Lazy as a piper's little finger ~ A pipe has three holes that when covered create different notes. Only the first three fingers are required to play the pipe.

Sew on your back, never have a tack. ~ Referring to one who is too lazy to remove an item of clothing before mending it. Such a person would never have a tack (worldly goods).

She's not lazy – she was born tired. ~ A sarcastic remark referring to a lazy woman.

Your claws will never maintain your jaws. ~ You are too lazy to earn enough to feed yourself.

L eaving

Batter to Moses and tell him I sent you. ~ Get out of here, beat it, get lost.

Give her the long main sheet. ~ To leave with no intention of returning.

I'm leaving the same way I came. ~ I'm leaving and I won't be back.

L ife

All my born days ~ All my life.

A man may live after losing his life but not after losing his honour. ~ One may die but his honour lives on. From Ireland.

Fish in summer, fun in winter. ~ Everything in its place.

Often does the likely fail and the unlikely prosper. ~ Life doesn't always turn out the way we expect it to. From Ireland.

The ugly are often lucky and the handsome unfortunate. ~ Life gives everyone a break at some time or another. From Ireland.

L og Driving

I was walking my catty. ~ I was jumping from log to log on a river drive.

L uck

Either a feast or a famine ~ There's no middle ground in life, things are either very good or very bad.

Good luck is better than early rising. ~ Luck decides most things in life. From Ireland.

Go to law with the devil and hold court in hell. ~ The odds are all against you.

Go to looward ~ To decline in fortune.

He that is born to be hanged needn't fear water. ~ Your life and death are plotted in advance. From Ireland.

If you look for one thing you'll find something else. ~ Lost items often show up at unexpected times.

Mail Order

Had it come ~ Got it by mail.

Marriage and Weddings

If you tie a knot with your tongue, you can't undo it with your teeth. ~ Referring to getting married – it is easier to say the wedding vows than to undo them later.

Marriages are all happy – it's having breakfast in the morning that causes all the trouble. ~ Loving is easy, it's the living together that's hard.

Stand up for ~ Be best man at one's wedding.

Master and Servant

Jack is as good as his master. ~ The hired hand is paid off at the end of the fishing season and is no longer a servant.

Out in service ~ Working as a domestic.

Men

Men are like bagpipes – no sound comes from them until they are full. ~ Men don't talk until they have been fed.

Mischievousness

He's the nevers. ~ He's full of mischief.

Misfortune and Misadventure

Arse over kettle ~ To fall down.

The arse fell out of her. ~ Things went wrong.

Up the creek with one oar ~ In a bad way.

You had your chips. ~ You're in trouble now.

Mistakes

When fools make mistakes they lay the blame on providence. ~ When some people make mistakes they point the finger of blame away from themselves.

Morals

She's on the road more than the pavement. ~ She is a woman of loose morals who is always walking the streets.

Naivete

I might have been born in the woods, but I never ate the boughs. ~ I know what's going on, even though some people might not think so.

Nerves

Me nerves is rubbed right raw. ~ I am very agitated. This expression is presently in jocular use in the province.

Oh, me nerves. ~ My nerves can't take any more. This expression is presently in jocular use in the province.

Noisy

Can't hear your ears ~ noisy.

Nothing Else

Nar nudder t'ing ~ Nothing else. From *not another thing*.

Opinion

You might opine. ~ You might have an opinion on the subject.

Overweight

He got a gut on him like a harbour tom cod. ~ He has a big stomach.

He's so big that when he backs up you hear a beep.

It's easier to go over her than around her. ~ She's short and fat.

Three axe handles across the arse ~ Having a wide posterior.

Oxymorons

Cute as the Christian ~ Referring to a very sly person. The word *Christian* one time meant *human*.

I knows you wouldn't ~ I believe you would. "I knows you wouldn't like one of them new skidoos."

I knows he wasn't going, was he. ~ He was moving extremely fast.

Stunned, like the fox ~ Smart.

Perspiration

I'm sweating bullets. ~ I'm perspiring profusely.

Perturbed

I'm poisoned with this. ~ I've had enough of this.

Poverty

Don't have a pot to piss in or a window to throw it out of ~ Without possessions and homeless.

I don't have a cent to my name. ~ I'm broke.

Neither meal nor malt ~ Living in poverty. Meal and malt both refer to grain which may be used to make bread.

Put a beggar on a horse and he will ride to hell ~ People who are not used to having money don't know how to handle it when they suddenly become well off.

The thief is no danger to the beggar. ~ The less you own, the less you have to worry about.

The well-fed belly has little knowledge of the empty. ~ The rich don't know the pain of poverty.

Praise

It's lovely, tell your mother. ~ It's very nice.

The best kind ~ Good, well. "Captain Kean treated me the best kind when I sailed with him."

You can cut a notch in the beam. ~ A compliment to someone when he or she does the unusual.

You're not easy. ~ You're extraordinary.

You're not too mouldy. ~ You're smart.

Predictions

That's a spoon you'll sup sorrow with yet. ~ That's something that will come back to cause problems. From Ireland, via the Southern Shore.

You are making a rod to whip your own back. ~ You are making choices that will cause you harm.

You'll come to a bad end. ~ Said to someone who does daring or foolish things.

You'll do it in the long run. ~ Eventually you'll succeed.

You'll wish your cake, dough. ~ You'll wish you were back where you once were.

Want will be your master ~ You are asking for things that you don't really need.

Pregnancy

Something under your pinny ~ Pregnant, a pinny being a pinafore or apron.

Preparedness

He who doesn't tie a knot will lose the first stitch. ~ To do something properly one has to prepare in advance. From Ireland.

The devil to pay and no pitch hot. ~ Service expected and no one ready to perform it. The devil is a seam in a ship at about water level. To patch this seam in stormy seas requires one to be under water for a period of time trying to apply the hot pitch to the leak.

'Tis no use to carry an umbrella if your boots are leaking. ~ If you're going to do something, do it right the first time.

Pride

Proud as Guilderoy ~ Very proud. Alluding to Guilderoy, a highwayman who was the subject of a Scottish ballad and who was hanged in 1638. He later became a motif for brave rascals who were proud enough to flaunt the English laws and make his people proud.

Put downs

Go home and hang on to your mother's petticoat! ~ You are a sissy.

Go home b'y – your mother got buns. ~ You don't know what you are talking about.

Go on with you ~ Don't be silly.

Grinning like a bitch fox in a thunderstorm ~ An insult.

He don't have enough sense to come in out of the rain. ~ He's senseless.

He don't know his arse from a hole in the ground. ~ He is stupid.

He don't know if he's punched or bored. ~ He doesn't know what's happening around him.

He don't know the war is over yet. ~ He doesn't know anything.

He haven't got a click nor a clue. ~ He's not very smart.

He is as stupid as Tom's dog, and he put his arse in the well to get a drink.

He's so crooked (cranky) **he could eat a four-inch nail and shit a corkscrew.**

He's so low he can walk under a snake's belly with a top hat on.

He thinks his shit don't stink but his farts tells on him. ~ He thinks he's better than everybody else, but his actions indicate otherwise.

He was behind the door when brains were passed out. ~ He's stupid.

I'd throw him an anchor. ~ I wouldn't do anything to save his life.

If it wasn't for your lack of sense, you'd have no sense at all.

If you had another brain it would be lonely. ~ You are stupid.

There's nobody home but your mother, and she's gone. ~ You come from a crazy family.

They're tarred with the same brush. ~ They are both bad.

Too big for your britches ~ Overconfident, assuming too much authority.

What are you like at all? ~ There is something strange or different about you.

Whoever knit you wasted their yarn. ~ You are useless.

Who knit you? ~ You're crazy.

Who owns you? ~ There is something wrong with you. Alluding to the possibility that the person referred to has strange parents, no parents, or no human parents, and wasn't raised properly.

You didn't show up when God was handing out sense. ~ You are a senseless person.

You'll never be the man your mother was. ~ You are not much of a man.

You're ugly and your mother dresses you funny. ~ You don't have much going for you.

Your mind is as sharp as a tack – hard tack. ~ You are too stubborn to learn.

Your tawts are too far aft ~ 1. You are mentally challenged. 2. Your opinion is a little off the mark.

You still got the slop pail ring around your arse. ~ Said by a Townie to a bayman who is fresh in St. John's from an outport.

Questioning

Don't you think I got either mouth on me? ~ You didn't ask if I was hungry.

What are you after doing now? ~ What have you done?

What do your father do? ~ What is your father's occupation?

Where do you belong to? ~ Where do you come from?

Who clipped your ears and made you skipper? ~ What makes you think you're the boss?

Recognizing Faces

I'd know him boiled up in a pot of soup. ~ I have no trouble recognizing him.

I know him all to pieces. ~ I know him exceptionally well.

I know him and I don't know him. ~ He seems familiar but I'm not sure if I remember him.

The face and eyes of ~ Identical to. "He's the face and eyes of his father."

Resting

I'm all in, so I going to have a blow. ~ I'm tired so I'm going to rest for a short while.

Seasons

The evenings are closing in. ~ It gets dark sooner in the fall.

Shortly

I'll be there the once. ~ I'll be there shortly.

I'll be there the rackley. ~ I'll be there shortly. *The rackley* is a corruption of *directly*.

Showing off

Big in himself ~ Showing off. "Since Harry got his new car he's some big in himself."

Similies

Big as Munn

Black as soot

Bold as brass

Brown as a berry ~ Suntanned.

Busy as a bayman with two chainsaws

Busy as a bayman with two wood stoves

Busy as a nailer

Busy as a one-armed fiddler with the lice

Busy as a one-armed nailer in a gale of wind

Busy as a one-armed paper-hanger with the itch

Cold as a turr on a battycatter

Cold enough to be anointed ~ So cold even the priest would think the person dead and could be given last rights.

Cold enough to clip you

Cold enough to shave you

Crazy as a loo (loon)

Cross as the cats

Cute as a rat

Dark as pitch

Darker than a cow's gut

Dead to the world ~ Sound asleep.

Deaf as a haddock

Deaf as a hatchet

Dirty as a duck's puddle

Dry as a bone ~ 1. Thirsty. 2. Completely without liquid content.

Far as ever a puffin flew ~ A long distance.

Flat as a pancake

Foolish as a capelin ~ Capelin were probably considered foolish because they ran ashore to spawn and die.

Foolish as odd socks ~ Acting silly.

Fresh as a rubber boot ~ not very salty. "This salt beef and cabbage dinner is fresh as a rubber boot."

Hard as the hob(s) of hell

Hard as the knockers of Newgate ~ Newgate was a notorious insane asylum/prison in London, England.

Hungry as a hound

Ignorant as a pig. ~ Having bad manners.

Leaky as a basket

Like a birch broom in the fits ~ Messy, unkempt, as in one's hair.

Like a cat on hot rocks ~ Don't know what to do next.

Like a Christmas turkey ~ All dressed up.

Like a fart in a wind storm ~ Flits about all over the place.

Like a fish out of water ~ Not comfortable in your situation.

Like a pig before thunder ~ Afraid.

Like a pig with a grunt ~ Has a sour personality.

Like a skinned rabbit ~ Very thin.

Like the cat. ~ He's quick and steady on his feet.

Lonesome as a gull on a rock ~ Possibly from the fact that the sight of a single gull on a rock is one of solitude.

Long as a wet Sunday ~ Very long. Possibly from the fact that work was forbidden on Sunday, which made the day boring and seem long. When it was raining on Sunday and you couldn't go outside it seemed longer.

Mute as a mouse

Old as Buckley's goat

Old as the North Star

Rotten as dirt ~ Not a nice person.

Rough as a dogfish's back ~ A dogfish is a small shark with a rough skin.

Round as a barrel ~ Rotund, fat.

Round as the bung of a cask ~ A bung is a plug in the hole in a cask through which the liquid contents are retrieved. The bung has to be perfectly round to make a good seal when fitted into the bung hole.

Salty as Lot's wife ~ Very salty. Alluding to Lot's wife in the Bible, who disobeyed God's command and looked back at the burning cities of Sodom and Gomorrah, for which God turned her into a pillar of salt.

Saucy as a black ~ Very saucy. Said by Roman Catholics of Protestants. Black being the state of one's soul who was not of the Roman Catholic faith.

Saucy as a crackie ~ A crackie is a small dog of mixed breed that barks a lot.

Sharp as the word of a fool ~ From Ireland.

Silly as a bag of nails ~ Very flaky or silly.

Slow as cold molasses ~ Very slow-moving.

Slower than the second coming (of Christ)

Smart as a bee

Smokes like a winter's tilt ~ Smokes a lot of cigarettes. A tilt is a temporary shelter or cabin. Often the stoves in these structures didn't draw properly and the cabins filled with smoke.

Smoky as a Labrador tilt

Smooth as a mill pond

Smooth as oil

Soft as a mummy

Soggy as lead

Solid as a rock

Sore as a boil

Sound as a bell ~ Strong and healthy.

Stiff as a poker ~ A poker is a long metal object used to stir the fire.

Straight as a ramrod

Straight as a whip ~ Very straight, especially as in the condition of one's hair.

Stunned as me arse ~ Stupid.

Thick as a brick ~ Stupid or dense.

Thick as tar ~ Very lacking in viscosity.

Thin as an eggshell

True as the gospel

Useless as tits on a bull

Welcome as the angels in heaven

Wet as dung

White as the driven snow ~ Very pale, especially in skin colouring.

White as the sheet ~ Very pale in the face and about to faint.

Wide as the devil's boots

Yellow as beaten gold

Yellow as ragweed ~ From Ireland.

S killed

He can put a arse in a cat. ~ Refers to a person who is very capable with his hands.

He could take a ball of steel wool and knit you a bike. ~ He is very capable with his hands.

S leep

He could sleep on a clothesline. ~ He could sleep anywhere.

Larry is crawling up your back. ~ You are getting sleepy.

S omehow

Between the jigs and the reels ~ One way or another, somehow. "We went through an awful storm, but between the jigs and the reels we made it.

S peaking Out

Don't want to hear tell of it ~ Don't want to know anything about it, referring to something one doesn't agree with. "Don't tell me the youngsters mooched from school, I don't want to hear tell of it."

I'll go bail for that. ~ I'll vouch for that.

It's just as well to say it as to have it on your mind. ~ If you're thinking a bad thought you've already committed the evil, so saying it won't make it worse.

S peed

He give it to her for all she was worth. ~ He ran (or attempted some endeavour) as fast as he could.

Take to your scrapers ~ To run away quickly.

Take to your taps ~ To run away quickly.

Took to wing ~ Ran away fast. "When Eli saw his father coming he took to wing." Referring to birds that fly away quickly upon approach.

Surprise

Came to his taps ~ Stood up quickly. "He didn't know there was a soul around until he looked up and saw me, then he came to his taps."

I didn't know whether to shit or go blind. ~ I was shocked.

Is you catching flies? ~ Why are you staring at me with your mouth open?

Well bless my britches and call me a frigger! ~ An exclamation of surprise.

Tardiness

It's no time to go for the doctor when the patient is dead. ~ Don't put off important things. From Ireland, via the Southern Shore.

I've got the sooners. ~ I'd sooner not do a certain thing than do it.

Thin

He was so skinny he could kiss a goat between the horns. ~ He was very skinny.

He's so skinny that if the door opens and nobody comes in, it's him.

He's so skinny you can see the sins on his soul.

He's so thin he has to turn around twice to make a shadow.

He's so thin you can see both sides.

There's more meat on Good Friday. ~ Refers to an exceptionally thin person.

Tired

You look like you were hauled t'rough a knot hole. ~ You look like you're worn out.

Time

An hour by sun ~ An hour before sunset.

Tongue

Lick out your tongue ~ Stick your tongue out.

Travel

Going out around shore ~ Going to a nearby outport. "I'm going out around shore to visit Mr. Watkins."

Going round shore ~ Going around the harbour by road.

Vamp the bottom ~ Walk around the harbour.

Wore me taps out ~ Walked a long distance.

Treachery

Treacherous as an Englishman ~ From Ireland.

Trickery

He's blind in one eye and can't see out of the other one. ~ He's pretending he doesn't understand, but he does.

He would cover a rock with hay and sell it for a haycock. ~ He's a good salesman, a smooth talker, a con man. From Ireland.

Vessels and Sailing

From anchor to anchor ~ For the duration of the voyage. "He's a good sailor from anchor to anchor."

I spent more time on one wave than you did on the water. ~ I've been to sea for many more years than you have.

I was further aloft than you were away from home. ~ You haven't sailed as far from home as I've been aloft in the mast.

I wrung more water out of me mitts than you sailed over. ~ I've been to sea for many more years than you have.

Swallow the anchor ~ To retire from a life at sea.

Those who would go to sea for pleasure would go to hell for pastime. ~ A sailor's life is a hard life.

Visiting

I'll never darken your doorstep. ~ I'll never come to your house.

The doorstep of a great house is slippery. ~ There's false welcome at the house of a rich man. From Ireland.

Water

Douse the killick. ~ Throw the killick (anchor) overboard.

I went slouse-oh. ~ I fell in the water.

Weather

A good day on clothes ~ Refers to a warm, windy day.

A jacket colder than yesterday ~ It's so much colder than yesterday that an extra jacket is required to keep warm.

A lazy wind ~ A cold, biting wind. Suggesting that the wind would rather blow through you than around you.

A warm smoke is better than a cold fog.

Blowing so hard it would take two men to hold down one.

I know it's not cold out, is it. ~ It is very cold out.

If the mar marnin' is ar bit like this marnin' it'll be some marnin' the mar marnin'. ~ If tomorrow morning is as good as this morning it'll be a good morning tomorrow morning. This expression is in present jocular use in the province.

It blows so hard there that even the cats have short legs. ~ It is a very windy place.

It was so cold that I looked out and saw the wood horse trying to get into the barn.

It would blow the horns out of a bull.

My goosebumps were so big I didn't know where to put me bra. ~ It was very cold.

Praise the weather when you're ashore.

Snowing by the reeves ~ Snowing hard.

The devil is beating his grandmother. ~ Refers to bright and sunny weather with rain falling at the same time.

The devil is dancing on his grandmother's back. ~ Refers to bright and sunny weather with rain falling at the same time, usually accompanied by a rainbow.

The fog is as thick as pea soup. ~ Split-pea soup is very thick in this province.

The old woman is picking her goose. ~ Refers to a snowy day. Snowflakes somewhat resemble the down from a goose whose feathers are being plucked.

The sun is splittin' the rocks. ~ It is very hot outdoors.

White horses on the bay. ~ Stormy weather. The white horses are the white-capped waves that occur when there is a strong wind.

You can cut the fog with a knife. ~ The fog is very thick.

omen

A fine leg for a skin boot ~ Meant as a compliment to a lady with nice legs.

A fine piece of gear ~ A good-looking woman. Gear refers to fishing equipment, in which men took great pride in keeping in good order.

He got the woman in his head, like the lobster. ~ He's always thinking about women. Alluding to the part inside the lobster's head that looks like a woman in a rocking chair.

There'll be white blackbirds before an unwilling woman ties the knot. ~ It's hard to change the mind of a woman.

W ork

A lick and a promise ~ Refers to a job done in a big hurry.

A man on a galloping horse wouldn't notice it. ~ Refers to a poor job of painting, carpentry, or other effort that can easily be seen as poor job by anyone in a normal situation.

Fit hands with ~ to accommodate or contend with. "I got more work than I can fit hands with."

Working harder than a one legged man in an ass kicking contest.

You'll never plough a field by turning it over in your mind. ~ Getting the job done requires effort as well as thought.

orry

I'm right afraid of myself today. ~ I'm worried.

In a hobble about it ~ Worried to the point of being distressed.

1 01 Colourful Place Names with Colourful Backgrounds

The sources of the material used in this section include the Encyclopedia of Newfoundland and Labrador, Volumes One and Two, published by Newfoundland Book Publishers; and Volumes Three, Four and Five, published by the Joseph R. Smallwood Heritage Foundation.
The material is also derived from the author's own personal knowledge, gleaned while visiting these places, as well as from a number of other publications listed in the bibliography at the back of this book.

Aguathuna {locally pronounced: *AIG - ah - TUNE - ah*} ~ Originally known as Jack of Clubs Cove because one of the eroding limestone pillars there resembled a club, this Port au Port West community got its present name from the manager of a mining company there in 1911. Arthur House, manager of the Dominion Iron and Steel Company, wanted to rename the site as it was felt a company in a place called Jack of Clubs Cove would not inspire serious respect and confidence to customers. Archbishop M. F. Howley suggested Aguathuna, believing it to be the Beothuk word for white stone that had been eroded into different shapes by the sea (it has since been suggested by linguists that the Beothuk "aquathoonet" in fact meant "grindstone"). The name Limeville was also suggested, but rejected. At peak periods the quarry employed 500 men, but has since closed. In 2001 Aguathuna and nearby Boswarlos had a combined population of 295.

Angels Cove ~ This Cape Shore community, like others in the area, was first settled in the early 1800s by Irishmen who worked for the firm of Sweetman's, and who decided to stay on in Newfoundland to settle the

Cape Shore. One of these men, James Coffey from County Waterford, along with his wife, Catherine McGrath, made his home at Angel's Cove and raised his family of 10 children there. The early settlers cleared the land and, until the 1870s, earned their livelihood solely from farming. Hay and potatoes were the main crops grown and sheep, cattle and pigs were the principal animals raised. In the 1870s the inhabitants began fishing as well, and by 1874, three fishing rooms had been established there.

B **areneed** {locally pronounced: *bar - NEED*} ~ This community at the base of the Port de Grave peninsula was originally known as Barren Head, which in West Country English dialect is pronounced: *bar - ren - EED*. Although Bareneed suggests poverty, the community has been a thriving one.

B **ar Haven** ~ This now-vacated island community situated on the northern part of the west side of Placentia Bay was earlier known as Barren Island. It is believed to have been settled in the late 1700s or early 1800s when the firm of Christopher Spurrier and Company of Poole, England, brought Irishmen over to fish from this island.

B **atteau** {pronounced: *BAT - toe*} ~ From the French, meaning boat, this summer fishing station is located on the southeastern end of the Island of Ponds off the Labrador Coast. Batteau Harbour was known as such as early as 1775 when George Cartwright referred to it by name. Batteau was almost always occupied on a seasonal basis, being used principally as a summer base for the settlers' cod, herring, salmon and seal fisheries. Until the mid-1950s the residents moved from Batteau every fall to the shores of nearby bays on the mainland of Labrador. There throughout the winter they trapped and hunted, returning to Batteau in early summer. As well as the livyers, large numbers of stationers and floaters from Newfoundland were regular summer visitors in Batteau from the early 1800s to the late 1930s. Since then seasonal fishermen from Newfoundland continued to go to Batteau, but in smaller numbers. From the mid-1950s the settlement was occupied year-round.

B **attle Harbour** ~ This summer fishing station, formerly a permanent settlement, is located between Battle Island and Great Caribou Island off the coast of southeastern Labrador. The name is believed by some to have derived from the Portuguese word *batal*, meaning "boat." According to legend

Montagnais Indians, aided by the French, fought their final battle against the Inuit around 1760 at Battle Harbour. A burial mound is supposed to mark the site and the name of the island and harbour is said by some to be derived from the event. According to Joseph Gilbert, in 1767 Battle Harbour was called *Ca-tuc-to* by the Indians. A mercantile saltfish premises was established there by the firm of John Slade and Company of Poole, England, in the 1770s. The population rapidly increased after 1820 when Newfoundland fishing schooners adopted Battle Harbour as their primary port of call. Battle Harbour developed into a thriving community, and for some time it was known as the Capital of Labrador. Battle Harbour is now the site of the national commemoration of the historic Labrador fishery and is designated a National Historic District.

Bay L'Argent {pronounced: *BAY - LAR - gent*} ~ the English translation of the French name of this Burin Peninsula community is "Bay of Silver" and possibly originated from the high cliffs which surround the bay. The faces of the cliffs appear to be silver coloured when the sunlight reflects off them. According to the *Encyclopedia of Newfoundland and Labrador*, "The first English settlers are thought to have been James Banfield (1799-1884) and Robert Thornhill (1817-1899) who arrived in the Bay in the 1830s and 1840s." In the 1836 census, the community then known as Bay Le John had a population of 32. In 2001 Bay L'Argent had a population of 320.

Beaumont {pronounced: *BO - mont*} ~ Originally known as Wards Harbour, this fishing community shares Long Island in western Notre Dame Bay with the community of Lushes Bight. It was renamed Beaumont soon after 1918, in hon-

our of the Newfoundlanders who died at Beaumont Hamel in France during a battle there on July 1, 1916. The first English settlers probably arrived shortly after 1800 and permanent settlement occurred by the 1820s or 1830s. The first settlers almost certainly had some contact with the Beothuk whose seasonal migration patterns took them out Indian River to the bottom of Halls Bay and then along the shoreline to the islands. In 2001 Lushes Bight-Beaumont-Beaumont North had a population of 308.

Belleoram {pronounced: *bell - LORE - am*} ~ The French who originally used the harbour at Belleoram extensively referred to the place as Bande de Laurier and variations such as Bande de l'Arier, Bande de l'Arriere, Bande de la Rier and Bandalore. The French were forced to leave the area by the provisions of the Treaty of Utrecht in 1713, after which English settlers moved in. It was reportedly given its present name by a French adventurer who is believed to have wintered there for 20 years. In 2001 Belleoram had a population of 484.

Bide Arm ~ Located at the far end of an indraft known as Bide Arm in White Bay, this fishing community was founded in 1969 by 186 of the 215 residents of Hooping Harbour under the community consolidation program. Under the leadership of Pastor Booth Reid of the Apostolic Faith Church, they chose Bide Arm over Englee because of a building lot shortage there and their desire to establish an independent community under resettlement. In 2001 Bide Arm had a population of 484.

Biscay Bay {pronounced: *BIS - key - BAY*} ~ This community located 5 km (3 miles) east of Trepassey on the Irish Loop was probably fished by the French, Basque and Portuguese in the 1500s. The name was first recorded in 1675. In 2001 Biscay Bay had a population of 52.

Blow Me Down ~ This fishing community in a small cove at the tip of the Port de Grave Peninsula was probably settled by 1750. It is likely that it got its name from a geographic feature, such as a high headland which would render vessels in the area especially liable to dangerous unpredictable winds. There are 30 localities around the province named Blow Me Down. This particular locale is now part of the community of Port de Grave. According to the *Encyclopedia of Newfoundland and Labrador*, "Blow Me Down was first reported in the Census of 1857 as an independent settlement. The community at that time numbered 169 people, 31 families, who were all adherents of the Church of England." Although Blow Me Down was first recorded as a separate community in 1857 the name was recorded as Blowmedown Cove as early as 1774.

Bonavista {pronounced: *BAWN - ah - VIS - tah*} ~ The name reportedly originated with John Cabot, the Genoese explorer, who made landfall there in 1497. Upon seeing the land, he was said to have exclaimed in Italian, " O Buona Vista,"

meaning "Oh happy sight." The town is situated at the end of the Bonavista peninsula on the northeast coast of Newfoundland. Explorer and cartographer Capt. James Cook, who made Bonavista his headquarters while mapping the coast in 1763, notes the area was settled on or before 1660. In 1677, Bonavista was the most northern community in Newfoundland was the second largest town on the island, with 18 houses compared with the present-day capital, St. John's, which had 45. It became the centre for the northern fishery and was attacked on several occasions by the French. In 1704 Michael Gill, a New Englander commanding a ship at harbour in Bonavista, made a brave stand against the French, whereupon the settlers came out of hiding and rallied to his support. The French were routed but returned again the following year. This time, although the Bonavista residents were well fortified on nearby Green Island, they were defeated. By the Treaty of Utrecht in 1713, Cape Bonavista became the eastern boundary of the French Shore, but this had little effect on the community. It was mostly occupied by English settlers and it continued to grow. A replica of John Cabot's ship, the *Matthew*, is now a tourist attraction at one of the harbour's wharves. In 2001 Bonavista had a population of 4,021.

Brighton ~ Located on the two islands of Cobbler's Island and Brighton Island in Badger Bay, Notre Dame Bay, this fishing community was originally called Dark Tickle. According to local tradition, when the post office was built in the community, Brighton was

chosen as the new name because of its optimistic connotations. The Palaeo-Eskimo and the Dorset Eskimo were the first settlers on the island of Brighton approximately 2,000 years ago. It was settled by the English in the 1800s. In 2001 Brighton had a population of 233.

Canada Harbour ~ The fact that Newfoundland was so close to Canada and later become a Canadian province would lead some to speculate that this resettled fishing community on the east coast of the Great Northern Peninsula got its name from that Dominion. In fact, the name had to do with the large number of wolves in the area at the time it was named. The name first appeared on French maps in the 1600s as Havre Canaries, and the harbour was frequently referred to as Canairies, Canaries and Canary Harbour by the French and English until the 20th century. According to Newfoundland historian E. R. Seary, the French word *canarie* is derived from the Latin "Canaria Insula" or "Isle of Dogs."

Carbonear {pronounced: *CAR - bah - NEAR*} ~ This large town on the west side of Conception Bay, probably got its name from either the Spanish word *carbonera*, which means a female who makes or sells charcoal, or from one of several French words. Among the first settlers were people from the Channel Islands  who, although they were part of England, spoke French. Charbonnier and Carbonnier were two Channel Islands' family names. Although English citizens who spoke French were among the early settlers, Carbonear and Carbonear Island were attacked by the French a number of times, as well as by privateers and pirates. The town is first mentioned in connection with raids by pirates in 1614. In 1696 and 1697, Carbonear was attacked by the French, who burned all 22 houses in 1697. Nearby Carbonear Island repulsed these attacks, as it did in 1704 and 1705 when Carbonear was again burnt by the French. The French raided the area again in 1762 and this time were successful in occupying the island for a short period of time. In 1775, Carbonear was attacked for the last time, carried out by American privateers. Among the well-known people from Carbonear are tele-journalist Rex Murphy; NHL hockey player Daniel Cleary; and the late Frank Moores, the second Premier of the province. Princess Sheila NaGeira also lived for a time in Carbonear. In 2001 Carbonear had a population of 4,759.

Catalina {pronounced: *CAT - ah - LINE - ah*} ~ According to historian E.R. Seary, the name Catalina probably derives from the French *Havre Sainte Katherine*, later superseded by the Spanish *Cataluna*. This name was established long

before the Pilgrim Fathers made their historic settlement after landing at Plymouth Rock in America, according to the *Encyclopedia of Newfoundland and Labrador*. "As early as 1534, when Jacques Cartier spent ten days in Catalina harbour, the name was well established as it is clear from Cartier's accounts that he already knew the place by name and did not name it himself." Situated on the eastern coast of the Bonavista Peninsula in Trinity Bay, Catalina adjoins the town of Port Union, home of the Fisherman's Union Trading Company established by Sir William Coaker. Catalina was the first community outside St. John's to set up a public library. Joseph Clouter, a former resident, donated 5,000 books and the library opened in 1937. In 2001 Catalina had a population of 995.

Champneys ~ This Trinity Bay community was known as Salmon Cove until 1904, when the name was changed to eliminate the confusion caused by the large number of Salmon Coves in Newfoundland. Although the good harbour, excellent facilities for curing fish, and proximity to the rich fishing grounds of Trinity Bay had probably attracted seasonal European fishermen as early as the early 1500s, the first known inhabitant of Champneys was a planter named John le Crass. In 1675 he ran a fishing establishment employing 12 men. On February 28, 1892, more than 200 men from Champneys and several surrounding communities were engaged in the seal hunt when a terrible blizzard descended without warning. This tragic event, in which 24 men lost their lives, became known as the "Trinity Bay disaster."

Chance Cove ~ Probably named for mischance or shipwreck, this fishing community in Trinity Bay comprises two adjacent coves: Big Chance Cove (formerly called Great Chance Cove) and Little Chance Cove (formerly called Lower Chance Cove). According to the *Encyclopedia of Newfoundland and Labrador*, "In 1873 J.F. Imray noted about the community, 'only fit for small vessels during the summer months.'" In 2001 Chance Cove had a population of 339.

Change Islands ~ Situated between Twillingate and Fogo in Notre Dame Bay, this group of islands is located along the narrow tickle separating the two largest of these islands (now connected by a causeway). Until 1783, Change Islands was part of the French Shore and unpopulated, but

with the beginning of the English Labrador fishery in the latter half of the 1700s and the setting up of establishments by the Bristol and Poole merchants, Change Islands began to be settled. By 1884 the population had increased to 934. Many of the fishermen from Change Islands went to the Labrador fishery, and in 1874 Change Islands was one of the focal points of the winter seal hunt prosecuted by landsmen. In 2001 Change Islands had a population of 360.

Codroy ~ Archbishop M.F. Howley suggests that the name of this community is a corruption of an incorrect spelling of the French for Cape Ray, " C. de Roy." This fishing community is located on the southwest coast of the Island, about 2.1 km (1.3 miles) southeast of Cape Anguille. It is not known when Codroy was first used as a fishing station, but it is known that by 1764 a British adventurer, John Broom, was fishing for salmon and cod there, and remained there until at least 1774. Following the Treaty of Versailles of 1783 the coastline of the west coast, including that of Codroy, became part of the French Shore. In 1822, William Epps Cormack (who, along with his Mi'kmaq guide, Silvester Joe, walked across Newfoundland) reported that the harbour between Codroy and Codroy Island was teeming with activity. According to the *Dictionary of Newfoundland English*, he wrote, "owing to the shelter and anchorage for shipping at Codroy... and to its immediate proximity to the fine fishing grounds about Cape Ray, it is the central point of the French fisheries in summer."

Coley's Point ~ Once known as Cold East Point, this community which became part of the municipality of Bay Roberts in 1965 was first settled in the late 1700s. The first settlers, who included John and William Snow, William North,

William Littlejohn, Peter Fradsham and James Bowering, moved into the south side of the settlement. Some of these early settlers came from nearby communities such as Port de Grave, but others came from England. Soon all the suitable areas for curing fish on the south side became taken up, and as early as the 1820s settlers started moving to the north side. By 1884, the population had reached its peak of 1,334.

Come By Chance ~ This incorporated community located near the head of Placentia Bay was originally called Passage Harbour by John Guy in 1612. It was settled by Thomas Adams from Devon, England, in 1822, according to local legend. The first written reference to the community as Come By Chance was in a dispatch dated September 13, 1706, from Major Lloyd, an officer prominent in Newfoundland for activity against the French between 1703 and 1708. In 2001 Come By Chance had a population of 265.

Comfort Cove ~ Located in the Bay of Exploits about 32 km (20 miles) northeast of Lewisporte, and now part of the incorporated community of Comfort Cove-Newstead, this fishing-farming community was one time occupied in the summer months by a  Beothuk band. The first reported settler of Comfort Cove was a John Cull of Barr'd Islands, Fogo, followed by others from the surrounding area looking for new areas to prosecute the cod and salmon fishery. In 2001 Comfort Cove-Newstead had a population of 484.

Conception Harbour ~ Known as Cat Cove until about 1870, this town is in the southwestern part of Conception Bay 64 km (40 miles) from St. John's. Tradition has it that Brian Collins was the first to settle there in the 1700s. By 1803 there were seven men with possessions there, and by 1836 the population was about 250. This town is home to pioneer Newfoundland musician, Wilf Doyle. In 2001 Conception Harbour had a population of 801.

Cormack ~ Named after the well-known Newfoundland explorer William Epps Cormack, this farming community situated 18 km (11 miles) north of Deer Lake at the base of the Great Northern Peninsula was created after World War II by the Commission of Government as an agricultural settlement for returning WWII veterans. Under the relocation scheme, each family was given 20 ha (50 acres) of land (a portion of which was to be cleared before the settler moved in); a six-room bungalow, and money for the construction of a barn, the purchase of livestock and equipment; and a maintenance allowance for the first winter. Two hundred and seventeen veterans applied and 163 were approved. All were required to have had previous farming experience or were sent on a 12-month training course in Canada. In 2001 Cormack had a population of 675.

Croque {pronounced: *CROKE*} ~ The name of this small fishing village south of St. Anthony on the Great Northern Peninsula is believed to be a corruption of the French word *croc* which means "boat hook." The bay is long, narrow and curving towards its head, shaped somewhat like a hook. It is believed that the name came from this physical characteristic. The area was part of the French shore, which meant that settlement was prohibited for French and English alike. Yet both French and English headstones dating from the 1700s can be found in the cemetery at Epine Cadoret. Some of the English settlers were "gaurdiens," hired by the French as winter caretakers of their stages and other property. Among those were two Irishmen, Patrick Kearney and James Hope, who settled in the mid-1800s. At this time Croque was also used as the headquarter station for the French warships employed in protecting the French fisheries. The settlement grew slowly, and although the French were banned from fishing in the area in 1904, a French warship continued to sail regularly to Croque until the 1970s to tend the graves of the French buried at Epine Cadoret.

Cupids ~ Known as Cupers Cove when it as settled in 1610, this Conception Bay community was the first post-Norse European settlement in Newfoundland, and holds two firsts for present day Canada. It was, the first English settlement, and the first child, a boy, was born there to Nicholas Guy and his wife on March 27, 1613. It was also one of the first European settlements anywhere in North America. In 2001 Cupids had a population of 775.

Deadman's Bay ~ This is a fishing community northwest of Lumsden on the "Straight Shore" of Bonavista Bay. The first record of settlement of Deadman's Bay was in 1845 when 24 people, two of whom were born in England, were reported in the Census. These fishermen were members of the Church of England. There was one Labrador banking vessel reported. By 1857 the population had doubled and 20 acres of land had been cleared as families moved to Deadman's Bay from Lumsden, Bonavista and Cape Freels.

Deep Bight ~ Although the name Deep Bight implies deep water, these depths are found offshore. Around the community itself are mud and sand flats which provide safe anchorage for small boats. This lumbering community on the western shore of the northwest arm of Trinity Bay was chosen as a millsite in the 1850s because of its fast-flowing stream, level land and excellent timber stands to supply lumber for the prosperous fishing settlements of Old Perlican, Hant's Harbour and Grates Cove – they were situated in prime fishing sites where the limited supply of timber had been exhausted.

De Grau {pronounced: *de - GRAW*} ~ De Grau is now part of the incorporated communities of Cape St. George-Petit Jardin-Grand Jardin, de-Grau, Marches Point-Loretto. Along with other communities at the extreme tip of the Port au Port Peninsula it was orig-

inally settled as a farming community. These settlers were reportedly made up mostly of deserters from vessels owned by French companies out of St. Pierre and the county of Breton in France. Although the sea around that part of the French Shore had lots of fish, the high cliffs and scarcity of proper beaches made it hard to fish from shore. Nearby L'Isle Rouge (Red Island), did have reasonable access to the sea and it was from there that the French companies operated. The land atop the cliffs around De Grau was level and fertile enough to raise crops and animals, and that's where these deserters started their families. This was illegal in the eyes of Britain, but that law was seldom on the English settlers in the Notre Dame Bay part of the French Shore, nor the St. George's Bay part. The French companies operating out of L'Isle Rouge left the settlers alone as long as they didn't interfere with the fishing. After France lost the rights to the French Shore, these settlers stayed on and some went back to fishing.

Dildo ~ The name for this town in Chapel Arm at the bottom of Trinity Bay comes from the pin on a rowboat to which the oar is attached, also known as a thole pin. Founded in the early 1800s as a fishing, whaling and sealing village, Dildo now has a fast-growing tourist industry. This very picturesque community won the *Harrowsmith Magazine* Award in 2001 as one of the 10 prettiest small towns in Canada. A giant squid was caught near Dildo in 1933.

Domino ~ Now part of the Local Service District of Black Tickle-Domino, this community on the Island of Ponds in Southern Labrador has a deep, protected harbour with an excellent holding ground and is mainly used as a summer fishing station. The first recorded settlement was 1891. In early July 1892, Wilfred T. Grenfell, aboard the hospital ship *Albert* on her maiden voyage, made his first landfall on the Labrador coast at Domino. The station became a regular port of call for the "Deep Sea Missions," and was serviced by the Labrador postal service. It supported a wireless station around 1940, and in 1965 a permanent wharf and a seasonal general store supplied by the Labrador coastal service were added.

Englee {locally pronounced: *ING - ah - LEE*} ~ This town is located on the east side of the Great Northern Peninsula in a sheltered harbour on the northern headland of Canada Bay. It was first settled in the early 1800s by four families, but most of the original settlers came between 1870 and 1900. The French were active in fishing operations there in the 1860s and 1870s. The first settlers were fishermen, builders and trappers. Each family grew its own vegetables and raised its own sheep and cattle. In 2001 Englee had a population of 694.

Fair Haven ~ This name was chosen as a positive sounding replacement for this fishing community's original name of Famish Gut. Located on the south shore of the Isthmus of Avalon, Fair Haven is a more appropriate name as it is situated at the head of Fair Haven, a pond into which boats may pass at high tide and obtain shelter from offshore winds.

Helen Kaulbach Photo

Ferryland ~ Some authorities believe that the name of this Southern Shore community is a corruption of "Veralum," which was the ancient name of St. Alban's in England. It has been written as "Forillon," "Foriland" and "Farilham." Ferryland was visited by French fishermen as early as 1504 and used by them as a base for the summer fishery. It was the French who called it *Forillon*, which meant "standing out or separated from the mainland." A few years later the French abandoned the site for Newfoundland's south coast, where fishing began a month earlier. English fishermen replaced the French as seasonal occupiers of the area. Then in 1922, Sir George Calvert, the first Lord Baltimore, set up a colony he called Avalon. The colony is "separated from the mainland" by a narrow isthmus that is not much more than a beach on either side of the road. There have been many archeological finds at the site in recent years, including, according to one archeologist, "North America's first flush toilet." Although not the conventional type invented by Thomas Crapper, but it had an outlet from the "washroom" to the sea that flushed itself twice a day, when the tides came in and out. In 2001 Ferryland had a population of 607.

Fleur de Lys {pronounced: *FLEUR - dee - LEE*} ~ Originally one of 40 French fishing stations spread around the vast French Shore, this community was first referred to as Petite Nord, the name given to the nearby fishing ground. In the well-protected harbour there's a striking rock formation over 800 feet high, which has three hummocks or hills resembling the national

symbol of France, the three-leafed fleur de lys plant. It was from this rock formation that this most northerly community on Newfoundland's Baie Verte Peninsula got its name. Fleur de Lys had one of the longest and most continuous associations with French fishing interests in Newfoundland. In 1706 the station had been the site of a clash between French and English interests. The *Falkland*, the *Nonsuch* and the *Medway*, all British warships, had been dispatched to Petit Nord to protect British interests on petition of the "inhabitants of St. John's." Off Fleur De Lys harbour they exchanged fire with *Le Duc d'Orleans*, a ship of 30 guns and 110 men from St. Malo. Between 1800 and 1850, a growing need to protect the interests of the French fishery year-round was met in the hiring of *gardiens* for Fleur de Lys. The French presence at Fleur de Lys continued on mostly friendly terms, until the 1880s when English settlers predominated. In 2001 Fleur de Lys had a population of 348.

Fogo ~ There are several theories on the origin of the name of this community on Fogo Island in eastern Notre Dame Bay. One theory is that it is derived from the Portuguese word *fuego* meaning fire, which might refer to early forest fires that occurred frequently on the northern part of the island. The other theory is that the word has the same roots as Funk, the name given to the

Charlie Prim Photo

islands to the east that now comprise the Funk Islands seabird sanctuary. This word means "bad smell" and comes from the droppings of the many seabirds

in the area. Like the Funk Islands, the shores around Fogo Island provided
nesting grounds for many seabirds. The earliest known inhabitants of Fogo
Island were Beothuks who summered there. Fogo was part the French Shore
when it was originally settled by English fishing families, making it illegal to
settle there. But by that time the English Shore, which ran south from Cape
Bonavista, was becoming overcrowded and the fishery was poor, so people
moved north to places like Fogo and Twillingate in spite of the law. The town
of Fogo with its two harbours (which between them provided shelter no matter the direction of the wind) was one of the most important bases for the
northern fishery beginning in the mid-1700s. In 1756, Britain and France
became involved in the Seven Years War. During those years, French fishing
vessels no longer came to Notre Dame Bay and many English settlers moved
into the bay, including Fogo Island. Britain was well aware of the value of
Notre Dame Bay – as well as Bonavista Bay, which was also part of the
French Shore – because the Treaty of Utrect, signed after the American
Revolutionary War in 1783, Britain gave up a large amount of coastline on the
west coast of the island to France in exchange for Bonavista and Notre Dame
bays. Today Fogo residents are involved in the crab fishery. A crab processing
plant, owned and operated by the Fogo Island Co-operative Society, employs
approximately 500 men and women at its peek season. A well-known attraction of Fogo is Brimstone Head, which the Flat Earth Society claims is one of
the four corners of the earth. The Brimstone Head Festival held every summer
attracts many tourists from around the world. In 2001 Fogo had a population
of 803.

Fortune ~ This town is situated on the western side of the
Burin Peninsula, near the mouth
of Fortune Bay. The name Fortune
is thought to have originated from
the Portuguese word *fortuna*,
which means "good fortune."

Although some historians believe it had satirical connotations and actually
meant "misfortune." According to the *Encyclopedia of Newfoundland and
Labrador*, "It appears on Spanish and Italian maps of the early Sixteenth
Century, including Majollo (1527), Verrazano (1528) and Ribeiro (1529),
which would indicate that Europeans, probably fishermen, were in the area
around that time." According to historian D. W. Prowse, "In testimony given
in Spain in 1697 by Captain Martin De Sapiain it is reported that Basque fishermen had frequented 'Fortuna' as early as 1650 and possibly earlier." In a
census of French settlements on the south coast of Newfoundland for the year
1687, a place listed as Baie de Fortune but believed to be Fortune itself, is
listed as having a population of 72 people. Fossils have been located at nearby

Fortune Head from the Precambrian era, about 530 million years ago. The first English settler is said to have been John Lake sometime after 1763, when a severe storm forced him to seek shelter in the harbour at Fortune. He was impressed enough to return the next year and build a house on the eastern side of the harbour, using logs cut in the vicinity. Many other families from the Placentia Bay area, including Lake's brother, soon followed and by 1836, the population had reached 163. Fortune is the ferry terminus for the French islands of St. Pierre et Miquelon. In 2001 Fortune had a population of 1,615.

Fox Roost ~ This fishing settlement situated on the shores of a short inlet east of Channel-Port aux Basques, to which it is connected by road, was claimed by writer Farley Mowat, to be a corruption of the French name *Fosse Rouge*, meaning "red gulley" or "red ditch." This was probably from the fact that there is indeed a narrow gulley in Fox Roost.

Francois {locally pro-nounced: *FRANS - way*} ~ First settled in the late 1700s, this postcard perfect fishing community is located on a small narrow strip of land at the head of a steep-walled, rocky fiord to the west of Hermitage Bay on the south-west coast of Newfoundland. The Friar, a cliff 207 m (680 ft) in height, overlooks the set-tlement from behind. A brook

runs through the settlement into the head of the bay. Apart from being pictur-esque, Francois is a vibrant community in every sense of the phrase. It has virtually no unemployment and everyone gets involved in its many communi-ty efforts. One of those efforts is the annual Francois Day, celebrated with events for children and adults. Francois is accessible only by boat or helicop-ter, and the community has no cars or roads, just lanes that are used for walk-ing, bicycling, or for using quadrunners (all-terrain vehicles). The voluntary fire department uses quadrunners as well.

G **allants** {pronounced: *gal - ANTS*} ~
This incorporated logging community located on the western banks of Harry's River, northwest of Stephenville, was originally known as Camp 7. It was later renamed after Stephenville businessman, A.V. Gallant, who established the camp and others like it in the neighourhood, including Harry's Brook and George's Lake. Mainly through the
efforts of James Collier, a foreman with the Gallant operation, Gallants was in many respects like a small company town. In Gallants Cupids had a population of 66.

G **arnish** ~ This incorporated fishing community on the west side of the Burin Peninsula in Fortune Bay is built on the western shore of Little Garnish Barrasway, a small natural harbour protected from Fortune Bay by a narrow stretch of land and two breakwaters. The name Garnish is of unknown origin but is a common one in the area, applying not only to the town, but to the barrasway and the river that empties into it. There is also Great Garnish Barrasway, a larger body of water several miles to the southwest. The name first appeared on a map by Captain James Cook, dated 1775, as "Little Garnish." The date of first settlement at Garnish is unknown, although it is believed that Grandys moved from St. Pierre to the area when British subjects were forced to leave St. Pierre in 1763. The earliest settlers in Garnish appear to have been Church of England adherents, but there was no regular clergyman stationed there until at least the 1880s. In 2001 Garnish had a population of 665.

G **aultois** {pronounced: *gall - TISS*} ~ This
fishing outport is located on the southern tip of Long Island, on the western shore of Hermitage Bay, which displays several rock pinnacles. The name of this fishing community was believed by historian H.W. LeMessurier to have come from an old Norman word *Galtas* which means "like a pinnacle or dome." Gaultois Harbour, which seldom freezes over except during the coldest winters with calm weather, is surrounded by high cliffs. Rocky outcrops with small, isolated patches of weathered
soil and sloping ground have limited both agriculture and building within the settlement. However, Gaultois's proximity to superb fishing grounds has made it a favoured site for settlement since the late 1700s. In 2001 Gaultois had a population of 321.

Charlie Prim Photo

Griquet {locally pro-
nounced: *CRICK - it*} ~
Now part of the incorporated
community of St. Lunaire-
Griquet located near the
northern tip of the Great
Northern Peninsula, this community is ringed around two
large, island-strewn harbours:
St. Lunaire Bay and Griquet

Harbour. Both harbours were being used by Breton fishermen as early as
1534, when they were visited by Jacques Cartier. They were French fishing
stations until the mid-1800s. The first English settlers at St. Lunaire-Griquet,
as elsewhere on the French Shore, were likely "gardiens" who oversaw the
French fishing premises during the winter months and were in return permitted to fish grounds that were normally reserved for the migratory French fleet.
The first settlers are said to be the Hills in 1849. Many of the first settlers
came from the Port de Grave-Cupids area of Conception Bay. According to
the *Encyclopedia of Newfoundland and Labrador*, "By 1872 it was noted that
the French had not been in the Griquet area in some years and their old rooms
were being occupied by about 10 fishing families." In 2001 St. Lunaire-
Griquet had a population of 822.

Happy Adventure ~
This settlement is
believed to have been named
after *The Happy Adventure*,
a ship owned by pirate captain, Peter Easton. It is located in the west bay of Happy
Adventure Bays on the
southern shore of the
Eastport Peninsula.

Residents survived by lumbering, and although it is situated far from the
prime fishing locations near the headlands of the Peninsula, it was also a fishing community. The area around Happy Adventure has a number of sandy
beaches, making the area attractive to tourists. In 2001 Happy Adventure had
a population of 245.

Harbour Grace ~ According to historian W. B. Hamilton, Harbour Grace
is "probably a transfer name from *Havre de Grace*, the name used for Le
Havre, France, when the place was founded in 1517." The town of Harbour
Grace is located about 45 km northwest of St. John's, just south of Carbonear.

Fishermen from the Channel Islands had connections with Newfoundland from an early date; tradition has it that they were driven to the shores here while on their way to Iceland sometime before Cabot's voyage of discovery in 1497. Channel Islanders were known to be fishing in Newfoundland waters in the early 1500s. In 1610, pirate Peter Easton made Harbour Grace his headquarters and established a fort overlooking the bay. Although it was attacked by the French the following year, the early settlement survived throughout the 1600s with a permanent, year-round population numbering a few dozen, and swelling to several hundred during the fishing season. The first English book written in North America, *Quodlibits*, was written there by Robert Hayman in 1628. The town, with a population numbering about 100, was destroyed by the French in 1697 and again in 1700. By 1771, the population had reached its peak of about 5,800 people. In 2001 Harbour Grace had a population of 3,380.

Heart's Content ~ The first recorded reference to Heart's Content (as Hartes Content) was probably made by John Guy, when he wrote in his Journal of a "voyage of discov-erie" from Conception Bay to Trinity Bay. According to the *Encyclopedia of Newfoundland and Labrador*, "At that time it appears to have been inhabited only by the Beothuk." Historian

E.R. Seary suggested the name may have been derived from that of a ship or may simply have been a euphemistic name like others in the Island given "to convey the idea of making a good impression or establishing favourable aus-pices." This incorporated coastal town is located on the east side of Trinity Bay, about halfway between Grates Point and the Isthmus of Avalon. Like most of the English settlements in southern Newfoundland, Heart's Content was attacked by the French under Pierre Le Moyne d'Iberville in 1697. In 2001 Heart's Content had a population of 495.

Heart's Delight ~ Now part of the incorporated community of Heart's Delight-Islington, this community located on the southeast side of Trinity Bay was given its name to create a favourable impression, according to historian E. R. Seary. In local lore, the name is said to have been applied by travellers passing through the area. As the story goes, some early travellers were making their first trip down the shore on foot. When they came to the area, they were "delighted" by the beauty of what they saw and gave it its present name. Heart's Delight was first settled in the late 1700s or early 1800s. As early as 1805 it appeared in Colonial Government fishery reports. The first settler is believed to have been a man named Bryant. In 2001 Heart's Delight-Islington had a population of 736.

Heart's Desire ~ A small fishing community located on the eastern shore of Trinity Bay approximately 7.2 km (4.5 mi) north of Heart's Delight, this community was first mentioned in Lane's Sailing Directions of 1775. Local tradition maintains that the Heart's Desire area was settled about 1786 by Irish fishermen named Walsh and St. George. According to tradition, the name is said to have been applied by the same travellers who named Heart's Delight who, after finding Heart's Delight were drawn by curiosity over the hill, where they found Heart's Desire. In 2001 Heart's Desire had a population of 298.

Highlands ~ The Scottish influence played a big role in the name of this fishing-farming community located on a level plateau near the low clay cliffs of southern St. George's Bay, southwest of Stephenville. The first settlers were of Scottish origin, either directly from Judique  and Inverness counties in Scotland, or via Cape Breton and other Gulf areas of Scottish settlement. Highlands is one of the few Scottish settlements in Newfoundland.

Hopedale ~ Named Arvertok (place of whales) in Inuktitut, this Labrador coastal community is the site of the most southerly mission station of the Moravian Church (Unitas Fratrum). Established in 1782, Hopedale is one of the

largest Inuit communities of the five existing settlements on the northern coast
of Labrador. Hopedale's history as a permanent settlement began with the
establishment of the mission station, and until 1926 the Moravians controlled
most aspects of life in the community. Archaeological studies of the region
indicate that the site of the Hopedale mission and settlement, selected by the
Moravians because of the good anchorage and landing site of its harbour, was
used by Eskimo populations, who are culturally ancestral to the present population, and by earlier Eskimo and Indian populations. During the early 1700s
the Hopedale Inuit were important as "middlemen" in the developing trade
between Europeans and Inuit throughout Labrador. In 2001 Hopedale had a
population of 559.

Indian Cove ~ Known locally as
Injun Cove for many years, this fishing community located on the west side
of New World Island (near the causeway that connects New World Island
and South Twillingate Island) was
named for migrating Beothuks, who
came to the area to fish and collect bird
eggs in summer. It first appeared on the
census of 1901, when it had a popula-

tion of 34: 15 Church of England members, 16 Methodists and three Salvation
Army soldiers. The fishermen pursued the inshore fishery and also caught
salmon, lobster and herring. They also raised cows, sheep and poultry, and
kept a number of dogs for hauling wood in the winter.

Ireland's Eye ~ This fishing
community on the northeast
shore of an island also called
Ireland's Eye, at the entrance to
Smith Sound, Trinity Bay, is
now vacated. The origin of the
place name is not known, but it
is recorded in documents from
1675 and appears on maps as

early as 1680. The earliest recorded resident of Ireland's Eye was a Nicholas
Quint, a planter who occupied at least part of the island in 1675, though he
may have moved to Old Bonaventure in the next year. Throughout the 1700s
Ireland's Eye was probably increasingly used by seasonal fishermen as an out-
post of Trinity. By 1857 the population had grown to 101. The residents later
resettled to other parts of Trinity Bay, particularly Trouty. There are 10 locations in the province that use the word Ireland in the name.

Irishtown ~ Located on the north shore of Humber Arm in the Bay of Islands, this community is believed to have gotten its name from a young Irishwoman named Margaret Piercey. She was among the early settlers before the place had a name, and when asked the name of the place, she replied "Irishtown," which was adopted by the

other residents. There are seven locations in the province that use the word Irish in the name. In 2001 Irishtown-Summerside had a population of 1,304.

Isle aux Morts {pronounced: *AISLE - ah - MORT*} ~ The name of this fishing community on the south coast, 10 km east of Channel-Port aux Basques, is French for Deadman's Island. It is believed to have gotten its name from the many deaths caused by the frequent ship-wrecks in the area. Two well-

known early inhabitants were George Harvey and his famous heroine daughter, Ann, who were responsible for saving many lives from the various wrecks. One of those wrecks occurred in 1828, when Ann was 17, and fishing with her father. George, who was born in Jersey, had moved to Newfoundland with his wife. They had eight children, of whom Ann was the oldest. On one July morning when the Harveys were the only residents of Isle aux Morts, Ann sighted a keg and a straw bed floating in the turbulent seas, and immediately realized a ship had been wrecked nearby. George and Ann fetched 12-year-old Tom, George's oldest son, and their Newfoundland dog, Hairy Man, and launched their punt with little regard for their own safety. On a beach nearby they found six men who had survived the wreck of the *Despatch* and set out to find more survivors. They found a large number of them on a tiny island that would be thereafter known as Wreck Rock. This rock, three miles from shore, was barely large enough to hold the remaining survivors of the 30 or more who had died from exhaustion or washed away and drowned. The Harveys got to this small rock by means of a mast they had cut away from the sinking vessel. George could not get closer than 100 feet of the survivors on account of the heavy seas. He threw them a billet of wood to which they attached a rope, and George got his Newfoundland dog to swim for it. Each of the 160 still-surviving passengers and crew were taken out of the jaws of death in this fashion by the Harveys. Ten years later, on September 4, 1838, the *Rankin* was sailing from Glasgow to Quebec and went aground near the same spot as the *Despatch*. This time the Harvey family saved the lives of 25 people. Isle aux Morts first reported an Anglican church in the census of 1911. Children at that time attended a small Church of England school, which had been built in the late 1800s. In 2001 Isle aux Morts had a population of 813.

Jerseyside ~ Named in the mid-1800s for the Jersey fishermen who occupied the site after the French departure in 1713, Jerseyside is located just across the harbour gut from Placentia's "Town Side." It was settled on a steep slope rising  upward from North East Arm to Castle Hill. Surnames associated with the area as early as the 1700s included Bruce, Blanche, Collins, Murphy, Power and Whelan, while Mulrooney, O'Keefe and Ryan families were also present by the early 1900s.

Joe Batt's Arm ~ Tradition has it that the name of the rock-encumbered harbour comes from the first settler, perhaps a crew member of James Cook who deserted, or the Joseph Batt who is recorded by E. R. Seary as being punished for stealing a pair of shoes at Bonavista in 1754. This community became the town of Joe Batt's Arm-Barr'd Islands in April 1980. While the first settlers were of West Country English stock, the prosperity created in the fishery by the Napoleonic Wars (1800-1815) brought an influx of Irish Catholics (early family names include Hackett and Higgins), who settled on the south side. By 1845 the population of Joe Batt's Arm stood at 329, with 114 of the inhabitants being Roman Catholic. Other common family names by 1871 included Brown, Coffin and Penton. This fishing community on the northeast shore of Fogo Island is the second largest community on the island after the town of Fogo. In 1972, Joe Batt's Arm and the contiguous community of Barr'd Islands were incorporated as a rural district. In 2001 Joe Batt's Arm-Barr'd Islands-Shoal Bay had a population of 889.

Keels ~ Although the surname Keel is found in Bonavista, the fishing community of Keels in Bonavista Bay

apparently predates that family. Local traditions about the name include suggestions that John Cabot's ship left the mark of its keel in the sand when stopping at the site for fresh water and that the first settlers found keel-shaped timbers on the beach. A more mundane explanation is that Keels Cove was named for the shape of the rocks at its entrance or for the family name Keough. In 2001 Keels had a population of 85.

Kippens ~ The popular local theory for the origin of the name Kippens is to a Captain Kippen, an Englishman said to have been shipwrecked around the time settlers first arrived in the mid-1840s. But another theory is that the community was named after an early settler named  Keeping. This fishing, logging and farming community at the bottom of St. George's Bay, near Stephenville, was first established behind a long, sandy beach. Settlement has since extended along the highway constructed to the Port au Port Peninsula in 1945. The Micmac from Cape Breton and the Montagnais from Quebec's Lower North Shore were likely among the earliest visitors to the Kippens area, for they were in St. George's Bay at least by the early 1600s (and much earlier according to Micmac tradition). French, and later English, migratory fishermen were frequenting the area by the 1700s, but permanent settlement did not occur until Acadians from Cape Breton began arriving. Local tradition maintains that the first settlers at Kippens were the Doucette family who, after having home and land seized to repay debts, left Cheticamp with their belongings, including several head of cattle. Another early settler was Hughie Campbell, who lived at Kippens before settling at Campbell's Creek in 1854. In 2001 Kippens had a population of 1,802.

Kitchuses {pronounced: *kit - CHEW - sess*} ~ This settlement is found on the western side of Gasters Bay, Conception Bay. Since 1972, Kitchuses has been part of the incorporated community of Conception Harbour. The origin of the name is uncertain. It has been suggested that it is a contraction of "Christopher Hughes's." In 1901, Archbishop M.F. Howley recorded that a local man had suggested that the name came from "Kate Gushue's." E. R. Seary has suggested that the name may originate in an Indian word for breast, *Quitouche*, the likeness of which can be seen in two hillocks behind the settlement. One local theory is that there was once a tavern there, operated by Kit Hughes, which in local dialect was pronounced "Kit Huses."

L'anse Au Loup {pronounced: *LANCE - ah - LOO*} ~ This fishing settlement located between L'Anse Amour and L'Anse au Diable on the Labrador side of the Strait of Belle Isle was once populated by wolves hence the name, which in English means "Wolf Cove." Initially, settlement occurred

both on the sandy beach where
L'Anse au Loup Brook flows into the
head of L'Anse au Loup Bay and at
Schooner Cove. The fur of the wolf
was one of the main attractions to
early settlers. In 1748 a Joseph
Deschenaux was granted trapping and
fishing concessions there. The English

firm founded by Andrew Pinson of Dartmouth and John Noble of Bristol had
established a station at Bear Cove (now Schooner Cove) by 1774. From then
to the early 1800s fishermen were brought from England seasonally. A court
of civil jurisdiction for Labrador was held there periodically, beginning in the
1820s, and in 1852 one of the two fishery protection officers appointed for the
Straits and Labrador was stationed at L'Anse au Loup. Permanent settlement
probably did not begin until the mid-1830s. According to local tradition there
was no resident family at L'Anse au Loup until 1835, when two employees
married and settled there. By the mid-1800s more people, including planters
from Newfoundland, were settling and establishing their own fishing rooms.
At first most people returned to the Island at season's end, but eventually
some settled permanently. The first of these, according to local tradition, was
a Thomas O'Brien of St. John's (but originally from Bonavista), who settled
there in 1855 with his wife Margaret (Hogan) and their four children. Other
early settlers included Thomas Linstead, John Barber, Jim Griffith and a Mr.
Lefevre. When L'Anse au Loup first appeared in the census in 1869 there
were nine families of 47 people: 24 born in Labrador, 19 in Newfoundland
and 5 in England. From then on the population increased gradually until it
reached 106 in 1921. The first settlers at L'Anse au Loup were Roman
Catholics and members of the Church of England. In 2001 Lanse Au Loup
had a population of 635.

L'Anse aux Meadows {pro-
nounced: *LANCE - ah - MED -
owes*} ~ This fishing community in
Épaves Bay on the northeast tip of
the Great Northern Peninsula got its
name from French migratory fishermen in the area during the 1800s and
1900s. They named the site L'Anse
aux Meduses, or Jellyfish Bay, which

later resulted in the English corruption based on local topography.
Archaeological evidence indicates that French and English presence at L'Anse
aux Meadows was predated by the Maritime Archaic Indians, the Dorset
Eskimo, and the Vikings or Norsemen, as well as the proto-Beothuk. The

community gained international attention in 1960 when Norwegian archaeologists Helge and Anne Ingstad excavated a Viking settlement near Black Duck Brook at L'Anse aux Meadows – a site surmised by W. A. Munn, a distinguished Newfoundland historian, as early as 1912 to be a Viking settlement. Scholars have since identified the site as probably the winter station of Leif Eiriksson described in The Vinland Sagas, and possibly even the mythical Vinland. L'Anse aux Meadows is the first authenticated Norse site in North America. Its sod buildings are thus the earliest known European structures on this continent; its smithy, the site of the first known iron working in the New World; the site itself the scene of the first contacts between native Americans and Europeans. The first record of permanent settlement appeared in the 1874 census when 46 people lived there, although family tradition maintains that a William Decker founded the community around 1835. A descendant, George Decker, first led archaeologists to the Viking site. L'Anse aux Meadows was declared a National Historic Park in 1968 and a World Heritage Site in 1978.

Lawn ~ According to one local tradition it was the lush landscape that inspired Captain James Cook to name the place Lawn Harbour. But it has also been speculated that a Frenchman named the community after a doe caribou he spotted there, believing it to be a donkey. Lawn became one of the best inshore fishing harbours on the Burin Peninsula throughout the late 1800s and early 1900s. In addition to the cod and capelin fishery, a salmon fishery was carried on: first by bar nets set across the entrance of two small rivers and then by schooners after the mid-1800s. Herring and sealing fisheries were also carried on there, and by 1891 a lobster factory employed eight people. In 2001 Lawn had a population of 779.

Leading Tickles ~ This community name originated with the name of the passageway between a group of three islands and a mainland promontory. A rock located at the narrowest section of Leading Tickles is known as the Ladle, probably because of its resemblance to a device used for bailing boats. When the community first appeared in the census in 1836, it was recorded as Ladle Tickles, and in 1845 as Lading Tickles. The incorporated community also encompasses the communities of Leading Tickles East and Leading Tickles South. The largest part of the population is in Leading Tickles West on Cull's Island, which is connected by causeway to the mainland communities of Leading

Tickles South on the western shoreline, and Leading Tickles East in Butlers Cove. The first settler in Leading Tickles was likely a member of the Rowsell family. In 2001 Leading Tickles had a population of 453.

Little Heart's Ease ~ Located on the south side of Southwest Arm, Trinity Bay, the well-protected harbour of Little Heart's Ease takes its name from the early fishing station of Heart's Ease. Some authorities suggest that Heart's Ease may have been named after an early fishing ship.

Lord's Cove ~ Historian E. R. Seary speculates that this name has no beginnings with nobility or deity, but was named after the Harlequin Ducks, locally called Lords and Ladies. Although Lord's Cove did not appear in the census until 1884, a family tradition holds

that a Bonnell came from England to Lord's Cove about 1800. Among the cemetery's legible grave markers is that of Thomas Hodge, who died in 1875 at age 52, indicating that Lord's Cove was inhabited well before the 83 residents of 1884 were recorded. Lord's Cove was one of the communities that felt the brunt of the 1929 tsunami. In 2001 Lord's Cove had a population of 234.

Nameless Cove ~ This community, as well as Mistaken Cove, are now a part of the incorporated community of Flowers Cove. All three were

mapped by Captain James Cook in 1764. Located on the northwestern side of the Great Northern Peninsula, the incorporated community became a fishing, business and administrative centre serving the area between Current Island and Eddies Cove East.

Nipper's Harbour ~ Local tradition holds that this community was named for its abundance of mosquitoes, or "nippers," as they are known locally. That theory was endorsed by Bishop Edward Feild in 1854 when he wrote that the "name is rather an alarming one, particularly to thin skinned Southerners, as the Nipper is the largest and most formidable of the mosquitoes." The Beothuk are believed to have frequented the Nippers Harbour area long before French and English migratory fishermen arrived in the late 1700s. Continuous settlement is thought to date from the late 1700s, when a West Country firm operating out of Twillingate, John Slade and Co., established a fishing post there. Two of the first known settlers in

1804 were Slade's agents, John Rideout and John Noble. Noble remained at Nippers Harbour. As many other families came to fish out of Nippers Harbour, the community came to be regarded as "the capital of Green Bay." In 2001 Nipper's Harbour had a population of 189.

Noggin Cove ~ A fishing and lumbering community, Noggin Cove is named after Noggin Island about 5 km off its eastern point, which bears some resemblance to an overturned half-cask, or noggin. There is also a local tradition that the first settler was a fisherman and cooper (who made barrels

and noggins), named Doyle from Tilting on Fogo Island. In the 1850s the Hamilton Sound area was being frequented by fishing crews from the north shore of Conception Bay, which may have provided a market for Doyle's trade.

Pacquet {pronounced: *PACK - it*} ~ This fishing and logging community on the north shore of the Baie Verte Peninsula, about halfway between Baie Verte and La Scie, was a French fishing station in the late 1700s. Earlier known as North East Pacquet when the neighbouring community of South West Pacquet was renamed Woodstock in 1935, the name Pacquet once again referred only to the older community. The first two year-round residents were recorded at Pacquet in 1857: a female of 10 to 20 years of age and a male over 70, who may have been employed as a "gaurdien" of a French company's property over the winter months. In 1869 two Roman Catholic families, those of Peter Dowdy and John McKay, lived there. But substantial permanent settlement did not occur until the French abandoned the harbour in the 1880s. In 2001 Pacquet had a population of 238.

Paradise ~ There are several theories as to how Paradise got its name. One tradition is that when the Rev. Colley, Church of England clergyman at Topsail was invited to minister to the people in the area, he asked how the community should be listed in the parish register. One man replied that the budding community had no name, but that compared to Upper Island Cove it was paradise; Colley then suggested that Paradise be adopted. Others have suggested that the name was purely the invention of Colley, or was the suggestion of a local politician. Originally a farming and logging settlement (now amalgamated with St. Thomas), Paradise is largely a dormitory suburb of St. John's. The town stretches from St. Thomas along the Horse Cove Line to Topsail Road. The opening up of the Paradise area was initiated by Governor Thomas Cochrane (1825-34), who believed that a road between St. John's and Topsail would allow residents of the south side of Conception Bay to more easily take their fresh produce to St. John's and would also open up potential farmland. The makeshift road was completed early in the 1830s and officially opened as a cart path in 1836. But poor soil and climate prevented agricultural development, and no one settled along the road until the 1890s. The town, because of its proximity and accessibility to St. John's, is now one of the fastest-growing in the province. In 2001 Paridise had a population of 9,598.

Path End ~ The community of Path End is located on a road, that was once a path. It extends 3 km inland from St. Mary's and ends at Holyrood Pond. For much of its history Path End was a satellite community of St. Mary's, but has been officially a part of the larger community since 1966. While the two communities are clearly linked, Path End's location on the shore of Holyrood Pond has distinguished it from St. Mary's. Of two dominant family names of Path End the Rowsells have probably been there since the mid-1800s; the Butlers arrived later, from Gaskiers.

Placentia {pronounced: *plah - SENT - shah*} ~ Once known as the old French capital of Newfoundland, the name of this community was originally, "Plaisance," which means "pleasant place." Although probably named by the Basques, in the 1600s the French and English began to vie for control of the beach and harbour at Placentia. It was an ideal location for fishermen at the time. Not only did it have one of the best beaches for drying fish anywhere in Newfoundland, but because of it's topography, could easily be defended against attack. In 1632 French fishing rights were acknowledged by the British, and three years later France asserted its right to dry fish on Newfoundland shores. When war broke out between the two nations, the French resisted repeated English attacks on Plaisance, and between 1696 and 1709 used the settlement as a base from which to attack the English capital of St. John's. The English takeover of Placentia in 1713, when France gave up all rights to Newfoundland, marked the beginning of a new mercantile era there, although some Channel Island businesses had existed during French occupation. By the 1760s Placentia was larger than St. John's, with ships coming from Bideford, Barnstaple and still more from the Channel Islands to share in the area's prosperity. In 2001 Placentia had a population of 4,426.

Port aux Basques {locally pronounced: *PORT - ah - BASK*} ~ Now part of the Town of Channel-Port aux Basques, this community got its name from whalers from the Basque region of the Pyrenees of France and Spain who sailed

to the area during the 1500s. Permanent settlement came from French fishermen who overwintered on this, the "French Shore," however, the 1713 Treaty of Utrecht saw France cede Newfoundland to England in exchange for the right to use coastal lands for the fishery. Later English setters moved in but French names such as AuCoin, Battiste and Beaucamp are still found there. Now known as the gateway to Newfoundland, Channel-Port aux Basques is the western point of entry for all people arriving from mainland Canada by boat. It was 65 km from this port that the SS *Caribou* sunk on October 14, 1942, by a German U-boat, taking the lives of 136 of its 238 passengers and crew. The town has since erected a monument listing the names of the victims of that tragedy. In 2001 Channel-Port aux Basques had a population of 4,637.

Port au Choix {pro-
nounced: *PORT - ah
- SHWAH*} ~ Translated
from the French, this
means "special, or
choice port." The French
weren't the only ones to
think the harbour, which
nearly bisects the penin-
sula that juts out into the

Strait of Belle Isle, a choice place; it was one time home to prehistoric peoples. In 1967, human remains were discovered in Port au Choix when the
foundations for a theatre and billiards hall were being dug by Theodore
Farewell. In total, the burial places of some 53 Palaeo-Indians were discovered. The culture represented is known to archaeologists as Maritime Archaic
and dates back to 3,200-3,900 years ago. In later years other cultures found
the harbour to be a choice place. According to the *Encyclopedia of
Newfoundland and Labrador*, "In an area known locally as Phillip's Garden
are the remains of a Dorset (Palaeo-Eskimo) village. About 50 circular depres-
sions on a raised, grassy terrace mark the location of what were probably sod
and skin huts. The Dorset lived there some 1,900 years ago, relying heavily on
harp seal, which must have been plentiful." Both sites were included within
the boundaries of Port au Choix National Historic Park, established in 1975.
The recorded history of Port au Choix begins in the 1700s, when in 1713, various English-French treaties, gave the French fishing rights to Port au Choix.
Basque vessels also fished there in the 1700s. Port au Choix became the main
French fishing station, and English settlement was not encouraged by either
nation. The French objected to competition in the fishery and the English
wished to avoid further conflict. However, by 1838 a few settlers were present
in Ingornachoix Bay, engaged in the salmon and herring fisheries. By the mid-
1800s, a small, settled population was established at Port au Choix. Relations
between the settlers and the French appear to have been cordial. A few of
these settlers may have been employed as caretakers or "gardiens" during the
winter. In 2001 Port au Choix had a population of 1,010.

Portugal Cove ~ It has been
conjectured that Portugal
Cove was discovered and
named in 1500 by Portuguese
adventurer, Gaspar Corte-Real,
but there is little evidence to
support this claim. It does
appear, however, that the

Portuguese were familiar with the Cove in the early 1500s. In the late 1500s and the 1600s, both the Portuguese and French fished along the shores of Conception Bay. Although no permanent settlement was established, the Portuguese may have used the Cove at some point to land and dry fish. Like the other six localities in the province that bears the name "Portugal," this fishing village is testament to the part the Portuguese played in our history. As it is located on the south side of Conception Bay, approximately 15 km (10 m) by road from St. John's, in the second half of the 1900s this fishing village increasingly become a bedroom community of St. John's. In 1992 Portugal Cove was amalgamated with St. Phillip's, Hogan's Pond and some previously unorganized areas as the Town of Portugal Cove-St. Phillip's, and in 2001 had a combined population of 5,866.

Pouch Cove {pronounced: *POOCH - cove*} ~ Located just south of Cape St. Francis, about 40 km north of St. John's by road, Pouch Cove has historically been a fishing and farming community. By 1992, however, Pouch Cove was largely a bedroom community of St. John's. The settlement is located at the top of cliffs, and the cove is exposed, especially to northeasterly winds. It is quite unsuitable as an anchorage for large vessels, while small boats have to be winched up over steep slipways at any threat of bad weather. In 2001 Pouch Cove had a population of 1,669.

Quidi Vidi ~ {pronounced: *KID - ee - VID - ee*, or *KWY - da - VIDE - ah*} ~ This small, picturesque community, now part of the City of St. John's, is north of St. John's harbour. It has a similar harbour, only much smaller, with a much tighter "nar-

rows." The name Quidi Vidi applies to the Gut (or small harbour), the village around it and the lake and small river feeding into it. The origin of the name has long been a matter of speculation. Historian E. R. Seary suggested that it originated with the French family and place name, Quidville. Early documents in English and French show variants from *que de vide* (Latin for "that which divides" – presumably the St. John's area from the wilderness around it), to Quimidity (having no apparent meaning) to Kitty Vittey, reputed to be a lady who was once well-known there.

Quirpon ~ {pro-
nounced: *car -
POON*} ~ A fishing com-
munity on the extreme
northeastern tip of the
Great Northern Peninsula,
about 35 km north of St.
Anthony, Quirpon
Harbour is the most
northerly sheltered har-

bour on the Island and has been frequented by migratory fishermen since the
1500s. Quirpon has been spelled a variety of ways, including Carpon, Carpunt
and Karpoon. The explorer Jacques Cartier probably knew the harbour by
reports from fishermen of Breton, France, before he anchored there in 1534
(and again in 1541). Though ice kept ships from arriving before early June,
during the summer large numbers of French boats fished the grounds less than
5 km from shore. In 1763 James Cook charted the area and described Little
Quirpon Harbour as "a very snug place for mooring ships." Quirpon was also
the site of one of the earliest meetings of Inuit people with a Moravian missionary. In 1764 the missionary Jens Haven was brought to Quirpon by an
English ship, and in September met with a small group of Inuit who came into
the harbour from Labrador. He followed them across the Strait to begin his
missionary work.

Rabbittown ~ This neighbourhood within the City of St. John's was, at
one time, outside the city. Several origins have been suggested for the
widely-used name. It is possible that it derived from the number of rabbits in
the area early in the 20th century, when people from the city went there to
snare them. Later, when scattered small houses were erected in an area that
had once been barrens and alders, it was derisively dubbed Rabbittown. The
boundaries of Rabbittown are generally considered to be Merrymeeting Road
on the south, Freshwater Road on the west, Empire Avenue on the north and
Newtown Road on the east. During the First World War early plans for the
development of the area showed the streets laid out in an orderly fashion, in a
general north-south and east-west pattern. Originally they were to be named
after trees. After the war, a co-operative housing program was begun in the
area to build homes for veterans. The Great War Veterans Association was
approached to pick the names of war heroes for the streets, but suggested
instead names of places associated with the Royal Newfoundland Regiment
overseas. These included Hamel Street and Liverpool Avenue, as well as Suez,
Suvla, Aldershot, Monchy and Malta streets. Development continued through
the 1950s and 1960s, and by 1960 there were 2,700 dwellings. In 1986
approximately 12,000 people lived in this area.

Red Bay ~ The name of this community is descriptive of the reddish cliffs along the shore. Red Bay has a long history and was the site of Buttes, a major Basque whaling station, between about 1550 and 1600. Aboriginal peoples also

occupied the area during this time, but it is uncertain whether there was any contact with the Europeans. Ancestral Innu and Inuit groups may have come to Red Bay to salvage iron and other goods left behind by the whalers each winter. Beneath the frigid waters of Red Bay are the remains of three ships and several smaller boats. One of these seems to be the Basque ship *San Juan*, lost in 1567. It is believed to be the oldest shipwreck north of the Caribbean and is one of the best preserved. After 1600, the Basques left Red Bay, largely because of the depletion of the whale population. In the 1700s, Red Bay was the site of a Canadian fur trading post and there were two English merchants operating out of the harbour by 1804. Early family names included Canning, Macey, Miner, Moores, Pike, Ryan and Yetman. In 1896, Dr. Wilfred Grenfell convinced the community to begin the first co-operative store in Labrador. The business was a success and even survived the economic collapse of the 1930s. In 2001 Red Bay had a population of 264.

Rencontre East {pronounced: *ROUN - COUN - ter - EAST*} ~ This fishing community located at the bottom of Fortune Bay takes its name from a French word for encounter or "meeting place." Before permanent settlement, Rencontre was likely visited by the French for bait and wood. In the early 1800s its ready access to timber and game made it a winter house for fishing communities further out the bay, such as Sagona and Blanchet. Tradition in the Mullins family has it that the first settler was Augustus Mullins, in about 1840. Other early settlers, including the Baker and Keeping families, likely decided to settle in the 1850s after some years of seasonal visiting from Sagona. In 2001 Rencountre East had a population of 202.

Renews {pronounced: *ren - OOZE*} ~ Now part of the two fishing communities which form the municipality of Renews-Cappahayden, this community is located on the Southern Shore, 83 km south of St. John's. Renews has been inhabited since the 1500s. It was obvi-

ously a thriving community in 1620, when the Pilgrim Fathers brought the *Mayflower* into the settlement for provisions there, on their historic voyage to Plymouth, New England. A plaque indicating the beach where they landed can be seen in Renews. Renews was home to one of the province's heroes. Captain William Jackman, who in 1867, together with others of the fishing fleet, sought a temporary haven at Spotted Islands on the bleak coast of Labrador. While the storm raged, some seaman's instinct urged Jackman to mount the crest of the hill above the harbour and scan the torn waste of water to seaward. According to the Newfoundland Grand Banks Web site, "His instinct was justified, for there, on a foaming reef some four hundred yards from shore, rolled a stricken ship – her boats and canvas gone – her crew clinging to the shrouds and shouting in wild despair. Save for Jackman, no one knew of their plight. There was no other aid in sight, but Jackman did not hesitate or pause to count the odds against him. Racing down the snowy wind-swept hill to the shore, he quickly stripped, flung his clothes beneath a boulder, and plunged into the seething, bitterly cold surf. He was an excellent swimmer, and his long powerful strokes soon brought him beyond the shore-long breakers where he could breathe more freely. Mounting the crest of each wave, he availed himself of every little advantage of wind and weather, and finally he reached the doomed schooner. Taking a man on his back he swam back to shore–buffeted by mountainous seas and half-blinded in the salt smother of foam. Once on shore he ordered the rescued man to hurry across the island for help, then he turned again to the self-imposed task which confronted him. When additional rescuers arrived, they found that the indomitable captain had, alone and unaided, already brought 11 persons safely to shore. Twenty-six times did Captain Jackman swim out to the wrecked ship, and 26 men were thus saved by his daring heroism. His strength was ebbing and he was on the point of exhaustion when one of the rescued seamen told him there was still one more person – a woman – aboard the wrecked vessel. 'With God's help, we will save her,' said the captain, and for the 27th time he plunged into the boiling surf to make another successful rescue." William Jackman's image appeared on a commemorative Canadian postage stamp in 1992. In 2001 Renews-Cappahayden had a population of 423.

R **igolet** {pronounced: *RIG - oh - LET*} ~ Originally founded as a trading post on the northwest side of the narrows, at the entrance to Hamilton Inlet, Labrador, this community takes its name from the French, *rigoulette*, meaning "channel." Continuous operation of trading posts at Rigolet likely dates from 1788, when the French Canadian trader, Pierre Marcoux, established a post there. Under a succession of Quebec-based traders, Rigolet became the hub for a network of Inuit and settlers trapping, hunting and fishing for salmon at a number of locations at the mouth of Groswater Bay, in

Double Mer and eastern Lake Melville. In 1836, Hudson's Bay Company agent Simon Macgillivray recognized the geographic advantages of Rigolet for trading and established a post there, in opposition to the Quebec trading firm of D.R. Stewart. Rigolet first appears in the census in 1901 with a population of 24. During World War II there were several hundred Canadian soldiers stationed at Rigolet to guard the Narrows and a small naval base to the south. The Canadian Army also built a school in 1944 for the use of local children. In 2001 Rigolet had a population of 317.

Mel D'Souza Photo

Rose Blanche {pronounced: *rose - BLANCH*} ~ The name of this community, about 35 km east of Channel-Port aux Basques, is a corruption of the French *roche blanche*, which means, "white rock," a reference to outcroppings of white quartz in the area. The first permanent settlers probably arrived around 1810. Local traditions have it that among the earliest settlers were families named Caines, Currie and Payne. Financed by Jersey merchants at Harbour Breton, they fished for some years at Burgeo or La Poile before moving to Rose Blanche and area. A stone lighthouse was erected at Rose Blanche Point in the 1870s. Now part of the incorporated community of Rose Blanche-Harbour le Cou, in 2001 it had a combined population of 668.

Rushoon ~ Geologist and historian James Patrick Howley suggested that the name of this fishing community may be a corruption of the French *ruisseau*, meaning "brook," or *roche jaune*, meaning "yellow rocks." Rushoon is located

at the base of steep slopes along the east side of the Rushoon River and on either side of a deep harbour, where the river runs into Placentia Bay. In 2001 Rushoon had a population of 359.

Salvage {pronounced: *sal - VAYGE*} ~ Located in central Bonavista Bay, at the tip of the Eastport Peninsula, Salvage has been named by *Harrowsmith Country Life* as one of Canada's 10 prettiest towns. Salvage was one of the earliest harbours to be employed by migratory fishermen from England. Originally inhabited by the Beothuks, it was then occupied by Basque fishermen in the early 17th century. As early as 1676 there were six English masters (family names Chambers, Knight, Pett, Pritchard, Stocks and Warren), making a summer population (with their families and servants) of 66 people. It's now recognized as one of the oldest continually inhabited communities in North America. In 2001 Salvage had a population of 203.

Seldom-Come-By ~ Now known simply as Seldom, this fishing community on the southern shore of Fogo Island, is one of the most frequently cited "colourful'" Newfoundland place names. Being the first sheltered harbour north of Greenspond, it was much resorted to by fishing schooners so the name may refer to this practice of seldom bypassing the harbour. During the heyday of the Labrador fishery the majority of vessels out of Conception, Trinity and Bonavista bays would put in at Seldom-Come-By. The first settler at Seldom was John Hodnett (Hoddinott), who had settled by 1828. Local tradition has it that he was a runaway from Kent, England, who subsequently changed the family name to Holmes in order to avoid detection. Most of the early settlers were people of Conception Bay who first became familiar with the harbour while engaged in the Labrador fishery and whose home ports were becoming overcrowded. Consequently the family names at Seldom are common in Conception Bay. These include, Anthony, Boone, Budden, Collins, Dawe, Penney and Rowe. In 2001 Seldom-Little Seldom had a population of 477.

Spaniard's Bay ~ This fishing and service community is one of six localities in the province that uses "Spaniard" or "Spanish" as part of its name. Spaniard's Bay was frequented  by Basque fishermen, who were often referred to as "Spaniards" by English fishermen because some Basques were actually from Spain. In 2004, Guy Narbonne, of Queen's University in Ontario, found fossils in Spaniard's Bay. The rare fossil creatures he found were 560-575 million years old and came from the Ediacaran era of history.

Sunnyside ~ This community is situated around the shore at the head of Bull Arm, in southwestern Trinity Bay. Originally called Truce Sound by John Guy, the arm was the site of a brief meeting between colonists from Cuper's Cove (Cupids) and a small group of

Beothuk on November 7, 1612, when the two groups exchanged gifts and shared a meal. Accounts of the 1612 meeting suggest that there was a considerable aboriginal presence in Bull Arm in the 1600s, and archaeological investigations have confirmed the early presence of Europeans and Beothuk, as well as an earlier Dorset-Palaeo-Eskimo presence on nearby Frenchman's Island.

Too Good Arm ~ Located on New World Island in Notre Dame Bay, this fishing community has sometimes been regarded as a part of Herring Neck and cannot be readily distinguished from other

communities in the area in early records. The name Too Good Arm was first employed in church records in the 1870s, with some of the first names recorded being the families of George Hurley, John Gillett and Samuel Russell. The Hurley family were originally Roman Catholics and it appears that they made up most of the Roman Catholic minority recorded at Herring Neck in the early census. Of 10 electors recorded in the community in 1889, seven were Hurleys (the others being Gillett, Russell and Moses Burton). The fishery out of Too Good Arm was by and large conducted away from the community, in schooners for which the arm and the Herring Neck area generally provided admirable shelter.

Turk's Cove ~ Local tradition has it that the small fishing community, located in an open bight on the southeast side of Trinity Bay, just to the north of New Perlican, was named for the Barbary pirates, also known as

Turks, who frequented the coast in the 1600s. Permanent European settlement at Turks Cove appears to have begun in about 1800, when John Antle and Manuel Carberry were recorded as living there. By 1835 the families of John and Joseph Antle, James Carberry, Philip Hearty, Thomas Peppy and Isaac Samson were resident. The following year, in the first census of the settlement, there were 69 people recorded.

Twillingate

{pronounced: *TWILL - in - GATE*} ~ Like many northeast Newfoundland communities, Twillingate was once part of the French Shore. The name comes from an English corruption of *Toulinguet*, a name it was

given by the French because it resembled a group of islets off the French port of Brest. Frequented by French crews in the 1600s and early 1700s, the harbour between north and south islands was later visited by the English. Local tradition identifies the first settlers as four English fishermen: Lawrence Smith at Young's Point on the Northside, the Young family at Southside, the Moores family at Back Harbour and a man named Bath at Jenkins Cove, who settled there in the early 1700s. By the winter of 1739, there were 152 people living in Twillingate. They were mostly fishermen and their families from the West Country in England. Twillingate became a thriving fishing community, and a busy trade and service centre for Labrador and the northern shore fisheries for more than two centuries. For many years it was known as the "Capital of the North." The *Twillingate Sun*, the local newspaper served the Twillingate district with local, Newfoundland and international news from the 1880's to the 1950's. Now being promoted as the "Iceberg Capital of the World," Twillingate is home to one of the oldest summer festivals in the province, the Twillingate-New World Island Fish, Fun and Folk Festival, attracting thousands of tourists from around the world annually. In 2001 Twillingate had a population of 2,611.

Virgin Arm

~ This community is located at the head of Friday's Bay, on New World Island. Its name probably originated in the fact that the narrow Arm was not settled until the 1870s, although it was used for winter woods work and schooner-building by fishermen from Tizzard's Harbour and Twillingate from the early 1800s. The first record of settlement at Virgin Arm is from Lovell's Newfoundland Directory of 1871, which identifies fisherman John Smith as a resident and notes a population of 10 people. Locally, the first settler is said to have been a Curtis of Snellings Cove, Twillingate. William Curtis was resident by 1876, and by 1882 had been joined by John Hicks and a family named Nicholas, also of Twillingate.

Wabana {pronounced: *wah - BAN - ah*} ~ This, the largest community on Bell Island, is closely tied to the development of the mines on the island got its name from the Abnaki words *wabunaki*, meaning "eastland" and *waban*, meaning "the dawn," because the mine was the most easterly in North America. In 1895 the Butler family of Topsail gained the rights to the iron ore deposit, which was subsequently developed by the New Glasgow Coal, Iron and Railway Co. The secretary of the company, Thomas Cantley, decided to name the area around the mine "Wabana." The mines at Wabana, some of which became submarine mines running several miles under the Atlantic Ocean, continued to operate until it no longer became feasible to bring iron ore up from such a distance. In April 1966, the last mine closed down. At the time of its closure, Bell Island was Canada's longest continually operating mining project. In 2001 Wabana had a population of 2,679.

Wabush ~ An iron ore mining town in western Labrador, Wabush is located 5 km south of Labrador City. The area to the south of Wabush Lake was known to contain minerals from the 1930s. However, mineral rights to this

Andrea Spracklin Photo

parcel of land were relinquished by the Labrador Mining and Exploration Co. (parent company of the Iron Ore Company of Canada) in the early 1950s, as it was felt that the deposits were not of high enough grade to be profitably mined. In 1953, John C. Doyle's Canadian Javelin Co. purchased the mineral rights in the area from a provincial Crown corporation. The next year Doyle incorporated Wabush Mines Ltd. to promote development of a mine at the site. Meanwhile, IOC had begun to take an interest in deposits at nearby Carol Lake. By the time IOC had established the townsite of Labrador City and had begun full production from their mine and concentrator in 1962 a pilot plant had been in operation at the Wabush deposits for two years and the decision had been taken to go ahead with production. Development of the Scully Mine and concentrating plant by Pickands Mather & Co. commenced in January of 1962, and the project was officially dedicated in 1965, when full production had been reached. In 2001 Wabush had a population of 1,894.

West St. Modeste {pronounced: *WEST - SAINT - mo - DESS*} ~ This fishing community on the Labrador side of the Strait of Belle Isle, on the southwest side of Pinware Bay, has retained the word "west" in its official name, even though East St. Modeste on the opposite side of Pinware Bay (also known as Little St. Modeste) has been abandoned since the mid-

1950s. In the 1560s, San Mandet or Semedet was a minor Basque whaling station, which would appear to have been located to the west of the Pinware River. Grand (or West) St. Modeste appears to have been known to the French as a fishing station in the early 1700s; in 1716, it was part of a grant given to Pierre Constantin, who maintained a cod fishery and sealing station on St. Modeste (MacDonald's) Island. The station was frequented by the French up until 1763, when they were excluded from the Labrador fishery. By 1774 West St. Modeste was owned by the Bristol firm of Noble and Pinson, which had their major Labrador premises at Chateau Bay and, after 1800, at L'Anse au Loup. West St. Modeste was never dominated by a merchant-based fishery. In the early 1800s the area was being frequented by increasing numbers of fishermen from Newfoundland, particularly from Bell Island and New Chelsea, Trinity Bay.

Whale's Gulch ~ This former community on the western tip of New World Island in Notre Dame Bay was located to the south of Western Head in a very unsheltered cove. In the 1950s the houses and fishing premises were built up the sides of a cliff. The residents of this community later moved the short distance to Valley Pond. When the first census was taken in 1836, the population of Whales Gulch was 18.

Wild Bight ~
Located on the
north side of Little Bay,
in western Notre Dame
Bay, this community was
probably used as a sum-
mer station by fishermen
from Twillingate prior to
being settled, in the
1850s. It takes its name
from prevailing sea con-

ditions. As noted in the book *Sailing Directions*, "with a light northeasterly
wind a swell sets in, and when the wind is strong the whole of the bight
appears to be breakers." The name of this community was later changed to
Beachside, because of postal problems with other communities of the same
name. In 2001 Beachside had a population of 174.

Winterhouses ~ Originally known as Maisons d'Hiver, which in English
means "winter houses," this fishing community on the northwest coast
of the Port au Port Peninsula was once used as a wintering site by French fishermen from Long Point (La Barre) and other fishing stations. The area was
ideal for winter habitation with its thick stands of spruce which provided shelter from winter storms as well as firewood. According to local tradition, the
area was first settled by the Duffenais family from Margaree, Cape Breton
Island, in the 1840s. But it does not appear in the census until 1921, at which
time it had population of 133. According to the *Encyclopedia of
Newfoundland and Labrador*, "Other early settlers were also Acadian, including the Felixes, Laineys and Youngs – and were joined in the 1890s and early
1900s by several families of deserters from French fishing vessels who married local women."

Witless Bay ~
Historian M.F.
Howley thought that
the name of this
Southern Shore com-
munity might have
derived from a shrub,
the northern wild
raisin, also known as
witherod or wittle.
Meanwhile historian
E.R. Seary suggested

that it could have been either a reference to the crazy, rolling motion of the sea or to a Dorsetshire family named Whittle. Although most residents of Witless Bay are now of Irish descent, the earliest inhabitants were West Country English migratory fishermen. There were 34 people recorded at "Whittless Bay" in 1675, including the families of Arthur Mahone, Humphrey Smith, Gilbert Martin and 26 servants. The following year, Mahone, Martin and Smith were joined by planters William Kile, Peter White and George Spark. The estimated summer population of Witless Bay in 1677 was 300 migratory fishermen. In the mid-1700s some Irish fishing servants began to settle, and by the 1760s there were 11 Roman Catholic families. Early family names include Dinn, Power, Carew, Norris, Burk, Madigan, Tobin and Mullowney. In 2001 Witless Bay had a population of 1,056.

Downhome Places

Do **Nipper's Harbour** nippers
Lately take a **Lushes Bight**
Do they lighten up in **Brighton**
And in **Triton**, outta sight?
Will you meet a prince in **Princeton** town
And in **Fox Roost**, feel foxey?
And if you doff your clothes in **Mose Ambrose**
Will they see your buff in **Boxey**?
If you cut hay all day in **Meadows**
In **Sheave's Cove** or in **Lawn**
Could you **Pacquet** up in **Haystack**
Then, on **Cow Path**, be gone?
If you scale a whale in **Whale's Gulch**
And in **Bird Cove** you take flight
Will you shed your shell in **Lobster Cove**
Or in **Seal Cove**, will **Seal Bight**?
But if you get goosed in **Goose Bay**
Try not to lose your dander
Just give your **Herring Neck** a stretch
At the gooser, take a **Gander**
If you **Fogo** the charm of **Joe Batt's Arm**
And **Seldom-Come-By Highlands**
You might miss a date in **Twillingate**
If at **Random**, you **Change Islands**
You could point out **Point Leamington**
Point May and **Point au Gaul**
Point of Bay and **Point la Haye**
Point Rosie, **Point au Mal**
For CFAs there's **English Harbour**
Frenchman's Cove and **Ireland's Eye**
Spaniard's Bay and **Portugal Cove**
And **Port aux Basques** me b'y

You can have a snack in **Snack Cove**
Plus there's tasty fare to please
In **Bacon Cove** and **Butter Pot**
Cape Onion, Bread and Cheese
If you lose your hair in **Hare Bay**
And your teeth down in **Deep Bight**
Will you wear spare hair in **Bluff Head Cove**
And will **Rose Blanche** at the sight?
You may come by chance to **Come By Chance**
Or find **Chance Cove** in your wanders
But to bide awhile in **Bide Arm**
You must **Branch** off past **Port Saunders**
If in **Angels Cove** you're grounded
'Cause your wings are out of joint
They mend wings and other things
In **Cupids** and **Wing's Point**?
If in **Lonesome Cove** your lonesome
For your sweetie in **Sweet Bay**
Would you pick her posies in **Flowers Cove**
Or roses in **Cape Ray**?
Should you spoon a lass from **Loon Bay**
Whose lover's from **Savage Cove** town
You might show your face in **Harbour Grace**
But not in **Blow Me Down**
Would you like to dwell in **Gargamelle**
Brigus or **Bauline**
Or in resettled **Harbour Deep**
Piccaire or **Merasheen**?
Could you be content in **Heart's Content**
Heart's Delight, Heart's Ease
Heart's Desire or **Comfort Cove**
Or places such as these?
If in **Paradise** you hear a voice
Directly from your Maker
You still can't stay in **Deadman's Bay**
They have no undertaker
If you nod off in **Noddy Bay**
And get stuck in **Muddy Hole**
Send the alarm to **Chapel Arm**
To have **Lord's Cove** save your soul

If you get drunk in **Gin Cove**
And rattled in **Rattling Brook**
Don't wear fur coats in **Bear Cove**
'Cause you might be mistook
If you're good while you're in **Glenwood**
While in **Deer Lake**, you leer
Would you be a giver in **Grey River**
And a barb in **Carbonear**?
If you broke your back in **Back Cove**
And your arm in **Durrell's Arm**
Would you venture into **Burnt Head**
Without fear of fiery harm?
If you felt "the pits" in **Pitts Harbour**
And got gonged while at **Long Point**
And then got blows at **Jerry's Nose**
Would YOUR nose be out of joint?
If you mistook **Mistaken Point**
For **Chanceport** on the ocean
Would you **Pushthrough** for **Exploits**
To keep **Swift Current**'s **Motion**?
If you are aground in **Harbour Round**
Or your **Keels** stuck in **Shoal Bay**
Will you lose your soul down in **Hibb's Hole**
Or for **Salvage,** will you pray
If you **Botwood** in **Birchy Bay**
Spruce Brook and **Aspen Cove**
In **Chimney Cove** or **Burnside**
Maybe **Glenwood** buy a stove
If you made soup in **Ladle Cove**
And in **Kettle Cove** made tea
Would you be hearty in **Cartyville**
And gleeful in **Englee**?
If you're unsteady in **Steady Brook**
And drunk while in **Bar Haven**
Would you milk a moose at **Cow Head**
Then at **Crow Head**, shoot a raven?
If you picked plums at **Plum Point**
And berries at **Berry Head**
Would you make preserves in **Canning's Cove**
As **Garnish** for your bread

In **Pope's Harbour,** will you cross yourself
Will you pray in **Parson's Pond**
Does **Holyrood** still fit your mood
And is **Bishop's Falls** "right on?"
Will you duck into **Black Duck Brook**
While in **Black Head**, you're abiding
Will you tack into **Black Tickle**
And slide into **Black Duck Siding**
Do you rush to get to **Rushoon**
Laze around in **Logy Bay**?
Do you know the charm of **Too Good Arm**
Down **New World Island** way?
If in **Famish Gut** you're famished
And **Bloomfield**'s gone to seed
Would you stay away from **Witless Bay**
And not go near **Bareneed**?
Would you catch a cod in **Codner**
Or a speckled in **Trout River**
Or would you race instead to **Riverhead**
For rainbow on a skivver?
If you rocked in **Rocky Harbour**
And was gross in **Gros Morne** Park
Would you clown around in **Clown's Cove**
In **Lark Harbour**, have a lark?
If you robbed a coach in **Coachman's Cove**
And put your **Fortune** in **Grand Bank**
And they caught up with you at **Path End**
Would they make you walk the plank?
If you were conceived in **Conception Harbour**
And then your parents moved away
And you were born on the **Mainland**
Would you still be from the bay?
If in later years, you should move back
And folks, without exception
Would stare and say, "There's a CFA"
Would you be a mis-**Conception**?

Bibliography

A Collection of Foolishness and Folklore, George H. Earle, Harry Cuff Publications, 1988.

A History of Newfoundland and Labrador, Dr. W. Fred Rowe, McGraw-Hill Ryerson Limited, 1980.

A Poem in My Soup, by Geraldine Rubia, Jesperson Press, St. John's, 1980.

A Rope Against the Sun: A Play for Voices, Al Pittman, Breakwater Books Ltd., St. John's, 1974.

Atlantic Guardian magazine, published by Ewart Young, St. John's Newfoundland, 1945 through 1955.

A Whale for the Killing, Farley Mowat, Little, Brown, Boston, 1972.

A Winter's Tale: The Wreck of the Florizel, Cassie Brown, Doubleday Canada, Toronto, 1976.

Beneficial Vapors, Ray Guy, edited by Eric Norman, Jesperson Press, St. John's, 1981.

Best of the Barrelman, William Connors, Creative Publishers, 1998.

Birds of North America at: http://bna.birds.cornell.edu

Book of Newfoundland, Volume 1, Newfoundland Book Publishers Ltd., 1937.

Book of Newfoundland, Volume 2, Newfoundland Book Publishers Ltd., 1937.

Book of Newfoundland, Volume 3, Newfoundland Book Publishers Ltd., 1967.

Book of Newfoundland, Volume 4, Newfoundland Book Publishers Ltd., 1967.

Book of Newfoundland, Volume 5, Newfoundland Book Publishers Ltd., 1975.

Book of Newfoundland, Volume 6, Newfoundland Book Publishers Ltd., 1975.

Collin's English Dictionary, HarperCollins Publishers, Glascow, Scotland, 2003.

Community Accounts Web site at: www.communityaccounts.ca

Death on the Ice: The Great Newfoundland Sealing Disaster of 1914, Cassie Brown, Doubleday Canada, Toronto, 1972.

Devine's Folklore of Newfoundland, P. K. Devine, Memorial University of Newfoundland, 1997.

Dictionary of Nautical Words and Terms, by C. W. T. Layton, Brown, Son and Ferguson Ltd., Glascow, Scotland, 1982.

Dictionary of Newfoundland English, G. M. Story, W. J. Kirwin, J. D. A. Widdowson, University of Toronto Press, 1990.

Don't Have Your Baby in the Dory: A Biography of Myra Bennett, H. Gordon Green, Harvest House, Montreal, 1974.

Downhome magazine, published by Downhome Inc., St. John's, 1988 - 2006.

Encyclopedia of Newfoundland and Labrador, Volume 1, Newfoundland Book Publishers Ltd., 1981.

Encyclopedia of Newfoundland and Labrador, Volume 2, Newfoundland Book Publishers Ltd., 1984.

Encyclopedia of Newfoundland and Labrador, Volume 3, Joseph R. Smallwood Heritage Foundation, Inc., 1991.

Encyclopedia of Newfoundland and Labrador, Volume 4, Joseph R. Smallwood Heritage Foundation, Inc., 1993.

Encyclopedia of Newfoundland and Labrador, Volume 5, Joseph R. Smallwood Heritage Foundation, Inc., 1994.

Extinction: The Beothuks of Newfoundland, Frederick W. Rowe, McGraw-Hill Ryerson Limited, Toronto, 1977.

Fables, Fairies and Folklore, Alice Lannon, Mike McCarthy, Jesperson Press, St. John's, Newfoundland, 1991.

Ferryland: The Colony of Avalon, Bernard D. Fardy, Flanker Press, 2005.

For Maids Who Brew and Bake, Sheilah Roberts, Flanker Press, St. John's, Newfoundland, 2003.

Folklore and Traditional Culture at www.heritage.nf.ca/society/folklore.html

Folklore, Old Remedies, and Newfoundland sayings at www.k12.nf.ca/discovery/Communities/acdrom/tourism/nfldsay.htm

Gazetteer of Canada: Newfoundland, Geographical Services Directorate, Surveys and Mapping Branch, Energy, Mines and Resources Canada, 1983.

Glossary of the Unfamiliar and Other Interesting Words in the Newfoundland Journal of Aaron Thomas, A. C. Hunter, 1970.

Harrap French Dictionary, edited by Patricia Forbes and Muriel Holland Smith, Chambers Harrap Publishers Ltd., Edinburgh, Scotland, 1993.

Historic Newfoundland and Labrador, L. E. F. English, M.B.E., the Province of Newfoundland and Labrador, 1985.

Home Medicine: The Newfoundland Experience, John K. Crellin, McGill-Queens University Press, 1994.

House of Hate, Percy Janes, McClelland and Stewart, Toronto, 1970.

My Newfoundland: Stories, Poems, Songs, A.R. Scammell, Harvest House, Montreal, 1966.

New Encyclopedia Britannica, 15th edition, Encyclopedia Britannica inc. Chicago Illinois, USA, 1996.

Newfoundland and Labrador Folklore at www.wordplay.com/tourism/folklore.html

Newfoundland and Labrador: Words and Sayings at www.explorenewfoundlandandlabrador.com/newfoundland-words-and-sayings.htm

Newfoundland Expressions at www.durham.net/~kburt/newfexpr.html

Newfoundland Folklore at www.ves.k12.nf.ca

Newfoundlandia Game, Cliff Brown, St. John's.

Newfoundland Sayings at www.geocities.com

Newfoundland's Grand Banks at http://ngb.chebucto.org

Newfoundland Word Game at www.nfld.com

Newfoundland Words and Their Meanings at www.wordplay.com

North American Mammals at www.mnh2.si.edu

Norton Encyclopedic Dictionary of Navigation, edited by Hewitt Schlereth, W. W. Norton & Company Inc., 1987.

Old-time Songs of Newfoundland, 3rd edition, Gerald S. Doyle, St. John's, 1955.

On Sloping Ground: Reminiscences of Outport Life in Notre Dame Bay, Newfoundland, Aubrey Malcolm Tizzard, edited by J.D.A. Widdowson, Memorial University, St. John's, 1979.

On the High Seas, John William Froude, Jesperson Press, St. John's, 1983.

Pathways through Yesterday, Michael P. Murphy, Town Crier Publishing Company Limited, St. John's, 1976.

People of the Landwash, George M. Story, edited by Melvin Baker, Helen Peters and Shannon Ryan, Harry Cuff Publications, St. John's, 1997.

Tales from Pigeon Inlet, Ted Russell, edited by Elizabeth (Russell) Miller, Breakwater Books, St. John's, 1977.

That Far Greater Bay, Ray Guy, edited by Eric Norman, Breakwater Books, St. John's, 1976.

The Boat Who Wouldn't Float, Farley Mowat, McClelland and Stewart, Toronto, 1969.

The Holdin' Ground, Ted Russell, McClelland and Stewart, Toronto, 1972.

The Story of St John's, Newfoundland, Paul O'Neill, volume. 1: The Oldest City, 1975, volume 2: A Seaport Legacy, 1976, Press Porcepic, Erin, Ontario.

Tomorrow Will Be Sunday, Harold Horwood, Doubleday & Company, Inc., New York, 1966.

White Eskimo: A Novel of Labrador, Harold Horwood, Doubleday Canada, Toronto, 1972.

Wikipedia Encyclopedia at http://encyclopedia.thefreedictionary.com

Words and expressions I remember from my past